Why Did They Kill?

CALIFORNIA SERIES IN PUBLIC ANTHROPOLOGY

The California Series in Public Anthropology emphasizes the anthropologist's role as an engaged intellectual. It continues anthropology's commitment to being an ethnographic witness, to describing, in human terms, how life is lived beyond the borders of many readers' experiences. But it also adds a commitment, through ethnography, to reframing the terms of public debate — transforming received, accepted understandings of social issues with new insights, new framings.

Series Editor: Robert Borofsky (Hawaii Pacific University)

Contributing Editors: Philippe Bourgois (UC San Francisco), Paul Farmer (Partners in Health), Rayna Rapp (New York University), and Nancy Scheper-Hughes (UC Berkeley)

University of California Press Editor: Naomi Schneider

Why Did They Kill?

Cambodia in the Shadow of Genocide

Alexander Laban Hinton

UNIVERSITY OF CALIFORNIA PRESS
Berkeley • *Los Angeles* • *London*

Maps 1 and 2 were redrawn from versions that
appeared in *The Tragedy of Cambodian History:
Politics, War, and Revolution since 1945*, by David P.
Chandler (Yale University Press, 1991). The Note
on Transliteration on p. 299 appeared originally in
Cambodian Culture since 1975: Homeland and Exile,
edited by May M. Ebihara, Carol A. Mortland, and
Judy Ledgerwood (Cornell University Press, 1994).

University of California Press
Berkeley and Los Angeles, California

University of California Press, Ltd.
London, England

Library of Congress Cataloging-in-Publication Data

Hinton, Alexander Laban.
    Why did they kill? : Cambodia in the shadow of
genocide / Alexander Laban Hinton.
        p.   cm. — (California series in public
anthropology ; 11)
    Includes bibliographical references and index.
    ISBN 13 978-0-520-24179-4 (pbk. : alk. paper)
ISBN 10 0-520-24179-7 (pbk. : alk. paper)
    1. Cambodia — Politics and government —
1975–1979.   2. Political atrocities — Cambodia.
3. Genocide — Cambodia.   I. Title.   II. Series.

DS554.8.H56   2005
959.604'2 — dc22   2005009189

Manufactured in the United States of America
13   12   11   10   09   08
11   10   9   8   7   6   5   4   3

Printed on Ecobook 50 containing a minimum 50%
post-consumer waste, processed chlorine free. The
balance contains virgin pulp, including 25% Forest
Stewardship Council Certified for no old growth tree
cutting, processed either TCF or ECF. The sheet is acid-
free and meets the minimum requirements of ANSI/NISO
Z39.48-1992 (R 1997) (Permanence of Paper).

For Nicole, Meridian, and Arcadia
Thank you for the light

Contents

Figures

Acknowledgments

This project would never have been possible without the help of a number of people and institutions. Enormous thanks go to Bradd Shore, my doctoral advisor in the Department of Anthropology at Emory University, for his support, encouragement, and critical insights about this project. He was extremely generous with his time, even when he was the department chair. The other members of my doctoral committee — May Ebihara, Charles Nuckolls, Robert Paul, and Carol Worthman — were similarly helpful, providing many excellent comments and suggestions that have helped shape the project into its current form. Fredrik Barth has been an inspiration and provided valuable feedback about this book. Finally, I want to thank Emory's anthropology department for creating a supportive and dynamic environment in which to undertake doctoral studies.

I am fortunate to have found a similarly stimulating atmosphere in the Department of Sociology and Anthropology at Rutgers University, Newark, where I have been a faculty member since 1998. The chair of the department, Clay Hartjen, has been wonderful, as have my other colleagues, Sherri-Anne Butterfield, Anne-Marie Cantwell, Ira Cohen, Brian Ferguson, Carol Henderson, Max Herman, Kurt Schock, and Janet Siskind. In particular, I have benefited from many conversations with Brian about violence and war. I have also enjoyed working in the Center for Global Change and Governance and would like to express my appreciation to the directors of the center, Richard Langhorne, Yale Ferguson, and Alex Moytl. Finally, I would like to thank my students at Rutgers for their engagement with issues and ideas related to this book.

I would also like to acknowledge the grants and fellowships that various institutions provided for my graduate education, fieldwork, and postdoctoral studies. My doctoral research was funded by a National Institute of Health NRSA Fellowship, a National Science Foundation Graduate Fellowship, a National Science Foundation Doctoral Dissertation Grant, an Institute for the Study of World Politics Scholarship, two Association for Asian Studies Southeast Asia Council Small Grants for Isolated Southeast Asia Scholars, an Emory University Doctoral Fellowship, and a grant from the Joint Committee on Southeast Asia of the Social Science Research Council and the American Council of Learned Societies with funds provided by the Andrew W. Mellon Foundation, the Ford Foundation, and the Henry Luce Foundation. Language training at the 1991, 1992, and 1993 Southeast Asia Summer Studies Institute was supported by Foreign Language Area Studies Scholarships. I am grateful to the Committee on Human Development at the University of Chicago for offering me a stimulating environment and a NIH Post-Doctoral Fellowship during the 1997–98 academic year. Two Rutgers University Research Council Grants provided funding that enabled me to return to Cambodia for follow-up research in the summers of 2000 and 2003. Finally, I would like to thank Rob Lemelson and the Foundation for Psycho-Cultural Research for awarding me a Book Writing Fellowship that enabled me to spend a semester completing the revisions to this manuscript in the fall of 2002.

My work would not have been possible without the assistance of various Cambodians and Cambodian institutions. During my 1994–95 doctoral research, the Ministry of Culture in Phnom Penh helped me to procure research approval to work in Kompong Cham and at Tuol Sleng. My thanks also go to the provincial government of Kompong Cham, which facilitated my research, and to the many schoolmasters, teachers, students, and officials who allowed me to videotape their classes and schools. I owe a great debt to the people of Banyan, the village where I conducted much of my research, for their time and assistance. Without their openness, patience, and compassion, this study would not have been possible. I want to thank my many informants from Banyan, Kompong Cham, and Phnom Penh — as well as my research assistants — for their help. I am grateful to Kurt Bredenberg and Seng Vanna for their friendship during my stay in Cambodia and for their help with my work. Thanks also to Phalla and Doung. When I returned to Cambodia in

2000 and 2003, Youk Chhang and his staff at the Documentation Center of Cambodia (DC-Cam), especially Vannak Huy, were extremely helpful, providing me with research space and ready access to key DK documents from the amazing archive they have assembled. My deepest thanks to Youk for his hospitality and help, which has continued since I returned from the field, and for his comments on this book.

I am lucky to be a part of a scholarly community that has done outstanding work on Cambodia and laid an important foundation for my research. The two "elders" of this community, David Chandler and May Ebihara, have been particularly supportive of my research and served as sources of inspiration. May graciously agreed to help me with my doctoral exams, fieldwork, and dissertation, despite living and teaching in New York. David also took an early interest in my work, providing encouragement and quickly reading and commenting on various chapters. His generosity as a scholar is illustrated by the time he devotes to other scholars and by his generous acts — such as his offer to provide me with his notes for his ground-breaking book on Tuol Sleng.

Two anthropologists, Judy Ledgerwood and John Marston, deserve thanks for their encouragement and their excellent work, which has set a high standard for junior scholars. Ben Kiernan has also been very supportive of my work and generous with his time. As the director and founder of the Cambodian Genocide Program (CGP), he invited me to come to Yale for discussions and to use the archives. His successor at the CGP, Sue Cook, and another CGP director, Toni Shapiro-Phim, were also sources of help. I am grateful to Sophea Mouth for his many valuable comments and to George Chigas for providing me with a copy of his translation of *Tum Teav*. Thanks also go to a number of other scholars of Cambodia and Southeast Asia, including Rich Arant, Lydia Breckon, Steven Collins, Howard DeNike, Penny Edwards, Craig Etcheson, Kate Frieson, Lindsay French, Anne Hansen, Steve Heder, Karl Heider, Doug Hollan, Charles Keyes, the late A. Thomas Kirsch, Ratha Tan, Frank Reynolds, and Frank Smith.

Numerous other people have influenced this project in direct and indirect ways. I want to thank audience members for their comments at the various departments and institutions where I presented parts of this book: the American Anthropological Association, the Association for Asian Studies, the University of California, Berkeley, the University of California, Los Angeles, the University of Chicago, Cornell University, the International Association of Genocide Scholars, Monash University, the New York Academy of Sciences, Northwestern University, Rutgers

University, the School of American Research, the Society for Psychological Anthropology, Vienna Public Broadcasting, the University of Wisconsin, and Yale University. While it is impossible to list everyone who has assisted me, directly or indirectly, in this project, I'd also like to express my appreciation to Beverly Achille, Lucy Anello, Joyce Apsel, Victor Balaban, Kevin Birth, Christen Carlson, Peter Carwell, Conerly Casey, Don Donham, Ian Edgewater, Paul Farmer, Helen Fein, Bruce Fischl, D. Harper-Jones, Karl Heider, Gil Herdt, Michael Herzfeld, Jane Huber, Richard Koenigsberg, Bruce Knauft, René Lemarchand, Aun Lor, Owen Lynch, Peter Maguire, Andy Marks, McKim Marriott, Holly Mathews, Jim McManus, Brian Marcus, Hannah Mitchell, Julie Monaco, Dirk Moses, Carole Nagengast, Carolyn Nordstrom, Elinore Olsen, Pou Sreng, Naomi Quinn, Antonius Robben, Samorn Nil, Victoria Sanford, Rick Shweder, Roger Smith, Charlie Swift, Chris Taylor, Thavro Phim, Neil Whitehead, John Wood, and Ronnie Yimsut. My apologies to anyone I have inadvertently left off this list.

I also greatly appreciate all that the University of California Press has done to make this book come to fruition. Naomi Schneider has been wonderful, providing encouragement and direction for the book. Her editorial assistant, Sierra Filucci, has been very helpful, as have other members of the editorial team, including Mary Severance and Elizabeth Berg. I am especially grateful to Rob Borofsky, the editor of the Public Anthropology series, for inviting me to place the book in his series. He has shown unflagging support for this book dating back to its earlier incarnation as a dissertation and has provided crucial feedback throughout the revision process. The reviewers of the book also gave the book an extremely thoughtful reading; their comments were critical to my revisions. Thanks also to Robert Jay Lifton for taking time from his busy schedule to write the preface to this book.

Of course, few books are published without the support of family members. My parents, Ladson and Darlene, created a warm and intellectually stimulating environment at home and have encouraged me in everything I have done. My brothers, Laddie and Devon, have been similarly supportive and are leading scholars in their fields. I have enjoyed many conversations with them and their family members, including Carina, Carolee, Devi, Kendra, Mikaela, and Susan. I also appreciate the support of my wonderful in-laws, Alissa, David, Jacki, Josh, Noah, and Peter.

Finally, my wife, Nicole, spent endless hours providing encouragement, reading over drafts of this manuscript, enduring absences while I was in the field, and helping me shape the book into its current form. It is, in a sense, her book too. Most importantly, she and our daughters, Meridian and Arcadia, brought me light during the many times I began to be dragged too deep into the darkness of the subject material. I dedicate the book to them.

. . .

Parts of this book were previously published, in different form, in the following places: "A Head for an Eye: Revenge in the Cambodian Genocide," *American Ethnologist* 25, no. 3 (1998):352–77; "Why Did You Kill? The Cambodian Genocide and the Dark Side of Face and Honor," *Journal of Asian Studies* 57, no. 1 (1998):93–122; "Agents of Death: Explaining the Cambodian Genocide in Terms of Psychosocial Dissonance," *American Anthropologist* 98, no. 4 (1996):818–31; "Under the Shade of Pol Pot's Umbrella: Myth and Mandala in the Cambodian Genocide," *The Vision Thing: Myth, Politics and Psyche in the Modern World,* edited by Tom Singer (New York: Routledge, 2000); "Genocidal Bricolage: A Reading of Human Liver-eating in Cambodia," *Yale University Genocide Studies Program Working Paper* [GS 06] (1998):16–38.

Timeline

September 1976 — *Revolutionary Flags* announces later founding date of CPK

September 20, 1976 — Ney Sarann arrested (marks purge of "Pracheachon" group)

December 20, 1976 — "Microbes" speech (signals intensification of purges)

January 25, 1977 — Koy Thuon arrested (marks purge of moderate intellectuals and Northern Zone)

February 1977 — Sreng arrested

April 10, 1977 — Hu Nim arrested

April–May 1977 — Purge of local Region 41 cadres intensifies (Southwestern cadres arrive and killing escalates)

September 1977 — Military conflict with Vietnam escalates

September 17, 1977 — Reap arrested (after attempting to instigate rebellion in Kompong Cham)

September 27, 1977 — Pol Pot's speech announcing existence of party

June 1978 — Sao Phim's suicide and Nhem Rhos's arrest

December 22, 1978 — Vietnamese invasion

January 11, 1979 — People Republic of Kampuchea (PRK) established

September 1989 — Withdrawal of Vietnamese troops

October 23, 1991 — Paris Peace Accords signed

July 1993 — UNTAC election (Royal Government of Cambodia established)

August 1996 — Ieng Sary faction defects

July 5, 1997 — Hun Sen coup

April 15, 1998 — Pol Pot dies

July 1998 — Election

late 1998 — Khmer Rouge movement ends (after Khieu Samphan and Nuon Chea defect)

May 13, 2003 — Passage of U.N. resolution on tribunal

July 2003 — Election

Personages

Boan — The chief at Trâpeang Trah, the Region 41 village where Vong resided during DK.

Chlat — A "new person" whose brother's family was executed at the Phnom Bros extermination center.

Duch — A former mathematics teacher who became the commandant of Tuol Sleng prison.

Euan — The commander of Division 310 and a native of Romeas, a village near Banyan. He was associated with Koy Thuon and purged in April 1977.

Grandmother Yit — A Khmer Rouge cadre from the Southwestern Zone who became the head of Kompong Siem district (in Region 41 of the Central Zone) during the purge of Koy Thuon's local network.

Hu Nim (aka Phoas) — A moderate revolutionary and DK minister of information who was purged in April 1977.

Hun Sen — A former Khmer Rouge officer who fled to Vietnam during the purges. He later became prime minister of the People's Republic of Kampuchea, the regime that succeeded Democratic Kampuchea. He has held power ever since and is the current prime minister of Cambodia.

Ke Pauk — The head of the Central Zone who helped to carry out the purge of Koy Thuon's local network.

Khel — A Khmer Rouge officer who was stationed at or near the Phnom Bros execution center during DK.

Koy Thuon (aka Khuon)	The former head of the Northern Zone and commerce secretary who was arrested and sent to Tuol Sleng prison in early 1977. Numerous members of his "string of traitors," including many officials from Region 41, were purged soon thereafter.
Lor	A Khmer Rouge cadre who worked at Tuol Sleng prison and oversaw the execution of its inmates at the nearby Choeung Ek killing field.
Neari	A "new person" who resided in Region 41 during DK. Her parents and seven siblings were killed by the Khmer Rouge.
Oum Chhan	A low-ranking Khmer Rouge cadre from the East Zone who was purged and sent to Tuol Sleng, where he confessed his "treason" after being tortured by Vaen Kheuan.
Reap	The commander of Division 174 who was in charge of the Phnom Bros execution center. After a failed rebellion, he was purged and sent to Tuol Sleng.
Rom	Grandmother Yit's younger cousin. She became the head of Krala subdistrict (Kompong Siem district located in Region 41) during the purge of Koy Thuon's Northern Zone network.
Sreng	The deputy secretary of the Northern Zone. He was associated with Koy Thuon and purged in February 1977.
Teap	A low-ranking cadre who worked under Rom.
Ung Pech	A "new person" who survived incarceration at Tuol Sleng because of his skills as a mechanic. He later became the director of the museum of genocide established at Tuol Sleng.
Vaen Kheuan	The Khmer Rouge interrogator who used torture to get Oum Chhan to produce a "confession" at Tuol Sleng.
Vann Nath	A "new person" who survived incarceration at Tuol Sleng because of his skills as a painter.
Vong	A Banyan villager who was caught stealing potatoes during DK. He likely survived because he was an "old person."

Foreword

The more closely one studies a particular genocide, the more one uncovers its special characteristics. But the careful scholar also becomes aware of certain general themes found in all genocides. Alex Hinton goes far toward connecting the particular with the universal in this most grotesque of realms.

His detailed study of the Cambodian genocide tells us much about its cultural roots in principles of honor, sanctioned rage, and disproportionate revenge. Yet he also makes clear that Maoist principles of mind manipulation or "thought reform" had a considerable influence. My own studies of Chinese thought reform attest to its potential for facilitating a broad socialization to genocide.

Indeed, the mass killing in Cambodia follows a sequence that has been observed in virtually every genocide: a sense of profound collective dislocation and humiliation, a historical "sickness unto death"; an ideological vision of revitalization and total cure, which comes to include a vast program of killing to heal; and the enlistment of a genocidal bureaucracy in an unending quest for national purification. I was able to observe this sequence in my study of Nazi doctors, and it is sadly but convincingly confirmed by Hinton's important work.

Genocide is apocalyptic, as it requires a form of world destruction in the service of a vision — or collective fantasy — of absolute political and spiritual renewal. In this way, studies such as Hinton's shed light on apocalyptic forces at play in our present world, whether found in relatively small cults like Aum Shinrikyo in Japan, in transnational terrorist groups like Al Qaeda, or even in America's "war on terrorism."

Hinton emphasizes the "high-modernist" pseudo-logic of the Khmer Rouge's murderous social engineering — a pattern that could be termed rationalist-apocalyptic — in combination with influences from Cambodian Buddhism (much as Maoism made use of Chinese Confucian principles). And toward the end of the book, in a grisly but profound segment, he suggests some of the primal passions that can underlie this "logic": he tells how two executioners eat the liver of their victim and then describes in revealing detail the many levels of significance of that act. Nowhere else has the bodily, literally visceral, dimension of genocide been so well illustrated.

Hinton's study contributes greatly to efforts, which must be continuous for all of us, to combat genocidal forces everywhere.

Robert Jay Lifton

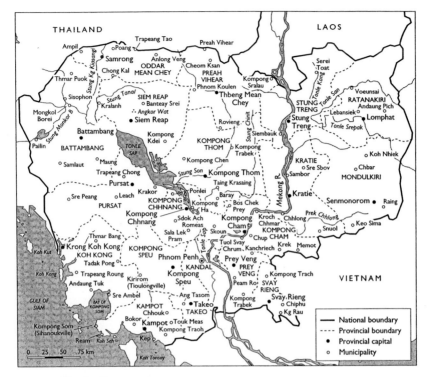

MAP 1. Cambodia, 1970

In the Shadow of Genocide

As long as I can still see my shadow while walking to the rice
fields, I will never be able to forget the slaughter committed by
the Khmer Rouge against my wife, children and the people of
Cambodia between 1975–1979.

Lay Ny, a farmer from Prey Veng[1]

Why did you kill? From the day I arrived in Cambodia to conduct
anthropological research, I wanted to pose this question to Khmer Rouge
who had executed people during the genocidal Democratic Kampuchea
regime, which lasted from April 1975 to January 1979. When the Khmer
Rouge, a radical group of Maoist-inspired rebels headed by Pol Pot,
came to power after a bloody civil war in which six hundred thousand
people died, they immediately set out to transform Cambodia into an
agrarian, communist state. In the process, they enacted policies that
resulted in the deaths of over one and a half million of Cambodia's eight
million inhabitants — more than 20 percent of the population — from
starvation, overwork, illness, malnutrition, and outright execution.

For most Cambodians, life during Democratic Kampuchea (hereafter
called DK) was like a giant prison camp in which basic rights and free-
doms were severely curtailed in the name of revolution. The cities were
evacuated; economic production and consumption were collectivized;
books were confiscated and sometimes burned; Buddhism and other
forms of religious worship were banned; freedom of speech, travel, resi-
dence, and occupational choice were dramatically curtailed; formal education largely disappeared; money, markets, and courts were abolished;
and the family was subordinated to the Party Organization, Ângkar.[2]
Cambodians I interviewed sometimes grimly described DK as "hell on
earth" *(norok lokiy)*, "the fire without smoke" *(phloeng et phsaeng)*, or
"the prison without walls" *(kuk et chonhcheang)*. One survivor explained

1

to me, "Everyone suffered as if they were in jail. We were ordered around and watched closely like prisoners. We were forced to work extremely hard, yet given little food. . . . There was no freedom. We weren't allowed to speak or move about freely. And, if there was a problem, a person would be killed and discarded. You always had to be prepared for death." Most Cambodians remember DK as a time of enforced, arduous labor, oppression, chronic starvation, prevalent illness and disease, widespread fear and terror, and death.

When I interviewed several Khmer Rouge cadres and soldiers about DK, they all denied killing people outside the battlefield. Finally, during my last month in Cambodia, I arranged an interview with a former soldier who had worked at Tuol Sleng, the infamous Phnom Penh prison where at least fourteen thousand people had been confined and then executed during DK, many after being tortured into giving a "confession." Finding this man, whom I will call Lor,[3] had not been easy. My research assistant, Bros, spent several days in an area south of Phnom Penh where a number of former Tuol Sleng cadres were rumored to live. One woman told Bros that she had worked at Tuol Sleng; when I formally interviewed her, however, she denied it. So, when Bros informed me that Lor openly admitted to working at Tuol Sleng and had agreed to come for an interview the next day, I was both intrigued and a bit apprehensive.

My feelings were exacerbated by rumors I had heard about Lor. An official at the Tuol Sleng Museum claimed that the man I was about to interview had admitted to killing four hundred people. One of the few prisoners to have survived Tuol Sleng told me that Lor had in fact executed more than two thousand men, women, and children. He said that Lor "was savage like an animal in the forest, like a wild dog or a tiger. I didn't dare look at his face. . . . We were terrified of him." Prior to the interview, I imagined Lor as a heinous person who exuded evil from head to toe. He was not what I expected. When he walked into the room, I saw before me a poor farmer in his late thirties, who greeted me with the broad smile and polite manner that one so often encounters in Cambodia.

After we had exchanged formalities, I began asking Lor about his life as a Khmer Rouge soldier. Lor denied being an interrogator or executioner at Tuol Sleng, but admitted to being a guard. In fact, he said he was eventually given responsibility for receiving new inmates and for transporting prisoners to a killing field located at Choeng Ek, a small village just outside of Phnom Penh. Lor emphasized that he did not execute people; he simply transported the prisoners to Choeng Ek and checked off the names as they were killed.

The method of execution Lor described was simple and brutal. One or two Khmer Rouge soldiers would lead a prisoner to a ditch in front of which he or she was ordered to kneel. A guard would then strike the prisoner once on the back of the neck with an iron bar. If the person didn't die immediately, the soldier would hit him or her repeatedly until the victim fell into the mass grave, which later was covered with dirt. Lor said that while the prisoners never tried to escape, they would often beg their executioner, "Please, don't kill me." Some prisoners went silently to their deaths; others screamed as they were killed.

As the interview continued, Lor explained that he had been arrested in 1979 and interrogated by district police of the new Vietnamese-backed government. Lor thought he would be killed so, when the police asked him how many people he had executed, he lied and said, "I am the killer, by myself, of one thousand people." Lor claimed he gave this false number in the hope that the police would kill him quickly. To his surprise, Lor was sent to prison for a year and then released. He returned to his native district, where he later married and had children.

At this point, I asked Lor, "So, during the Pol Pot period you never killed anyone?" Lor hesitated momentarily and then responded, "I did kill one or two people, but I did this so that others wouldn't accuse me of being unable to cut off my heart." While Lor's comment that he had killed "one or two people" suggested that he had killed many more, I decided not to press him on the matter for fear he would stop giving detailed answers, a pattern I had encountered in other interviews with former Khmer Rouge. Instead I asked him to explain why he had killed the "one or two" prisoners. Lor replied, "At the time, my boss was also present. . . . As we walked he asked me, 'Have you ever dared to kill one of them, Lor?' I responded, 'I never have, elder brother.' So he said, 'Like your heart isn't cut off *(chett min dach khat)*, go get that prisoner and try it once. Do it one time so I can see.'" Lor told the soldier who was about to execute the prisoner to give him the iron bar and then "struck the prisoner so they could watch me. I hit him one time with the iron bar and he fell to the ground. Afterwards, I threw the bar aside and returned to the place where I marked off the names. When my boss asked me to do this, if I didn't do it [pause] . . . I couldn't refuse."

· · ·

Lor's chilling story highlights the key problematic of this book: How do perpetrators like Lor come to commit murderous acts in such situations?

Was Lor a sadistic monster who was drawn to killing and reveled in it? Was he an ideological fanatic who raged against the despicable "hidden enemies burrowing from within" that Khmer Rouge speeches and radio broadcasts incessantly warned were subverting the revolution? Was he a strategic calculator who saw an opportunity to rise in rank in the new society and took it, regardless of the fact that he would be required to kill other human beings? Or, as Lor explained to me, was he merely "following orders" in a highly constrained environment and a difficult historical moment that victimized Lor by forcing him, on pain of death, to do things that he would otherwise not have chosen to do? These are highly controversial issues that have dominated debates in academic circles, journalistic accounts, and the popular imagination, and which I will explore in subsequent chapters of this book.

How are we to resolve the paradox of perpetration? It is best to resist simple, reductive explanations; while often containing some truth, they provide partial answers to the complex processes that move human beings to kill. A more complete answer requires that we consider a number of factors and leads us to other questions, in particular those dealing with the origins and dynamics of genocide.[4] The second key question with which this book is concerned is: How does genocide come to take place? How did the Khmer Rouge rise to power in the first place? Why did people like Lor join the revolutionary movement? Why did the DK leadership enact genocidal policies that resulted in the death and suffering of so many people? These issues in turn demand discussion of the conditions of life in this horrifying "prison without walls."

Such questions are notoriously difficult to answer. A number of people, many of them survivors of the Holocaust and other genocides, have warned that social science can never capture the experiential horror of genocide, suggesting that explanations of genocide risk oversimplification, and may lessen or even absolve guilt — a concern that is accentuated when perpetrators assert that they were "only obeying orders." Hannah Arendt's book, *Eichmann in Jerusalem*, generated enormous controversy precisely because it raised questions about the banality of evil and the moral culpability of Nazi bureaucrats like Adolf Eichmann. These matters are important ones, highlighting the importance of looking at multiple modalities of representation, from poetry to the visual arts, and of recognizing the limits of explanation.

Silence poses its own dangers, however. If we do not seek to analyze genocide, then it becomes a floating signifier of evil, appropriated at will for moral condemnation or contained in ways that make us feel more comfortable. Genocide has too often been associated with the "barbaric" in a sort of twentieth-century stage theory of mass violence in which "barbaric" acts of violence are linked to modes of being antithetical to and lower than those of "civilization." This conception is evident in the writings of Raphael Lemkin, the scholar and advocate who coined the term *genocide*. Lemkin originally proposed calling genocidal acts "crimes of *barbarity*."[5] His later search for a neologism was inspired, in part, by a speech in which Winston Churchill proclaimed, "We are in the presence of a crime without a name."[6] In one of his unpublished notebooks, Lemkin drew a line connecting "THE WORD" to "MORAL JUDGEMENT"; elsewhere he stated that the new term would serve as an "index of civilization."[7] In other words, his signifier would index a type of "modern" morality — and a type of "civil" society governed by international law — by marking its binary opposite. Through its association with barbarity, *genocide,* the signifier that Lemkin ultimately selected, implicitly diverted attention from the possibility that something all-too-modern was involved in this mass violence. The Nazis could more comfortably be viewed as an atavism, a throwback to a more "primitive" state of being that seemingly produces frenzies of mass violence in places like Bosnia and Rwanda — thus the frequent depiction of these conflicts as a primordial clash resulting from a seething cauldron of "ancient tribal hatreds."

This position is highly problematic.[8] There is a deep and complex relationship between genocide and modernity,[9] which are bound by tropes of "progress," projects of social engineering, the reification of group difference (often in terms of racial categories), capitalism and the pursuit of profit, bureaucratic distanciation, the rise of the nation-state and its highly increased centralization of power, technologies of mass murder, and crises of identity and the search for meaning in a world of upheaval. Moreover, to ignore this relationship is to overlook a deeply troubling implication — that some of the processes that help generate genocide are operative in our everyday lives, a point that was vividly illustrated by Stanley Milgram's obedience experiments, which I discuss in the Conclusion.[10]

To reflect on genocide, then, is not just to explore evil but also to gain greater insight into ourselves and the society in which we live. Furthermore, if we do not attempt to understand the etiology of genocide, we will be unable to prevent its recurrence. Analysis also provides a basis for advocacy, as the international community in general, and the United States in particular, has too often stood by as genocide unfolded, claiming ignorance or disbelief.[11] Rwanda and Bosnia are recent examples of this tragic trend.

For all of these reasons, it is crucial for us to try to understand perpetrator motivation and the origins of genocide. In doing so, we must bear in mind warnings about the limits of analysis and representation. Clearly, exegesis has limitations: it can never fully convey the experience of genocide and provides only a partial and positioned perspective. Moreover, no account can be complete, meaning that the picture the analyst constructs will inevitably have gaps. Having stated these caveats, in what follows I attempt to fit together a number of analytical "pieces" of the puzzle about why people kill and how genocide comes to take place. The book is also meant as an example of how anthropology can engage with pressing public issues like genocide, about which the discipline has much to say and much remains to be said.

. . .

When I first traveled to Cambodia as a graduate student in 1992, I did not expect that I would study genocide and meet people like Lor. I had just completed my second year of doctoral studies and planned to do language training and preliminary research on the embodiment of emotion in Cambodia. Upon my arrival, I was immediately struck by the devastation the country had suffered. The signs of a quarter-century of civil war and genocide were omnipresent. Urban shantytowns, beggars, roads scarred with potholes that were sometimes impassable, a lack of electricity, tattered clothing, and malnourished children suggested a debilitated infrastructure and endemic poverty. One was reminded of the prevalence of mines by the frequent sight of the maimed and the many red skull-and-crossbones signs reading "Danger! Mines!" Cambodia was also awash with munitions, ranging from handguns and AK-47s to unexploded ordnance (much of it from U.S. bombing raids during the Vietnam War) in villages and rice paddies. Later I developed an eye for more subtle signs: bullet holes in the side of a building, the large number of female-headed households, the vague contour of a bomb crater in a rice field, the difficulty of finding expert informants, or a slight tensing of the body when "the Pol Pot period" was discussed.[12]

Statistically, Cambodia ranks in the world's bottom tier in terms of poverty, infant mortality, life expectancy, and per capita income.[13] In 1995, the per capita income was $260 (a figure that has barely risen since); according to the World Bank, Cambodia was then one of the twenty poorest countries in the world. The country had the dubious distinction of having almost one unexploded mine for every Cambodian man, woman, and child (Cambodia also has the highest percentage of amputees in the world) and, more recently, of having one of Asia's highest rates of HIV infection. While the Cambodian genocide did not cause all of these problems (many of which were exacerbated by a U.S.-led international embargo of the Vietnamese-backed People's Republic of Kampuchea during the 1980s), it has been a major contributor to the difficult life conditions so many Cambodians confront.

The year 1992 was a time of hope. The United Nations Transitional Authority in Cambodia (UNTAC) was preparing to oversee an election that would allow the various Cambodian factions that had been fighting since the end of DK to become part of a new, democratically elected government. Still, the wealth of thousands of foreign UNTAC officials and soldiers stood in strong contrast to Cambodia's endemic poverty. White cars, trucks, and sports utility vehicles, stamped in black with "UN," filled the roads of Cambodia, contrasting sharply with the mopeds and pedicabs that most Cambodians used for transport. Many U.N. officials received a per diem of $145, an amount that seemed outrageous given Cambodia's per capita income. Although an election eventually was held, it was hampered by the pullout of the Khmer Rouge, political violence, and a threatened secession that enabled the ruling government to effectively maintain their hold on power despite losing at the polls.

During this time, I lived with a Cambodian family and took Khmer classes at the University of Phnom Penh. I was struck by the fact that, despite the suffering they had endured, most of the people I met were extremely friendly and warm. This social demeanor, which is partly linked to local conceptions of face, honor, and social harmony, no doubt contributed to colonial and postcolonial characterizations of Cambodia as a "gentle, smiling land" — stereotypes formed in ignorance and belied by Cambodian history.

Almost inevitably, most Cambodians I got to know eventually began to tell me about their experiences during DK, often quite unexpectedly. These recollections often began with a description of the March 18, 1970 overthrow of Prince Sihanouk, who had ruled Cambodia since 1953, when he led the country to independence from French colonial rule. This was a landmark event since, within days of the coup, Sihanouk had joined his former enemy, the Khmer Rouge, in calling upon his rural "children" to fight the "illegitimate" Khmer Republic (1970–75), which had been established after Sihanouk's overthrow by his former general,

Lon Nol.[14] While the coup was supported by many urbanites, particularly the middle class, the educated, traders, and merchants, Sihanouk's speech galvanized large numbers of peasants to follow their beloved, charismatic, fatherly king in joining the Khmer Rouge movement. Although the Khmer Rouge had been active in Cambodia for over fifteen years, it was only after the Vietnam War intensified and Sihanouk was overthrown that they began to gain the legitimacy and support that would bring them to power.

During the next five years, the U.S.-backed Khmer Republic engaged in a fierce civil war with the Khmer Rouge, who were supported by communist China and, at least initially, North Vietnam. Life in Cambodia became increasingly difficult as the economy collapsed, foreign soldiers (Vietcong, South Vietnamese, and U.S. troops) encroached and skirmished on Cambodian soil, and bullets, artillery shells, and bombs rained from the sky. The destruction wrought by ground battles was compounded by intensive U.S. bombing.[15] Between 1969 and 1973, nearly 540,000 tons of bombs — over three times the tonnage dropped on Japan during World War II — were dropped on Cambodian soil, almost half of it in 1973. On the local level, the bombing resulted in enormous suffering, impoverishment, displacement, and perhaps as many as 150,000 deaths. Hundreds of thousands of rural Cambodians fled to the cities. Phnom Penh, which had had a prewar population of around six hundred thousand people, held roughly two million refugees by the end of the war. In total, perhaps six hundred thousand Cambodians had perished by the time the Khmer Rouge achieved victory in April 1975.

Upon taking power, the Khmer Rouge set out to achieve a "super great leap forward" into socialism that would be unprecedented and would supposedly create, as a May 1975 radio broadcast announced, "the cleanest, most fair society ever known in our history."[16] They immediately ordered the urban population to evacuate the cities "for a few days." The urban dwellers would not be allowed to return. Hundreds of thousands of Cambodians streamed out of Phnom Penh and other cities, a journey that urbanites remember for the sweltering heat, the stench, the times when the masses moved at a crawl, the fear of armed Khmer Rouge soldiers, the loss of their homes, the uncertainty of the future, the panicked attempt to make it to a familiar village, the first "disappearances" of loved ones, and the unusual and sometimes bizarre sights — swollen corpses, hospital patients being pushed along still hooked to IVs, women giving birth by the side of the road, isolated executions, and even the occasional suicide of people who would rather die than live under the Khmer Rouge. Peng, a boy at this time, recalled:

> I remember when my family made the journey from Phnom Penh . . . and took a boat to Prek Kdam. While riding in the boat, I heard people speaking about the corpses they saw floating on the water. I looked and saw lots of corpses floating in the river. When the boat arrived at Prek Tam, my family got out and journeyed onward. There were many people walking in groups along National Highway 6. Some pushed small carts loaded with things, some carried possessions, some held small children in their arms. Everyone walked from four o'clock in the morning until ten o'clock at night, when they all rested along the side of the road. The road really stank from the corpses of soldiers and people who had died from illness along the road, since they didn't have access to medicine or a doctor. Because at that time, people drank water that was not hygienic, water from a pond next to the road that had corpses and feces in it. There were a lot of corpses along the road creating a stench; no one had buried the bodies.

When they were eventually settled in rural villages, such urban dwellers, including both longtime urbanites and peasant refugees who had fled to the cities during the civil war, discovered that they were labeled "new people" *(brâcheachon tmey)*, "1975 people," or members of "the April 17 group" *(puok dap brampir mesa)*. The rural villagers who had resided in Khmer Rouge zones during the war, in turn, were called "old people" *(brâcheachon chas)* or "base people" *(brâcheachon moulâdthan)*.

Both "new people" and "old people" found themselves living in a radically changed world. The Khmer Rouge initiated radical structural transformations, which were inspired, despite Khmer Rouge assertions about the uniqueness of their revolution, by Soviet, North Vietnamese, Thai communist, and, especially, Maoist models.[17] As in these cases, the preexisting "exploitative" relations of production were fundamentally altered through collectivization and the creation of cooperatives *(sâhâkâr)*, though more rapidly than ever before. The party's 1977 Four-Year Plan proclaimed that the regime had "achieved a socialist society straight away. The situation is completely different from other countries. . . . We are faster . . . we are four to ten years ahead of them. We have new relations of production; nothing is confused, as it is with them."[18]

Collectivization strongly undermined three key features of traditional peasant life: the family, whose members jointly engaged in economic production and consumption; the village, which was composed of friends and relatives who shared a sense of identity and sometimes assisted one another; and Buddhism, which provided a social, moral, and educational locus for everyday life.[19] In the new society, Buddhism was banned and the means and relations of production communalized. Cambodians soon were working and dining in collectives that provided the large labor pool needed to accomplish the key economic goal of the new regime: dramatically increasing rice production to yield enough food to "raise the standard of living of the people" and generate capital needed for imports, defense, and the development of industry.[20] The Khmer Rouge calculated that they could attain the requisite rice surpluses by increasing the average rice yield per hectare from one to three metric tons of paddy, a goal that was stressed in the Khmer Rouge refrain, "Three tons per hectare."

To achieve this goal, the DK regime mobilized the entire population to increase production. Throughout the country, people were divided into work "forces" *(kâmlang)* based on sex and age.[21] Mobile work teams *(kâng châlat)*, consisting of young, unmarried teenagers and adults, engaged in strenuous labor (for example, digging dams and canals or clearing large swaths of land), often traveling great distances to work with thousands of other Cambodians on huge Khmer Rouge projects. Married adults also labored hard, but tended to reside in villages and work for their cooperative. The elderly and the very young, in turn, performed light tasks for the cooperative, though children were sometimes sent away to live together in camps. This division of labor often separated family members.

The work groups were sexually segregated and organized along military lines into "squads," "platoons," "companies," "battalions," and "regiments." Such military metaphors were omnipresent in Khmer Rouge discourse. Just as an enemy would be defeated in battle, so too would the revolutionary spirit of the people "defeat" the problems facing the country and enable them to "become masters of the lands, the rice paddies, harvests, indeed, of the fruits of their labor."[22] Units *(kâng)* of workers from the cooperatives were sent to "launch offensives" *(veay sâmrok)*, "struggle" *(brâyut)*, and "fight heroically" *(tâsou)* on the economic "front lines" *(sâmârâphoum mukh)*. As Haing Ngor explains:

> "Struggle" was military talk, like "front lines." It reflected the idea that the nation was still at war. On the front lines we didn't just work, we "struggled," or else "launched offensives." We were to "struggle to cultivate rice fields vigorously," "struggle to dig canals with great courage," "struggle to clear the forest," and even "struggle to solve the manure problem." We

were to "launch an offensive to plant strategic crops," and "launch an offensive to perform duty with revolutionary zeal." . . . The goal of this struggling and launching of offensives was "victory," or "mastery." We were going to achieve "victory over the elements." We would become "master of the rice paddies and fields and forests," "master of the earth and water," "master of the canals," "master of the flood problem."[23]

Victory would be achieved when the people had mastered nature and achieved the "super great leap forward." The Khmer Rouge did not hesitate to move large numbers of people to achieve this goal. In late 1975 and early 1978, hundreds of thousands of Cambodians — most of them "new people" — were relocated to underpopulated (and sometimes barely habitable) areas, particularly in the northeast and northwest, that allegedly had rich agricultural potential.

Despite its ambitious plans, the DK regime quickly ran into problems that derailed the revolution and ultimately fueled mass murder.[24] Although it made some gains, the regime failed to attain its economic objectives. To meet their large, inflexible production quotas, local cadres sometimes sent rice to Phnom Penh that should have been set aside for consumption. When the party leadership heard reports that people in the countryside were suffering, they decided that subversion was to blame. Thus a December 1976 political speech, thought to have been given by Pol Pot, stated that "hidden enemies seek to deprive the people of food, while following our orders to an extent. . . . They take our circular instructions and use them to mistreat the people and to deprive them, forcing them to work, whether they are sick or healthy."[25]

The existence of such "hidden enemies" confirmed the necessity of the political purges already underway. The DK regime decided to "purify" the general populace, targeting hundreds of thousands of "class enemies" for elimination. At the same time, "bad elements" within the ranks of the party had to be purged. Tens of thousands of cadres were eventually arrested and killed, many after being forced to "confess" their crimes at interrogation centers like Tuol Sleng. If many of these confessions referenced alleged economic sabotage and membership in traitorous networks, they also increasingly included mention of ties to Vietnam — particularly after 1976, when tensions between DK and Vietnam escalated, resulting in military clashes that culminated in Vietnam's overthrow of the DK regime in early January 1979.

The ease of Vietnam's victory was facilitated by the DK purges, which had resulted in the execution of many of the country's best-trained cadres, already in short supply. In addition to losing experienced cadres, the Khmer Rouge had trouble building the local infrastructure necessary to indoctrinate the masses. The DK regime explicitly recognized this "problem of cadres," which prevented the party line from "being absorbed" by the people and thereby transformed into proper revolutionaries. As the December 1976 speech states, "The line must seep in everywhere until it is effective. When we solve this problem, we can solve any others that arise."[26] The "problem of cadres" was evident at the frequent political meetings people had to attend, where local cadres, many of whom were uneducated and barely understood the party line, often spoke in an unconvincing manner, reciting a litany of clichéd slogans. Unable to inspire the populace, such cadres used fear and force to ensure compliance.

Not surprisingly, most Cambodians, including many "old people" and members of the Khmer Rouge, became increasingly dissatisfied with this repressive regime, which created a society characterized by unrelenting work, malnutrition, starvation, illness, familial rupture, the loss of Buddhism, a lack of rights, brutality, terror, and death. Chlat, a "new person" who returned to his home village in Prei Chhor district after the Khmer Rouge took power, described some of the difficulties he endured:

> The mobile work force performed the really hard labor. They called us the "shock troops" and we often slept in the countryside. . . . My suffering greatly increased when I was working on the mobile work team. . . . For instance, when we were working at a dam site, we were required to carry four cubic meters of earth each day. Sometimes we could do it and other times we couldn't. If you were short, the head of our mobile work group would have the others come and help us finish. It was really difficult. They would walk around inspecting to make sure that we had transported all four meters of earth. At mealtimes, a gong would sound and we'd go get a plate of food. Everyone had one spoon to eat with. . . . When I first joined the mobile work team, we were just given rice gruel. Sometimes things were better, sometimes they were worse. In my district, things got better during harvest season. We'd get a ladle of rice. But a little later the rice would become scarcer, and we'd just get rice gruel again. . . . In some places, people would receive as little as a half a [condensed-milk] can of rice gruel.
>
> And there was so much sickness. No one had any strength and people became emaciated. . . . But at the hospitals, [the staff] didn't know how to do anything. They just guessed at it. Sometimes they would just grind up some tree bark and mix it with something. When they had enough, they'd inject it into people. . . .
>
> Once I came home to visit and found that my parents were ill. That night I had a dream that I had lost a tooth. I thought, "My parents are ill, surely one of them will die." Before I left again, I whispered to my sister, quietly so that my father wouldn't know and become frightened, "Elder

sister, please try really hard to care for mother and father or anyone else who becomes ill." When I left, my mother felt very bad for me. She was standing there under a tree in front of the house watching me go. After I had traveled a kilometer, I turned back and she was still there watching me. She did that until I was out of eyesight. . . .

My mother was sick for three months. I went around pleading for medicine, telling them, "I'll give you anything, even my arm, if you give me some medicine for my mother." But I couldn't get any. My mother eventually died after drinking a bit of water and then throwing it up. I was really angry [at the Khmer Rouge]. There was only one monk left in our village. He helped us perform some brief rites. The next day, Pol Pot's plan to get rid of all monks was implemented, and the monk was disrobed. . . . Still, my mother was lucky that she died before the Khmer Rouge ordered my brother's entire family to get into a truck and drove them off to be killed. If my mother had experienced this event, it would have surely driven her mad.

Given such suffering and privation, it is not surprising that, despite their traditional fears of the Vietnamese, few Cambodians opposed the Vietnamese army when it invaded Cambodia in late December 1978: most felt relief and joy when the DK regime fell in early January 1979.

Unfortunately, life has not been easy for Cambodians since that time. When the Vietnamese-backed People's Republic of Kampuchea (PRK) took power in early 1979, it was confronted by a number of problems, including a severely damaged infrastructure, a flood of refugees fleeing to Thailand, and a possible famine.[27] Social services, including health care and education, were practically nonexistent, and much of Cambodia's civil service had to be rebuilt from scratch. To its credit, the PRK regime moved quickly to address many of these problems, an impressive feat given the internal chaos and the international isolation the country faced because of its association with Vietnam. Buddhism reemerged, though in a limited form at first, and the economy was reorganized in a semisocialist manner, which was later abandoned. Meanwhile, the international community imposed an embargo on Cambodia, while assisting the Khmer Rouge and other groups that were waging civil war against the PRK. Despite its genocidal past, the Khmer Rouge was even given a share of Cambodia's seat at the United Nations, while the PRK regime was excluded.

Formal and informal peace negotiations began in the mid 1980s, culminating in the 1991 Paris Agreement, which called for a United Nations–sponsored election in 1993.[28] By this time, the PRK regime, headed by Hun Sen, had renamed itself the State of Cambodia (SOC) and initiated a number of reforms to liberalize the economy, privatize property, and make Buddhism the state religion. Despite pre-election political violence and intimidation and a threat that the Khmer Rouge, who were boycotting the election, might disrupt the polls, the 1993 elections were held in a relatively "free and fair" manner and elicited high voter turnout. Although the royalist party, FUNCINPEC, won the most seats in the National Assembly, it was forced by a threatened secession to accept a power-sharing agreement with the Cambodian's People's Party (CPP), the political arm of the SOC regime. A new constitution restored the monarchy and established the Royal Government of Cambodia (RGC), nominally headed by King Sihanouk, who "reigns but does not rule." After roughly a quarter-century of armed conflict and five different governments, Cambodia was welcomed back into the international community, regaining its seat in the United Nations and worldwide legitimacy.

Problems remained, however.[29] While open-market policies enabled some people to become extremely wealthy, many more continued to live in poverty and suffer from a lack of adequate social services. Political tensions also persisted between FUNCINPEC and the CPP, whose leader, Second Prime Minister Hun Sen, wielded true power due to the CPP's organizational base and disproportionate influence over the police, army, and judiciary. These tensions culminated in a July 5, 1997 coup in which FUNCINPEC and its leader, Prince Ranariddh, were routed. The international community once again intervened, and new elections were held the following year. With the opposition in disarray, Hun Sen's CPP won the 1998 election and has held power since.

The year 1998 also marked the final demise of the Khmer Rouge. After boycotting the 1993 election and continuing to fight the new government, the Khmer Rouge leadership gradually lost support due to a RGC program that enticed Khmer Rouge soldiers tired of war to defect. The 1996 defection of a large faction of troops associated with Ieng Sary, Pol Pot's brother-in-law and longtime comrade, left the Khmer Rouge with a much smaller force and diminished territorial holdings. When Pol Pot heard rumors that another longtime associate, Son Sen, might defect in June 1997, he ordered the execution of Son Sen, his wife, and a dozen other family members. His actions ignited an internal feud within the Khmer Rouge that ended with Pol Pot's overthrow by his former general, Ta Mok.

Pol Pot became a captive of his own movement and a month later was convicted by a "People's Tribunal" to life imprisonment (house confinement) as crowds of former followers shouted at him, "Crush! Crush! Crush! Pol Pot and his clique!" Pol Pot sat with his head bowed, "an anguished old man, frail eyes struggling to focus on no-one, watching his life's vision crumble in utter, final defeat."[30] When asked if he felt responsible for what had happened during DK, Pol Pot told journalist Nate Thayer, "My conscience is clear. Everything I have done and contributed is first for the nation and the people and the race of Cambodia. . . . I came to carry out the struggle, not to kill people. . . . Even now, and you can look at me: Am I a savage person?"[31] Pol Pot died less than a year later without having taken responsibility or been held accountable for the death of more than 1.6 million Cambodians.

The Khmer Rouge movement came to an end at the close of 1998, when Nuon Chea and Khieu Samphan, two senior Khmer Rouge leaders, agreed to end their armed struggle and disbanded their troops. After thirty years, Cambodia finally had peace. In early 1999, Ta Mok and the former head of Tuol Sleng, Duch, were arrested. They have remained in prison since then, awaiting a decision on whether they and other senior Khmer Rouge leaders will be tried before a U.N.-sponsored criminal court, an eventuality that now looks likely with the signing of an agreement between the United Nations and Cambodia on June 6, 2003.

While Cambodia's recent history is filled with devastating moments, I was strongly affected by the testimonials people gave about DK. Many Cambodians spoke of this period with tears in their eyes; a few broke down in sobs, unable to continue. These stories, like so many I subsequently heard, have stayed with me, demanding explanation: How could this happen? Why did so many people suffer and die under the Khmer Rouge? What could motivate a person to participate in mass murder?

Such questions are particularly vexing in the Cambodian case, since much of the killing was perpetrated by ethnic Khmer against ethnic Khmer — thus the occasional characterization of the Khmer Rouge period as an "autogenocide." While this label is problematic (it overlooks the fact that the Khmer Rouge also targeted ethnic minorities, including Muslim Chams, Vietnamese, and Chinese, and that ethnic Khmer were manufactured into different sorts of political beings), it does foreground a contrast with other cases, including the Armenian genocide, the Holocaust, and the Rwandan genocide, where the killing more directly followed the lines of preexisting communal divisions that, while fluid and malleable, were more easily crystallized into rigid differentiations that could serve as a basis for mass murder in particular historical contexts. Thus, as I discuss in Chapter 5, while genocidal regimes usually make intensive efforts to manufacture difference, the Khmer Rouge leadership did so to an even greater degree, since the political and class differences it asserted were often quite difficult to discern on the local level.

. . .

I returned to Cambodia for a year from 1994 to 1995 to conduct my doctoral fieldwork. While I had initially intended to live and work in a rural
village, I quickly found that this would be difficult because of security
concerns. Just before my arrival in Cambodia, a group of Khmer Rouge
soldiers (the Khmer Rouge were still active in parts of Cambodia more
than fifteen years after the end of DK) had seized three Western tourists,
whom they would later execute. Shortly thereafter, Khmer Rouge radio
announced that the group was putting a price on the head of people from
several Western countries, including the United States. Because of this
event and other safety problems, I decided to do a multi-site ethnography, residing in Kompong Cham city and conducting research there, in
Phnom Penh, and in a nearby rural village, which I will call Banyan.

Much of my research was carried out in Banyan, which is located at
the intersection of two small dirt roads roughly seven kilometers from
Kompong Cham city. Several days a week, I would travel to the village
by moped, a journey that took about twenty minutes. Banyan is moderately large, comprising over five hundred villagers (246 men and 268
women at the time of my census) living in ninety-five homes. Almost half
of the villagers (250 people) were under the age of eighteen, a demo-
graphic that is not uncommon in Cambodia and that, along with the
large number of female headed households, reflects the country's recent
violent past.

Although the villagers primarily practice single-crop, wet rice farming,
they supplement their income by growing sugarcane, potatoes, corn,
peanuts, and various types of beans. Many also have small vegetable gardens and fruit groves. A small number of villagers earn extra cash in
other ways, such as extracting sugar palm juice, selling cigarettes and
snacks at a stall in front of their homes, or working in construction or as
police. While a few Banyan villagers are destitute, most are able to eke
out a living each year. In general, Banyan is slightly better off than more
remote villages. A modest number of relatively large homes have wood
and tile roofs, more than one room, and entrance steps made of concrete
and wood (as opposed to the sugar palm thatch roofs, single-room
dwellings, and spare wooden ladders of the poor). In Khmer fashion, the
homes are raised on wooden piles set in concrete, with the homes of the
wealthy typically larger and higher up. With a few exceptions, the homes
line the two roads, which form a "T," and are surrounded by gardens
and lush, green paddy fields sprinkled with sugar palms.

For the most part, the life of the villagers follows the seasonal cycle. With the arrival of the rains in May or June, the earth softens and villagers begin to prepare their rice fields (the seasonal cultivation of fruits and vegetables varies somewhat depending on the crop). Over the next few months, they plow the fields, sow the rice seed, and eventually transplant the seedlings from nursery beds to the main fields. The crops are usually harvested in December, just as the rains taper off. During the dry and increasingly hot months that follow, many villagers engage in part-time work while awaiting the next rainy season.

The farming cycle in Banyan also provides grim reminders of the past, as the plows sometimes pull up pieces of cloth, teeth, or shards of bone marking the village's location next to Phnom Bros, an enormous DK killing center where over thirteen thousand people were executed and then buried in dozens of mass graves and even a couple of village wells. The villagers, however, were not allowed to reside in Banyan while Phnom Bros was being used as an extermination center. In 1973, the Khmer Rouge overran the village as they battled Lon Nol soldiers for control of the nearby Kompong Cham airport. They ordered the villagers to evacuate Banyan.

While the experiences of the villagers varied dramatically, many provided testimonials that broadly resembled that of Vong, a man who was in his early thirties during DK. Vong recalled that, like other families in Banyan, he and his wife lived in constant fear of being killed in crossfire between the Khmer Rouge and Lon Nol soldiers guarding the Kompong Cham airstrip, which was located a kilometer up the road. By 1972, most of the villagers had dug bunkers near their houses and would scramble into them when artillery fire began. Some families slept in the bunkers at night. When the Khmer Rouge entered Banyan in 1973 and told everyone to leave, Vong and his fellow villagers obeyed. Although a few families with military ties fled to Phnom Penh, most were sent to live in villages in western Kompong Cham that were already under Khmer Rouge control.

In 1973–75, Vong lived in Chomkar Loe district. Aside from rampant malaria, life in the district was not as difficult as it was in some Khmer Rouge zones. People were allowed to dine and, for the most part, work on their own. During this period, the Khmer Rouge sold rice to the villagers at cheap prices, and sometimes even helped them with their work. Vong explained, "At first, the Khmer Rouge were good. Perhaps 70 to 80 percent of the rural population liked and believed in them because the Khmer Rouge were honest and helpful. Many people hated Lon Nol at this time." After the Khmer Rouge seized total control of the country in April 1975, Vong wanted to return to Banyan. Local officials gave his family permission to do so. When Vong arrived at the road leading to Banyan, however, soldiers informed him that he could not live there. The entire area around Phnom Bros, including Banyan, had been secured by Khmer Rouge soldiers. Later, Vong discovered that the Khmer Rouge had used the site as an execution center where thousands of Cambodians were brought by truck and then killed. Vong's family was told to go live in a nearby village, Trâpeang Trah.

Vong found life in Trâpeang Trah quite different from what he had experienced previously. Even the name of the region in which he lived had changed — instead of Kompong Cham, his home was now referred to as Region 41 of the Northern Zone. In the Khmer Rouge territorial-administrative system, old provincial designations were replaced by a new "zone" (phoumipheak) system that, by 1975, included: the South-west Zone, the Eastern Zone, the Northeastern Zone, the Northern Zone (later divided off from a newly created Central Zone that included Regions 41, 42, and 43), the Northwestern Zone, the Western Zone, and a Special Zone around Phnom Penh. As illustrated on Map 2, each zone was composed of several numbered "sectors" or "regions" (tombuan). After they took power, the Khmer Rouge formalized and expanded this territorial administrative system so that it incorporated the traditional subdivisions (below sectors) of districts (srok), subdistricts (khum), and villages (phoum), which were later combined into cooperatives (sâhâkor) for economic purposes.

The changes, however, went far beyond the territorial administrative system. As opposed to farming his own land, Vong now had to work on communal work teams according to the long hours set by local officials. In addition to laboring all day, Vong was also ordered to work at night during the harvest season. By the beginning of 1976, eating was communalized, and Vong's family dined in a large hall with many other families. A bell signaled mealtime. At first the villagers were given rice in the morning and rice gruel at night. By the end of the year, however, they were served small portions of rice gruel at both meals. People became thinner and thinner, and a few of the elderly died of starvation.

The villagers were required to attend frequent meetings at which local cadres told them that they should love the party and obey its directives without question. Vong recalled, "They told us that if the plan called for rice-farming, we had to do it. If Ângkar ["the Organization"] said to do something, we had to do it without argument." The cadres also some-

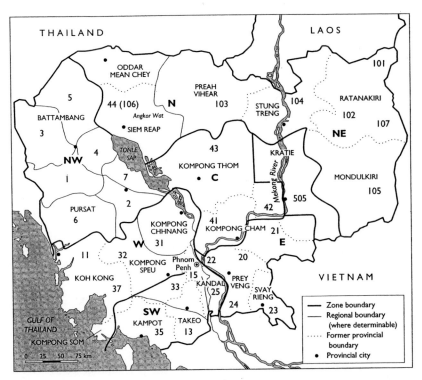

MAP 2. Divisions of Democratic Kampuchea, 1975–79

times discussed politics, warning that the Vietnamese coveted Cambodian land or that enemies still lived among the populace. Ironically, cadres sometimes asked the assembled villagers if they had enough food. Vong explained, "We didn't dare say were weren't full, even though we weren't. We responded 'full' or 'yes.' Once a man named El told them that the people weren't receiving enough food. He disappeared a few days later." Vong also recalled that the Khmer Rouge employed a common DK refrain during the meetings. "They said if we protested or didn't follow Ângkar's instructions, there wouldn't be a profit in keeping us. They'd say, 'To keep you is no profit, to destroy you is no loss.' That made everyone scared."

When cadres from the Southwest Zone arrived in 1977, a political purge began and the killings intensified. The village head, Boan, had at first governed in a relatively benign manner. Over time, Vong explained, Boan was brainwashed by Khmer Rouge ideology and became increasingly angry at the "enemies" his superiors told him were still living in the villages. More than thirty of the village's three hundred inhabitants were taken away to be killed after Boan reported their "suspect" backgrounds and activities. Most were Muslim Chams, "new people," or "old people" who had been soldiers. An atmosphere of terror pervaded the village. Vong explained, "We were all terrified. Even though I was exhausted from work, it was hard to sleep at night because I feared they would come take me away to be executed. We didn't even dare look at the faces of the big cadres. If one passed by, I would turn my face away or look down. We were so scared." People were afraid to gather in groups for fear that they would be accused of "talking against Ângkar" and then disappear.

Even terror could not prevent the people from trying to find food to fill their empty stomachs. One evening, while Vong was attempting to steal two potatoes, he was caught by Boan and sent to the local detention center. Vong was sure he would be executed. The next day, Vong was interrogated by one of Boan's superiors, a Southwest cadre named Leuang. Leuang asked Vong if he was a "new" or an "old person" and told him to describe his background. Vong complied and told Leuang: "I love the revolution and am willing to die for it. I stole the potatoes so I would have the strength to work hard for the revolutionary organization." Perhaps because of this explanation and the fact that he was an "old person," Vong was released. Leuang warned Vong that if he tried to run away, his wife and children would be executed.

A few months later, Boan, who had been selected by a cadre named Krauch, was purged by the Southwest cadre. The new village head, Saun, was friendly with Vong and showed him a list containing the names of some living residents of Trâpeang Trah, including Vong, as well as those who already had been executed. Saun then erased the names of the living from this list of "enemies." Life under Saun's rule was much better: only one person was executed, and that death was due to information gathered by a female cadre from the Southwest, Rom, and her secret police. People continued to live in hunger and fear, but their intense terror decreased.

Following the Vietnamese invasion, Vong's family, which had survived DK intact (many other Banyan villagers lost family members to starvation, illness, or execution), returned to Banyan. Although Vong had observed trucks filled with people driving down the road toward the Phnom Bros, he was not fully prepared for what he now saw. First he and his wife found a place where the clothes of the Phnom Bros victims had been burned. "Then we found all the graves, some of which still had limbs sticking up through the dirt. The place stank." Initially, many Banyan villagers were scared to live so close to the mass graves, some of which had been dug in their rice fields. The Khmer Rouge had even dumped corpses into nearby village wells. Gusts of wind occasionally carried the stench of death.

After a while, however, the villagers' fear lessened, and they settled back into life at their old home. Some even joined the dozens of people who dug through the mass graves to find the gold that some victims had sewn into the lining of their clothes when they journeyed to their "new home." Twenty years later, the killing fields were a distant memory to the Banyan villagers, though even today they unearth gruesome reminders — teeth, shards of bone, and pieces of cloth — of the victims. Vong says that at such times he pities the victims and thinks about how close he came to death when he stole the two potatoes.

In addition to recording these riveting testimonials, I used traditional ethnographic methods, living with Cambodians and participating in their daily lives. Besides Banyan, I conducted interviews in Kompong Cham city and the outlying areas, and in Phnom Penh. In Kompong Cham city, I lived with a relatively affluent family, renting a room large enough to also serve as an office and interview space. This arrangement enabled me to meet privately with Banyan villagers, former DK cadres and soldiers, urbanites, and teachers. I also used my Kompong Cham home as a base from which to visit local temples, provincial government offices, and both urban and rural primary and secondary schools.

I spent my last month of fieldwork living in a rented apartment in Phnom Penh. During this period, I worked at the Tuol Sleng Museum of Genocidal Crimes, gathering such documentary material as forced confessions, a study guide for interrogators, cadre notebooks, and DK propaganda. The staff at the museum provided me with leads that enabled me to interview Lor. I also used this time to conduct interviews with journalists, human rights workers, politicians, and acquaintances. In total, I collected over one hundred hours of tape-recorded interviews on violence, culture, socialization practices, life histories, and the DK period. I also gathered research data from Cambodian school texts, books on Cambodian socialization practices, didactic poetry, proverbs, videos, and newspaper articles.

Much of my analysis is based on original Khmer Rouge documents that were unavailable or difficult to obtain during my fieldwork. Thanks to the hard work of the Cornell University Document Preservation

Project, the Cambodian Genocide Project, and the Documentation
Center of Cambodia (DC-CAM), such documentation has become
increasingly available. Many new caches of documents have been discovered, particularly since 1998. This new material has been central to
the revision of my dissertation into a book.[32]

· · ·

If I had originally gone to the field with the broad intention of studying
genocide, by the time I returned to the United States I knew that my
ethnography would focus on perpetrator motivation and the dynamics of
genocide. As I searched for ways to frame the findings that had emerged
from my research, I was struck by how little anthropologists had written
on the topic of genocide. Anthropologists were vocal in defending indigenous peoples from the onslaughts of modernity, but enormous gaps
remained. I have yet to find an anthropological article written on the
Armenian genocide, and with a few exceptions, anthropologists
remained silent about the Holocaust until the mid 1980s — over forty
years after the fact — and since then have published only a handful of
book chapters and articles on the subject.[33] Much more helpful was a
growing body of anthropological work on political violence, particularly
work on the cultural patterning and bodily inscription of violence,[34]
though this literature has not fully grappled with the issue of perpetrator
motivation.

I am also fortunate to have conducted research in a country where a
number of excellent scholars, including anthropologists, have done prior
research. My project builds on the invaluable work of historians and
political scientists who have provided crucial insights about the many
ways in which political dynamics, international affairs, socioeconomic
conditions, and historical processes ("macrolevel" analysis) contributed
to the Khmer Rouge genocide.[35] However, while such scholars have provided rich and valuable insights into the events that took place prior to
and during DK, they have paid less attention to the local, experiential,
and motivational aspects ("microlevel" analysis) of the genocide. Several
anthropologists have partially addressed this issue in important chapters
and articles,[36] but there has yet to be written a book that focuses explicitly on the cultural dimensions of the genocide.

As a result of this bias toward macrolevel analysis, the scholarship on
the Cambodian genocide has also not yet dealt fully with the crucial
issue of perpetrator motivation. Scholars sometimes slip into an over-

simplified line of analysis that portrays perpetrators as ideological automatons. The following passage, written by a scholar and former ambassador to Cambodia, Kenneth Quinn, is illustrative:

> What emerges as the explanation for the terror and violence that swept Cambodia during the 1970s is that a small group of alienated intellectuals, enraged by their perception of a totally corrupt society and imbued with a Maoist plan to create a pure socialist order in the shortest possible time, recruited extremely young, poor, and envious cadres, instructed them in harsh and brutal methods learned from Stalinist mentors, and used them to destroy physically the cultural underpinnings of the Khmer civilization and to impose a new society through purges, executions, and violence.[37]

Although Quinn's chapter, entitled "Explaining the Terror," provides an excellent analysis of Khmer Rouge ideology and policy, it overlooks the complexity of individual motivation and agency. Quinn portrays perpetrators as generic automatons who, after being imprinted with a violent ideology and trained in "harsh and brutal methods," willingly commit genocidal atrocities. From this perspective, perpetrators are uniformly motivated by external forces (ideology) or narrow self-interest (advancement). Such an account is unable to provide a complete understanding of why someone like Lor killed, and it takes us back to questions raised by his actions. What were the cultural frames through which Khmer Rouge killers interpreted their lethal tasks? What did it mean, from a Cambodian perspective, for Khmer Rouge perpetrators to "cut off their hearts"? How were executioners influenced by local contexts? Clearly, an analysis of ideology is central to answering these questions. A more complete explanation, however, would demonstrate how the very effectiveness of genocidal ideologies is dependent on their ability to play upon a variety of emotion-laden local understandings. While much that is new may be introduced through the global flows of Marxist-Leninist and Maoist ideas, these bodies of knowledge are always localized. Otherwise, these ideas would remain both incomprehensible and unattractive to people whom ideologues seek to convert into followers. Ideologies are palimpsests in which new concepts — at once transforming and transformed — are sketched upon the lines of established cultural understandings.

Reading through the literature on genocide, I noticed that, while a number of scholars in this interdisciplinary field — particularly those working on the Holocaust — had addressed the issue of perpetrator motivation, almost nothing had been written on the cultural dimensions of genocide and that the motives of perpetrators were too often oversimplified. This tendency was highlighted by the enormous controversy that broke out over Daniel Goldhagen's book, *Hitler's Willing Executioners,* which argued that previous analyses of the Holocaust had ignored the complexity of perpetrator motivation.[38] Goldhagen contended that the historical and ideological development of a single German cultural model — "eliminationist antisemitism" — was ultimately responsible for the extreme loss of life during the Holocaust. When given the opportunity by the Nazi state, ordinary Germans, inspired by a genocidal ideology that played upon preexisting and highly motivating anti-Semitic values and beliefs, willingly and enthusiastically participated in the "extermination" of millions of dehumanized Jews.

Goldhagen's argument is reminiscent of older anthropological paradigms that portray culture as a hegemonic entity that imprints all members in a similar manner. Thus Goldhagen assumes that the internalization of eliminationist anti-Semitism during Nazi Germany was "near universal/deep" because such models were "automatically incorporate[d]" and accepted as natural "self-evident truths."[39] As many anthropologists have shown, this type of argument is questionable in a number of respects.[40] First, it assumes that the transmission of cultural knowledge is unproblematic, thus ignoring potential variation in the distribution, content, saliency, and motivational force of cultural knowledge. Second, it essentializes and reifies "culture," leading to oversimplified and stereotypical portrayals of the "other." Third, it overlooks the ways in which people may resist or contest the dominant ideas in a society. And fourth, by viewing culture as a bounded system, it fails to account for transnational and global flows of knowledge across these boundaries.

Of course, almost everyone would agree that anti-Semitism played a key role in the Holocaust. Therefore, a key objective for an analysis of the cultural dimensions of genocide is to describe such salient forms of local knowledge in a manner that avoids the aforementioned problems. Anthropologists have offered a number of suggestions for dealing with such a problem, sometimes arguing that cultural knowledge should be viewed as distributed within and across populations.[41] To understand how perpetrators like Lor come to commit genocidal atrocities, then, I have sought to develop an approach that (a) can account for the complex local understandings that motivate people to act, (b) remains sensitive to the many ways in which these local understandings are nevertheless linked to and influenced by macrolevel processes, (c) avoids depicting perpetrators as homogenous automatons, and (d) uses a distributive view of cultural knowledge.

For example, drawing on scholarship ranging from cognitive anthropology to practice theory, I examine how cultural models are strategically manipulated by or more tacitly motivate genocidal regimes. By cultural models, I refer to those processually generated and recursively enacted local knowledge structures that are variably distributed and internalized by the members of a social group and that mediate their interpretation of experience in given social contexts, albeit in potentially disparate ways.[42] Arguing that cultural phenomena cannot be fully comprehended by an exclusively psychological or social account, cultural models theorists assert that the key to understanding meaning is to examine the dialectical relationship between the intrapersonal and extrapersonal realms.

To this end, Bradd Shore has shown how cultural models have "two births" — one as "instituted models," or socially produced public forms, and the other as "mental models," or the subjective appropriations of these conventional public forms by meaning-seeking individuals participating in intentional social worlds.[43] For example, in the next chapter, I describe a cultural model of disproportionate revenge enacted in one of the most popular stories in Cambodia, *Tum Teav*.[44] In this violent tale, King Reamea exacts disproportionate revenge against a disobedient and disrespectful governor by obliterating seven generations of his family line. The cultural model of disproportionate revenge enacted in *Tum Teav* constitutes an instituted model, since the story is a public artifact "in-the-world" that is read in book form, discussed in schools, dramatically enacted, and recounted verbally. Individual Cambodians, however, construct various mental representations of this instituted model based both on their reading of *Tum Teav* and their encounters with disproportionate revenge in other social contexts (the media, gossip, games, drama, and eye-witness accounts). Cultural models are thus characterized by a dialectical duality — what Anthony Giddens has called "the duality of structure"[45] — as the individuals who develop such mental models subsequently participate in the enactment (or modification) of their public, instituted forms, which in turn may reinforce or subtly change their own mental models over time.

This dialectical perspective provides an important way of explaining cultural change. In addition to "conventional mental models" derived from instituted models, people have idiosyncratic "personal mental models" not shared by other members of their community.[46] At times, these personal models may significantly influence a person's modeling of public forms, leading him or her to enact instituted models in distinctive ways, thus contributing to cultural diversity and change.[47] Under appropriate historical conditions, cultural innovators may find themselves in a position to successfully spread their new understandings to other members of the community and thereby transform cultural knowledge — in the short or long term.[48] Thus, the Khmer Rouge revamped the cultural model of disproportionate revenge in accordance with Marxist-Leninist views of class resentment and contradiction. This new Khmer Rouge ideological model, which encouraged poor peasants to seek vengeance against the capitalist and reactionary classes that had traditionally oppressed them, was publicly instituted in Khmer Rouge speeches, radio broadcasts, political training, songs, slogans, and policy. Some forms of cultural knowledge, however, are relatively durable due to their generalized schematic features, their widespread distribution in the population, and their enactment in multiple public domains. Consequently, we can see a family resemblance between some past and present forms of Cambodian cultural knowledge, including the cultural model of disproportionate revenge, because of this durability and the relatively short duration of Khmer Rouge rule.

By acknowledging the dialectic between instituted and mental models, cultural models theorists are also able to account for individual variation, thereby avoiding what Claudia Strauss has called "fax models of socialization"[49] — such as the ones implicit in Kenneth Quinn's and Goldhagen's accounts of perpetrator motivation — which assume a one-to-one correspondence between instituted and mental models. In other words, there is always potential "interference" built into the dialectical interplay between instituted and mental models. Despite being members of the same community, people have different backgrounds and experiences that may lead them to construct divergent mental models of similar public forms. Thus, a seasoned Khmer Rouge cadre who had received extensive political training would be more likely to develop a complex understanding of the Khmer Rouge model of disproportionate revenge than an illiterate peasant recruit who previously had had minimal contact with urbanites and little exposure to Khmer Rouge propaganda. As a result of such interference, mental models always have an open-ended, dialectical relationship to instituted models, ranging from fairly direct approximations of these public forms to highly idiosyncratic understandings. Of course, a person's mental representations may change over time. After years of fighting for the revolution, a new recruit might develop a more elaborate understanding of the Khmer Rouge model of disproportionate revenge that, while still distinct, might be closer to that of the seasoned cadre and more or less approximate the instituted forms of the Khmer Rouge model. The dialectic between instituted and mental models therefore provides a way of explicating both individual variation and change over time.

Moreover, even in situations in which people share similar mental models of given public forms due to social constraints, the motivational force of these models may vary from indifferent familiarity, through clichéd understanding, moderate belief, and guidance, to the highly salient instigation of action.[50] Such variation in the motivational force of cultural models arises from a variety of interrelated sources, including associations with rudimentary sensorimotor schemas that serve as developmental building blocks; emotion-laded experiences and understandings; the directive force of personal goals and public pressures; local understandings of being; and the felt experience of acting in social worlds.[51] In this study, I discuss the "ontological resonance" of cultural knowledge, or the ways in which these understandings come to have motivational salience for actors as a result of resonances with local ontologies and embodied experience (the patterns of being-in-the-world constituted as people engage in social practices over time).[52]

In the dialectical interplay between instituted and mental models, a variable constellation of factors will strengthen or weaken the motivational force of cultural models for individuals whose understandings are shaped by their distinct backgrounds and experiences. Thus the Khmer Rouge model of disproportionate revenge would likely be more highly motivating to a landless peasant who felt deep resentment over the shameful and exploitative way in which he or she had been treated by a rich merchant or the loss of family members to U.S. bombing raids. A richer peasant who owned land or had suffered much less might be more indifferent to this Khmer Rouge model. Not surprisingly, at times there was a great deal of such "interference" in the reception of many Khmer Rouge ideological models, thereby limiting the degree of "take" they had among the general populace.

This dialectical focus on variation and change shifts us toward a more distributive view of cultural knowledge. Gender, class, wealth, ethnicity, residential area, education, religion, and occupation constitute some social axes that may alter a person's access to and understanding of instituted models. For example, during the Cambodian civil war, poorer peasants in rural areas were exposed to the Khmer Rouge model of disproportionate revenge to a much greater extent than people living in urban areas, since the rural poor were the primary target of Khmer Rouge propaganda and political training and lived in areas where the Khmer Rouge exerted influence or control. To account for such variations in the distribution and internalization of instituted models, it is helpful to view the individual as a "distributive locus of culture."[53] Each individual occupies a variety of social roles and moves within a set of social contexts that expose him or her to distinct constellations of cultural knowledge, based on which he or she constructs mental models and acts in meaningful ways.

From this vantage point, people are viewed as meaning-makers who draw upon a given repertoire of personal and cultural knowledge to comprehend and construct meaning out of their social lives. Some of this knowledge may be highly idiosyncratic. Some may be more or less shared with members of local communities. And some may come from the larger regional and global communities to which they belong — national, religious, ethnic, professional, and ideological. In constructing a mental representation of the Khmer Rouge model of disproportionate revenge, then, Khmer Rouge soldiers drew upon their personal experiences, their (more local) earlier understandings of disproportionate revenge, and their (more global, but localized) knowledge of Maoist and Marxist-Leninist philosophy, which they had learned in political training sessions and propaganda. And again, knowledge about Maoist and Marxist-Leninist ideas would be distributed across certain Cambodian groups, including the educated and those living within the Khmer Rouge (or communist Vietnamese) spheres of influence, as well as communist groups and people knowledgeable about communism in other countries (though these global schemes would be localized in different ways).[54]

Finally, in addition to variation among individuals, historical moments, and social groups, cultural knowledge varies across social contexts. The knowledge involved in one situation (for example, a DK political meeting) may be quite different from that invoked in another (for example, mealtime at a DK communal dining hall). Even within a situation such as a DK political meeting, the relevant cultural models shift as the topical focus fluctuates (for example, as the speaker moves from a diatribe about the necessity of seeking out and destroying "internal enemies" to a discussion of agricultural quotas at a work site). Moreover, since each individual brings a distinct set of understandings to the context, participants must negotiate meaning with one another. Part of the openness of such situations arises from the fact that cultural concepts are often loose containers for many cultural (and personal) models.[55] When discussing "revenge" (sangsuk), for example, two Cambodians may invoke widely different cultural knowledge, ranging from models of disproportionate revenge to notions of "justice" and "law" adopted from Western legal discourse to Buddhist ideas about the origins, consequences, and elimination of such violence.

This perspective provides an insightful way of examining large-scale genocide in general, and the actions of perpetrators like Lor in particular. Genocides usually take place when a state is going through a period of social, economic, or political upheaval. In many cases, a genocidal regime gains popular support and power by promising to revitalize the country. Unfortunately, such promises of renewal usually accentuate structural divisions in the state by blaming a victim group for the country's woes and legitimating violence directed toward such sources of "contamination." The Holocaust provides a clear illustration of this process of "genocidal priming," as the Nazis came to power in the wake of enormous socioeconomic turmoil. Much of their popular appeal arose from Hitler's charismatic pledge to usher in a new era of glory for the German race. In the Nazi "diagnosis," Jews were portrayed as a "disease" that gave rise to social illnesses and woes. After this process of "genocidal priming" is underway, the state initiates genocide by introducing policies that further stress social divisions and facilitate violence (the Nuremberg Laws), altering the social contexts in which violence takes place (placing Jews in ghettos and concentration camps), establishing policies that enable its minions to kill the regime's "enemies" and giving such orders (Hitler's authorization of "the final solution to the Jewish problem"), and disseminating an ideology of hate that legitimates and promotes the destruction of these victim groups (the Nazi regime's extreme anti-Semitic rhetoric, notions of "blood and honor"). As will become clear in the course of this book, DK was characterized by a similar process of genocidal priming and activation.

Because perpetrators are not automatons who, for identical reasons, blindly carry out the ideological dictates of the state, genocidal regimes almost always blend the old with the new in such a way as to make their lethal ideologies effective and reasonable to people.[56] Thus genocidal regimes usually co-opt preexisting cultural knowledge, dressing it up in new ideological guises that maintain familiar and compelling resonances while legitimating new structures of domination and violence against victim groups. The Khmer Rouge model of disproportionate revenge provides an illustration of this point, as the Khmer Rouge revamped preexisting knowledge about disproportionate revenge in accordance with its Marxist-Leninist views to sanction the killing of "class enemies." In this study, I will describe a number of Khmer Rouge models that were similarly constructed out of preexisting instituted models to facilitate genocide. Ironically, some Khmer Rouge models played upon Buddhist themes — despite the fact that the DK regime banned the religion and executed many monks.

Local responses do not necessarily follow the path laid out by such "state-level initiatives." Because of the dialectical duality of cultural knowledge, there are always degrees of interference between such instituted ideological models and individual understandings. Even perpetrators are active meaning-makers who, when put in a position to kill, make their own "individual-level response" based on the situation, their prior experiences and personal mental models, the meaningful interpretive frames available to them, and their immediate feelings and goals, although all of these factors may be strongly influenced by state-level initiatives and situational constraints. Consider, for example, a newly trained Khmer Rouge cadre who, after assuming a position of power, is asked to compile a list of former Lon Nol soldiers, ethnic Vietnamese, and "capitalists" living in his cooperative. Because he has lived in the area all his life, the list is bound to contain the names of people he knows and has been friendly with for years. Suddenly, his superiors give the order for such "reactionary" elements to be destroyed. It is likely such individuals will experience "psychosocial dissonance"[57] as their understanding that it is bad to harm others, especially friends, comes into conflict with the order to kill. At such times, people make an individual-level response in which they reinterpret their actions in terms of available meaningful forms (for example, reconceptualizing a former friend as a traitorous reactionary who is out to subvert the revolution, and deciding it is necessary to "cut off one's heart" from enemies, even those who were formerly friends or family).

When making such individual-level responses, perpetrators engage in a meaning-making process that loosely resembles what Claude Lévi-Strauss calls "bricolage."[58] For Lévi-Strauss, bricolage consists of instances in which something, like mythical thought, is built from an available set of resources; a "bricoleur" is a kind of "jack of all trades" in the sense that he or she uses whatever materials are at hand to perform given tasks.[59] Like bricoleurs, perpetrators such as Lor — whom we might call "genocidal bricoleurs" — draw upon a toolkit of personal and cultural knowledge to overcome their hesitations and to make sense of the murderous deeds they are carrying out. By linking their lethal ideologies to preexisting cultural knowledge, genocidal states provide perpetrators with an array of compelling discourses that may be used, consciously or unconsciously, in their genocidal bricolage.

In this study, I explore several of these linkages, arguing that the Khmer Rouge attempted to motivate its minions — who were differentially constrained in various contexts — to kill by invoking ideological discourses that played upon Cambodian cultural models related to revenge, power, patronage, status, face, and honor. Because of the dialectical duality of cultural knowledge, variation existed in the way these instituted Khmer Rouge models both were understood by and had motivational force for individual perpetrators. Nevertheless, in different contexts and in varying combinations, the Khmer Rouge models I discuss seem to have been an important part of the genocidal bricolage of many DK perpetrators, and effectively motivated them to kill.

Cultural models theory as inflected by practice theory, then, provides a strong theoretical basis for viewing perpetrators as meaning-making genocidal bricoleurs. This perspective enables us to examine perpetrator motivation in a way that accounts for the complex local understandings that motivate people to act, remains sensitive to how these local understandings are nevertheless linked to and influenced by macrolevel processes, avoids depicting perpetrators as homogenous automatons, and uses a distributive view of culture. By framing my argument in this manner, I hope to demonstrate how scholars can account for the actions of perpetrators like Lor in a more complex manner, one that weaves macrolevel and microlevel analysis to comprehend local motivation and the cultural patterning of mass violence. Few studies of genocide have done so. By regarding perpetrators as bricoleurs and not passive ideological automatons, we can gain a better understanding of their motivations for committing genocidal atrocities. Even if perpetrators are highly constrained in some circumstances, they remain active subjects who construct meaning and assert their self-identity through their violent practices.

· · ·

The first part of this book, "The Prison without Walls," consists of three chapters that examine the origins of and motivations for the Cambodian genocide. I begin with a preamble that describes the experiences of Khel, a Khmer Rouge soldier who worked at the extermination center adjacent to Banyan. Why, I ask, were revenge killings so prevalent in DK and why did the Khmer Rouge purge so many of their own followers? To answer such questions, this first section explores how the pattern and scope of the DK purges were shaped by historical events, an ideological blending of the old and the new, and local motivations. While strongly influenced by global schemes of Marxist-Leninist, Maoist, and high-modernist thought, I argue, Khmer Rouge ideology and practice interpreted these frames in local ways, often fusing them with preexisting, emotionally salient cultural models in a manner that contributed to an escalating spiral of violence.

Chapter 1, "A Head for an Eye: Disproportionate Revenge," examines the role that a local Cambodian model of disproportionate revenge played in this violence. If Buddhism and local understandings of anger management provide a powerful alternative to violence in Cambodia, people may sometimes find these strategies unsatisfactory and instead seek vengeance against their enemies. Drawing upon peasant anger over intensive U.S. bombing, widespread poverty, and the disrespectful and exploitative way the rich treated the poor, the Khmer Rouge gave this "burning rage" a focus (class struggle) and a target (the "oppressor classes"). Lon Nol soldiers, police, and government personnel were initial targets of revenge just after the Khmer Rouge came to power; later on, DK propaganda attempted to keep the "burning rage" of its soldiers and cadres inflamed. The result was the decimation of numerous "class enemies," and often their families.

The second chapter, entitled "Power, Patronage, and Suspicion," argues that, in order to fully understand why the purges took place, one must understand Cambodian notions of patronage and power, which hold that power comes to be invested in certain "potent centers" around which a network of followers develops. Because anyone can potentially be invested with the merit that legitimizes a rise in rank, however, the periphery tends to be unstable and is frequently characterized by power struggles, as people strive to increase their status. The "center," in turn, vigilantly guards against betrayal by such subordinates, often by undercutting or destroying their power.

As the third chapter, "In the Shade of Pol Pot's Umbrella," illustrates, these dynamics were clearly manifest during DK and helped motivate violence. Pol Pol and the Party Center constituted a raised "center" in which an enormous amount of power was gradually concentrated. Nevertheless, Pol Pot and his allies felt threatened by other DK chiefs, including some members of the Central Committee. In order to crush potential dissent, the Party Center destroyed the entire patronage networks of these rivals, and often many civilians living under their jurisdiction.

Part 2, "The Fire without Smoke," focuses more exclusively on the question of perpetrator motivation. The section begins with a preamble that presents the recollections of Vann Nath and Ung Pech, two of a handful of former prisoners who survived incarceration at Tuol Sleng. Their devastating stories depict a social institution characterized by extreme brutality, as dehumanized prisoners were beaten and tortured until they confessed. More broadly, these accounts touch upon several key, interrelated issues that are at the heart of this book, including questions about political identity, the construction of the "other," the structure and function of institutions like Tuol Sleng, and extreme cruelty. The next three chapters tackle these questions from different angles, moving between microlevel and macrolevel analysis to explain the complex motivations of perpetrators.

Chapter 4, "The DK Social Order," begins with the interrogation summary of a Tuol Sleng cadre that is replete with dehumanizing language and repeated references to torture. To understand such chilling spaces of violence, I argue, we need to examine how ideology is linked to local knowledge and psychocultural processes. During DK, social status was largely correlated with "revolutionary consciousness" *(sâtiarâmma),* a notion that was itself forged out of an amalgam of Marxist-Leninist ideas and the Buddhist conception of "mindfulness." A person with "pure" revolutionary consciousness applied the party line "mindfully," maintained an attitude of renunciation, and was completely loyal to the party. If a person betrayed the DK regime, it meant that he or she had a "regressive consciousness" and therefore occupied the lowest rungs of the new DK social order. This new conception of hierarchy, however, was blended with preexisting notions of hierarchy that were more salient for most Cambodians.

Chapter 5, "Manufacturing Difference," continues this line of analysis. I begin by discussing how genocidal regimes construct essentialized categories of identity and belonging, a process I refer to as "manufacturing difference." Difference is manufactured as genocidal regimes construct, essentialize, and propagate sociopolitical categories of difference, crystallizing what are normally more fluid forms of identity (the "crystallization of difference"); stigmatize victim groups in accordance with the differences that are being crystallized (the "marking of difference"); initiate a series of institutional, legal, social, and political changes that transform the conditions under which the targeted victim groups live (the "organization of difference"); and inscribe difference on the bodies of the victims (the "bodily inscription of difference").

Beginning with an analysis of a Khmer Rouge radio broadcast entitled "Who are 'We'?" I devote much of the chapter to describing how the DK regime manufactured difference. Ultimately, however, an analysis of ideology has difficulty accounting for the rage that Khmer Rouge perpetrators seem to have experienced while working in violent spaces like Tuol Sleng, where they sometimes beat prisoners to death. One way of explaining such excesses, I suggest, is to take an approach that links perpetrator excess to existential fear, dread, and anxiety. From this perspective, victims may be viewed as mimetic icons onto whom perpetrators project their anger, fear, and disavowed qualities and who serve as a medium for perpetrators to try to fortify their vulnerable sense of self (the "mimetics of difference").

In Chapter 6, "The Dark Side of Face and Honor," I focus largely on intrapersonal dynamics, exploring how cultural models related to face and honor motivated Khmer Rouge soldiers and cadres to kill. Despite the DK call for the renunciation of such "private sentiments," face and honor continued to influence interactions during DK. Although the criteria by which face and honor were achieved had changed, Cambodians continued to be highly concerned about peer evaluations. Negative evaluations could result in execution. More broadly, Khmer Rouge ideology linked honor and killing. Everyone had to demonstrate the purity of their revolutionary consciousness and their unquestioning loyalty to the party, which entailed, as one Khmer Rouge tract proclaimed, "struggl[ing] to clean up hidden enemies burrowing from within . . . so that they are completely gone, cleansed from inside the ranks of our revolution."

In the concluding chapter, "Why People Kill," I reconsider my two objectives in light of the preceding analysis. Extrapolating from the Cambodian case, I propose that genocides are generated through a process of "genocidal priming" and "genocidal activation." On the one hand, a given country may become primed for genocide due to structural divisions, the absence of an international response, socioeconomic upheavals, structural change, moral restructuring, manufacturing difference, and effective ideological manipulation. As these "primes" begin to coalesce, the possibility of genocide increases. On the other hand, even a "hot" situation that is highly primed for genocide still requires a "push," usually from ideologues who help create a climate of fear in order to trigger mass violence. These two processes can be seen to occur in a variety of situations, particularly in cases genocide scholars often refer to as "ideological genocides." The remainder of the conclusion returns to the issue of perpetrator motivation. Drawing on a chilling story of human liver-eating during DK, I argue that obedience is only one of the complex motivations that move human beings to kill in contexts like DK. To go beyond the overly reductive accounts of perpetrator motivation that too often appear in explanations of genocide, we need to examine the complex inputs, ranging from macrolevel ideology to psychocultural dynamics, that both constrain and propel human action.

PART ONE

The Prison without Walls

Preamble

In 1973, when Khel was fifteen, the Khmer Rouge set up a loudspeaker in his village, located in Speu district in Kompong Cham province, and began urging people to fight against General Lon Nol, saying that Lon Nol had betrayed the country when he seized power from Prince Sihanouk. Khel said he volunteered to enlist with the Khmer Rouge "because I saw others doing this." During basic training, Khel learned how to shoot a gun, to crawl along the ground, and to duck down quickly when under fire. The Khmer Rouge gave the soldiers lectures on political ideology, instructing them about the basic tenets of communism and the class struggle between the poor and their capitalist oppressors. Khel recalled, "They educated us so that we would be seized with painful anger against the Lon Nol regime and the oppressor class."

Khel fought against Lon Nol troops in Kompong Cham, and later near Phnom Penh, and was eventually promoted to second-in-command of a company of soldiers. After the Khmer Rouge won the war, however, they began researching backgrounds and discovered that Khel's father, who was separated from his wife, had driven an orange juice truck in the Phnom Penh area during the war and therefore was considered a supporter of Lon Nol. This association raised doubts about the purity of Khel's revolutionary consciousness. Khel and other soldiers with potentially counterrevolutionary "tendencies" were sent to do farm work near Phnom Bros. While the rest of these soldiers were eventually sent to fight the Vietnamese in 1977, Khel was more fortunate. Chien, a former private in Khel's old company, had become the head of the army battalion stationed around Phnom Bros and the nearby Kompong Cham airstrip. When Chien discovered what had happened to Khel, he transferred Khel to his battalion.

Khel soon discovered that, like many other temples around Cambodia during the DK period, Phnom Bros was being used as an execution center. An officer named Reap headed a regiment of Northern Zone soldiers that was charged with "sweeping clean" *(baos samat)* the enemy during the first part of 1977. Khel explained, "The Khmer Rouge wanted to kill people who had worked as government officials, those who had been on the side of the Lon Nol regime — soldiers, police, civil servants, intellectuals, teachers, doctors, and so on." Reap's troops first "cleaned up" in Kompong Thom province and the Chomkar Loe district of Kompong Cham. Perhaps to expedite such killings, Phnom Bros temple and its environs were turned into an extermination center — one of many in operation during DK — run by Reap. Most of what follows is based on Khel's observations while he was a soldier there.

In just over one month in mid 1977, Reap's troops executed somewhere between five thousand and ten thousand people at Phnom Bros. The victims, many of whom were told they were "going to a new village" *(tov phoum thmey)*, were loaded into trucks that held thirty to forty people. Upon arriving at Phnom Bros, the trucks drove directly to one of two killing sites: one at the base of Phnom Bros, the other at the outskirts of nearby Banyan village, which remained unoccupied. After exiting the trucks, the victims found themselves surrounded by Reap's armed soldiers. They were ordered to form a straight line and take off their outer garments before being marched a short distance to the killing field, where they were murdered by members of a twelve-person execution squad. Khel commented, "If they had fought back, perhaps some could have escaped. But they were terrified. The guards were pointing their guns at them the entire time. . . . The people were killed immediately upon arrival, though sometimes a truckload took more than an hour." Adults and children were killed by a blow to the back of the head; large trees at the site were supposedly stained with the blood of babies who were bashed to death there.[1] The bodies of the victims were placed in rows in the many mass graves at Phnom Bros, the outlines of which can still be seen. After a hole was full, it was covered over with dirt by another squad of soldiers.

While the frequency of truck arrivals varied, victims were delivered to Phnom Bros almost every day. At the peak of the killings, four trucks would each bring in two loads of people in a single day, thus resulting in the execution of about three hundred individuals. The vehicles would sometimes arrive in the evening, making it necessary to execute people by the light of the moon or the truck's headlights. Khel noted, "The killing was usually over by nine or ten o'clock at night. Afterward, the killers washed off the blood."

While Reap's soldiers were performing their murderous duties, larger political processes, which I discuss in subsequent chapters, resulted in a local-level purge in the area where Phnom Bros was located, Region 41 of the Central Zone (the part of Kompong Cham that lies west of the

Mekong River). Many Khmer Rouge cadres native to the area were executed and replaced by new officials from the Southwest Zone in early to
mid 1977. For example, the head of the district, Seuan, and his family
disappeared one day, only to be replaced by a woman from Takeo
province called Grandmother Yit. After assuming power, Yit gradually
killed off most of the people whom Seuan had appointed to local political positions. Thus Krauch, a former student and monk who had been
the head of Krala district since the Khmer Rouge took power, was killed
and replaced by Rom, Yit's younger female cousin. Rom's husband and
other relatives were members of the local "security" *(sântesokh)* force —
roughly equivalent to secret police — which quickly executed any "enemies" it discovered.

Many local officials did not survive the purges that ensued. Khel's
friend Chien shot himself in the head just before he was to be arrested by
cadres from the Southwest Zone. After some of his associates were jailed,
Reap realized that his days were numbered and plotted an uprising
against the head of the zone, Ke Pauk, known as "Grandfather Pauk."[2]
Reap apparently detonated some mines at the jail and a munitions store-
house, but local troops were too scared to follow the orders of Reap and
his coconspirators to attack Kompong Cham city. Khel explained, "The
plan was that after the explosion they should attack Grandfather Pauk.
But their soldiers didn't dare. They were too scared because other troops
were loyal to Pauk and he had placed heavy weaponry around his headquarters." Following the failed rebellion, Pauk immediately had the
rebels arrested and sent to Tuol Sleng. After being tortured for a day and
a half, Reap confessed his faction's traitorous "plan to kill our superiors."[3] Reap's troops were sent to fight the Vietnamese, and work at the
Phnom Bros extermination center came to a halt. Khel once again was
lucky when Chien was replaced by Chuon, an old acquaintance from
Speu. Khel and Chuon became quite close and roomed together in a
small office in front of Phnom Bros.

The murderous activity at the temple was not dormant for long.
About two months after Reap's arrest, around November 1977, the
head of Central Zone security, Phal, began to execute people at Phnom
Bros. While Reap's victims had been members of the general populace,
the majority of Phal's were Khmer Rouge cadres from the East Zone
who had been accused of being pro-Vietnamese traitors. Phal transported his victims by car and truck during the day and at night. The
people, many of whom had been previously interrogated and tortured at
Phal's Kompong Cham city headquarters, arrived at Phnom Bros blind-

folded and bound and were immediately killed. A few times, Phal's soldiers brought in tractors to cover the mass graves into which the corpses had been dumped. Occasionally extra dirt had to be piled on top of the graves because the corpses had swollen up in the heat, though the limbs of corpses could still sometimes be seen sticking out of the killing fields. Although Phal did not execute people as rapidly as Reap had, he continued to kill people at Phnom Bros until the end of DK, and Khel estimates that in the end Phal killed about the same number of people as Reap. Local documents, based on a count of skulls found at Phnom Bros, estimate that 13,450 people were exterminated at the site during DK. Some local residents claim that the number is far too low, however, because many corpses remain buried and were not included in the count.

Chuon, whom Khel described as a good person who was popular and "laughed often," was apparently disturbed by the killings at Phnom Bros. When he saw Phal bringing victims to Phnom Bros, he would shake his head and tell Khel that the killers had "excessive hearts." Because of the purges and suspicion, even high-ranking soldiers like Chuon were scared and had difficulty sleeping at night. Khel says that Chuon dreamed of escape: "He would sniff the stench of the corpses and shake his head and tell me, 'I brought you to work in the land of death.' Chuon secretly listened to the Voice of America. He would say, 'The two of us should run away to Thailand and cross the ocean to America. We could expose what Pol Pot is doing in Cambodia.'" To get away from the stench and killing at Phnom Bros, Chuon and Khel sometimes took trips to Ângkounh Dey village, about one kilometer down the road from Phnom Bros. There they became friendly with Neari's family.

. . .

Neari's family had fled from Ângkounh Dey village to nearby Kompong Cham city in 1973 to avoid the fighting between the Khmer Rouge and Lon Nol government forces. The family lived at the Kompong Cham market, and they were terrified by the artillery shells that the Khmer Rouge fired into the city. After the Khmer Rouge occupied Kompong Cham city in April 1975, the family returned to Ângkounh Dey and found themselves labeled "new people." Despite working the same amount as "old people," Neari's said that her family received less food and had fewer rights than their fellow villagers who had lived under Khmer Rouge rule during the civil war: "They were much more lenient with old people and told us that we should respect old people, that we should do what they said."

In contrast to many other "new people," Neari's family did have a connection that initially provided them with security. Seuan, Grandmother Yit's predecessor, was a relative and protected Neari's family. When Seuan and his faction were purged by the Southwest Zone cadres, however, the family became vulnerable again. Moreover, Neari's family was marked for elimination because it was widely known that her father had worked as a teacher under the Lon Nol government. The family was slowly killed off. Neari explained that the Khmer Rouge "had a grudge against my family. They hated us and wanted to kill us all so that no one in our family would remain."

After her father, mother, and three siblings had been killed, Neari developed a high fever and went to the hospital. Despite the fact that her parents had died there, Neari said, "I wasn't scared [of what might happen to me] because my mother, father, and most of my siblings had already been killed." She had begun to give up hope. At about nine o'clock in the evening, Neari's only surviving sister came and told her they had to flee or she would be killed. Neari's parents had been friendly with Chuon, who sometimes visited the family in Ângkounh Dey. After the death of Neari's parents, Chuon had told the sisters that they should work hard and stay out of trouble, but if they were about to be killed, he would help them. Having nowhere else to turn, the girls fled to the small building where Chuon and Khel resided.

When Neari and her sister arrived, Chuon told them he could help them more easily if Neari was married. Khel, who was tired of life at Phnom Bros and wanted to leave, agreed to marry her. Neari, however, was already engaged. She didn't reply when asked if she would marry Khel. Instead she began to sob. Her younger sister answered for her: "Whoever helps us can take her as his wife." Chuon hid the sisters in the attic of Phnom Bros temple for three days. Khel said that if they had dared to look out the small attic window, they would have seen Phal executing people in the killing fields below. Chuon didn't tell them about this murderous activity, thinking it would only further frighten them.

Four days later, Chuon arranged for all of them to drive to Speu district. He asked the local cadres if Khel, Neari, and Neari's sister could live there. The officials, who knew Chuon's high rank, didn't dare deny his request. The three of them lived in Speu until the end of DK. Chuon returned to Phnom Bros, where he stayed until the Vietnamese invasion. At that time, local villagers, who had seen Chuon entering and leaving

Phnom Bros and assumed he was the head executioner, reported him to the new authorities. After being arrested, Chuon committed suicide by diving in front of an oncoming tank as he was being led along a road by Vietnamese soldiers.

. . .

In addition to providing information about the atrocities committed in the region around Banyan, Khel and Neari's experiences, like those of other perpetrators and survivors, raise important questions about the DK period. Why did massive purges occur in places like Region 41 during DK? Why did the Khmer Rouge kill the family members and associates of the people they were purging? How did perpetrators like Reap and Lor come to be involved in mass murder? Why were the purges so virulent? To answer such questions, this book section explores how the pattern and scope of the DK purges were shaped both by historical events and by an ideological blending of the old and the new. While strongly influenced by global schemes of Marxist-Leninist, Maoist, and high-modernist ideology, Khmer Rouge ideology and practice interpreted these frames in local ways, often fusing them with preexisting cultural knowledge in a manner that contributed to an escalating spiral of violence.

CHAPTER ONE

A Head for an Eye

Disproportionate Revenge

To outsiders, and often to ourselves, Cambodia looked
peaceful enough. The farmers bound to their planting cycles.
Fisherman living on their boats. . . . The wide boulevards
and the flowering trees of our national capital, Phnom
Penh. All that beauty and serenity was visible to the eye.
But inside, hidden from sight the entire time, was *kum*.
Kum is a Cambodian word for a particularly Cambodian
mentality of revenge — to be precise, a long-standing grudge
leading to revenge much more damaging than the original
injury. If I hit you with my fist and you wait five years and
then shoot me in the back one dark night, that is *kum*. . . .
Cambodians know all about *kum*. It is the infection that
grows on our national soul.

Haing Ngor, A Cambodian Odyssey

We cannot cut off their heads in revenge following our
anger. I myself used to taste that taste. . . . [Let the matter]
be processed in a court case.

Chairman of the Cambodian Military Court
on prosecuting Ta Mok and Duch[1]

In April 2000, the *Phnom Penh Post* published an interview with a former Khmer Rouge cadre who had studied in Paris with Pol Pot and
helped to found the Communist Party of Kampuchea (CPK). When
asked why Pol Pot killed millions of people, the former cadre, who chose
to remain anonymous, replied, "As far as the killing is concerned, I don't
think it was only Pol Pot. It was more about revenge — the revenge with

Lon Nol [soldiers] for killing their husbands and wives before 1975."[2]
Later in the interview, the cadre (hereafter referred to as "anonymous
cadre") expanded on this assertion, which seemed to be related to his
view that Pol Pot was a "gentle man" with a "good heart" who ultimately shouldn't be blamed for the killing:

> So, when Lon Nol soldiers knew that someone was a former Viet Minh
> [agent], they would shoot and kill them without trial. Then, you can
> understand that in the Pol Pot regime, they would kill people even though
> Pol Pot didn't tell them to kill. They just took revenge for their husbands or
> fathers and put the blame on Pol Pot. . . .
>   [Local Khmer Rouge cadres] just had the anger with the fact that their
> wives or children had been killed. Then, they hated all those from the
> city. . . .
>   [B]efore 1975, there was also a war crime: what happened with the
> B-52s? . . . I am from Svay Rieng and Prey Veng, where a lot of my rela-
> tives were sad. I saw my relatives taking revenge with people from Phnom
> Penh. They just waited for people from Phnom Penh: if they had a chance
> to kill, they would kill. . . . I saw that there was more revenge [by people]
> than official order [from the top].

As the former cadre contends, revenge was an important motivation
behind some DK violence. In fact, revenge was invoked repeatedly by
perpetrators and victims I interviewed to explain why the Khmer Rouge
killed so many people. However, the cadre's assertion that Pol Pot and
other top officials were unaware of and lacked responsibility for the violence (an assertion that these leaders have also tried to make) is dubious.

This chapter argues that Khmer Rouge leaders directly and indirectly
called for their followers to take vengeance upon the "class enemies"
who had formerly "oppressed" them. I begin by examining the historical
development of the Khmer Rouge party "line" *(meakea)*, suggesting that
Pol Pot and his colleagues came to believe that the "science" of Marxist-
Leninism enabled them to discern the origins of and devise a solution for
the impoverishment and oppression of the Cambodian people. While
Marxist-Leninist and Maoist notions of exploitation made a certain
sense to many of Cambodia's poor, the Khmer Rouge leadership
attempted to couch such philosophical abstractions in terms that would
inspire them to embrace the Khmer Rouge movement and to take arms
against its enemies. To do so, the Khmer Rouge combined the new and
the old into ideological palimpsests, in which Marxist-Leninism was
sketched upon the lines of local understandings, at once transforming
and transformed.

A key ideological palimpsest centered on the notion of class rage, which played upon ontologically resonant local understandings of disproportionate revenge that were salient for many Cambodians. In contrast to the oft-cited Biblical conception of "an eye for an eye,"[3] the Cambodian model of revenge involves disproportionate retaliation against one's enemy — what we might call "a head for an eye," since disproportionate revenge is usually linked to issues of face, and sometimes even decapitation. In an extreme situation like DK, disproportionate revenge could involve an attempt to kill a foe or even his or her entire family.

For example, Vann Nath, a survivor of Tuol Sleng, told me that in 1996 he had encountered Lor at the site of the former interrogation center, where Lor was being interviewed for a documentary film. After an initial reaction of stunned outrage, Vann Nath decided that he had to speak to Lor: "I went up and asked him *(vea)*, 'Lor, do you know who I am?' Lor replied, 'I don't.' I told him, 'I know you with certainty. I know that you worked in a high position here. You were in charge of over a hundred guards.' " Lor began to get nervous and tried to deny this, but Vann Nath knew too much and began questioning Lor:

> First of all, I wanted to know what happened to the little children who were taken from their mothers. I could hear both the mothers and children crying and screaming when this happened. I asked Lor, "Where did you take the children? Where were they taken care of?" He replied, "There wasn't any plan [to care] for them. They were taken away and killed." I didn't know that they had been killed! I imagined that the children had been cared for at some center. I couldn't believe it. Some of the children were newborns, others four or five months old, others five or six years old. They killed them all! I was astounded. I never guessed that even this place was *that* brutal.

Lor's explanation is supported by surviving documentation: the Khmer Rouge recorded not just the execution of prisoners, but also of their spouses and children. On July 2, 1977, for example, an execution schedule from Tuol Sleng lists the names of eighty-five children of detainees who were "smashed," most likely under Lor's supervision.[4] The annihilation of entire families was not restricted to Tuol Sleng. Throughout Cambodia, entire families were taken to extermination centers like Phnom Bros and executed en masse. Sometimes the Khmer Rouge destroyed a family line more slowly on the local level, as happened to Neari's family. This chapter, then, suggests that the violence during DK — including, in the extreme, the Khmer Rouge attempt to annihilate the families of some enemies, ranging from former Lon Nol soldiers and

government workers to suspected counterrevolutionaries and traitors —
was partly motivated by preexisting understandings of disproportionate
revenge *(karsângsoek)* that were revamped and incorporated into Khmer
Rouge ideology.

CLASS HATRED AND THE KHMER ROUGE PARTY LINE

The American imperialists and their lackeys
Their lackeys owe us blood as hot as fire.
The hot and angry war ensured that Kampuchea
    will never forget the enmity
Will not forget the severe oppression.
Seize hold of guns to kill the enemy quickly.

                              Khmer Rouge song,
                    "The Motherland of Kampuchea"[5]

To understand the origins of this ideological palimpsest, it is necessary to
examine some of the historical processes through which the DK party
line was forged. On September 27, 1977, for example, Pol Pot gave a
speech, broadcast throughout the nation, to celebrate the seventeenth
anniversary of the founding of the CPK. The speech constituted the first
clear public acknowledgement of the CPK's existence, Pol Pot's leadership, and the history of the struggle that had brought the regime to
power. Like all party histories, which reconstruct the past to confirm a
desired image of the present (for example, Pol Pot's speech excises an
alternative history of revolutionary struggle and association with
Vietnam dating back to the fight for independence), Pol Pot's is sugges-
tive about the emergence of the party line and the high-modernist orientation of the DK regime.

By "high-modernist orientation," I refer to James Scott's concept of an
overweening confidence in the possibilities of progress, mastery of
nature, and human emancipation through the use of science, reason, and
social engineering — a faith that has sometimes inspired authoritarian
regimes to attempt to use their highly abstract and oversimplified
schemes as a blueprint for radical sociopolitical transformation.[6] Because
they tend to oversimplify complex on-the-ground realities, these projects
of social engineering have often ended in catastrophe. As was the case
with the Khmer Rouge, high-modernist faith and vision may also provide
the building blocks for a revitalization movement, which, in a context of
stress and upheaval, may attract followers through promises of a new

and better life. I should also note that in Cambodia transformative knowledge is viewed as a form of power and may confer on the bearer an aura of potency. If, in the past, revitalization movements in Cambodia and its Southeast Asian neighbors had often been led by charismatic leaders claiming a special endowment of merit and power, Pol Pot and the CPK similarly claimed a sort of high-modernist potency that legitimated their claims to power and their subsequent attempt to radically transform and revitalize Cambodian society.

These threads are evident in Pol Pot's 1977 speech, as well as numerous other Khmer Rouge documents, such as the 1976 Four-Year Plan. After a brief preamble, the speech begins with a discussion of how Cambodia had passed through eras of slavery, feudalism, and, most recently, capitalism. Each epoch was characterized by exploitation and class struggle that ultimately failed because the masses had not found a "clear and correct" political line. Without such a line, which provides "judicious guidance, one becomes blind. Even with great strength and determination, one cannot win. One loses one's orientation, one doesn't know what to hold onto, one proceeds toward certain defeat and, in the end, ruin."[7]

To remedy this problem, Pol Pot stated, the Cambodian communists established a committee in 1957 to prepare the party's political line based on Marxist-Leninism and the "study and research" both of other revolutionary movements and of Cambodia's history and socioeconomic situation. This assertion was contentious, denying a history of association with Vietnam dating back to the struggle for independence from French colonial rule, in which a number of longtime revolutionaries (many of whom had been purged by the time of Pol Pot's speech) had fought. While these revolutionaries had initially been exposed to Marxist-Leninism by Vietnamese communists and were linked to an alternative party genealogy involving participation in the Vietnamese-backed Indochinese Revolutionary Party and the Khmer People's Revolutionary Party (established in 1951), another set of revolutionaries, including Pol Pot, Ieng Sary, Son Sen, and Khieu Samphan, had received their initial training in Marxist-Leninism while studying in Paris in the 1950s.[8] Many of them became members of the French Communist Party, which had strong Stalinist, anti-American, and anti-colonial streaks. This anti-colonialism appealed to the students, who had come of age in a time of protest and indignation about French colonial rule. The "anonymous cadre" explained that the French communists "helped French colonial countries to be freed from the yoke of colonial rule. . . . As we wanted independence for the country and when we saw them helping us, we joined with their ideas. . . . And when we learned, we saw that this ideology was good and just. . . . it helped protect the poor from oppression. Therefore, we loved it, because we had been oppressed for 100 years."[9]

It is important not to overstate the differences between the two origin points for Cambodian communism, since the students later returned to Cambodia to foment revolutionary struggle and worked closely with the Cambodian communists who had fought the French and with communists from China and Vietnam. Still, these historical trajectories were salient because they could mark, real or perceived, different networks of association and views of the DK party line.

For Pol Pot, the key to revolutionary success seems to have been total commitment to the DK party line, a high-modernist, abstract set of principles that had been determined through "scientific analysis." This perspective not only fit well with Maoist doctrine, but may also have appealed to his student background and the conviction that proper "study and research" would yield a correct party line that should be inexorably followed. When others dissented, arguing for the more gradualist approach that had been used in other socialist countries, Pol Pot and his inner circle perceived the weakening of their "stand" as treachery and a sign of a "regressive" consciousness.

Their conviction that they had discovered the key to ending oppression and revitalizing Cambodian society seems to have given Pol Pot and his associates a sense of omnipotence and grandeur, which can be read in the lines of speeches and documents that assert the unique and unprecedented nature of their revolutionary movement. Like Buddhists who had achieved enlightenment, they had attained secret knowledge that would transform Cambodia and enable its inhabitants to reach a higher state of being. In fact, the Khmer Rouge ideology often played upon the theme of enlightenment when it depicted Ângkar using metaphors of clairvoyance and omniscience. Yet another strand in this sense of grandeur was the French reconstruction of Cambodian history, which provided a narrative of decline from the magnificence of the Angkorean era, when Khmer kings built impressive stone monuments and were a dominant military presence in the region, to the contemporary period, when Cambodia had become a weak country dominated by others.[10] Driven by feelings of inferiority and inflation about what was possible, the Khmer Rouge proclaimed that their revolutionary society would surpass even Angkor in greatness, moving more rapidly and successfully toward a communist utopia than had any other communist regime.

These views and experiences were to shape the development and

application of the party line. Pol Pot's 1977 speech asserts that a pro-
posal for the party line was approved at the September 1960 Party
Congress, which his speech marks as the birth of the CPK, "a genuine
Marxist-Leninist party."[11] Since "a correct analysis . . . allows for the
correct definition of the tasks of the revolution," the attendees "analyzed
and defined the real nature of Kampuchean society at that time." The
"conclusion of our analysis," ascertained through the "science" of
Marxist-Leninism, was that Cambodia was plagued by two major contradictions. On the one hand, there existed a contradiction with imperialism, especially U.S. imperialism. Cambodia remained a "semi-colony,
in a situation of dependency" on exploitative imperial powers that
impoverished the poor and corrupted Cambodian society. On the other
hand, Cambodia was plagued by internal class contradictions. While
contradictions existed between various classes (workers versus capitalists, petty bourgeoisie versus capitalists, capitalists versus peasants), the
dominant one, Pol Pot asserted, was between the landowners and the
peasantry, who comprised 85 percent of the population.

The solution to these contradictions was to drive out the imperialists
and their lackeys, the "feudal-capitalist" government that supported the
exploitation of the poor. The DK party line held that, upon attaining
power, the Khmer Rouge would impose new relations of production that
would end exploitation. Through this structural reorganization and
indoctrination — what the Khmer Rouge called "seepage" *(karchreap)* —
the masses would gradually absorb party ideology and be transformed
into passionate revolutionaries guided by a proper political consciousness.

In addition, the country would avoid foreign dependency and influence by adhering to a strict line of "independence-mastery" *(aekâreach
mâchaskar)*, a crucial stance given centuries of foreign involvement in
Cambodian affairs, culminating in the Vietnam War. During DK, Khmer
Rouge ideology constantly invoked this refrain, as Haing Ngor, a "new
person," noted:

> The key concept for the new society, as we were told all the time in propa-
> ganda sessions, was "independence-[mastery]." One word made out of
> two, independence-[mastery]. For Democratic Kampuchea, this meant
> being absolutely free of other countries — free of their aid and even of their
> cultural influence. We Khmers would make it on our own. By reorganizing
> and harnessing the energy of our people and by eliminating everything that
> distracted from our work, we would become an advanced, developed
> nation almost overnight.[12]

The Party's Four-Year Plan provides an illustration of Haing Ngor's
point, as it boasted that in contrast to socialist regimes like China, North

Korea, and Vietnam, DK received "no assistance from outside for industry or agriculture. . . . This is our Party's policy. If we go and beg for help we would certainly obtain some, but this would affect our political line. . . . [I]f we asked [for] help. . . . a little or a lot, there would be political conditions imposed on us without fail."[13]

Pol Pot's 1977 speech contends that "the key problem, the fundamental problem which was decisive for victory" was to "arouse the peasants so that they saw [contradictions], burned with class hatred and took up the struggle."[14] If, in the past, such hatred potentially existed, Pol Pot asserted, it was "buried" because of the false consciousness of the masses, who were "deceived" by ruling-class ideology into thinking that their status was due to karma. The party line provided the means of helping the masses see the "contradictions" and the ways in which they were oppressed. For Pol Pot and his colleagues, then, one basic strategy for successfully waging revolution was to make the masses "hot and angry," feelings that would ultimately be transformed into "class hatred" and "class fury."

In retrospect, Pol Pot tried to make the process appear natural and ineluctable, yet another illustration of the correctness of the "all-knowing" Party Center and its "line," and of the inevitability of the revolution. Thus he proclaimed:

In 1964 and 1965, the movement was already strong. In 1966, it became even more powerful. In 1967, it became an extraordinary force. By the thousands, by the tens of thousands, the peasants demonstrated, rose up, marched on the administrative offices of the communes, districts and provinces, in order to regain control of the land. Every form of struggle was used, including petitions and meetings with deputies. But what is especially important, the peasants armed themselves with scythes, knives, axes and hatchets, and other traditional weapons. Weapons in hand, the peasants surrounded police stations and military posts, resorting to revolutionary violence because the ruling classes refused to solve the problem of the lands which they had grabbed from the poor peasants in collusion with the landlords. How could they satisfy the demands of the peasants? They couldn't. Their lies and their deceit could only help them for a time. When, after several actions, the peasants still had not recovered their lands, this discontent was transformed into anger, then class hatred, hatred arising from the class contradictions. At this stage, how could the problem be solved? There was nothing left for the peasants but to take up their scythes and axes and drive out the landlords, who had grabbed their land. From that point on, they no longer feared death, because they had nothing, and this was already like death for them.[15]

In this passage, Pol Pot refers to an incident that took place in early 1967, when hundreds of peasants from the Samlaut subdistrict in Battambang province revolted. Fed up with the government's policy of directly purchasing rice from farmers at prices far below the black market rate, high levels of debt, heavy-handed treatment by local soldiers, corruption, and the reallocation of their land, peasant rebels murdered two soldiers and stole their weapons on the morning of April 2.[16] Carrying banners denouncing the government and U.S. imperialism, the peasants destroyed a youth agricultural camp, attacked two government outposts, and later that day, killed a local official. During the next few weeks, the revolt quickly expanded. To put down this threat to civil order, Sihanouk's government sent additional troops into the area and used increasingly brutal tactics to suppress the "red" rebellion. Peasant villages were razed. Suspects were beaten, imprisoned, and summarily executed. There were even rumors that the government had paid a bounty for the severed heads of rebels.[17] Estimates of those killed by government forces ranged into the thousands.

According to Pol Pot, this incident convinced the Khmer Rouge leadership that it was time to initiate "armed struggle" throughout the country. The class situation was allegedly reaching a "boiling point," and if given guidance and leadership by the Khmer Rouge, the masses would erupt in revolutionary fervor—just as "dry straw in the rice fields in March and April" needs only "a small spark to set it on fire."[18] To support such claims, Pol Pot proclaimed that the party had conducted "scientific analysis of the society" that revealed the "true nature" of the socioeconomic situation. This endeavor included "direct investigation for several years" in communities like Thmor Koul in Battambang, where, in 1957–58, "some 90 percent of the farmlands were in the hands of the landowners. Of the tens of thousands of people in Thmor Koul, only four in ten persons were landowners, who monopolized 90 percent of the land. Tens of thousands of peasants shared the remaining 10 percent of the farmlands."[19] This example illustrated the inevitable "process of impoverishment in the countryside," whereby landlords became increasingly rich while the number of poor peasants rapidly grew. Such "contradictions," Pol Pot proclaimed, existed "everywhere in Kampuchea."

Pol Pot's assertions were problematic. W. E. Willmott, for example, has argued that this class analysis was strongly influenced by erroneous assumptions in Khieu Samphan's doctoral dissertation.[20] Khieu Samphan contended that the Cambodian economy had stagnated under the domination of French colonialism, U.S. imperialism, and foreign-controlled "capitalist networks," remaining mired in an undeveloped "feudal mode of production" in which peasant families grew "rice mainly for paying off land rents and debts," with the remainder going "toward meeting subsistence need, not for exchange or for monetary gain."[21] Drawing on Maoist categories (and 1930–31 data), Khieu Samphan divided the Cambodian peasantry into poor smallholders (those owning less than two hectares of land), middle peasants (two to seven hectares), rich peasants (more than seven hectares), and big landlords (owners of ten or more hectares). He noted that the majority (60 percent) of the rural landowners were "middle peasants," who owned 40 percent of Cambodia's paddy fields, in contrast to the poor (30 percent, owning 20 percent of the land) and rich peasants and landowner classes (10 percent, owning 40 percent of the land).[22]

While acknowledging that this socioeconomic situation was different from Vietnam (as it was from prerevolutionary China), where land-lordism was much more prevalent, Khieu Samphan argued that middle peasants "lack operating capital," which they were forced to obtain "from village usurers who are also large landowners or traders. They are then often unable to escape the grasp of these people. Property owner-ship is no more than the appearance of ownership for a substantial num-ber of middle peasants."[23] Because they had to pay interest rates that were sometimes as high as 200 to 300 percent per year, many of these middle peasants were effectively divorced from the product of their labor "as if they were working the land of usurers." Middle peasants lived in a state of false consciousness, deluded by the ruling classes into believing in the value of "ownership" and expecting that their lot would improve in the future.

Cambodian peasants were exploited by usury,[24] a point that neither Pol Pot's speech nor the DK party line emphasized. Many of these mon-eylenders were ethnic Chinese. In fact, part of the reason ethnic Chinese perished in disproportionately large numbers during DK (almost 50 per-cent of the ethnic Chinese "new people" by one estimate)[25] was their widespread involvement in trade and usury prior to DK. Many of them lived in Phnom Penh or had fled to Phnom Penh during the civil war and were therefore labeled "new people."[26] When cadres began to search for "class enemies," ethnic Chinese came more readily under suspicion because of their stereotypic associations with "capitalist" endeavors, par-ticularly shop-keeping and money-lending. Nevertheless, the Khmer tended to have ambivalent attitudes toward ethnic Chinese, admiring perceived Chinese attributes such as light skin and industry, while some-times resenting their wealth, power, and cultural differences.[27] Many of these attributes, particularly light skin and former wealth, came to signal a regressive consciousness during DK.

The ethnographic record nevertheless throws a number of Pol Pot's and Khieu Samphan's assertions into question. If usury was a serious problem for Cambodian villagers, its prevalence varied depending on the location and year. In survey research in the 1950s, Jean Delvert found that rates of interest approached the figures given by Khieu Samphan, though the severity of indebtedness ranged from 10 percent to almost 80 percent of the population in various parts of Cambodia.[28] Areas closer to major cities, particularly Phnom Penh, tended to have lower rates of indebtedness because peasants had the opportunity to earn money by performing seasonal labor tasks.

Delvert's argument was largely supported by May Ebihara's study of Sobay, a village in Kandal province located 30 kilometers southwest of Phnom Penh, where "indebtedness tends to be infrequent and/or rela-tively minor."[29] Far from passive victims of an oppressive set of structural constraints, those villagers who did go into debt, Ebihara found, were active strategists who tried to "avoid borrowing if at all possible by tight-ening their belts when necessary, by seeking means of earning extra money, or by selling some valuable item."[30] Those who chose to borrow money would first seek to obtain a low-interest loan from family or friends. If forced to borrow from merchants or moneylenders (at high rates of interest), the villagers would try to pay back the loan "as quickly as possible. . . . Often he is successful in clearing his debts within a year or so." Only a couple of families from the village were unable to escape the cycle of debt.

Similarly, these studies suggest that class divisions were not as severe or widespread as Khieu Samphan and Pol Pot assert. Willmott points out that Khieu Samphan's dissertation improperly generalized from the three provinces (Battambang, Prey Veng, and Svay Rieng) in which class divi-sions were most extreme.[31] Delvert, whose 1956 research is based on a broad sample of the Cambodian countryside, estimated that 92 percent of the peasantry owned five hectares or less of the rice fields, with the vast majority owning less than two hectares.[32] The national average was 2.2 hectares.[33] Kompong Siem district, where Banyan is located, was a rough snapshot of this national pattern: 98 percent of the peasants owned less than five hectares of rice fields, and 70 percent owned less than one hectare, with an average holding of 1.7 hectares.[34]

Such statistics do not support the DK party line, which assumed that
the second major contradiction existing in Cambodia was between the
peasantry and landlords. Pol Pot pointed out that peasants were exploited by "capitalists. . . . However, it was from the landlords that the
peasants suffered the worst, most varied and most direct exploitation.
Thus, 85 percent of the population, that is, the peasants, were in contradiction with the exploiting class which oppressed them directly, the
landowners."[35] While almost 20 percent of peasants owned 5–50
hectares of land in Battambang, Prey Veng, and Svay Rieng (resulting in
more tenancy and sharecropping), the situation was quite different in the
rest of the country, where most peasants owned enough land to subsist
upon — although often barely — and there was greater socioeconomic
homogeneity.[36] Pol Pot's assertion that places like Samlaut and Thmor
Koul were typical of the "process of impoverishment in the countryside"
and of contradictions that existed "everywhere in Kampuchea" was
therefore mistaken. The revolutionary potential of the Cambodian peasantry does not seem to have been as great as it had been in China and
Vietnam, where there were more poor and landless peasants, land was
more concentrated in the hands of rich peasants and landlords, and consequently, there was more economic exploitation.

To be sure, few Cambodian peasants had an easy life. Most were poor
but not completely destitute, eking out a living on small plots of land that
produced low yields of rice. In the village hamlet Ebihara studied most
intensively, for example, the average landholding was just under one
hectare per household, below the national average.[37] The hamlet, which
was in many respects "typically" Cambodian,[38] was composed of thirty-
two households. Four of these owned no land. One household owned
four hectares of rice paddy, while the remainder owned two hectares or
less (fourteen households, or almost half the hamlet, owned less than one
hectare). There was no absentee landlordism or land rental, though the
household that owned four hectares of land, which would have classified
them as middle (or upper- middle) peasants in the Khmer Rouge class
analysis, had a traditional sharecropping arrangement with eleven of the
families that owned little or no land.

Ebihara notes that such arrangements were viewed as "mutually beneficial, not as exploitative rent extracted by the rich from the poor," and
that "relative affluence has no significant influence on daily interaction
within the community."[39] Most of the villagers, including those who
were relatively well off, referred to themselves as "poor people," a designation that made sense given that differences in wealth between villagers

were minimal compared to the differences between villagers and urban-ites. Life in the hamlet was characterized by an ethos of egalitarianism, a tradition of mutual aid, and a lack of significant class stratification. Thus, Ebihara concludes, "social classes did not exist in Sobay in 1960," though she notes that villagers did distinguish between rich people, or "those who have" *(neak mean)*, "those who have enough" *(neak kuorsâm)*, the poor *(neak krâ)*, and the destitute *(neak toal, neak toal krâ)*.[40] While a handful of villagers were destitute, the majority were poor, living a precarious existence that could be upset by droughts, floods, or emergencies that might force them into debt. Most were able to get out of debt by supplementing their incomes with seasonal or part-time work; a few might eventually be forced to sell their land.

What emerges from these ethnographic studies is a picture of a Cambodian peasantry that was poor and sometimes indebted but not riven by landlessness and landlordism. Class stratification was a prob-lem in some areas, but in general it was not severe when compared with the situation in China and Vietnam. The peasants in villages like Sobay (which was poorer than average) resemble but also differ in important ways from the population Pol Pot describes in his 1977 speech. This fundamental error in the DK party line was likely an important reason the Khmer Rouge initially had trouble recruiting peasants to their movement.

During the last half of the 1960s, the number of recruits began to slowly rise as the Vietnam War intensified and the Cambodian economy stagnated. More peasants confronted economic difficulties, forcing them into (greater) debt or to sell their land. Ben Kiernan has estimated that, between 1952 and 1970, the proportion of landless peasants rose from 4 to 20 percent.[41] The Samlaut rebellion illustrated that, at least in some areas, the socioeconomic situation had deteriorated to the point that there existed a moderate number of disaffected peasants who could be incited to join the Khmer Rouge given the right circumstances. While scholars continue to debate the size of this pool of recruits, the extent of landlessness, and the overall degree of peasant support for the Khmer Rouge, most would broadly agree with Kiernan's assessment that the number of disaffected peasants "probably never formed a majority in the Cambodian countryside. But they *were* numerous enough for Pol Pot to build a viable recruitment strategy targeting poor peasants, and particu-larly their teenage children"[42] — especially after the overthrow of Sihanouk and the ensuing civil war. Without these events, which took place in the context of the Vietnam War, it is doubtful the Khmer Rouge would have come to power; economic conditions alone were not severe enough to generate widespread support for the movement.

The flood of recruits who came to the Khmer Rouge in the early 1970s bore malice toward the Lon Nol regime for a variety of reasons. A smaller number were disaffected intellectuals or members of the middle class who were drawn to Khmer Rouge ideals. A larger number of peasant recruits were incensed by the devastation caused by the war, particularly U.S. bombing, which contributed to economic destabilization, the death of up to 150,000 people, and the displacement of tens of thousands of others.[43] Many Cambodians joined the Khmer Rouge out of anger over the destruction of their homes and the death of loved ones. Khel explained, "The American B-52s dropped too many bombs. The people became seized with painful anger *(chheu chap)* and wanted to fight against the Lon Nol regime." The excesses of some South Vietnamese and Lon Nol troops were another source of discontent.

Other recruits were incensed by the 1970 overthrow of Prince Sihanouk, who appealed to his rural "children" to take arms with him against the "traitorous" and "illegitimate" Lon Nol regime. Khel recalled that he and many other youths in his village joined the Khmer Rouge because "in general the people loved the king and he was the head of the Khmer Rouge military front." Prince Sihanouk's actions can also be partially explained as the result of a grudge, as the prince openly admitted: "I want to avenge myself for having been slandered, cursed and humiliated in such a cowardly, low and wicked fashion by my enemies of the extreme right."[44] To pay back Lon Nol and Sirik Matak for their "bad deed" and to restore his honor, Prince Sihanouk allied himself with the Khmer Rouge, who he believed could provide him with the revenge he desired. Saruon, a man whose family lived in Kompong Cham at the time, explained, "Sihanouk was the one who gave Lon Nol power, but Lon Nol deposed him. Sihanouk was really angry and had a grudge against Lon Nol. . . . The people loved King Sihanouk and fled into the forest to struggle with him. The Khmer Rouge would never have defeated Lon Nol if they had not had Sihanouk on their side."

Finally, some peasant recruits resented the wealth and status of the rich. Even if they had not yet fully developed "class consciousness," these men and women were angered by their own poverty, landlessness, and debt. They worked hard but remained poor, while the rich lived a life of relative luxury. Such animosity toward the rich still persists, albeit in a more moderate form, partly explaining why the Khmer Rouge continued to enjoy popular support in some rural areas long after the DK regime was deposed. In the mid 1990s, a peasant told me, "The farmers feel that they work hard but only get a little for their effort. They only have a little money to purchase things. Rich people, in contrast, have it easier and have lots of money. They also make a profit from the farmers they sell and buy from." Another source of resentment was the perceived disrespect with which the rich often treated the poor, particularly given the importance of face in Cambodia.

Even if the DK party line was flawed in its assessment of the socioeconomic conditions in Cambodia, then, by the early 1970s the Khmer Rouge were nevertheless able to attract an increasing number of recruits who were angry for a variety of reasons, including poverty, landlessness, civil war, U.S. bombing, disrespect, foreign invasion, the destruction of their homes and death of loved ones, economic turmoil, and Sihanouk's overthrow. As I discuss in Chapter 5, it is precisely at such moments of upheaval that people often undergo a process of "cognitive constriction" as they seek the new types of meaning that revitalization movements offer.

At the same time as they promised to create a new, utopian society, the Khmer Rouge attempted to give their recruits' anger and resentment a common ideological focus (class struggle) and target (the oppressor classes). Political education was geared to instill ideological conceptions that would generate the "class ardor and fury" or "burning material force" that would lead the revolution to victory over this enemy. Recruits were taught basic Marxist-Leninist doctrine, particularly the idea that the suffering of the poor *(vonnah âtun)* was due to the exploitation *(kar chih choan)* of the oppressor classes — an enemy that abstractly included "imperialists," "feudalists," and "capitalists," and more concretely comprised the Lon Nol regime, the urban population it controlled, and the capitalists and imperialists with which it was allied.[45]

Perhaps the most basic ideological concept, and one that could in some sense be understood by almost all of the Khmer Rouge's followers, was the notion of oppression. In Khmer, the term for "oppression" or "exploitation," *chih choan* (or sometimes *sângkat*), literally means "to be ridden" or "stepped upon," and implies being "pressed and squeezed," "dominated," "crushed," "ground up," and "invaded and robbed."[46] Some Cambodians, particularly the destitute and the poor, likely felt that they were "stepped upon" and "dominated" by the wealthy and powerful. Khmer Rouge notions of class oppression could also play upon preexisting local distinctions between those who are "rich," those who "have enough," and those who are "poor." Moreover, the idea of oppression could help make sense of the existential threat that many people, particularly destitute and poor peasants, felt as their already marginal subsistence was severely strained by fighting and economic upheaval and by the bombs that rained down on the countryside, destroying their homes, livestock, and crops and killing their friends and families. This notion could therefore potentially lead Cambodian peasants to feel a "burning rage," an ontologically resonant feeling into which Khmer Rouge ideology tapped.

ANGER AND NONVIOLENCE

When anger controls us, we harm ourselves and the
people around us. Anger burns the mind and body. The
face becomes flushed, the heart weakens, and the hands
tremble.

Maha Ghosananda, *Step by Step*

To understand the motivational force of such anger metaphors, we need to turn to local understandings of anger, ethnopsychology, and as suggested by the epigraph above, Buddhist ontology. Nonviolence is a central part of Buddhist tradition and an important theme in Cambodian society. Buddhist doctrine provides an explicit ontology that explains how violence originates in ignorance and desire. If the effects of violence are manifest in overt signs, such actions also have long-term consequences. On the one hand, violence may lead others to seek vengeance against you. On the other hand, harming others is considered to be a Buddhist sin that results in a loss of merit and diminished status in the next life. A person who kills is reborn in one of the Buddhist hells, such as the Lohakumbha hell, where sinners are repeatedly decapitated and boiled.[47] In other hells, people are boiled in cauldrons, have their eyes or livers picked out by crows, are burned, have their hands hacked off, are skewered on a tree of thorns, or are chopped into pieces.

Besides providing an etiology of violence and its consequences, Buddhism offers a remedy to avoid this toxic state of being — the middle path. Cambodians are enjoined to follow five moral precepts *(seyl bram)*, the first of which is the injunction not to kill. Ebihara notes that the precepts "exercise a powerful influence on village behavior, though often they are followed with varying degrees of fidelity. . . . The murder of human beings is universally regarded as the greatest sin and horror. . . . [T]he slaughter of animals is also abhorred, and this task is [in many cases] delegated to Cham and Chinese butchers."[48] Monks preach that one must learn to control and extinguish one's anger, which arises from ignorance and desire and leads to violence and suffering. In Buddhism, the mindful way of dealing with anger is to recognize its source and to allow it to dissipate, since anger, like everything else in the world, is impermanent. Thus, Maha Ghosananda, a peace activist who was elected Supreme Patriarch of Cambodian Buddhism, gave the following sermon on anger:

> Our first duty is to protect ourselves, so we say, "May I be free from harming myself, may I be free from anger." Then we say, "May I be free from harming others, may I be free from anger." When we analyze anger, we find that it has no substance of its own. It is always conditioned by something else. There is no "I" to be angry. There is only the Dharma.
>
> When we are angry, our faces become ugly. Anger is fire, and it burns hundreds of cells in our brain and our blood.
>
> If we have loving kindness, our faces become brilliant, radiant, and beautiful. Loving kindness is like water. If we leave boiling water sitting for some time, it naturally becomes cool again. Sometimes we may boil with anger, but we can cool down gracefully by contemplating loving kindness, anger's opposite. The nature of water is to cleanse. When the mind is angry, it becomes soiled. Using the water of loving kindness, we can cleanse our mind. Like water, loving kindness flows everywhere.
>
> "Bodhi" means to wake up, to see things as they are. When we wake up to our anger, it loses all of its force. Then anger gives birth to its opposite — compassion, the compassionate heart of the Buddha.[49]

In this sermon, anger is ultimately depicted as a form of delusion that creates psychic and physiological disequilibrium, the opposite of the ideal Buddhist states of equanimity and balance. If anger is like a burning fire, it may be "cooled" through mindfulness and loving kindness, which are represented by the Bodhi tree.

Young children learn these Buddhist norms of nonviolence and methods for overcoming anger both at home and at the temple. Such lessons are reinforced by morality tales that illustrate how people who are "quick to anger" *(chhap khoeng)* encounter misfortune.[50] The importance Cambodians place upon managing anger is reflected in an elaborate vocabulary of emotion control. Thus Khmer includes such terms as "to block/control the heart" *(tuap chett)*, "to destroy/calm the heart" *(rumngoap chett)*, "to lose/cool one's anger" *(rosay kamhoeng/chett)*, "to turn/cleanse one's heart" *(puat chett)*, "to melt/calm one's anger/heart" *(roleay kamhoeng/chett)*, "to press down/calm the heart" *(sângkat chett)*, "to become cool in one's feelings" *(nay)*, "to extinguish anger" *(rumluat)*, "to keep one's temper" *(tâmkal chett)*, and "to disperse/demobilize one's anger/heart" *(rumsay kamhoeng/chett)*. Likewise, a person with a "heavy heart" *(chett thnguan)* is said to be slow to anger.[51]

The Khmer Buddhist term for anger, *tosah* (Pali *dosa*), has a wide range of connotations, implying agitation, malice, hatred, ignorance, and sin.[52] When used with the Buddhist term for delusion, *mohah* (Pali *moha*), *tosah* suggests the "violent anger" that drives combatants to kill each other in a blind rage. Among its synonyms, the *Khmer Dictionary* includes *kamhoeng*, the colloquial Cambodian term for "anger." The *Khmer Dictionary* further defines the verb form of *kamhoeng*, *khoeng* ("to be angry"), as "to be moved by a pressure" when the "object of one's mind *(arâmma)* is unsatisfied. . . . This causes choking heat to arise in one's heart *(chett)*."[53] As this definition suggests, anger, which is hyper-cognized in Khmer, is often described through metaphors of heat: an "angry" person is described as "hot" *(kdav)*, having a "hot heart" *(kdav chett)*, or being "hot and irritated" *(kdav krâhay)*.

Cambodian conceptions of anger have parallels to those advanced by some Western scholars. Richard Lazaraus, for example, has proposed that people experience anger when their self-implicating goals are blocked by someone or something that can be blamed.[54] Lazarus's perspective is interesting, since he directly links anger to self-identity: people become angry when goals related to their sense of self are threatened or blocked. Buddhism follows an analogous line of thought, linking anger to a self-inflation that is ultimately illusory (though the ontological status of self is radically different in Buddhist and Western psychology, an illusion in the former and a reality in the latter).

There are also differences between Cambodian and Euro-American notions of anger. For example, while metaphors of heat are central to both conceptual systems, Cambodian anger is linked to a different ethnophysiology, which centers on the notion of equilibrium and has been strongly influenced by Buddhist, animistic, Ayurvedic, and Chinese medical traditions.[55] In this humoral system, well-being is linked to physiological balance, particularly the balance between "hot" and "cold." The various humors have "heating" and "cooling" properties; thus "phlegm" tends to be associated with disorders linked to overheating and "bile" with excessive "cooling."[56] "Wind" *(khyal)*, the central humor in Khmer ethnophysiology, has cooling properties and, through its movement of the blood, directly affects the balance of hot and cold.[57]

For example, after giving birth, a Cambodian woman is considered to be in a "cold" state (pregnancy is a "hot" state), in part because of the obstructed flow of her blood vessels *(sârsai)*, which are believed to be damaged or lost during birth. Cambodian women traditionally take a number of steps to restore bodily equilibrium and protect themselves during this vulnerable time, when they are susceptible to postpartum ailments *(toas)* and spirit attack.[58] Both during and after birth, a traditional healer may try to ward off spirits by reciting incantations and prayers, placing thorns on the ground, or tying a string around the wrist.

Just after delivery, Cambodian women are often "roasted" *(ang phloeng)*, a tradition in which the woman is taken to a closed room (thereby avoiding cold drafts) and placed on a platform under which hot coals have been set.[59] This exposure to heat, it is thought, helps to regenerate the blood vessels and restore proper balance. In addition to "roasting," new mothers may wear warm clothing, cover their body so as to minimize exposure to wind and cold, consume "hot" foods, get injections of "hot" medicines, and place hot rocks on their abdomens.

Such practices illustrate the equilibrium that is crucial to well-being for Cambodians, both in terms of social relations and bodily health, the two being closely interrelated in Cambodian ethnopsychology. Emotions like anger can disrupt this balance and signal a disturbance in the social fabric in which a person is embedded, producing "felt" somatic manifestations, such as pain *(chheu)*, discomfort *(min sruol khluon)*, dizziness *(vil)*, or "heat" *(kdav)*, symptoms for which Cambodians constantly scan.[60] The "choking heat" of anger, then, metaphorically references the felt "pressure" of an animating but potentially disruptive psychosocial process that strongly "moves a person's heart" to act.

Each person, of course, has choice in negotiating his or her course of action when angered. Cambodians may have a Buddhist response and follow the spirit of Maha Ghosananda's sermon to overcome the "burning heat" of anger by trying to mindfully adjust their hearts and "cool down"; some may succeed in transforming their anger into loving kindness. Nevertheless, people may not have the mindfulness, desire, or ability to let their anger melt away, particularly when the perceived offense is significant and has caused them pain and suffering. There are other ways, both conscious and unconscious, in which individuals may manage their anger, strategies that are negotiated within social contexts in which importance is placed on mutual face-saving, avoiding public exposure and shame, observing Buddhist moral codes, "having friendly relations with others" *(roap an knea, reak teak)*, maintaining balance in one's interactions and relations, avoiding direct conflict, and controlling one's emotions. Anger may be expressed through somatic complaints, be redirected into more socially approved forms (including spirit possession, cockfighting, or striking animals), or be expressed in an indirect manner, such as through avoidance, teasing, or gossip.[61]

DISPROPORTIONATE REVENGE

To the Khmer, questions of honor and personal dignity
are of extraordinary importance. That which diminishes
personal honor is unacceptable — "*awt ban*" (cannot be
done). . . . Inflexible positions and uncompromising
stands are tied to honor and face. To yield diminishes
honor; to compromise is a form of surrender. When
compelled to accept an undesired end, the Khmer can
have a long memory. Old wounds may be passed from
one generation to another. . . . Some seek revenge to
"cleanse" their honor until their last breath.

> Abdulgaffar Peang-Meth, "Understanding the Khmer"

Cambodians, then, have a variety of strategies to manage anger. In some situations, however, particularly when honor and shame are at stake, a person may hold onto his or her anger and follow a path of violence. As Haing Ngor notes in the quote that began this chapter, such individuals may come to harbor a "grudge" *(kum, kumkuon, kumnum, kongkuon)* against their foes that lasts until they exact revenge *(karsângsoek)*, ideally in a manner that is disproportionate to the precipitating offense.

In Khmer, the word *kum* means "to wish to do bad or harm someone, to have a heart that is tied in malice *(pyabat)* with someone, to be tied in a grudge *(châng kumnum)*," which leads one "to prepare to take vengeance *(sangsoek)* in return."[62] One women's rights worker succinctly described the origins of a grudge to me as follows: "A person will hold a grudge when he or she understands that another person has done something very bad to him or her; he or she will have this one thought kept inside his or her heart." While such a grudge most often arises when another person or group makes the individual in question or that person's group suffer (for example, by murdering a family member), lose power (for example, by deposing that person from office), or lose face (for example, by dishonoring that person with a slight), it usually involves a degree of anger, shame, and the desire to "defeat" *(chneah)* a foe through an act of vengeance.

A grudge may arise from a single incident *(preuttekar)* or a series of smaller events. On the one hand, a person may seek revenge when someone else does "something very bad" to him or her. Many Cambodians continue to bear malice toward the Khmer Rouge, whose actions resulted in great suffering and the death of family members, relatives, and friends. On the other hand, a grudge may develop gradually as a person endures a series of small yet memorable incidents. While usually able to manage their anger so that open disputes do not break out, people do not always simply forget a matter.

A variety of Khmer phrases express the idea of storing away the memory of events that angered them. Cambodians sometimes say that a person takes such anger (or a grudge) and "hides it inside the body" *(leak tuk knong khluon)*, "puts/keeps it in the head" *(tuk knong khuor kbal)*, or "buries/hides it in the heart" *(bângkap/leak knong chett)*. When these feelings of anger and resentment persist, a person may become "seized with painful anger" *(chheu chap, kamhoeng cheu chap)*. As we will see, a buildup of class resentment proved lethal during DK, when Khmer Rouge ideology encouraged the poor to take revenge upon the rich.

The above examples of malice share a pattern in which an event or a series of small incidents causes a person to suffer and feel shame, which in turn leads to anger, resentment, and possibly the desire for revenge. Cambodians who have a big grudge are sometimes said to want to "eat the flesh and sip the blood" *(si sach hot cheam)* of their enemy. Despite this desire to take revenge, however, most Cambodians recognize that it is often not propitious to repay a bad deed immediately. A grudge thus contains an element of potentiality and is frequently long-lasting, as illustrated by the *Khmer Dictionary*'s definition of the term *kum kuon*: "A long-lasting grudge *[kum]* that one can't forget, as in 'he has harbored *kum kuon* for a long time already, secretly preparing to strike his old rival.' "[63] By hiding their animosity from a foe, people who hold a grudge may be able to maintain an element of surprise and prevent their adversary from taking the initiative. During everyday interactions, a person may therefore smile and act politely toward an enemy; when the appropriate occasion arises, however, they will act.

Those unable to exact revenge in person may decide to hire a killer or order a subordinate to perform the deed. Several Cambodian journalists have been murdered by assassins weeks or months after having written insulting articles about government officials or businessmen. Alternatively, people may hire sorcerers to cast a spell on their adversaries. Many Cambodians worry about black magic, which they believe can make a person fatally ill, and try to protect themselves by wearing magical objects such as a pig fang, a fragment of elephant tusk, a piece of gold, a magical string, an inscribed cloth, a Buddha amulet, or some combination of these items.

Despite its duration, a grudge often continues to involve intense feelings. One religious lay expert explained, "A grudge is packaged anger that has not yet come out; it remains inside, always hot, but it doesn't leave. It keeps waiting until 'I' [ânh] have the opportunity to strike immediately." As this remark suggests, anger lies at the center of the desire for revenge, generating a felt "heat" that moves one to act when the appropriate time arrives. This heat also symbolizes the social and bodily disequilibrium caused by an offense that angers, shames, and dishonors the person, disrupting the (ideally) balanced flow of their self-implicating interpersonal interactions.

The expression *chheu chap* captures this sense of imbalance. The word *chheu* means "to be sick," but is also used to denote pain, torment, suffering, and a felt "hurt" signifying humoral imbalance. *Chap* means to seize, grab, catch, or hold tight.[64] This is also the word used for "arrest" (as in being "held" or detained); the "list of traitorous strings" in Tuol Sleng confessions contain annotations stating whether or not a person was *chap*. *Chheu chap* therefore signifies being caught in a frustrating, lasting, and possibly intensifying state of painful agony that disrupts the balance and flow of social and emotional life. The "heat" of anger is often crucial to the experience of *chheu chap*, which, in contexts of malice and violence, connotes being "seized with painful, agonizing anger." People who are angry or upset are sometimes said to have a "hurt/painful heart" *(chheu chett)*, a state that also implies imbalance and heat; in fact, the *Khmer Dictionary* defines *chheu chett* as having a "hot heart" *(kdav chett)*.[65] It is precisely because a grudge involves "painful agony," the "heat" of anger, somatic and social disruption, a loss of face and honor, and deeply felt shame that the desire for vengeance comes to have such strong emotional and motivational force.

Revenge *(sângsoek)*, however, has other ontological resonances, particularly because of its linkages to the moral order, interpersonal ties, and reciprocal exchange. The root of the word, *sâng*, refers to the obligation "to return (an object), to pay back (debt), to pay for damage."[66] While *sâng* can imply an impersonal transaction, such as a market exchange, it is often used in the context of personal exchanges that imply a moral relationship between the parties involved. As in all societies, exchange is a fundamental dimension of Cambodian daily life. Many forms of exchange promote social solidarity and mutual obligation, such as the generalized reciprocity within a household or more balanced exchanges with friends, villagers, and neighbors (mutual assistance, labor exchanges, contributions to life ceremonies, and the lending of money, rice seed, or livestock).[67] The participants in a reciprocal relationship are sometimes metaphorically portrayed as being "tied" *(châng)* together. For example, during a Cambodian wedding, guests are literally said to "tie the hands" *(châng dai)* of the bridal couple by making a monetary gift that signifies their bond to the newlyweds and their families.[68]

Such bonds may also be forged by unequal or disproportionate exchanges, particularly when status issues are involved. In a cosmos in which all beings are hierarchically ranked, some people are able to give more and therefore perform deeds that are difficult to repay. Exchange may thus involve the negotiation of status, since the act of giving and receiving inscribes relative standing.[69] Thus, while the amount of a wedding gift can signify social distance, it can also mark the status of the giver — a wealthy individual may *châng dai* a large sum of money that the parents of the couple would have difficulty reciprocating. Disproportionate exchanges are manifest in many contexts, ranging from the offerings a person makes to monks (which are insignificant compared to the merit and blessings the lay person receives in return) and spirits (which are also trivial compared to the protection and good fortune one may gain) to the services one provides to a patron (whose power enables the person to offer relatively greater resources and protection). The notion of disproportionate return is initially learned at home, where parents are idealized as performing good deeds that are almost impossible for their children to repay.

Regardless of the difficulty, one is morally obligated to strive to repay *(sâng)* the "kindness" or "good deeds" *(kun)* of others. It is considered a virtue for someone to "know" *(deung kun)* and to "repay the good deeds" *(sâng kun)* of their parents, relatives, teachers, and patrons; an ingrate who ignores or takes lightly this debt *(bamphlech kun, romil kun)* commits a moral offense that may generate feelings of malice. Thus, when Lon Nol overthrew Prince Sihanouk, the prince bore ill will toward this former client, whom he characterized as an "ingrate." In most contexts, those who receive a good deed are expected to acknowledge their debt through greater respect, loyalty, or attachment to the benefactor, although the intensity and structure of the bond varies according to the situation and the respective status of each person in the dyad. The increased respect given to the person who does the good deed signals the benefactor's elevation in hierarchical standing vis-à-vis the debtor.

Revenge is largely premised on this logic of debt and reciprocal exchange, but in a manner that is the inverse of a relationship based on gratitude and good deeds. Just as a person should return a good deed, so too should they repay a bad deed, ideally in a disproportionate manner that "defeats" the offender and elevates one's honor (which was diminished by the instigating offence). The Khmer term for "revenge," *karsângsoek,* literally means "to pay back" *(sâng)* "the enemy" *(soek).* Moreover, the injured party's obligation to repay the enemy for whatever this foe has done creates a bond between the dyadic pair. Thus, a Cambodian bearing malice is often said to be "tied" or "bound" to his enemy by anger or vindictiveness *(châng kamhoeng, châng kumnum, châng pear).* The *Khmer Dictionary* defines *sângsoek* as not just "to return evil, to destroy in return," but "to be tied in malice *(châng pear)* [with the desire] to make a return"; similarly, the term *kumnum* is defined as "a grudge *(kum),* desire for vengeance: a grudge *(kumnum)* that is the origin of a knot of malice *(chamnâng pear)*; a tie of vindictiveness *(karchâng kumnum)* that leads the *chett* to be irritated and hot [like sticky, humid heat], almost all of the time."[70] Because of its strong ontological resonances, ranging from this felt "heat" to local understandings of reciprocal exchange that are first learned and enacted in early childhood, the cultural model of revenge has been a prominent theme in Cambodian politics, as various groups, including the Khmer Rouge, attempt to blend it into their ideological pronouncements.[71]

• • •

Why, then, does a Cambodian grudge sometimes lead to revenge that, as Ngor notes in the epigraph that opened this chapter, is "much more damaging than the original injury?" If the desire to exact disproportionate revenge resonates ontologically with the experience of physiological, emotional, and social "imbalance," it also resonates with other forms of disproportionate exchange, particularly those that involve the negotiation of status. If benefactors gain respect, elevate their status, and generate moral debts by performing good deeds, those who perform bad deeds show disrespect toward, lower the status of, and "defeat" *(chneah)* the recipient, who in turn has a moral obligation to repay the bad action. On the one hand, the person doing the "bad deed" asserts his or her superiority over the recipient; on the other hand, the bad deed results in a loss of face, since it undermines the self-implicating "line" asserted by the recipient, particularly in public contexts, where the offender may lead other people to lower their esteem of the recipient.

Merely to repay this bad deed with an equivalent act would leave the parties on an equal footing. Those who take disproportionate revenge for bad deeds "defeat" their foes, elevate their standing vis-à-vis the offenders, restore (in part or in whole) their previously diminished honor *(star ketteyos)*, and symbolically display that an exchange with them is not to be taken lightly. The head of a Khmer Buddhist Society told me that people who hold a grudge "desire to take vengeance in a manner that exceeds the initial offense because they want to win and not to be ashamed before others. When they win, they have honor and others will look at them and stop thinking that they are inferior."

The second crucial reason why a Cambodian grudge may result in disproportionate revenge is the view that a person must "completely defeat the enemy" *(phchanh phchal)* to deter further retaliation. The phrase *phchanh phchal* literally means to defeat others in such a manner that they will not dare to continue the matter out of fear or because they are completely crushed.[72] Drawing on an analogy with boxing, Bun Chân Mol describes the spirit of *phchanh phchal* as follows:

> If a person knocks down his opponent, he will not stand quietly by the side. Instead, he will run forward and begin kicking his foe in order to add on to the injury, sometimes doing so until the loser is knocked unconscious or perhaps even dies. . . . He does not consider himself to have won until his opponent has fallen down unconscious or dies. . . . [If not completely defeated], the loser, in turn, will not be content to remain defeated and will develop a grudge against his opponent and the matter will go on. . . . A person might even secretly stab his foe in the back.[73]

Similarly, those who bear a grudge know that after they have exacted revenge, their adversary will in turn desire to repay the bad deed. To prevent the cycle from continuing, it may be in the avenger's interest to make a preemptive strike that will mute this desire by fear or death. As one informant explained, "*Phchanh phchal* means that you want the enemy to see what you have done and to be scared and respect you . . . to be so afraid that they won't dare to fight back."

Acid attacks provide a particularly brutal illustration of completely defeating a foe. One evening, for example, Bros, who sometimes worked as a nurse at a local hospital, told me that the previous evening a woman was admitted to the hospital with acid burns on the right side of her face and on her upper torso. Her right eye and ear were severely burned. Her younger sister did this to her! This younger sister, who had become wealthy because of her business skills, had invited her older sister to come live in her house. She had just helped her older sibling with the marriage of the older sister's virgin daughter when the older sister ran off with the younger sister's husband, who was a schoolteacher. So, the younger sister had a grudge *(kumnum)* against her sibling. She took revenge *(sangsoek)* by throwing acid on her sister's face.

In a notorious case in December 1999, Khourn Sophal, the wife of Svay Sitha, an undersecretary of state in the Council of Ministers and a former Hun Sen advisor, allegedly attacked her husband's young lover, the actress Tat Samarina. In broad daylight in a busy market, Khourn Sophal and her two bodyguards poured a five-liter container of nitric acid on Samarina's torso and head, resulting in severe disfigurement and burns over half her body.[74] By carrying out these brutal acid attacks, the perpetrators exact revenge against their "enemies" (women who have done a "bad deed" to them by stealing their husbands). In doing so, they "completely defeat" the victim by obliterating her beauty and ensuring the end of the extra-marital affair. Moreover, the victim will forever have to deal with her injuries, disfigurement, and loss of (figurative and literal) "face."

The most extreme form of *phchanh phchal* consists of killing one's enemies, and possibly their families. While people may exact revenge in such a manner that their adversary is completely defeated for the moment, it is possible that the vanquished foe's fortune may change for the better at a later date and provide them with an opportunity for revenge. In fact, several Cambodian proverbs warn of the danger that a person who currently shows fear and respect may rise to a powerful position in the future.[75] One way to prevent such potential retribution is to suppress its root cause:[76] to kill the enemy and thus preempt the possibility of retaliation. A further problem arises, however, since someone in the deceased foe's family may seek disproportionate revenge for the death. The head of a Cambodian nongovernmental organization pointed out, "When a son sees people kill his father, he will be seized with painful anger *(chheu chap).* After he has grown up, he will try to kill all of the people connected to the matter of his father's death. He won't just kill one person, he will kill many."

The most extreme Cambodian solution to this predicament, only possible in situations where a person has great power, is to kill the enemy and "cut off" or "destroy" their "seed" *(phtach pouch, sângsoek suor pouch, prâlay pouch sas); pouch* is the agricultural term for "seed," which is metaphorically extended to describe a group of people such as a family, clan, or nationality).[77] The genealogy of this practice goes far back in Cambodian history to accounts of victorious Cambodian kings who, after winning a war, would attempt to kill opposing kings and their entire family lines.[78] As we will see, much DK violence can be viewed as a Khmer Rouge attempt to "cut off the family line" of their enemies.

Other parallels exist.[79] During political upheavals of the late 1990s in Cambodia, for example, several incidents of "cutting off the family line" were rumored to have occurred. Pol Pot, in a desperate attempt to hold onto power in June 1997, ordered the execution of Son Sen (the former DK minister of defense), his wife Yun Yat, and ten of their family members and relatives.[80] Some reports held that, after killing them, Pol Pot's troops ran over their heads with a truck. Similarly, during the July 1997 coup, rumors abounded that Hun Sen's troops had killed the families of some of Prince Ranariddh's loyalists.[81] Finally, from 1993 to 1997, the Khmer Rouge supposedly conducted internal purges in which entire families were annihilated.[82] Krom Khuon, a former Khmer Rouge soldier, recalled, "Sometimes I would see a car full of soldiers come. . . . They would take the whole family into the forest in a truck. Then the soldiers would come back without the family."[83] Thousands of these victims are supposedly buried in a massive killing field called Gravel Hill.

Such examples illustrate the Cambodian cultural model of disproportionate revenge, albeit in its most extreme form, of "completely destroying" the enemy. Revenge may be carried out in person or with the "backing" of a powerful patron who helps exact revenge against a foe who has done "something bad" to the perpetrator, a pattern that is manifest in the Cambodian legend *Tum Teav*.[84] Based on this information, we may schematize the cultural model of a grudge leading to disproportionate revenge in the following manner:[85]

> *Cambodian Revenge (karsângsoek):*
> *"A Head for an Eye" ("Disproportionate")*

EVENT:	A does a bad deed to B
JUDGMENT:	B loses face and suffers
	A is now "higher than" and "looks down upon" B
	B must return *(sâng)* the bad deed to A (grudge/*kum*)
	B should try to "completely defeat" A *(phchanh phchal)*

COMPLICATION:	A tries to prevent B from returning the bad deed
EXPECTATION:	B should return the bad deed to A (disproportionately)
MORAL INFERENCE:	B has an obligation to disproportionately return the bad deed to A
	A should receive B's disproportionate bad deed
STATUS INFERENCE:	B will be "higher than" A
	B's honor will be cleansed *(star ketteyos)*
	A will (hopefully) not attempt further retaliation against B

In the next section, I show how disproportionate revenge provided a legitimating and highly motivating basis for violence during DK.

DISPROPORTIONATE REVENGE IN DK

To develop ideology, so that there is always the
revolutionary attitude and the class (proletarian)
attitude in the party . . . is to conduct internal
ideological indoctrination so that the initial attitude
taken is conserved firmly, and the Marxist-Leninist
class leaning and devotion to class struggle is retained
always to win power by annihilating the enemy
regime . . . and to create class ardor and fury. This
ardor and fury must be aroused according to the
contradiction of the day whether it be large or small.
Thus, ideological force will be converted into a burning
material force which will dare to engage in struggle,
attack the enemy and win final victory over the enemy
even if he is very strong.
              Pre-1975 Summary of Annotated Party History[86]

To dig up grass, one must also dig up the roots.
                                    Khmer Rouge saying

To "create class ardor and fury," the Khmer Rouge used notions like exploitation as an ideological "hook," tapping into preexisting feelings of dissatisfaction, unrest, anger, and spite and providing a foundation upon which revolutionary consciousness could be built. Simple sayings, songs, refrains, and leaflets provided a rudimentary class explanation for this sense of oppression; thus one pre-DK propaganda leaflet explained that capitalists "live in affluence at the expense of the working class and the masses," who "live in misery, bled by them." [87] The revolution, the leaflet asserted, would "liberate" the people from this oppression and revitalize Cambodian society.

More thorough political education texts elaborated upon these points. For example, a August 1973 tract published in the youth periodical *Revolutionary Young Men and Women* asserted that "human society is divided into . . . the oppressor class and the oppressed."[88] The tract went on to discuss who the oppressors were (imperialists, feudalists, capitalists, and reactionaries) and how they exploited the oppressed. Through such instruction, the tract proclaimed, the revolutionary youth would "awaken and become aware of the national problem [and] the class problem." Ultimately, such an understanding was supposed to result in rage: "Khmer youth, upon receiving this education in the political principles, the revolutionary consciousness of the party, all found rage strongly mounting. [Their rage] manifested itself as a struggle movement to contest American imperialists and the oppressor classes in whatever guise."[89]

Ith Sarin, who spent nine months with the Khmer Rouge in 1973, provides a detailed example of how such indoctrination proceeded, as the regime attempted to instill "bloody" or "mortal hate" in its followers.[90] At political education seminars, for example, recruits would study a number of documents, including ones on "Class Struggle" and "Revolutionary Hate." Such instruction was supplemented by criticism and self-criticism sessions at which recruits were assessed in terms of their "state of morale [and] feelings." In addition to explicit discussion, revolutionary meetings included artistic performances (and even funerals of those who had been killed in battle) that were designed to foment "revolutionary violence" so that the attendees "burned" with hatred toward the enemy.[91] The ninth of fifteen Khmer Rouge revolutionary precepts even read, "One must maintain a burning rage [*kamhoeng chap cheh*] toward the enemy."[92]

To recruit cadres and soldiers and increase their support among the population, then, the Khmer Rouge relied heavily on notions of class struggle and oppression. As Pol Pot noted in his 1977 speech, the goal was to transform popular discontent into class rage that would propel the revolution to victory. By giving preexisting resentments a focus and target and attempting to transform these feelings into a "burning force," the Khmer Rouge effectively encouraged people to hold a class grudge *(kumnum vonnah)* against their "oppressors." Thus, while a person like Khel might have joined the Khmer Rouge originally because Sihanouk was overthrown, he was quickly indoctrinated into communist ideology: "Their political education consisted of telling us to be seized with painful anger against the oppressor class. They spoke about this all the time." The Khmer Rouge drew upon and transformed preexisting understandings of disproportionate revenge to create a new model of revenge that was adapted to their doctrine and the particular historical moment in which they lived.

The logic of the Khmer Rouge model of disproportionate revenge was that oppressors had done "something bad" to the poor by making them suffer and lose face. One or more of these incidents led the poor to be "seized with painful anger" *(chheu chap)*, which they stored inside themselves. The Khmer Rouge inflamed this hidden resentment into a "burning" class grudge to motivate the poor to want to "eat the flesh and sip the blood" of this enemy. The poor, however, needed a powerful patron to help them exact disproportionate revenge against this hated enemy. Ângkar fulfilled this role. Drawing on the format I presented earlier, this Khmer Rouge ideological model can be schematized as follows:

DK Class Revenge: "A Head for An Eye" ("Disproportionate")

EVENT:	Oppressors do bad deeds to the poor
JUDGMENT:	The poor lose face and suffer
	Oppressors are "higher than" and "look down upon" the poor
	The poor must return *(sâng)* the bad deed to the oppressors (class grudge, *kumnum vonnah*)
	The poor should try to "completely defeat" the oppressors
COMPLICATION:	Oppressors prevent the poor from returning the bad deed
EXPECTATION:	The poor should return the bad deed to the oppressors (disproportionately)
MORAL INFERENCE:	The poor have a moral obligation to return disproportionately the bad deed to the oppressors

Oppressors should receive the disproportionate
bad deed from the poor (Ângkar as the powerful
patron)

STATUS INFERENCE: The poor will be "higher than" their former
oppressors

The honor of the poor will be cleansed (*star
ketteyos*)

The oppressors will (hopefully) not attempt
further retaliation against the poor

It is important to note that the distribution, understanding, internalization, and motivational force of this model could vary. A person living in
a Khmer Rouge zone, where various Khmer Rouge indoctrination methods had been instituted, would have much greater exposure to this model
than a rich person living in Phnom Penh, which is part of the reason why
there was so much interest in Ith Sarin's book when it was published in
1973 — many people in Phnom Penh were getting their first look at
Khmer Rouge practice and ideology.

Similarly, depending on their personal histories and the social fields in
which they moved (for example, their educational, class, or political
background), a person might have a relatively deep understanding of
such Khmer Rouge ideological models. Pol Pot, who had been studying
Marxist-Leninism since his years in Paris and who was a formulator of
Khmer Rouge doctrine, no doubt had a more complex understanding of
the regime's ideology than did Ith Sarin. As an educator, Ith Sarin, in
turn, likely understood the nuances of Khmer Rouge ideology more
deeply than Lor, a moderately poor peasant who had little formal schooling and who had received less political training. Reflecting on the way he
was indoctrinated, Lor recalled that the Khmer Rouge "told us that the
poor were poor because of the rich and the rich were rich because of the
poor. They wanted us to become seized with painful anger about this
exploitation, to hate and fight bravely against the capitalist, feudal, and
landlord classes, the rich big people who harmed the poor." His basic
understanding of class oppression, struggle, and rage was probably similar to that of many poor peasants in Khmer Rouge zones.

The motivational force and contextual salience of Khmer Rouge ideology also varied. Thus the Khmer Rouge model of disproportionate
revenge was likely more compelling to landless peasants who worked the
fields of a landlord who paid them little and treated them with disrespect

than it was to the landlord or a relatively wealthy peasant. Similarly, Khmer Rouge ideology was less appealing to most wealthy, educated urbanites, who were classified as "oppressors" and whose relatively privileged life experiences often made it difficult for them to sympathize with the plight of the poor. Moreover, because of the structural position in which "new people" typically were placed (having low status, being subject to dehumanizing discourses and practices, losing their wealth and homes, lacking former rights and access to power), this group had much less reason than poor peasant "old people" (whose structural position typically improved) to "take" and be motivated by Khmer Rouge ideology. This is part of the reason why so many "new people" viewed Khmer Rouge slogans, songs, and meetings with indifference or hostility — in contrast to the recruits that Ith Sarin observed.[93] Even within a given socioeconomic group, the motivational force of the Khmer Rouge model varied depending on life history, personality, and context. In some situations and for some cadres — like those the "anonymous cadre" observed — class hatred appears to have been a strong motive for violence. In other contexts and for other cadres, different motives, such as the ones I discuss in subsequent chapters, might be more salient.

Still, the Khmer Rouge model of disproportionate revenge was a strong motive for many cadres, partly because it was sufficiently abstract to encompass a variety of sources of resentment and discontent (the "bad deeds"): debt, impoverishment, hunger, shame, the destruction of one's home and property, being bombed, the killing of loved ones, and so forth. These experiences provided an ontologically resonant base into which Khmer Rouge ideology could tap. Through the logic of disproportionate exchange, the "oppressors" who had done these "bad deeds" deserved to receive "something bad" in return. Until this was achieved, the oppressed would remain "tied in malice" with them, a state characterized by feelings of disequilibrium and heat. By stoking the flames of this "burning rage," the Khmer Rouge were tapping into these ontologically resonant dimensions of anger and malice and effectively promoting revenge.

The abstractness of this model also enabled the Khmer Rouge to direct this "burning rage" toward disparate groups at different times, with targets ranging from various oppressor classes within Cambodia to oppressive foreign powers. During the civil war, the Khmer Rouge attempted to focus these feelings primarily on the Lon Nol regime and the urban areas it controlled. For the Khmer Rouge, the Lon Nol regime was a corrupt enemy "lackey" that militarily defended the interests of the oppressive social classes and imperialists and protected the capitalist system used by these groups to exploit the poor. As the 1973 *Revolutionary Young Men and Women* tract stated, this "traitorous . . . clique is a militarist, fascist representative for the feudal, capitalist, and unparalleled reactionary class that serves as traitorous, country-selling valets of American imperialists."[94] A current government official told me, "The Khmer Rouge brainwashed people into believing that the Lon Nol regime was a capitalist regime, and that the very poor, who had been oppressed and swindled by the rich, had to fight bravely to defeat Lon Nol." Lon Nol had overthrown Sihanouk. He could be blamed for the death and devastation caused by the bombing. His soldiers engaged in close combat with Khmer Rouge forces, killing friends and comrades of the cadres. Such brutality was memorialized in songs such as this one, which was taught to children after the war:

> Baribo village sheds it tears;
> The enemy dropped bombs and staged a coup.
> The screams of a combatant; friend, where are you?
> The hated enemy killed my friend.
> When you died away, friend, you were still naked,
> Chest and stomach asunder, liver and spleen gone,
> You floated them away like a river's current.
> Removal of liver and spleen is cause for sadness.
> The ricelands of my mother are far in the distance.
> The sun slants over the green hills.
> When you died away, friend, you reminded me
> That the hated enemy had swallowed Cambodia.[95]

Through such ideological discourses and practices, the Khmer Rouge helped further inflame emotions, leading many cadres to become "seized by painful anger" and to maintain a "bloody" and "mortal hate" for the Lon Nol regime.

The cities were similarly vilified as corrupt and immoral centers of undue foreign influence. Even before the war, many peasants felt disconnected from and wary of cities. Structurally, there were few institutional links between the urban and rural populations. In her study of Sobay, Ebihara found that most villagers lived in a fairly insular world that revolved around family, relatives, neighbors, and the temple, or *wat*.[96] Although Sobay villagers did travel and have contacts beyond the village (the frequency decreasing dramatically with distance), most remained highly distrustful of strangers.[97] Strangers were often suspected of being "people of bad character," including "robbers, rapists, [and] murderers."[98] If some Sobay villagers, particularly the young, viewed Phnom Penh as exciting, many others found it "a welter of noise, confusion, crowding, unsavory characters, immorality, danger, and expense, to be endured only when absolutely necessary. Some people . . . [brought] back stories of immodest women, attempted or accomplished thievery, physical violence, and other lurid accounts or varied complaints."[99]

This peasant distrust of cities and the structural condition of urban-rural disconnect allowed the Khmer Rouge to crystallize and mark the differences between the urban and rural populations. The Khmer Rouge depicted urbanites as corrupt beings who lived in luxury and sin — residing in huge homes, eating well, drinking cognac, and visiting prostitutes — while the masses were exploited and suffered. Thus, in a broadcast on May 12, 1975, Phnom Penh Domestic Radio proclaimed that in the areas that Lon Nol controlled, "injustice, corruption, hooliganism, burglary, banditry, and prostitution were overwhelming and became a natural and even legal way of life." The "rotten culture" of U.S. imperialism, the broadcast proclaimed, had "poisoned" the urbanites, whose immoral practices were opposed to those of the "clean" peasantry.[100] Such discourses constructed urbanites and peasants as different sorts of beings. A broadcast three days later described how, upon entering Phnom Penh, the revolutionary army was "taken aback" by the sight of "long-haired men and youngsters wearing bizarre clothes" such as "skin-tight pants with oversized bell-bottoms," an attire that stood in stark contrast to the traditional garb of Cambodians.[101]

Such images of strangeness and difference were reinforced by assertions that the cities contained "American lackeys" and foreign imperialists. In fact, most foreigners resided in the cities, which contained a disproportionately large number of ethnic minorities. A 1962 monograph reported that Phnom Penh was 42 percent Khmer, 30 percent Chinese, and 27 percent Vietnamese.[102] Such structural divisions resonated with the preconceptions of peasants who viewed strangers with suspicion and regarded cities as locales in which sinful deeds took place.

Ideologically, the Khmer Rouge stigmatized the urbanites as capitalist oppressors who exploited the poor. Slogans and sayings like "Trees in the country, fruit in the town" were used to inflame the anger of the peasantry toward the urbanites. According to Soth Polin, this common Khmer Rouge saying was "cast in the form of an old saying and profit[ed] from the good sense attributed to traditional maxims." He explains that this slogan "engender[ed] jealousy among the peasants against the city-dwellers. Repeated a thousand times, it convinced the former that eliminating the latter was within their rights — better still, an imperative of their culture. Repeated a thousand times, this adage has 'devised' an inextinguishable hatred."[103]

For many peasants, usurers, "those who have" *(neak mean)*, or, less frequently, landlords were the familiar oppressors who could serve as a sort of experiential point of reference for abstract Khmer Rouge pronouncements about "class oppressors" — even if their understandings did not always exactly parallel the formal DK party line, which underemphasized usury. Like usurers, who charged high rates of interest, the urbanites consumed the "fruits" of the peasants' land and labor to support their comfortable and "immoral" lives. In all of these ways, Khmer Rouge ideology helped manufacture urbanites into an "other" marked as corrupt and targeted for revenge. City people were not only capitalist exploiters, they also were not quite "real Khmer" — instead they represented a hated enemy who should be "crushed" by "class ardor and fury." A "new person" explained that the Khmer Rouge "sometimes called this [type of indoctrination] 'igniting class anger.' They made people in the countryside have a grudge against the urbanites by teaching them about class contradiction. When we left the cities, the rural population considered us their enemies."

Given the intensity of some peasant resentments and the centrality of class rage to Khmer Rouge ideology, it is not surprising that so much violence occurred after liberation. As the "anonymous cadre" suggests, by the end of the brutal civil war, the "ignited class anger" was burning at full force and many Khmer Rouge soldiers and cadres were firmly tied in malice toward their enemy. In Battambang province, for example, Khmer Rouge appeared "contemptuous and aloof" just after liberation and later reportedly admitted that they had been "fired by 'uncontrollable hatred' for members of the 'old society.' 'We were so angry when we came out of the forest,' one speaker allegedly said, 'that we didn't want to spare even a baby in its cradle.' "[104] Some of these cadres even ripped apart with their hands a Lon Nol military jet in the Battambang airport.

As this incident suggests, Lon Nol soldiers, police, and government personnel were targets of revenge during the first wave of DK killings. Throughout Cambodia, the Khmer Rouge set out to identify and detain members of the Lon Nol regime, particularly those who had held high rank. In his confession, Sreng, a high-ranking Northern Zone cadre who had close connections to Region 41, where Banyan was located, asserted that at this time the Party Center "put forward a policy of successively smashing officers, starting from the generals and working down through the lieutenants, as well as government investigative agents, policemen, military police personnel and reactionary civil servants," an order that was later extended to include lower-ranking Lon Nol soldiers.[105]

After taking Phnom Penh, Khmer Rouge radio ordered "all ministers and generals to come to the Ministry of Information at once to organize the country."[106] Dari, a Banyan villager who had fled to Phnom Penh, where she lived across from the ministry, noted that many of these people looked scared, despite Khmer Rouge assurances that they were to help in the reconstruction of the country. Many people thought that the top "supertraitors" of the Khmer Republic would be executed, but few suspected that the Khmer Rouge would execute the entire leadership of the former regime. This is exactly what happened. According to You Kim Lanh, a technician who reported to the ministry, the Lon Nol officers and officials were asked to write their life histories and then taken to the Monorom Hotel, which was used as a detention center.[107] For several days, according to You Kim Lanh, hundreds of people continued to arrive at the hotel, most of whom were loaded into trucks at night and driven away. When You Kim Lanh asked a Khmer Rouge officer he knew what happened to these people, the cadre replied: "We kill them all because they're traitors and deserve to be shot."

As the cities were evacuated, the Khmer Rouge appealed to high and low-level soldiers and officials to identify themselves, suggesting that their skills would be of help in the reconstruction of the country or that they would receive an equivalent rank in the new regime. Urbanites being evacuated from the cities were asked to give background information about their former occupations. Many people who told the truth were taken away to be killed. Others who remained silent, such as Chlat's brother-in-law, a Lon Nol officer, were recognized or discovered through investigations. Chlat described what happened to his brother and other Lon Nol personnel who were killed:

> There was a Pol Pot [cadre] who knew that my brother-in-law had been a major [in the Lon Nol army]. The man had been one of my brother-in-law's men before he defected to serve Pol Pot. He reported my brother-in-law's rank, an accusation that meant death. The Pol Pots detained my brother-in-law and told us to go on. My elder sister and their four children sobbed and sobbed, knowing that the Pol Pots wouldn't let him live and that they would be separated forever. We walked on, stunned by his death, with dried out, sad faces. We had lost a family member whom we all loved dearly.
>
> We traveled on northward, before stopping in front of Bateay Mountain [located in Region 41] for the night. Throughout the evening,

until dawn, trucks passed by carrying people to be killed on Bateay Mountain. Some of the trucks were closed; others were not. But there were a lot of people taken there, because once in a while we'd see two or three trucks depart and then return. A little latter it would happen again. This went on all night. . . . Such activities fulfilled Pol Pot's objective. They hated Lon Nol soldiers. . . .

So we can see that the activities of Pol Pot included a plan to kill soldiers. Some they extracted while they journeyed on the road [just after the Khmer Rouge had come to power]. The others they had seized at their military posts or ports. At that time, they began to send these soldiers to be killed. I saw it with my eyes. There was a group of [former Lon Nol] soldiers at Taung Raung village who were sent to be killed on a secluded hill by Lovea village.

While I was rice farming, a long line of these soldiers passed by me, perhaps five meters apart. The line was really long. There were maybe two kilometers of soldiers. A person would pass, then five meters later another, five meters another. . . . And the line did not just include the soldiers, but also their wives and children. They were all marched to an old temple perhaps one hundred meters to the west of Lovea village. From this place, they were taken to be killed [on the hill] above Lovea village, where [the Pol Pots] had already dug [graves to put them in]. At night, they'd take five, ten, fifteen people at a time. There were a lot of them.

And, on this hill above Lovea, there were two wells, which . . . the Pol Pots completely filled with the corpses of [Lon Nol] soldiers! There were eight or nine mass graves as well — big ones, each perhaps ten meters in length with a width of five, six, seven, eight meters. . . . This occurred around the end of 1975 or beginning of 1976. They didn't let people go near this [killing field]. . . . I don't know how many people were killed there, but they were all soldiers, along with their wives, children, and grandchildren.

As the events Chlat witnessed illustrate, the mass killings of former Lon Nol soldiers and government personnel (and sometimes their families and other "reactionaries") took place throughout Cambodia just after the Khmer Rouge came to power.[108] Many were killed by the truckload immediately after the evacuation; some were executed after being rounded up and held in detention centers. Still others were sent to be "reeducated" in special camps or through rural peasant life, though they remained targets of suspicion throughout DK.

Up to two hundred thousand people — ranging from Lon Nol soldiers to civilians who made "mistakes" — may have perished during this first wave of DK killing, immediately after the regime took power.[109] For many Khmer Rouge cadres, the Party Center's call to "execute all leaders of the Lon Nol regime beginning with the top leaders"[110] provided them with a warrant to take revenge upon the "oppressor enemy" to whom they were tied in malice for so many reasons.

· · ·

Instead of ending the vengeance after this initial period, the Khmer Rouge attempted to keep the class grudge inflamed. "Burning rage" remained a central part of revolutionary consciousness. Sometimes this connection was explicit, as in the July 1977 issue of *Revolutionary Flags*, which stated that, as "one's standpoint" *(kol chumhor)* was "clarified and sharpened," one would be "pushed" to have a political conscious-ness *(sâtiarâmma)* that included:

> 1. A constantly burning rage *(kamhoeng chap cheh)* for the enemy.
> 2. An extremely deep revolutionary sentiment toward the oppressed classes.
> 3. A strong spirit of love for the nation, revolution, collective, and Party.[111]

These three forms of consciousness constituted the "basis" of the "daily fighting spirit," which would ideally make one "hot" *(kdav)* so that one would "stand on the base of anger toward the enemy." Ultimately, this revolutionary consciousness, including "anger for outside enemies, class enemies, and enemies burrowing from within," would inspire one to "work hard to research, investigate, seek out, and clean up these enemies."

More concretely, the DK regime attempted to generate this "con-stantly burning rage" through frequent reminders of the "bad deeds" the oppressor classes had done to the oppressed. On the local level, cadres were instructed to continue emphasizing oppression in their political propaganda. A deputy secretary of Region 21 stated that this meant encouraging the peasantry to remember that the city people "had an easy life" in contrast with their own suffering, "were exploiters," "shirked productive work," and were "not pure and clean."[112] Khmer Rouge speeches, publications, and radio broadcasts reinforced this mes-sage. Thus a radio broadcast on January 20, 1976 reminded its listeners of how the city people had caused them to suffer and feel humiliated:

> Our brothers and sisters lived a most miserable life, enduring all manner of hardships, including shortages of food and clothing, while under the most barbaric, ferocious and fascist oppression of the imperialists, colonialists and their lackeys of all stripes, including their ringleader, Lon Nol. They never had enough food, never were happy and never had an opportunity to

receive [an education]. Our brothers and sisters were looked down upon, regarded as animals or as the most ignorant class in national society. Remembering all this, our brothers and sisters have a great hatred for the traitorous clique.[113]

Similarly, in a speech marking the first anniversary of the revolution in April 1976, Minister of Information Hu Nim harped on the devastation inflicted in the rural areas during the war by guns, napalm and other chemical agents, and bombs. Hu Nim's speech is striking for its detailed and exaggerated statistics: four hundred thousand peasants killed, more than twenty thousand maimed or disabled, and two hundred thousand injured; 80 percent of Cambodia's factories destroyed; and 80 percent of the fields and almost all of the homes close to battlefields ravaged.[114] On the same occasion, Khieu Samphan proclaimed: "Nothing can erase or make us forget . . . [this] dark past."[115]

Such discourse was incorporated into Khmer Rouge song and dance. To help keep the class grudge inflamed, for example, Khmer Rouge dances, performed at meetings, frequently involved harsh, militaristic demeanor and violent imagery. Sometimes the theme of revenge was explicit. Haing Ngor recalled how, at the end of one propaganda dance, costumed cadres — some of whom wore red headbands and red *krama* sashes around their waists — formed a line and began shouting:

> "BLOOD AVENGES BLOOD!" at the top of their lungs. Both times when they said the word "blood" they pounded their chests with clenched fists, and when they shouted "avenges" they brought their arms straight out like a Nazi salute, except with a closed fist instead of an open hand.
> "BLOOD AVENGES BLOOD! BLOOD AVENGES BLOOD! BLOOD AVENGES BLOOD!" the cadres repeated with fierce, determined faces, thumping their fists on their hearts and raising their fists. They shouted other revolutionary slogans and gave the salutes and finally ended with "Long live the Cambodian revolution!"
> It was a dramatic performance and it left us scared. In our language, "blood" has its ordinary meaning, the red liquid in the body, and another meaning of kinship or family. Blood avenges blood. You kill us, we kill you. We "new" people had been on the other side of the Khmer Rouge in the civil war. Soldiers of the Lon Nol regime, with the help of American weapons and planes, had killed many tens of thousands of Khmer Rouge in battle. Symbolically, the Khmer Rouge had just announced that they were going to take revenge.[116]

Besides the overt call for vengeance, this dance embodies movements signifying "burning rage" — loud shouts associated with anger; fierce faces showing that one was *dach chett* (resolute); clenched fists indexing the "knot" of malice; chest pounding (with the clenched fists), evoking the image of a person who is "seized with painful anger."

Blood imagery was also central to this dance. In fact, the color of blood was a prominent theme in Khmer Rouge propaganda, providing a metaphoric call for revenge. The DK national anthem contained numerous references to spilled blood, which provided a reason for people to maintain their "unrelenting hatred." In a speech delivered on September 27, 1977, Pol Pot explained that a "blood call has been incorporated into our national anthem. Each sentence, each word shows the nature of our people's struggle. This blood has been turned into class and national indignation."[117] Similarly, the Khmer Rouge flag was red, and was glorified by "The Red Flag," which was often sung in unison before meetings:

> Glittering red blood blankets the earth —
> Blood given up to liberate the people:
> Blood of workers, peasants, and intellectuals;
> Blood of young men, Buddhist monks, and girls.
> The blood swirls away, and flows upward, gently, into the sky,
> Turning into a red, revolutionary flag.
>
> Red flag! Red flag! Flying now! Flying now!
> O beloved friends, pursue, strike and hit the enemy.
> Red flag! Red flag! Flying now! Flying now!
> Don't leave a single reactionary imperialist (alive)
> Seething with anger, let us wipe out all enemies of Kampuchea.
> Let us strike and take victory! Victory! Victory![118]

Like the national anthem, "The Red Flag," with its analogy between blood sacrifice and the color red, and its encouragement to "seethe with anger" and "strike and hit the enemy," urged cadres to maintain their class grudge until not "a single reactionary imperialist" was left alive.

The invocation of blood imbues such songs with powerful ontological resonance. On the one hand, blood is central to health. In Khmer ethnophysiology, the proper flow of blood leads to a balanced state of well-being. The disruption of this flow signifies social and somatic disequilibrium, often diagnosed as maladies of excess heat or cold. Anger, in turn, is conceptualized as having heating properties and, as Maha Ghosananda notes in the passage cited earlier, may make the blood "burn." More concretely, the loss of blood signifies injury and a threat to one's well-being, possibly even the loss of one's life. Blood is also a powerful, embodied symbol of violence, which often results in bloody injury or death.

Through frequent invocations of spilled blood, then, Khmer Rouge

songs, ideological discourses, and symbols condense a number of powerful themes: existential threat, bodily and social disequilibrium, anger and
rage, sorrow and loss, and violence against the enemy. Moreover, as
Haing Ngor notes, blood is also a kinship idiom signifying similarity and
difference. By focusing on the spilled blood of beloved comrades, Khmer
Rouge ideology implied there was a kinship-like bond between the revolutionaries (Ângkar being the "parent") that opposed them to the enemy
"others" — the oppressor classes. Blood imagery thereby helps to manufacture difference, providing a symbolic manifestation of more explicit
us/them discourses. In the context of the dances and songs, blood
imagery implies that "something bad" has been done to the person, a
sentiment that leads to imbalance and makes one become hot and
"seized with painful anger." The ensuing knot of malice in turn generates
hatred and a desire for vengeance or, as the Khmer Rouge dancers cried
out, for blood to avenge blood. The threat of revenge was clear to Haing
Ngor, leaving him, and many other members of the "oppressor enemy"
who listened to the performance, terrified.

While such ideological messages clearly had a different "take" among
different segments of the population, they were effective in motivating
many cadres, particularly poor and uneducated cadres like Boan, the village chief at Trâpeang Trah, where Vong stole the two potatoes, to seek
revenge against their class enemies. As Vong noted, "At first Boan was
like us. After they had brainwashed him, however, his heart and thoughts
changed. He became angry at the people, particularly the rich and soldiers. Boan was an ignorant person and couldn't write much . . . but he
loved Ângkar and would report on people who were then killed."
Similarly, the relatives of the "anonymous cadre" were likely influenced
by such discourses when they took "revenge with people from Phnom
Penh" because of their anger over the loss of loved ones and the B-52
bombings: "They just waited for people from Phnom Penh: if they had a
chance to kill, they would kill." (His assertion that such revenge killings
were not driven by an "official order [from the top]," however, is problematic given the DK leadership's explicit policy of annihilating "hidden
enemies" and its ideological call for vengeance.) Haing Ngor once joked
to some "new people" in his work group that such Khmer Rouge cadres
were not "communist" (kommuyonis) but "revenge people" (kum
monuss): " 'That's what they are at the lower level,' I said, 'revenge people.' 'All they know is that city people like us used to lord it over them
and this is their chance to get back. That's what they are, communist at
top and kum-monuss at the bottom.' "[119]

In one sense, the poor took revenge upon their class enemies through the reversal of status in DK. If the poor had suffered disproportionately in comparison to and been looked down upon by the rich, the situation was now reversed. "New people" received less food, were treated more harshly, had fewer rights, and were killed more readily than "old people." Khmer Rouge cadres told "new people" that they had enjoyed an easy life in the old society — while the poor were exploited and bombed and while Khmer Rouge soldiers endured great hardships in the jungle — and that it was now their turn to suffer. Sometimes "new people" were even referred to as "war slaves," as Haing Ngor discovered when he heard a nurse ask someone if they had "fed the war slaves yet. . . . It was a chance remark, but it stuck in my ears because it explained the Khmer Rouge better than anything else. . . . The Khmer Rouge had beaten us in the civil war. We were their war slaves. . . . They were taking revenge."[120]

Long work hours, starvation rations, lack of freedom, miserable living conditions, and constant terror soon erased their humanity. As Someth May recalled, "We were hungry, too tired to wash or clean our clothes, and we lost all sense of hygiene. We didn't care what we ate as long as we could put something in our stomachs. We didn't mind where we had a shit, or who saw us. Disease spread through the village — cholera, malaria, dysentery, diarrhoea and skin infections."[121] Such conditions often reduced a person to an animal-like state of being. Like water buffalo, "new people" were sometimes required to pull a plow or cart and might be whipped if they failed to work hard enough.[122] A soldier told one "new person" that it would be better that her sick mother die "than a cow. The cows are good. They help us a lot and do not eat rice. They are much better than you pigs."[123] Since "new people" were less than fully human, there were fewer moral inhibitions in harming them. A "new person" who did something wrong could be "discarded" *(veay chal)* — a euphemism for execution — without many qualms, an attitude captured by the chilling Khmer Rouge threat, "To keep you is no gain; to destroy you is no loss" *(tuk min chomnenh yok chenh min khat)*.

This dehumanization, combined with Khmer Rouge ideology that fomented malice against the oppressor classes and glorified revolutionary violence, were key factors that contributed to the revenge killings that continued to take place long after the first wave of DK executions had ended. Having annihilated most of the Lon Nol government's leadership, the Khmer Rouge began to seek out and kill off other "class enemies," such as rich "capitalists," intellectuals, professionals, and lower-ranking Lon Nol soldiers, police, and government employees. By the end of

March 1976, the Party Center had made the decision to authorize the use of violence to "smash" people "inside and outside" the revolutionary ranks,[124] initiating a second wave of violence, which peaked in 1977 in most areas but continued to ebb and flow until the end of DK. All over Cambodia, orders were passed down the Khmer Rouge civilian and military chain of command instructing local cadres to research the backgrounds of the people under their control and find the "hidden enemies burrowing from within."[125]

Former Lon Nol soldiers remained at the top of the target list. In his 1977 confession, Sreng, the deputy secretary of the Northern Zone, recalled how lists of these suspected enemies were compiled on the grassroots level and then passed to higher administrative levels, often reaching the zone office, where decisions were made about who should be executed:

> The grassroots area [had] all successfully implemented these Party instructions [of successively smashing officers]. Every sector has implemented them at the levels of general officer, field-grade officer, and junior officer, and then also down to the level of enlisted men (those who were active), who the Zone stated were also to be swept out. There was quite a powerful dynamism with regard to this matter. Each sector drew up list after list, which was proposed to the Zone and sorted out one after the other. Actions to search for these officers have continued constantly right up to the present . . . they were discovered not because the Zone Committee knew who they were. Rather, they were discovered by the grassroots' inquiries and investigations among the masses.[126]

Many Banyan villagers living in Region 41 were directly affected by this process of investigation.

Upon arriving at Ampil Krânhanh village in Region 41, for example, the Khmer Rouge questioned Dari's husband and her brothers — most of whom were soldiers — about their previous occupations. Yum, Dari's sister-in-law, explained that a cadre "asked my husband what he had done. He lied and told them he had ridden a cyclo bike and guarded a house. The cadre said, 'If so, why are your hands, legs, and face so nice?' They asked him to prove that he was really from the countryside by plowing a rice field and doing other peasant tasks." Because he had grown up performing such labor in Banyan, Yum's husband was able to do what the cadre asked. In the end, however, the Khmer Rouge discovered that her husband had been a soldier. Yum added, "There were people from Banyan living there who knew my husband's occupation. Whoever hated us told the Khmer Rouge that my husband had been a soldier." (As Yum's remark suggests, many people strategically used such situations to settle old scores.) After learning this, the district security office gave orders for the family of Lon Nol soldiers to be executed.

Neari's family experienced a similar tragedy, illustrating how the Khmer Rouge took revenge upon other types of class enemies. When local officials began researching people's backgrounds, Neari's family could not hide the fact that her father, Tak, had been a teacher during the Lon Nol period because he had taught in the area. This "oppressor" class background made him a potential target to be "smashed." Neari recalled, "The Khmer Rouge slowly killed people off. First they took former government workers, then intellectuals, then people who were lazy. . . . They killed a lot of [new] people, maybe fifty families from our village alone."

Soon after the family's relative and protector, Seuan (head of Kompong Siem district, where Banyan is located, and a member of Sreng's "string"), had been purged by cadres from the Southwest Zone, Tak went to the Ângkounh Dey hospital because his stomach had become bloated from malnutrition. A few days later, Tak and some other patients were told to gather their possessions because they were to be transferred to the regional hospital due to the seriousness of their illnesses. Instead, the patients were led behind the hospital and executed:

> Some of the other patients saw them being taken away. When [the cadres who had led them behind the hospital] returned, they had blood all over their bodies and went to bathe. . . . There were twenty people who were taken at that time, all of them police and teachers who were in the hospital. . . . Everyone knew my father had been a teacher because he had taught at Ângkounh Dey school. . . . Everyone knew. A group [of cadres] had come and asked our village head if there were any former government workers living there and, if so, how many families. They wanted to know who had been a soldier, policeman, teacher, or landlord and who had been [a peasant]. The pure people were the ones who hadn't done any of this work. [The Khmer Rouge] got their information and selected [their victims] in this manner. They knew everything. We couldn't hide our backgrounds. The village head researched our life histories. When we arrived [at Ângkounh Dey], he asked us what we had done during the Lon Nol period and wrote down the information . . . and kept it in a book. So they could say, "This one was a teacher, this one a policeman, this one a soldier, this one a MP," and so forth.

One of the executioners, Hean, was a disgruntled former student of Tak's. Neari continued, "My father was a very strict teacher and would frequently hit his students in order to make them want to learn. Hean was a particularly lazy and disobedient student and was beaten often.

These beatings really hurt, so Hean became angry at and held a grudge against my father. . . . So he killed my father." Afterward, Hean was overheard bragging that, before executing Tak, he told Tak (using superior to inferior prefixes), "When you *(hâ'aeng)* were my *(ânh)* teacher, you beat me and made me hurt. Now, I will repay your 'good' deed *(sângkun)* in turn. I will kill and discard you, so that you can no longer be such a mean teacher."

Two months after her father's death, Neari's mother was completely exhausted from overwork and went to the hospital to see if she could get an injection to increase her energy: "She said [to a cadre], 'Comrade, please give me a good shot so I'll get well. . . . I don't want to die and abandon my nine children.' The cadre replied, 'No problem, we'll give you a shot and you'll get well immediately.' But they didn't give her anything for the entire day. Some cadre from the Southwest Zone inquired, 'Aunt, aren't you the wife of Tak the teacher?' " Neari's mother responded affirmatively. That evening, a cadre named Dr. Khon inquired about her identity and then "filled a syringe with a white liquid and gave it to my mother. As soon as she got the shot, the wind left her body. She was dead within ten minutes. . . . They dumped her body in a ditch, like a dog." Neari has no doubt the Southwest cadre ordered Khon to kill her mother; upon learning that Neari's mother was going to the hospital, Southwest cadres had gone to speak with Khon. She explained, "They had a plan to destroy my entire family, bit by bit. . . . They wanted to completely destroy us, to cut off our seed."

Three of Neari's sisters were killed next. The oldest, Kolap, had a silk scarf that had been used in their parents' wedding ceremony. The subdistrict head, Rom, saw the scarf and "suggested" that Kolap give it to her, but Kolap refused because of the scarf's sentimental value. Neari explained, "When my elder sister didn't give the scarf to her, Rom became very angry with this new person who thought she was better than an old person. Rom held a grudge against my sister and waited for an opportunity to get back at her." After that, Kolap was constantly followed. One day while Kolap was plowing a field, she became angry and swore at one of her oxen. Rom was nearby and claimed that Kolap had sworn at her. That evening, a woman arrived and told Kolap, " 'Elder Rom has called for you.' My sister asked, 'What does she want me for at night?' The woman replied, 'I don't know what she wants. Maybe she's calling you to get something or to plant vegetables. . . . Hurry up.' Kolap told her to wait a moment. She knew that they were going to kill her." Another sister insisted upon coming along because it was dark and she was afraid something bad would happen to Kolap. They took along their nine-month-old baby sister, whom they had cared for since their mother was killed.

After the end of DK, a person who had worked for Rom at the sub-district office told Neari that Kolap and her sister were tied up and taken by Rom and five or six subordinates to a killing field by Tuol Beng village, where district and subdistrict cadres from Kompong Siem killed thousands of people during DK. Rom reportedly said to Kolap (using superior-inferior prefixes), "So, you were trying to act tough with me and wouldn't give me your scarf. This is what you get." Upon hearing this, Kolap, despite having her arms tied, began to kick wildly at her captors, managing to tear some of their clothes. Rom was incensed. Neari continued:

> My elder sister's heart was such that she wanted to fight back and punch her captors so they couldn't touch her. Her hands were tied but she ran forward and kicked at them. But there were too many of them. They seized her and stripped off all her clothes . . . making her stand there naked in front of the group, some of whom were men. . . . [Her captors] were all people with good backgrounds, the children of the poorest of the poor, who hadn't had enough food to eat [before DK]. These people, who were ignorant and had dark skin, were considered to be the good people, the ones who could cut off their hearts and dare to kill. . . . My other sister begged Kolap, "Don't fight with them. Let them kill us since that's what they intend to do. We're certain to die." One of them then grabbed my infant sister and smashed her head against a tree stump. Her head burst open with a pop and she died instantly. They killed my little baby sister like this! Next, they took a chunk of wood and clubbed my other sister on the back of the neck, killing her immediately.

After forcing Kolap to watch the execution of her sisters, Rom and the executioners began beating and kicking Kolap: "Rom told my sister, 'It's going to be a long time before you are dead.' They punched and kicked all over until she was finally finished off. Rom was really angry. . . . My family suffered so much. It's so sad." A few days later, Neari and her younger sister made their dramatic escape from the village. Unfortunately, Neari's four younger brothers were still living in the area. Rom sent for them and had them work at Ângkounh Dey temple, which was being used by the Khmer Rouge as a prison. Their job was to carry out the prisoners' excrement. Just before the end of DK, the boys were executed.

The destruction of Neari's family illustrates how the Khmer Rouge attempted to take disproportionate revenge so as to "completely destroy" (phchanh phchal) their enemies. Because the Khmer Rouge were so powerful, they were able to engage in the most extreme form of *phchanh phchal*—killing off the enemy's line. Neari sadly explained:

> The Khmer Rouge had a grudge against my family because we were petty bourgeoisie and because my father had been a government worker in the previous regime. My father had been a mean teacher as well. They hated him to the point of hating his wife and children. The people hated us. The cadres hated us. Everyone hated us. . . . [The Khmer Rouge] wanted to eliminate us, to cut down our family seed, to reduce it to nothing so that no one would remain. If they allowed someone to remain, they were afraid that person would . . . have a hurt heart and be seized with painful anger that would lead them to seek revenge in turn. . . . So they tried to kill all of us at once.

Many other Cambodian family lines were destroyed during DK. For example, while Dari survived, all eight of her siblings (seven of whom had been in the army) were executed. Every member of four of these siblings' families was killed. In some cases, the Khmer Rouge would simply load families of "new people" into trucks and take them to execution centers like Phnom Bros. The Khmer Rouge adopted a Maoist saying that encouraged such slaughter: "To dig up grass, one must also dig up the roots" *(chik smav trauv chik teang reus)*.[127] Echoing the explanation of many others, a former DK chief of Neari's village told me that this phrase meant that cadres were supposed to "dig up the entire family line. Not just the [nuclear family] of husband, wife, and children, but the entire line of descent, the entire clan, from the grandparents on, to take the entire string at once." He confirmed that he was ordered to research the background of people living in the village and that, at meetings, Rom spoke of a plan to seek out "soldiers, the rich, and government workers and to kill all of them and their families." The village chief explained that this was done so that "none would be left to take revenge on a later day."

Thus, much of the killing that occurred during DK was motivated by a Khmer Rouge ideological model that drew heavily upon preexisting notions of disproportionate revenge. Many of the poor were angry at the rich and powerful "oppressors" who looked down upon them, exploited them, and made them suffer. The Khmer Rouge used this ideology to inflame the feeling of resentment even further, trying to make its followers "burn with rage" and be "seized with painful anger" *(chheu chap)*, feelings that would motivate them to seek revenge and destroy their class enemies. Khieu Samphan's brother explained, "The destruction of the Cambodian people can be understood in terms of the resentment *(chheu*

chap) of the destitute *(neak ât)* who suffered and were looked down
upon. . . . Their resentment became a grudge that was repaid *(sâng)*
when they had power. . . . They repaid [this debt] by killing people in
return."

Although they attempted to "completely destroy" these enemies, the
Khmer Rouge were not completely successful in preventing future retaliation: many revenge killings took place at the end of DK. Thus, if Rom
and Grandmother Yit fled before the Vietnamese invasion, other cadres,
like Phat, a woman who was known for her brutality, were not able to
escape. After hiding in the jungle for a few days, Phat tried to sneak into
a village to steal food one night and was shot and wounded. A crowd
gathered and beat her to death. A Banyan villager whose husband had
been killed by Phat recalled, "More and more people kept coming, including grandfathers and grandchildren. They really hated her because she
had killed so many people. I hit her two times, too. I hated her because
she had killed my husband. We wanted revenge." Many Cambodians
witnessed post-DK revenge killings of former Khmer Rouge cadres.

These incidents sometimes involved decapitation, a symbolic act
indexing the avenger's desire to take "a head for an eye." Although the
head has a wide range of signification for Cambodians, it is related to
vengeance in a number of ways. On the one hand, the head is an icon of
status. In colloquial discourse, Cambodians often speak of the head as an
almost sacred part of the body, a center of intelligence that must be
respected. To touch or strike someone's head is considered a serious
insult in many contexts. The lay religious specialist at Banyan explained:
"The head is the most esteemed part of the body because they say that
the seat of intentionality and consciousness is located in the head. If
someone touches one's head . . . it is offensive, . . . it makes one hurt and
become hot." Here Doeung links the head to "hurt" and "heat," two key
feelings associated with vengeance. Such views are reinforced by the
notion that the body is a mirror of the cosmos, with the head — the highest point of the body — representing the higher planes of existence.[128]
Similarly, in Buddhism, the head may signify enlightenment and dharma
(dhamma). On the other hand, the head is crucial to dyadic exchange,
since it contains the eyes, ears, nose, mouth, and facial expressions that
are so important to social interaction. Moreover, these interactions are
both regulated by and involve the negotiation of "face," itself an embodied symbol of social status.

The head is thus symbolically linked to issues of status and reciprocity that are at the core of disproportionate revenge.[129] As a locus of social exchange, the head may symbolize the reciprocal ties binding adversaries through ill will. Since the head is a signifier of status, decapitation signifies both one's own diminished status and the destruction of the status of one's enemy. To strike off the head of an adversary is to "completely defeat" them by obliterating their honor, their capacity to engage in social interactions, their ability to seek revenge in turn, and their life itself. It sends a powerful message of intimidation to potential enemies, warning them not to do "something bad" to the perpetrator lest it lead to a horrific end. In yet another sense, decapitation is a form of punishment for someone who has done something bad, as illustrated by the beings in Buddhist hells who repeatedly have their heads cut off. Decapitation also manufactures difference, transforming a human being into a headless corpse — an enemy whose body has been inscribed with a message stating that the person is no longer fully human and is completely different from the pure "us."

In a variety of ways, then, decapitation serves as an ontologically resonant marker of revenge, drawing on the powerful symbolism of the head. This association between revenge and decapitation helped to motivate beheadings during the civil war (by both Lon Nol and Khmer Rouge forces), during DK (by Khmer Rouge), and after DK (in revenge attacks on former cadres); more recently, it also led the chairman of the Cambodian Military Court to say, referring to Ta Mok and Duch: "We cannot cut off their heads in revenge following our anger."

· · ·

Given the enormous loss and suffering they experienced during DK, it is not surprising that many Cambodians continue to hold a grudge against the Khmer Rouge, who did "something [extremely] bad" to them. Chlat and Neari, for example, continue to bear strong feelings of malice toward the perpetrators who killed their family members:

> [Chlat] I continue to think of revenge. But this thought of revenge, it doesn't know how to stop. And we should not have this thought or the matter will grow and keep going on and on for a long time. We should be a person who thinks and acts in accordance with dharma. [A person who seeks revenge] only creates misery for our society. It is a germ in society. But I continue to think of revenge. . . . The people who killed my brother, who put down his name to get into the truck, are all alive, living in my village. To this day, I still really want revenge. I keep observing them. But I don't know what to do. . . . The government forbids it.

[Neari] When I see Hean [driving his moto along the road], I get angry. But I don't know what to do about it. I'm a woman. I think to myself, "This despicable person killed my father but didn't die himself." When I see him, I become angry in my heart. In one part of my heart I want revenge. . . . When I recall [what he did], I get hot and angry. I want to kill him. I want to ask him, "What did my father do to you to make you kill him? You were beaten because you were lazy." When I think about him, I get so angry. I have an angry heart. But I have another thought out of laziness. I think to myself, "Don't take revenge upon that despicable one. Let him suffer from his karma. 'Do good, receive good. Do bad, receive bad'" . . . My heart wants to harm and kill him. But another part of me thinks that this is not necessary. I expect that another person who hates him *(vea)*, who is tied in malice with him, will make him croak. They will do this to console themselves [about what Hean did to their family]. So if I don't do it, another person will.

These narratives reveal the complex moral and emotional struggles survivors endure. We see the clash of competing cultural models, as they weigh their desire for revenge against Buddhist proscriptions and legal repercussions. Chlat even describes vengeance as a disease that leads to further social suffering and misery. In the end, both Neari and Chlat remain tied in malice to the perpetrators who harmed their loved ones. It is not easy for such individuals, when standing before the killers of their family, friends, and relatives, to simply allow this painful anger to "melt away" or to "forgive and forget" their hated enemy.

How might justice be found for victims like Neari and Chlat and the members of their families? How might future cycles of revenge be prevented? These are just some of the many complex questions that Cambodians face since the demise of the Khmer Rouge movement. Buddhism provides an important method of dealing with anger and resentment. Ultimately, as Neari notes, the law of karma states that sinners will suffer the consequences of their action. Thus Neari expects that Hean will one day be punished — perhaps even murdered — for his bad deeds. She told me that she believes Pol Pot and other Khmer Rouge leaders will go to hell or be reincarnated as a *bret* or some other hideous, despicable, and evil spirit. Buddhism also teaches that feelings of anger arise from ignorance and that one should choose "to block/control one's heart" or to "disperse one's anger." On an institutional level, legal and educational practices could be made more effective. If corruption within the Cambodian judicial system were reduced, for example, some people might not feel as compelled to exact revenge when someone has done "something bad" to them. Alternatively, teachers could put greater emphasis on understanding revenge and the social misery to which it leads. Finally, the U.N.-sponsored trial of the Khmer Rouge leaders may make it easier for some Cambodians to let their anger toward the Khmer Rouge "melt away" and to cope with their suffering and loss. Perhaps the trial will even serve as a symbolic severing of the collective Khmer Rouge "head." The hard work being done by Youk Chhang and others at the Documentation Center of Cambodia, a local nongovernmental organization dedicated to gathering legal evidence and creating a historical archive about DK, will be crucial to the success of this trial. [130]

In the end, reconciliation will ultimately involve more than a trial: it will require a change of attitude. Just as Buddhism teaches that each person must discover the path to enlightenment, so too must each Cambodian decide what to do if a "knot" of malice still ties him or her in anger against the Khmer Rouge. As Maha Ghosananda has stated, the path to peace is a "step-by-step" process of increasing understanding, compassion, and forgiving. To change one's attitude one must become more mindful — in the Buddhist sense of the word. Part of becoming more mindful, in turn, is to broaden one's understanding of the conscious and unconscious understandings that guide one's actions, including local notions of anger, begrudgement, and revenge that may motivate violence.

CHAPTER TWO

Power, Patronage, and Suspicion

In 1976, for example, speaking only of internal Party
matters, while we are engaged in a socialist revolution, there
is a sickness inside the Party . . . We cannot locate it precisely.
The illness must emerge to be examined. Because the heat
of the people's revolution and the heat of the democratic
revolution were insufficient at the level of people's struggle
and at the level of class struggle among all layers of the
national democratic revolution, we search for the microbes
within the Party without success. . . . Contradictions exist.
If we scratch the ground to bury them, they will rot us from
within. They will rot society, rot the Party, rot the army. . . .
We must expose them.

Party Center Report, 1976[1]

In December 1976, Pol Pot is thought to have made the above remarks at
a meeting of the Party Center. While the Khmer Rouge had periodically
purged its ranks in the past, Pol Pot's obsession with finding the "sickness" that was "rotting society" marked a rapid escalation of this
process. The Party Center's paranoia quickly reached places like Region
41 of the Central Zone, where suspect cadres and soldiers were purged.
Some, like Reap, the head of Phnom Bros, ended up at Tuol Sleng, where
they were forced to confess their supposed treason, thereby confirming
the Party Center's suspicions and further catalyzing the search for other
"microbes." As this paranoia grew, almost everyone became suspect and
was subject to sudden arrest. In the next two chapters, I argue that the
Khmer Rouge purges were not simply the result of a universal type of
"power struggle" or a straightforward replica of the purges that took

place in other communist regimes. While the Moscow Show Trials and the Maoist and Vietnamese "reeducation" campaigns certainly influenced Pol Pot and his associates, these models were localized and enacted in culturally distinct ways that had ontological resonances, and thus motivational force, for the actors.[2]

Specifically, I argue that the Khmer Rouge purges were linked to the Party Center's attempt to establish itself as a potent center, a desire heightened by their high-modernist ambitions. This encounter with modernity, however, was a local one, in which the Khmer Rouge constructed a government infused with patronage ties. The Party Center ultimately came to view these networks as a threat to its authority and set out to eliminate numerous "strings of traitors." As their suspicions of betrayal increased, so too did the fervor of the purges with which the Party Center tried to eradicate the "microbes" that were supposedly contaminating the new revolutionary society. If the purges that took place under other communist regimes served as a general model for the Party Center, then, the Khmer Rouge purges were nevertheless patterned in terms of local knowledge about power, patronage, and suspicion. This chapter explores Cambodian understandings of power, patronage, and suspicion; the next illustrates how these understandings shaped and motivated the DK purges in a distinctive manner.

"POWER" AND THE POTENT CENTER

Power is the intangible, mysterious, and divine energy
which animates the universe. It is manifested in every
aspect of the natural world, in stones, trees, clouds, and
fire, but is expressed quintessentially in the central
mystery of life, the process of generation and
regeneration.

Benedict Anderson, *Language and Power*

Many Cambodians, like other Southeast Asian peoples, view the cosmos as permeated by an animating energy or divine radiance that is unequally distributed and continuously in flux. Since everything has a differential capacity to contain this divine energy, it becomes concentrated to a greater or lesser extent in objects, places, and persons. Such understandings have been shaped by a syncretic amalgam of animistic, Hindu, and Buddhist traditions. Before Indian traders frequented Southeast Asian coastal towns, bringing new goods and Hindu-Buddhist ideas, people living in the area we now call Cambodia are thought to have viewed their world as being animated by immanent energies. Powerful spirits and beings, many of which in one form or another are still worshipped in Cambodian villages today, were thought to inhabit the forests, mountains, waters, jungles, and fields.[3] Some, like the territorial spirits *(neak ta)*, resided in local mounds, trees, wooden images, or stone icons. Others, like serpent gods and earth spirits, vitalized the environment through their connection to the soil and rain. Human beings (along with rice and select objects, plants, and animals) were believed to be animated by nineteen *broleung,* which gave them their "vital essence." Like the world around them, human beings were differentially endowed with *mana*-like energies, leading to the emergence of powerful "men of prowess," or charismatic leaders, who distinguished themselves through outstanding deeds and accomplishments.[4]

Such animistic conceptions of power were subsequently inflected by Hindu notions of divine energy. O. W. Wolters, for example, has argued that early Khmer chiefs were attracted to Hindu devotionalism because it fit nicely with local understandings of prowess.[5] Hindu *bhakti* priests taught that, through ascetic practices and devotion to Siva, one could attain access to Siva's *sakti,* or divine power. By claiming a special relationship to such Hindu gods, Khmer kings enhanced the idiom of prowess and established a cosmic basis for their rule. (In fact, two contemporary Khmer terms that reference power, *sâkti* and *sâktesetthi,* are etymologically derived from the Sanskrit term *sakti.*) This linkage between the king and cosmic energies helped lay a foundation for the localization of other Hindu notions related to power, including the notion of micro-macrocosmic parallelism.[6]

Theravada Buddhism, which gained ascendancy in Cambodia during the thirteenth century, operated under an analogous set of assumptions, as the universe was viewed as being infused with the vitalizing force of *dhamma.* The term *dhamma* has an array of meanings, ranging from ontological reality to moral law. It is etymologically related, through the Sanskrit term *dharma,* to the root *dhr,* which means "to support," as in "that which forms a foundation and upholds."[7] Similarly, *thomm,* the Khmer term for *dhamma,* is defined as "ultimate reality" or "dhamma, the nature of being including merit, sin, virtue, evil; cause; state of being, nature, wisdom, kindness; progress; mental perception."[8] Thus *dhamma* commonly refers to the ultimate reality or cosmic foundation of existence that the Buddha perceived and preached about to his followers. On another level, *dhamma* connotes an animating energy that generates vitality and power; the splendor of life on earth depends on the extent to which everyday action accords with cosmic *dhamma*.

The Buddha himself acts as a micro/macrocosmic conduit for the spread of *dhamma*, bringing prosperity and mindfulness to the human realm. After the Buddha was born, all the world benefited from the power of his *dhamma*: "At the moment of incarnation the heavens and the earth showed signs, the dumb spoke, the lame walked, all men began to speak kindly, musical instruments played of themselves, the earth was covered with lotus flowers, lotuses descended from the sky, and every tree put forth its flowers."[9] As such descriptions of his life suggest, the Buddha is viewed as an extraordinarily powerful being because of his connection to *dhamma*. The Buddha's perfection of the dhammic virtues endows him with power, authority, and charisma *(bareamey)*.[10] Through his mastery of mind, the Buddha obtains potency and magical powers *(etthi)*, often referenced by a mandala symbol — the miraculous "sixfold rays" of light the Buddha's body emits.[11] This image portrays the Buddha as a potent center, who, as a cosmic axis, spreads the power of *dhamma* outward in all directions. Even after his death, the Buddha's radiant energy endures, invested in his relics, in amulets and statuary that bear his likeness, and in his sermons about *dhamma*.

This syncretic blend of animist, Hindu, and Buddhist conceptions has contributed to local Cambodian understandings of power as an animating energy that shifts and flows through time and space. Since beings differ in their ability to contain and accumulate this power, certain individuals and objects inevitably become centers in which power is disproportionately concentrated. Cambodians often say that such beings have *etthipol*, a term that is etymologically derived from the Pali root *etthi*, which means "potency" and "psychic power."[12] Like other Khmer terms for "power," *etthipol*, which I hereafter translate as "potent power," is used in a variety of ways in colloquial conversation. Many of the usages connote individual potency or a forceful inner capacity that enables one to be effective, to accomplish (often extraordinary and sometimes supernatural) deeds, and to influence others. One of my research assistants likened *etthipol* to the concentrated quality of a drug that effectively cures a patient's illness. Similarly, powerful individuals who have "potent saliva" *(teu moat brei)* are sometimes described as having *etthipol*, in the sense that their words or orders are listened to and obeyed. Through ascetic practice, meditation, and understanding, religious figures — from the Buddha to a forest monk — gain *etthipol* that enables them to accomplish magical feats.

Etthipol may be differentiated from the power that comes from having *amnach*. This term is related to the verb *ach,* meaning "to dare, to be able (to do something) . . . to not be afraid, to not shrink back, to not hesitate, to not be obstructed."[13] *Amnach* implies "raw power," or the ability to act without hesitation or constraint because of one's political "authority," connections, or wealth. Cambodians often use the term to describe the actions of ruthless officials who utilize their political authority to carry out their desires, sometimes abusing the populace in the process. One Cambodian official differentiated this "raw power/authority" from "potent power" by stressing its external locus: "*Amnach* comes from the law, while *etthipol* comes from the person himself." The two terms are highly interrelated, however, since a person who is able to rise to a position of authority or wealth is often said to have potent power. Thus Pol Pot may be characterized as having both potent power and despotic authority. Some Cambodians use *amnach* as an all-purpose term to connote power or political authority. Other words that are associated with power include merit *(bon)*, skill/effectiveness *(poukae)*, and strength/influence *(kâmlang, khlang)*.

The meaning of many of these terms was all too clearly illustrated by the brutal murder of a Cambodian journalist in Kompong Cham during my fieldwork. Just after one o'clock in the morning on December 8, 1994, Chan Dara, a reporter for the *Island of Peace* newspaper, was shot dead while riding his moped along a dark Kompong Cham city street. The first person who told me about the incident said that Chan Dara was inadvertently struck by gunfire intended for a fierce army colonel, Sat Suen, who possessed a magical string *(khsae kânta)* and a Buddha amulet that deflected bullets, and who had been drinking with Chan Dara that night. He added that an enemy of Suen's had once fired a bazooka at him, but the blast had only left a small rip in Suen's shirt because of his magical items. Since Suen had a long history of such legendary exploits (including the ability to walk unharmed through minefields), he was popularly referred to as "Suen of the Earth" *(Seuan Phan Dey)*. By linking Suen to the earth, which is associated with mighty beings ranging from Siva to naga serpents and territorial spirits, Suen's nickname signified great strength and power.

As it turned out, Chan Dara was shot twice in the back at close range after he and Suen had reportedly consumed sixteen bottles of beer at local drinking establishments. The two were seen leaving the last restaurant-bar together. Suen quickly became a suspect when his alibi and explanation of the events did not corroborate the facts established by the police investigation, and the bullet serial numbers matched those belonging to his military unit. Four days after Chan Dara's murder, Suen was arrested and taken to Phnom Penh to await trial because the police feared the actions of Suen's powerful friends if he remained in Kompong Cham.

Many newspapers speculated that Chan Dara's murder was related to the perception that he was behind a series of anonymous articles that had appeared in the *Island of Peace* and another newspaper, the *Courier Pigeon,* and were critical of corruption in the Kompong Cham provincial government. In particular, the articles claimed that Governor Hun Neng (Hun Sen's older brother), Forestry Chief Pal Ren, and Police Commander Man Saran were illegally transporting timber and rubber out of the country. One article included the following allegations:

> Mr. Hun Neng is seeking the person who gave information about him, Pal Ren (head of forestry), and Man Saran (head of the military police) to a newspaper. Hun Neng believes that the person who gave out the information is someone who works and does business with him. . . . Pal Ren is a person who puts Hun Neng behind his back *(khnâng).* He uses the name "Hun Neng" to facilitate his [illegal] business. . . . [T]he people in Kompong Cham really hate Hun Neng because they work legally while Hun Neng allows people who work illegally and who are corrupt and savage to go about their business. (*Courier Pigeon,* Dec. 7–8, 1994)

As noted in this passage, on the day of Chan Dara's murder, the *Courier Pigeon* alleged that Governor Hun Neng was looking for the source of the articles. Chan Dara had already told his editor at the *Island of Peace* that he was resigning.

As is common in Cambodia, Suen's trial lasted only one day. After hearing the evidence, the judge retreated to his chambers for fifteen minutes. He returned and delivered a fifty-minute speech explaining his reasons for deciding that Suen was innocent. Clearly, the verdict had been determined in advance.[14] Rumors swept through Kompong Cham that Suen had bribed the judge with thousands of dollars in gold. Because of Suen's fearsome reputation and high-placed connections, the judge also likely feared that he would be killed if he delivered a guilty verdict. The Cambodian minister of the interior at that time, You Hockry, publicly stated that "there is no doubt at all that [Suen] is the one who committed (the murder). . . . The Kompong Cham court was decided by some kind of fear . . . there was something, but I would prefer not to talk about it."[15] The national police chief confirmed that the judge had been bribed. Suen celebrated that night by throwing a big party. Chan Dara's widow, the plaintiff in the case, went into hiding because she feared that Suen might seek revenge against her. Several months later, Suen was implicated in the vigilante slaying of a teenage boy who was trespassing on private property.[16] Fearful local officials never arrested Suen for this incident or two other murders he allegedly committed, though in 1998 Suen was finally "relieved of his military duties," and the police confiscated his collection of two hundred guns.[17]

In the weeks after Chan Dara's murder, Cambodian newspapers published numerous pieces about the case, including an article in the *Island of Peace* that discussed Suen's legendary life:

> Despicable little Suen of the Earth was born in Prey Veng province in the village of Sambuor, a place notorious for its savage people and thieves. From birth, he was called despicable little Lieung. During the genocidal Pol Pot regime, despicable little Lieung worked as a spy in Sambour village. (As you already know, throughout the reign of the despicable Pol Pot, such spies had the right to kill people as they pleased.) From 1979 to 1980, when Mr. Teng was the subdistrict head, despicable little Suen was selected to continue working as a policeman because he was a person who dared *(hean)*. In 1981, the subdistrict head, Mr. Teng, sent despicable little Suen to serve in the army. Despicable little Suen separated from his superior and fled to Kompong Cham province. He took shelter with a sorcerer named Sarom, who knew magical incantations. In addition to wearing a magical string, Suen had magical tattoos placed all over his shoulders and chest. Despicable little Lieung changed his name to Sat Suen and started working as a provincial soldier.
>
> Because he was fearless and daring, they had Suen walk at the head of his squad when they went into the jungle to fight enemies. One time when he was walking ahead a bit, the soldiers behind him stepped on mines. The others said, "Sat Suen is really powerful *(poukae)*. He steps on mines but they don't explode." This continued, so the members of his squad gave him the name "Suen of the Earth." Later on, the provincial authorities had despicable little Suen come work for them, and he eventually was promoted to the rank of lieutenant.
>
> Because he was very well taken care of by the provincial authorities, despicable little Suen turned into the killer of countless numbers of people and worked on "complicated" matters. To help in these tasks, he was equipped with soldiers, machine guns, and light artillery, which also enabled him to earn a lot of money by illegally transporting lumber to the Vietnamese border for businessmen.
>
> Despicable little Suen's activities became too complicated, so the provincial authorities kicked him out of the provincial army. But just a few months later, despicable little Suen of the Earth purchased the rank of colonel, changing his name to Chan Chaeng. But even if he had changed his name to that of a dog or a cat, they would never have called him anything but despicable little Suen of the Earth.
>
> Some of our journalists who went to the main ferry crossing to Vietnam were told the following story. Several days before [Suen] married his sec-

ond wife, [he] became extremely drunk after eating and drinking a great deal. At that time, he announced to everyone that he had already killed fifty-six people and was just five murders short of reaching the [magical] number specified by his sorcerer. Oh my, these were the words that came out of his mouth. We are in awe *(kaot)* of the provincial authorities in Kompong Cham province who allowed despicable little Suen of the Earth to kill people according to his heart's desire. Everyone was scared *(khlach)* of despicable little Suen of the Earth and didn't dare to arrest him. . . .

At the ferry crossing, the police were afraid *(khlach)* of despicable little Suen of the Earth, to the point that their butts shook [when they saw him]. One time a policeman named Li Chhor was seized and beaten by despicable little Suen of the Earth until he was lying on the ground. [Suen] then started shooting around Li Chhor's body so that he couldn't get up, telling him, "If you dare to get up I will shoot and kill you." He then ordered the policeman to get on his knees and offer obsequious salutations to [Suen] in front of the many people who were watching. Who could see this and not be afraid of despicable little Suen of the Earth to the point that their butts shook? This is what happened to a policeman who had dared to stop one of [Suen's] trucks that was illegally transporting rubber. Any other policeman at a control post who dared to stop one of [Suen's] trucks that was illegally transporting timber or rubber would likewise be completely broken without fail. *(Island of Peace,* Jan. 4, 1995)

This newspaper article recounts events serving as signs that Suen is a man of great power. First, Suen is reported to have gained knowledge and power from his mentor, Sarom the sorcerer. In addition to teaching Suen magical incantations, Sarom provided Suen with magical strings and tattoos that supposedly protected him from bullets and other dangers. As noted earlier, people in Kompong Cham also believed Suen carried a Buddha amulet that was powerful enough to deflect a bazooka blast. There were even rumors that Suen possessed a "desiccated human fetus" *(kaun krâk)* — a grisly amulet that supposedly consists of a fetus that a husband cuts out of his wife's stomach when she is several months pregnant and then dries by the heat of a fire.[18] After being ritually prepared, the desiccated fetus is placed in a small container and worn on the chest or waist. In times of danger, the fetus is said to whisper warnings and advice to the bearer.[19]

Second, Suen is said to be powerful in the sense of being *poukae,* a word that suggests the force and efficacy gained from skill, knowledge, or the possession of potent objects.[20] While a person like Tum, the hero of the famous Cambodian tale *Tum Teav,* is described as verbally skilled *(poukae samdey),* Suen is *poukae* with regard to matters of violence. One person told me that Suen "is *poukae* because bullets can't hit him. . . . When such a person possesses objects like a magical string or a desiccated fetus amulet he becomes very *poukae.*" Likewise, Sarom told an *Island of Peace* reporter that Suen's "tattoos are really *poukae.*" Such objects supposedly helped Suen walk through minefields untouched, for which he was given his nickname, "Suen of the Earth."

Finally, people often referenced Suen's power by describing him as *khlang,* a word that can be translated as "extremely strong," "mighty," or "forceful" in the sense of having *kâmlang,* or "force, power, strength, energy, vigor, authority, [or] influence."[21] The word *khlang* refers to a person who is physically strong or brave, to the concentrated intensity of a strong drink or hard work, or to a person who has power, connections, or influence that causes others to fear and obey him. I translate *khlang* as "hard power" because the term implies a coarse (and often ruthless) toughness and stands in contrast to the qualities of an ideally "soft" *(tuan)* female. In fact, most of the Khmer terms for power that I have mentioned are less often used to characterize women, whose feminine potency is more likely to be evaluated in terms of a gender ideology that stresses virtuous comportment, sexuality, and behavior.[22]

Suen is *khlang* in several respects. As demonstrated by his life as a soldier and his beating of Li Chhor, Suen is regarded as having great strength and force. His bravery is demonstrated by his supposed fearlessness in battle, his illegal transport of timber and rubber, his murders, and his consumption of human gallbladder, which is said to increase an individual's daring. Even the police are scared of Suen. He is a person who cannot be defeated, because of his strength and bravery, the high-placed connections who protect him, and his leadership of a brutal troop of soldiers.

All of these factors show that Suen of the Earth is popularly perceived as a center in whom great power is concentrated. The forms of power with which he is associated have connotations of amorality — beings choose to use their "raw power/authority," "hard power," "potent power," and "skilled efficacy" in good or bad ways. There is, however, a moral source of potency that comes from the religious merit *(bon)* that a person has accumulated in past lives and that rises or declines depending on how one acts in the present life.[23] This association of merit, rank, and authority is evident in Cambodian words like "merit rank" *(bon sâk)* and "merit authority" *(bon amnach).* In Theravada Buddhism, the law of karma *(kâmm)* holds that one's station in the present is determined by one's virtuous or sinful actions in the past. Because everyone's store of merit varies, people differ in their relative status, degree of suffering, and efficacy of action. Thus the Buddha and the gods have more merit than humans, while humans are more virtuous than beings who reside in the

Buddhist hells. Likewise, within the human realm, each person has more or less potency than others. Because of their great virtue *(kun)*, certain charismatic individuals emerge as powerful centers who are extremely effective in their actions. Unlike Suen, though, such "people having merit" *(neak mean bon)* tend to use their potency in moral ways and provide an ethical counterbalance to morally neutral forms of power. In fact, from the Theravada Buddhist perspective, the "wheel of power" *(anacakka)* is viewed as dangerous and in need of constant moral guidance from the "wheel of righteousness" *(dhammacakka)*; only when these "Two Wheels of Dhamma" are in sync will society flourish.[24]

Since merit and power are amorphous qualities, they are difficult to detect and must be discerned from signs.[25] The various descriptions of Suen's power, for example, focus on his amazing feats of prowess (for example, walking through minefields unharmed, defeating foes, acting in a virile manner) and possession of potent objects (for example, Buddha amulets, magical strings, tattoos, a desiccated human fetus). Similarly, Cambodian villagers might infer a person's store of merit from his or her wealth, efficacy, virtuous accomplishments, ethical conduct, and respectful treatment.[26] A Cambodian king's power, in turn, was indexed by his fecundity (harems, offspring, prosperity), ceremonies, success in war and absorption of potential adversaries, cosmic temples, and possession of powerful regalia, such as the royal sword, crown, umbrella, betel boxes, and silver trays. Cambodians frequently search for signs of such potent centers both to avoid offending these potentially dangerous beings and because they may hope to increase their own power and status through association with them.

PATRONAGE

The patron-client relationship — an exchange between roles — may be defined as a special case of dyadic (two-person) ties involving a largely instrumental friendship in which an individual of higher socioeconomic status (patron) uses his own influence and resources to provide protection or benefits, or both, for a person of lower status (client) who, for his part, reciprocates by offering general support and assistance, including personal services, to the patron.

> James Scott, "Patron-Client Politics and Political Change in Southeast Asia"

Since power is a largely amoral force that concentrates differentially in various objects and beings who exercise it for good or evil purposes, Cambodians tend to view the world as a dangerous place. Ordinary people are threatened by potent individuals like Suen of the Earth who choose to use their power in brutal ways. Even local officials and policemen, who have "raw power/authority," are typically feared and either avoided or dealt with in a cautious and respectful manner. In addition, people may fear powerful spiritual beings. In Banyan, for example, the villagers were concerned about incurring the wrath of powerful territorial spirits *(neak ta)*, nagas, ghosts *(khmaoch, areak)*, and ancestral spirits *(meba)*, many of whom may stalk, possess, or inflict illness upon a person, sometimes resulting in death. Similarly, Banyan villagers frequently worried that an unknown adversary would enlist the services of a sorcerer *(krou tmuap)* to afflict them with magic. Because of the dangers posed by such powerful forces, most Cambodians feel a need for some sort of protection.[27] One way to protect oneself is to increase one's potency, through education, moral or spiritual discipline, asceticism, training, or the acquisition of items such as amulets, magical strings, and tattoos. Thus Suen supposedly spent a long period of time receiving training from his mentor, Sarom, and obtained a number of powerful objects. However, this is difficult to do, since there is only a limited amount of power distributed throughout the universe and people vary in their capacity to contain it. Cambodians therefore more often attempt to gain the protection of powerful beings by entering into relationships of personal dependency with them.

If possible, people establish such protective relationships in a number of domains, ranging from the supernatural to the political. As I noted, Cambodians worship territorial/local spirits, or *neak ta,* who are thought to reside in trees, mounds, or iconic objects. Some of these spirits, particularly those that live in "wild" contexts like the jungle and woods, are viewed as extremely dangerous and are to be avoided at all costs. Others, however, are more "civilized," in the sense that they live within or on the outskirts of an inhabited area.[28] Like a powerful individual, the more "civilized" *neak ta* can provide protection to those who pay homage to them. The ritual lay specialist at Banyan, Doeng, described the relationship between the villagers and their local *neak ta*:

> People pay homage *(korop)* to neak ta so that the neak ta will take care *(thae roksa)* of their well-being. People know that the neak ta have supernatural potency *(etthirritthi)*, so they entreat the neak ta, saying "Please give me health and security. Help me earn a livelihood and gain property. Please

don't allow me to fear anything. Help protect me." The people strongly believe this. . . . But the neak ta can harm people as well. If we forget them or don't pay homage or make offerings to them, the neak ta will come and afflict us. . . . So the people are also really scared *(khlach)* about what the neak ta might do to them.

Doeng's comments illustrate some crucial dimensions of the idealized relationship of dependency Cambodians sometimes attempt to establish with these territorial spirits. The villagers pay homage and make ceremonial offerings of food and incense to the *neak ta,* who, in return, use their potent power to protect and care for their devotees. Nevertheless, everyone must act respectfully toward and avoid offending these powerful benefactors, who are known to be whimsical and easily angered if offended. When villagers suspect that a *neak ta* is responsible for making a person or domesticated animal gravely ill, they go to the spirit's abode and make a special offering to it.

Buddhism provides another source of protection for Cambodians. On a strictly doctrinal level, the Buddha is understood as an extremely virtuous individual who discovered the path to enlightenment and, because of his kindness and compassion, shared his insights with his fellow human beings. From this perspective, Buddhism offers salvation from suffering and asks for nothing in return. In practice, however, many Cambodians view the Buddha and the members of the religious order he founded as extremely potent beings who, because of their asceticism and connection to *dhamma,* can provide protection from the dangers of the world. Not surprisingly, the relationship between the lay populace and Buddhism is one of personal dependency. People pay homage to the Buddha and monks through bodily prostration, virtuous conduct, respectful greetings, honorific speech registers, offerings, and chants.[29] In return, worshippers gain merit, understanding, and the protective force of *dhamma,* which is a prominent theme in Buddhist symbolism and illustrated by the ability of monks to make magical strings and to use holy water and magical incantations to heal those who are ill, afflicted by black magic, or possessed by spirits.

In the world of everyday life and politics, many Cambodians seek to establish an analogous relationship of personal dependency with more powerful individuals, though their opportunities to do so vary. Such patronage relations constitute a key structural dynamic of Cambodian sociopolitical life. Patrons and clients are bound by a negotiated exchange that, while instrumental in significant ways, may also involve moral authority, emotional bonds, and kinship ties.[30] Because of their relative power and resource base, patrons are ideally positioned to protect their clients, and possibly to provide them with important resources (for example, knowledge, skill, property, lucrative positions, wealth) that may enable them to rise in status. In return, clients are expected to show deference, make offerings, and provide general support, loyalty, and service to their patron. Through such ties, then, clients gain crucial allies and life opportunities, while patrons increase their base of support and receive symbolic affirmation of their high status.

While patronage assumes a wide variety of forms, the following example illustrates of some of its key features. During the late 1980s, a man named "Nuon" became the chief of police at a strategically located highway town, which I will call Caek, in Kompong Cham. One of my close informants, who is from Caek, described what happened afterward:

> Nuon is from a nearby village, Samot. When he first started working in Caek, Nuon began replacing many of the people who worked in lucrative positions — like the control post, accounting, rice distribution, and traffic control — with his relatives and close friends, most of whom came from Samot. (The policemen who were removed from these positions became angry and frequently quit working at the police station soon thereafter.) Nuon's deputy was from Samot. Likewise, the traffic division, which was headed by Nuon's younger brother, Kim, consisted entirely of their relatives. This was a very lucrative post because traffic police have the opportunity to skim money when they fine cars and motos or mediate traffic disputes (if two people get in an accident, one may give the policeman some money in order to "win" the dispute). When Kim first began working at the police station, Nuon placed him in the control post (another lucrative position, where officers collect money from taxis and take payoffs from people who are illegally transporting rubber or lumber — people working the control post often get even more money than traffic police). Perhaps three months later, Nan increased Kim's rank and appointed him as the head of the traffic division. Other policemen who had been working at the police station since 1979 had never been promoted. Kim came and, after working for only three months, rose to this high rank!

This example illustrates some prototypical aspects of patronage, as a higher-status patron (Nuon) uses his position to place his (lower-status) relatives and friends in lucrative positions (traffic control, the control post, accounting), where they can gain prestige and wealth. Moreover, Nuon may use his influence to protect or assist his clients with other matters (getting a travel permit, avoiding military conscription, winning a dispute, or even engaging in illicit commerce). Nuon's clients, in turn, are expected to be loyal, respectful, and supportive. If he asks them to do a special task, they must do it or risk severing the relationship. Moreover,

Nuon's brother, deputy, and other subordinates will honor and present him with money or food in a manner that often parallels the way villagers pay homage and make offerings to *neak ta*.

Such patronage circles exist at several interconnected levels that form a sort of "pyramid."[31] A patron like Nuon may be the client of an even more powerful person or persons; his clients, in turn, may serve as patrons to their own client circles. Thus Nuon sometimes went to the provincial capital to make offerings of food and other items to his superior, the head of the provincial police office. My informant explained:

> When you make such offerings to your patron *(me)*, it keeps your boss happy. In addition, if your patron has a problem, you should help and support the patron. When the boss falls in rank or the boss's faction falls from power, the people who are below the boss may very well fall in rank, too. In return for such offerings and support, the big person will find places where his subordinates can flourish. These clients will quickly rise in rank and work "big" in a place where they can get a lot of money. When they become "big," these clients will develop their own strings of clients on the next level down. So the governor selects the district chief; the district chief in turn will place his friends and relatives in positions of power. A given individual may have more than one patronage network or faction. If the district chief gets his relatives and friends appointed as the head of police or to other important offices, he will have many of these patronage strings *(khsae)*, just as the provincial governor has.

Cambodian sociopolitical life is replete with such patronage networks, though their importance has usually been greater in more formal urban and institutional contexts than in everyday village life.

Cambodians often describe the linkage between people in a patronage network as a "line" or "string" *(khsae, khsae royeah, khsae chrâvak)*.[32] This metaphor refers to a specific chain of individuals connected by personalized ties of dependency and exchange — such as Nuon's string, which consists of his deputy, Kim, and other relatives and friends at the police station. Nuon and his clients, in turn, are part of the provincial police chief's "string," though at one level of remove. As we move up such a patronage pyramid, a string may reach the top echelons of government. Thus, at yet another level of remove, the police chief is likely a client of the provincial governor, who himself may be the client of the prime minister or another top-ranking government official. Ultimately, then, a police officer in Samot may be (in)directly linked to the prime minister. (This string could extend even further, since the police officer may have his own clients in Samot or Caek.)

This cultural idiom of patronage has important political implications in Cambodia, since various high-ranking officials may have strings of police and military units that are loyal to them (as well as strings of civil service personnel).[33] In the next chapter, we will see that the severity of the Khmer Rouge purges was directly related to their desire to destroy the (perceived or real) strings/pyramids of their (perceived or real) enemies, which represented a (perceived or real) threat to the DK regime.

The personal nature of Cambodian patronage ties stands in contrast to impersonal, generalized interests around which groups in legal bureaucratic systems often form: a Cambodian client owes allegiance to his or her patron, not to the other members of the patron's circle. In many ways, this contrast parallels the distinction Max Weber made between two ideal types of authority: patrimonial domination and legal domination.[34] In systems of legal bureaucracy, which are idealized in industrialized capitalist countries like the United States and Western European states (clearly, other systems of authority also exist), authority is invested in an office that functions in accordance with general rules (for example, technical qualifications for hired personnel, promotion based on merit, and codified, routine, predictable norms for task performance). Moreover, the bonds between the members of a corporate group are supposed to be impersonal; a person's loyalty should be to the office itself and his or her actions guided by an impersonal code of conduct.

Patrimonial systems are predicated on a very different set of premises. Authority is derived from personal ties of loyalty. While ability is a consideration, patrimonial chiefs choose to place their personal retainers in key offices; their decision is arbitrary and based on informal norms of familiarity and trust. Although Weber's description of patrimonial authority is quite broad, it dovetails nicely with some features of patronage in Cambodia and other Southeast Asian societies. Nuon's actions, for example, resemble those of Weber's patrimonial chief. After becoming police chief, Nuon arbitrarily placed relatives and friends with whom he had a personal connection in positions of power — regardless of the experience, qualifications, and abilities of the officers who were already working in the station. As Scott's definition of patronage emphasizes, such patron-client relationships have a *"face-to-face,* personal quality" that is usually rooted in a history of association and trust. [35]

Despite the fact that their real-life manifestations are complex and may involve negotiation and ambivalence, these ties of personal dependency are idealized in an idiom of hierarchical encompassment that is manifest in a number of Cambodian social contexts, including myth, ritual, art, and bodily understandings.[36] This cultural model of hierarchical encompassment is embodied in mandala images, which convey the idea of a potent center providing integration, order, protection, purity, and benefits to the peripheral space/followers that it encompasses. Thus the Buddha took seven steps upon his birth, thus symbolically encompassing the cosmos with the purity of *dhamma*. More recently, during the 1990s, Cambodia's supreme Buddhist patriarch, Maha Ghosananda, led annual peace walks through troubled parts of Cambodia. Along the way, the marchers planted small bodhi trees that symbolically purified and re-encompassed the territories under the shade of *dhamma*.[37] These examples suggest an idealized state in which dependent beings are encompassed by more powerful beings who provide their followers (whether religious or political) with protection and enable them to prosper and gain fulfillment. At times, the encompassed are portrayed as almost a part or extension of the encompassers, who uplift their subordinates with potent power through the act of hierarchical encompassment.

In Cambodia and elsewhere in Southeast Asia, the sunshade is often used as a metaphor for such idealized relationships of hierarchical encompassment. This metaphor references the mandala-like structure of the patronage system, as powerful patrons (the raised centers/poles of the sunshade) are linked (the connecting ribs) to a peripheral circle of clients (the perimeter). A traditional signifier of rank, the umbrella is also an emblem of power. Just as the sunshade provides refuge from the sun and the elements, so too does a powerful patron offer protection from the dangerous world. Such protection is likened to the cool "shade" of an umbrella or tree, an extremely evocative image in the hot climate of Southeast Asia. Thus a mother who defends, helps, and cares for her children is said to provide them with comforting "shade."[38] Opposition politician and human rights activist Kem Sokha, fearing for his life in the aftermath of the 1997 coup, used a similar metaphor in describing why he sought protection from Prince Ranariddh's FUNCINPEC Party, "FUNCINPEC is like the big tree, I can stay without the sun, [it's] not so hot for me."[39] Similarly, ancient Cambodian inscriptions and chronicles speak of how the realm prospered in the "shade" of the king's parasol.[40]

Relationships of personal dependency are also idealized through the use of kinship idioms, which imbue them with ontological resonance. The nurturing bond between children and their caretakers, particularly mothers, often serves as a rudimentary prototype upon which later ties of personal dependency are modeled. Thus, a mother cares for, nourishes, protects, and provides moral support for her child in times of need; the father, while often an increasingly distant figure during a Cambodian child's youth, nevertheless offers material support and helps take care of his sons and daughters; and older siblings, especially sisters, and relatives fulfill supplemental caretaking roles.[41] Cambodians frequently refer to the close ties between family members using terms that signify care and affection, nurturance, protection and guardianship, provision, supervision, and nourishment *(thae, thae roksa, roksa, chenhchoem, beybach, kruap krong)*.[42] While these terms imply mutual caring, they usually connote hierarchical difference, since an elder/superior who has the means and ability assists a younger/subordinate/dependent family member.

In Khmer gender ideology, women are commonly portrayed as the paradigmatic nurturers. A mother "cares for, oversees, and protects" *(thae roksa)* her children, attending to their needs and providing them with the love, guidance, and sustenance that will enable them grow into mature adults. As noted above, this protective, nurturing quality of mothers is sometimes likened to "shade," such as when a Khmer interviewer described one of her female interviewees as "the 'shade' for her children and the 'shade' of happiness for her family."[43]

From the child's perspective, the mother and other caretakers are benevolent individuals he or she can "depend upon" *(peung)* to fulfill the child's needs. For example, Tuol Sleng survivor Vann Nath explained that, after he was arrested by the Khmer Rouge, "I didn't think much about my own life, I thought about and pitied my family who wouldn't have anyone to *peung*." Vann Nath was lamenting the fact that he would no longer be able to take care of his wife and children, who were dependent upon him to protect and provide for them. As his comments imply, Cambodians often view this state of personal dependency in a positive way, since it implies that one stands within the comforting shade of a potent benefactor.[44]

From the perspective of others, however, relationships of personal dependency may be viewed negatively precisely because the individual has the protection of such a benefactor. Cambodians often use the word *ang*, which similarly means "to depend/rely upon," to describe a person who relies on a benefactor to act in a transgressive manner. Once, when the parents of a Cambodian family I lived with were out of town, the eldest son was given responsibility for taking care of his younger siblings. I asked him if his brothers and sisters misbehaved more when his parents were gone. He replied, "No, they behave better. They're scared that I'll hit them. When our mother is around, they rely upon *(ang)* her because she is more lenient." Similarly, when I asked a primary school headmaster if teachers hit students in class as often as in the past, she responded:

"No, nowdays students *ang* their mother and father to protect them." In politics, this term is similarly used to describe people who act with impunity because they have the "backing" *(khnâng)* of powerful people.

As recipients of the protection and overall benevolence *(kun)* of their parents, children incur a great moral debt "to repay their good deeds" *(sângkun)*. Children are therefore expected to respect *(korop)* and obey *(stap)* their parents without hesitation. Upon reaching adulthood, a son can partially repay his parents by entering the monastery and earning merit for them. Likewise, a daughter who remains chaste and marries into a good family increases the status of her parents. Children can also *sângkun* their parents by supporting them in old age, presenting them with gifts and tasty food, and achieving successes that give the parents prestige.

In sociopolitical life, relationships of personal dependency frequently involve the use of kinship idioms in an attempt to play upon the ontological resonances of these early childhood experiences. Ideally, patrons, like parents or elder siblings, benevolently protect and provide resources to their clients, who, like a child or younger sibling, repay the resulting moral debt through support, respect, and obedience. Hok, a Cambodian human rights worker, argued that this analogy between parents and patrons is a fundamental aspect of Cambodian sociopolitical life:

> We live in a society of "parents" and "grandchildren." In this society, whoever is born second must respect and obey *(korop)* whoever is born first, their elder. Within the family, the child *(koun)* must respect whoever is the mother *(me)*. A person who doesn't show gratitude to their mother and father, who isn't grateful to their siblings, is a person who is an ingrate *(romilkun)* and lacks morality. As for society in general, whoever is "big" is like a parent and the person under them is always called a "grandchild" *(kaunchav)*. This "grandchild" must respect and obey the parent, just like in the family. . . . Do you know the word "to know a good deed" *(doengkun)*? It's really important for Cambodians. Let's say I'm the boss *(me)* and give a lot of resources to my grandchildren. Or, perhaps my nephew comes to live with me. I get him work at my office, nourish *(chenhchoem)* him at home, and help him with his affairs. This is the goodness *(kun)* that I do for him. It's enormous. As for those who receive such favors from another person, well, if that patron *(me)* later has a problem and suffers, the grandchild will try to do something about it in order to repay their benefactor's kindness *(sângkun)*.

Hok's comments, which invoke familial idioms of respect, debt, nurturance, and gratitude, illustrate how Cambodian patronage relationships ideally involve obligations and duties that parallel relationships of personal dependency within the family. Cambodians sometimes even refer to patrons as the "mothers" *(me)* of their client "children" *(koun)* or "grandchildren" *(kounchav, chav)*, though the term *me* can be used more generally to refer to any "chief, leader, head, master; owner; guard; supervising officer," as in a village headman *(mephoum)* or a military commander *(metoap)*.[45] For example, when my informant discussed how Nuon brought offerings to his patron, the provincial police chief, he described the provincial police chief as Nuon's *me*. Patrons are also sometimes referred to as "fathers" *(puk)* or "elder siblings" *(bâng)*.

Hok's remarks suggest another dimension of patron-client ties: they are "diffuse, 'whole-person' relationships rather than explicit, impersonal contract-bonds."[46] In contrast to the ideal type of legal bureaucratic authority, in which employees perform specific tasks based on impersonal contractual obligations, patronage ties are flexible and diffuse and involve a personalized negotiation between the dyadic pair. Patrons may provide a range of benefits to their clients, just as the patron Hok finds employment for, cares for, and helps out his "grandchild." The obligations of clients are also generalized, usually involving a range of possible acts based on circumstances. For Hok, an ideal client "knows the kindness" *(doengkun)* of his benefactor and is prepared to repay these good deeds *(sângkun)* by supporting, showing respect to, and performing tasks for the benefactor. Some clients may even be willing to perform extreme acts — including harming or killing another person — to show their gratitude to patrons who have done an "enormous" number of good deeds for them.

Several newspaper articles, for example, suggest that Suen of the Earth killed Chan Dara on behalf of a patron. On December 19, 1994, an *Island of Peace* cartoon depicted Suen shooting Chan Dara in the back, with the caption, "Now that I have fulfilled my duty I can report this to my boss." Clearly, the newspaper is alleging that Suen was ordered to murder Chan Dara by a superior. Six days earlier, an *Island of Peace* article had asserted that Suen was Forestry Chief Pal Ren's "right hand man" and was illegally escorting timber to the Vietnamese border with his heavily armed subordinates without being stopped by the terrified police. While Suen and Pal Ren supposedly garnered thousands of dollars in profit from each logging shipment, their lucrative illicit business (as well as their honor) was threatened by newspaper revelations for which Chan Dara was thought to be the source. This *Island of Peace* article concluded, "Thus despicable little Suen of the Earth, who shot and killed [Chan Dara], surely must have received the order [to do so] from his boss, despicable little Pal Ren. If they hadn't killed [Chan Dara], the profits . . . that were making them rich men would have been cut off."

According to the allegations of *Island of Peace* and other newspapers, Suen and Pal Ren constituted a patronage dyad. Pal Ren gave Suen the opportunity to become rich by illegally transporting lumber to Vietnam and reportedly protected Suen from being convicted. Suen ensured that Pal Ren received a steady stream of money and, if *Island of Peace* is correct, obeyed his patron's orders to murder Chan Dara. Pal Ren, in turn, had his own patron (Governor Hun Neng), while Suen maintained a circle of loyal soldier-clients who helped him conduct his corrupt affairs. When people like Suen and Pal Ren can "rely upon" *(ang)* a powerful patron for protection and assistance, Cambodians often say that they have a "back" *(khnâng)*.[47] Other articles in the December 13, 1994 edition of *Island of Peace,* for example, state that "the group that killed the reporter has a back *(khnâng)* to hide behind" and that "Pal Ren relies upon *(ang)* and hides behind the back *(khnâng)* of the provincial governor, who is more powerful *(khlang)* than an ancient warlord, so no forestry officials dare to speak out about him."

Such statements depict a "back" as a powerful figure who provides protection and support to clients when they encounter difficulty. Hok described the importance of gaining the support of such a patron:

> An ordinary person must always seek a supporting back *(khnâng)*, one that's big *(thom)*, a person who has raw power *(amnach)*. . . . If we don't have a big protector like this, others will start to look down on us. They won't really fear *(khlach)* us and will abuse us because they can do so. But, if we have a back, they really won't dare. They'll fear our back. So, in Cambodian society today . . . anyone who doesn't have a back has a really difficult life. A back is a protector.

The importance of finding a *khnâng* was implicit in my informant's comments about Nuon when he noted all the ways that Nuon protected his clients. He commented, "If a person has a back, no one will dare to look down on them." However, Cambodians frequently use the term *khnâng* in a resentful, negative manner to refer to others who use their "back" to do as they please. The various newspaper accounts expressed outrage that Suen could so blatantly flaunt the law. Hok expressed a similar sentiment about Suen: "Mr. Sat Suen is a soldier who has rank *(bon sâk)*, guns, raw power *(amnach)*, and a back *(khnâng)*. In our society, when people like Suen have a big back, they have raw power and often abuse those who don't have backing." Relationships of personal dependency thus have a double edge: they both offer protection in a dangerous world and provide "backing" that sometimes makes the world a more dangerous place.

SUSPICION

From ancient times onward, Cambodian leaders have been constantly suspicious *(sângsay)* of one another. This doubt has led to there being merciless killings between them. Those who are in the process of holding power *(amnach)* never trust *(min tuk chett)* those who work with them, always fearing: "That person is inclined to quietly try to seize my *(ânh)* authority! That person will try to secretly kill me in order to take over my position!" . . . When a person thinks in this panicked manner and stops trusting a person, if one of his subordinates inflames his suspicions a little bit, telling the leader that a colleague or longtime friend has in fact betrayed him, the leader will believe him at once. Immediately after this, the leader will find a pretext to accuse this colleague or friend of doing something bad so that the person can be killed and discarded.

Bun Chân Mol, *Châret Khmaer*

At their root, patronage ties involve an exchange, as resources, services, and benefits flow from one individual to another and back again. This exchange may be mixed with moral authority and genuine affection, particularly when kinship is involved, but it retains an instrumental dimension. Moreover, patron-client relationships are asymmetrical and unbalanced: patrons act from a position of greater wealth, status, and power and provide benefits that their clients cannot return in full. In their dyadic interactions, the client is expected to give "face" to the patron by acting in an obedient and respectful manner. It is important, however, not to view these relationships as static, mechanical exchanges. John Marston has noted that patron-client ties involve negotiation, particularly in places like Cambodia, where relationships of personal dependency tend to be less institutionally formalized and characterized by greater flux.[48] Thus, in different times and places, the symbolic and material exchange between patrons and clients may be renegotiated. As clients develop their own power bases, for example, they may show less respect to their patron and eventually even switch allegiances or attempt to displace their patron, thereby bettering their position. Patrons, in turn, must guard against such threats to their power.

The more fluid and unstable nature of relationships of personal dependency is illustrated by the following example of how one patronage network in a Provincial Educational Office (PEO) carried out its corrupt affairs just prior to the UNTAC period. From 1987 to 1993, the Cambodian educational system was plagued by rampant corruption. The term for "corruption," *puk roluoy,* implies rot and decay, as in a rotten piece of fruit or wood. However, some of the behaviors that a person in the United States might consider "corrupt" are accepted by Cambodians as a necessity or as a privilege of office. It is only when an official "feeds on bribes" *(si somnauk)* to an excessive extent that the derogatory term *puk roluoy* is used.[49] The following account of educational corruption is based on interviews I conducted with people who worked in the provincial education sector. In order to protect their safety, I refer neither to them nor the province by name.

The PEO was run by its chief, "Luoy," and his small circle of loyal associates. During the annual entrance examination period, Luoy's group made a list of people whom they could trust — usually relatives and lower-ranking educational officials — and selected some to serve as exam graders or local intermediaries. The intermediaries, sometimes called "head winds" *(me khyal),* worked in outlying districts, where they or their designated local headmasters, district educational officials, and teachers collected bribes directly from parents or, less frequently, from the students themselves. In 1990, it was not uncommon to find that over 90 percent of the students who passed an exam had paid such a bribe. Bribes for the eighth grade exam ranged from $70 to $150; a place in the provincial Teacher Training College (TCC) could cost anywhere from $400 to $600. The results were often disastrous. As one informant, "Mol," explained, "Many students stopped trying to study. Poorer students worked to raise pigs and cows so they could get money to buy their degrees. Learning did not have much meaning. If these students spent time on their lessons, they wouldn't pass the exam."

Grading the exams was an intricately designed process. To give the appearance that the tests were graded anonymously, each student was assigned a number that served as the only indication of their identity. Exams were first graded fairly by a group of teachers and then passed on to a "middle commission" that verified the scores in a private room. The middle commission, consisting of a few trusted individuals whom Luoy and his colleagues had carefully selected, was given a master list that matched the exam numbers to names and indicated who should be passed. One person who served on a middle commission explained, "We were the ones who gave the final passing grades. If I opened the exam of a student who was supposed to pass and saw that he or she was short five points, I would secretly add on the extra points."

While extremely variable in its exact proportions, the distribution of the bribe money typically followed the Cambodian saying, "In accordance with their station, the little eat little, the big eat big" *(tauch si tam tauch, thum si tam thum)*. Mol described how money flowed from the bottom of the patronage strings (teachers, headmasters, and local officials) toward the provincial education office (the "head winds," exam graders, the "middle commission," the PEO chief and his "inner circle"), all the way to the upper echelons of the provincial and national governments (the provincial governor, the Ministry of Education). At the peak of corruption, the PEO chief supposedly earned enough money from the Teacher Training College entrance examinations alone to build a new villa (approximately twenty thousand dollars); some of his top subordinates could do likewise after two or three years. Mol complained:

> If you look, you will see that the top officials in the Provincial Education Office all have cars and villas. But their income is just a little above my own. How did they get their villas, cars, and the money they lend with interest at the market? Where did the money come from? It came from the student entrance examinations. This corruption is what makes children stop trying in their studies. Why should they learn? If they study and know the answers, they still will not pass their exam.

In fact, in the province in question, PEO officials have constructed a number of villas for themselves on the same city block.

This example illustrates how patronage operates within the government bureaucracy. As the head of the provincial education office, Huoy is able to appoint an inner circle of clients to prominent positions within the PEO and to delegate lucrative projects to them. Cambodians sometimes refer to the immediate members of a patronage circle as a *bâk puok*, though the term has a wide range of meanings and may also be used to describe a political faction or group of (more or less equal) close associates. Huoy's subordinates are thus placed in a position to make money through corrupt activities, such as gathering bribes for exams, selling off a certain percentage of the educational supplies donated by UNICEF, giving a European Union–sponsored nongovernmental organization a dramatically marked-up price for the cost of constructing classroom blackboards, or pocketing money that was supposed to be dispersed to schools or civil servants in the PEO. In return for Huoy's benevolence, the members of his *bâk puok* are expected to support, obey, and be loyal to him. While allowed to take a cut of the corrupt money they gather, Huoy's clients must give him the larger share of this wealth.

As noted earlier, such a patronage circle is often part of a larger "pyramid" or "entourage." Thus Huoy may be a client of the provincial governor or the minister of education, who are themselves likely the clients of the prime minister or another top official. Huoy's clients, in turn, are the patrons of people for whom they arrange work on special projects, as "head winds," or as lower-level civil servants, headmasters, or teachers in the provincial or district education sector. A patronage "string," then, may consist of relatives who have positions of power within an institutional framework (for example, Prime Minister Hun Sen and his brother Hun Neng, the governor of Kompong Cham during my fieldwork), a *bâk puok* of close associates (for example, Huoy's trusted "inner circle" at the PEO), or a pyramid (for example, a prime minister or minister of education who controls a long line of graded patronage circles in the education sector that theoretically extends all the way down to students and their families). With increasing distance, the bond between a patron and a member of his or her string tends to become less nurturing and more instrumental.

Such personal networks, however, are often filled with uncertainty, negotiation, and distrust. As the head of the PEO, Luoy attempts to maintain the loyalty and support of his clients by giving them the opportunity to become wealthy through corruption. Even within this circle of clients, Luoy places the greatest trust in a few individuals to whom he allocates the most power. Luoy also attempts to prevent betrayal from within by meeting periodically with his inner circle to construct a list of the workers they can trust. Whenever they need additional people for their corrupt activities, Luoy's group first hires people from this list, many of whom are their relatives or friends. The ethos of secrecy and mistrust that characterizes the workings of the PEO is shown by their procedure at the end of the examinations. Mol explained: "After the exam officials had returned to their districts, Luoy's group gathered all of the master lists and burned them. Luoy and one of his closest associates were the ones who did the actual burning." Unable to fully trust his subordinates to dispose of evidence that they could potentially use against him, Luoy made certain that he personally witnessed the destruction of the incriminating materials.

From a client perspective, Mol had ambivalent feelings toward his patron, "Bunruen," an official who was part of Luoy's inner circle. At one point, Mol asked Bunruen if he could arrange to have Mol's younger sibling pass an exam. Bunruen turned down the request. Mol said, "From that time on, I stopped believing in him. But I tried to act in such a way that he wouldn't know about my feelings. I was friendly toward him, but I tucked away in my heart the thought 'I can't trust this person.'" Later on, Bunruen lost his position because Luoy suspected that he or one of his subordinates was responsible for information that had surfaced about the group's corrupt work. Because he was one of Bunruen's clients, Mol's name was placed "on the list of people who could not be trusted. . . . I was one of Bunruen's 'grandchildren,' though the least powerful one. Because they got rid of Bunruen, they stopped using me in their work afterward. They suspected that one of us was responsible for the leaked information." Here, in the realm of education, we find an analog of the purges of "strings of traitors" that claimed so many lives during DK.

This example shows that the relationship between patrons and clients is subject to negotiation and change, as their perception of one another's needs, loyalty, trust, and deserved return alters over time.[50] A patron may suddenly decide to drop a client because of expediency or, in the case of Luoy and Bunruen, suspicion. Because patrons have limited resources, they must choose to allocate them in the most beneficial manner. Bunruen no doubt made this type of assessment when he denied Mol's request. Clients, in turn, may stop following a patron if they don't feel they are receiving their due. Mol was initially quite satisfied to be Bunruen's client. During the early 1990s, he earned well over one hundred dollars for his participation in the examination scheme, an amount then regarded as large. He recalled, "We were really happy if they gave us even fifty or sixty dollars because we were so poor. . . . But we knew that if we said anything we might have an 'accident.'" When Bunruen refused to help Mol's sister, however, Mol was upset and became dissatisfied with the relationship. Because he lacked alternatives, Mol somewhat reluctantly continued to serve Bunruen until he fell from power. At that point, Mol searched hard for and eventually found a new patron. Mol's experience also demonstrates that patronage networks tend to be less stable at more distant levels of remove. Luoy was able to maintain the loyalty of his inner circle by carefully managing the opportunities and resources that flowed to them. He was less able to control the clients of his clients, who received fewer benefits and were more peripherally connected to him.

Like energy, power is thought to ebb and flow, accumulating for a time in one location before scattering to the winds. The possibility of flux means that powerful beings may lose their potency over time as weaker beings increase theirs. For clients, particularly in high-level political patronage networks, this precarious state of affairs means that their benefactor may suffer a "fall" from power, thus enabling the client — if their own store of power has increased — to usurp their patron's place at the center of the "umbrella" or necessitating that the client be ready to suddenly switch allegiances to a new patron so that he or she is not left in the open without protective shade (for example, Mol's abandonment of Bunruen soon after Bunruen fell from power). The instability of such relations is reinforced by the Buddhist view that a person's store of merit may suddenly "kick in" or expire, thereby resulting in a sharp rise or decline in standing. While there are mechanisms that provide stability to patronage relations (for example, genuine affection and respect, feelings of moral debt, the difficulty of finding new patrons, fear of retribution, kinship bonds), these relationships, particularly in the political domain, are nevertheless often characterized by uncertainty and, in the extreme, chronic mistrust.

Cambodian understandings of the instability of patronage relationships resonate with Buddhist ontology.[51] The Buddha taught that life is suffering (tukkha) and that this suffering originates from ignorance (avichchea) and desire (tânha). To liberate oneself from ignorance and desire and thus, ultimately, suffering, one must see that, at root, all things are impermanent. Nothing lasts. One becomes attached to people and objects, but it is the nature of things to change. Therefore a person you love leaves you or dies and you suffer because you are attached to them. This fundamental doctrine of impermanence (ânichcha) is related to another key tenant of Buddhism, non-self (ânatta). Our sense of self is an illusion. What we perceive to be the self is really just a momentary aggregation of five interdependent elements — form/body, feeling/sensation, perception, mental formation, and consciousness — that continuously appear, disappear, and are generated anew. Suffering arises because one becomes attached to this (nonexistent) sense of self and the elements from which it arises.

On an even more metaphysical level, Buddhism describes this state of suffering, impermanence, and non-self in terms of the principle of dependent origination (bâdechchâsâmobbat), understanding of which provides the key to the cessation of suffering. Dependent origination refers to the psychophysical process by which twelve interdependent elements give rise to a ceaseless cycle of birth, death and decay, and rebirth. We suffer because, in our ignorance, we continue to desire impermanent things, which fuels our greed *(loph)*, anger/hatred *(tosah)*, and delusion *(mohah)*, and continues the cycle anew. The principle of dependent origination is often symbolized through mandala images in which the twelve constituent elements form a circle without beginning or end.[52] According to this principle, then, existence is characterized by impermanence and flux, as interdependent elements briefly cohere and then pass away. Suffering arises as we ignorantly crave and cling to illusory and impermanent phenomena; the cessation of suffering can only be attained by seeing this reality for what it is and extinguishing desire. Nirvana *(nipvean)*, the cessation of suffering, "can only be found in the present moment . . . [when] there is no clinging, no expectation, and no desire."[53]

Despite being characterized by impermanence, the process of dependent origination does generate some continuities, perhaps the most important of which is the law of karma *(kâmm)*, or of the appropriate consequences of action.[54] Each of our actions is performed with greater or lesser mindfulness. Because of their craving and attachment to transient phenomenon, the ignorant perform impure actions that have morally negative consequences; those who are mindful, in contrast, perform good deeds that have positive consequences. These actions condition our future actions and rebirths into the world. In everyday life, Cambodians, like other Theravada Buddhists, frequently think of the law of karma in terms of merit *(bon)*, which is viewed as a sort of moral banking system. People are born into the world with a store of merit based on their good or bad karma from past lives. Based on their performance of good or bad deeds, each person's store of merit will rise or decline, thereby resulting in a higher or lower rebirth in the future. Cambodians often succinctly refer to this state of affairs with a saying: "Act meritoriously, obtain merit; act sinfully, receive demerit" *(thvoe bon ban bon; thvoe bap ban bap)*. On an ethical level, therefore, the ideas of karma and merit provide a motivation for moral action. On a spiritual level, these Buddhist doctrines offer an explanation for social hierarchy and social suffering, since one's actions in the past are viewed as conditioning one's life in the present. Thus, many Cambodians interpret their suffering during DK in terms of bad karma. Finally, on a political level, they offer hope of rising in rank and fear of falling from power, since one's store of merit may suddenly catalyze or diminish.

Cambodian understandings of dependent origination, power, merit, and karma contribute to a deep sense of impermanence in other dimensions of Buddhist doctrine as well. For example, a state of integration, order, and hierarchical encompassment, while a longed-for ideal, is viewed as difficult to achieve and always transient. Just as individual existence is characterized by a cycle of birth, decay, and rebirth, so too does the cosmos undergo a cyclical flow between states of coherence and fragmentation.[55]

This conception of temporal oscillation may underwrite or undermine sociopolitical authority. In the shade of a potent center, people benefit and flourish. Since all things are impermanent, however, all orderly conditions of coherence and encompassment must inevitably degenerate. Invisible and in a state of flux, power and merit must be inferred from signs, such as the ability to control large numbers of people, the possession of magical objects, and the wealth and benefits they generate. Ultimately, anyone from a prince to a pauper may exhibit the appropriate signs and make a claim to authority. This temporal sensibility is conducive to millennial movements, particularly during times of socioeconomic upheaval, when there are signs of entropy.[56] Cambodian history is replete with episodes in which a charismatic leader claiming to be a "person of merit" (neak mean bon) has led a movement that attempted to revitalize a sociopolitical order they perceived as degenerate. The Khmer Rouge revitalization movement, while operating from a very different set of ideological assumptions, parallels these millennial revolts in many respects: Pol Pot and his associates believed they had attained a secret form of knowledge (Marxist-Leninism) that increased their potency, enabling them to regenerate and purify Cambodian society.

The notion of impermanence contributes to a sense that interpersonal relations are transient. From a Buddhist perspective, mental states, like everything else in the cosmos, are contingent and labile. A person's thoughts and feelings come and go and are likely to change over time, thus introducing a degree of uncertainty into relationships, since it is possible that someone who is close to you will suddenly become distant. Such unease about the feelings and intentions of others is exacerbated by local norms of social interaction, which may lead people to protect their "face" by hiding disruptive feelings "inside their heart" (leak knong chett ke).

Cambodians have many sayings and proverbs that reflect this sense of wariness and impermanence. Many of these didactic expressions encourage suspicion directly or indirectly: "Don't trust the sky; don't believe the stars;/don't believe your daughter when she says she has no lover;/don't believe your mother when she says she has no debts"; "If the tiger lies down quietly before you/don't say it respects you"; "An evil heart, but an angel's mouth"; and "Just as the water never ceases to flow, so you should not believe the promises of a man."[57] Others warn about the impermanence and fluidity of social status: "The stupid person, scorned by neighbors/may suddenly become wealthy and wise"; "When the hollow gourd sinks, the clay pot floats"; and "When the cat is not around, the mouse ascends the throne."[58] The latter two proverbs are particularly interesting, since they figuratively signify that a superior must constantly be on guard to prevent a subordinate from usurping his or her position.

As these expressions suggest, patronage relationships are often characterized by suspicion and distrust, particularly in the political realm, where the stakes for power, money, and prestige are high. In Cambodia, which has traditionally been characterized by a lack of enduring extrafamilial social institutions linking villagers to the state,[59] relationships of personal dependency represent a crucial means of gaining access to resources and increasing one's status. Ideally, this relationship replicates the familial bond of the nurturing "parent-patron" and the morally indebted and loyal "child-client." Such a situation benefits the patron by increasing his or her control over his or her subordinates, and the client by creating the potential for social advancement and providing a protective "back." In practice, however, patronage relationships are negotiated exchanges and are often undermined by the possibility that a cunning client may switch allegiance or attempt to take over the patron's position. Bros, one of my research assistants, explained,

> If there is a problem, a person will hide it inside themselves. They won't tell others because they are afraid people will lose honor. . . . Thus, a person must lie. If another individual comes and speaks with us, we will think that they are lying to us also, because we are accustomed to lying to others. . . . Moreover, many Cambodians are extremely ambitious, desiring rank *(bon sâk)*, power *(amnach)*, and honor *(ketteyos)*, wanting only to win. This leads them to betray and seize the position of people to whom they are close. But when they have rank, they too will fear that others will try to seize their power and defeat them. . . . Thus, there is a saying, "One should not trust other people."

Bros's comments suggest why Cambodian patronage relations are frequently characterized by suspicion and instability. First, these relationships often have a competitive structure, since subordinates may desire to increase their social standing. Second, the possibility of such a rise in rank is implicitly legitimated by local understandings of hierarchical mobility, which maintain that an individual's status rises or declines in accordance with the ebb and flow of their store of power and merit. Third, patrons are often uncertain about the loyalty of their clients because it is difficult to know the heart of another person; patrons realize that their clients may be concealing feelings of resentment and ambition. And finally, this distrust and wariness about the intentions of others resonates ontologically with socialization practices and Buddhist notions of impermanence.

While patrons and clients often do feel mutual affection and loyalty, these dyadic pairs nevertheless tend to vigilantly monitor one another because of the perceived instability of patronage relationships. Clients look for signs of their patron's potency and assess their own possibilities for advancement; patrons constantly watch out for subordinates who may betray or seek to displace them. This tension may be diffused by continuous validation involving the allocation of resources, the exaggerated use of hierarchical registers, and the invocation of idealized idioms of kinship and hierarchical encompassment.[60] Since patronage relations ultimately retain a competitive, instrumental, and unstable structure, however, Cambodians often attempt to enlist their relatives into their personal networks.

In Cambodia, kinship is reckoned bilaterally — Cambodians recognize relatives on both the maternal and paternal sides of the family without the formal rules of preference that group people in matrilineal and patrilineal societies.[61] Although the primary Cambodian social unit is the household, which may be composed of nuclear, stem, and extended family members, a person usually includes other cognatic or, more rarely, "fictive" relations within his or her circle of "relatives" *(bâng b'aun, nheate, trâkoul)*. Because the ties of personal dependency are stronger between relatives, particularly core family members, Cambodian patrons often place their relatives in key positions of power within their sociopolitical networks.[62] Thus Nuon gave his relatives lucrative positions in the police station and appointed his younger brother, Kim, to be the head of an important office. Luoy similarly privileged relatives in his corrupt patronage network. By stocking their networks with relatives, powerful Cambodians both help members of their family move up in the world and, they hope, gain more trustworthy followers who can potentially offset some of the structural instability of patronage networks. Despite such measures, Cambodian patronage, particularly in politics, is often beset by suspicion and instability, a pattern that was taken to the extreme during DK.[63]

CHAPTER THREE

In the Shade
of Pol Pot's Umbrella

When the Khmer Rouge came to power, they took control of a society that had been devastated by war, social upheaval, and economic collapse. Such circumstances are conducive to the emergence of high-modernist authoritarianism, since high-modernist regimes are often willing to use coercive force to implement a radical program of social engineering, and the devastated populace usually lacks the ability to resist these plans.[1] Although the Khmer Rouge faced factional disputes that helped catalyze the DK purges, they nevertheless found themselves in a situation in which they could rapidly centralize control and begin implementing communist reforms.

In one sense, therefore, the DK regime's program of centralization and social transformation resembled that of other communist, high-modernist, and authoritarian states. In other ways, however, this process of centralization and change was a distinctly local phenomenon, patterned by a set of social institutions and political understandings about power, patronage, and relationships of personal dependency. Ultimately, all communist and high-modernist regimes blend the new with the old both to maximize the "take" of their ideological models among the general populace and because the leaders themselves interpret global models through local categories, thereby giving rise to synthetic new formations.

ÂNGKAR AND THE EYES OF THE PINEAPPLE

A key symbol of the new order, Ângkar, constitutes a Khmer Rouge ideological palimpsest linking high-modernist thought, communist ideology, and local understandings to idealize a new potent center. The term *Ângkar* may be translated as "organization" but includes an array of connotations not captured by the English word. Ângkar is derived from the Pali term *anga,* meaning "a constituent part of the body, a limb, member," and proximately from the Khmer term *ângk,* which has the primary meaning of "body, structure, physique; limb of the body" but is also used to refer to "*mana*-filled" objects such as monks, royalty, religious statuary, or Siva lingas.[2] The *Khmer Dictionary* defines *ângkar* as "a type of structure, an orderly institution that arranges the state of affairs of the government or a governmental [administrative] group created in order to achieve prosperity — as in a 'political organization' or a 'state organization.' " Thus, *Ângkar* can be properly glossed as "the organization," but it also connotes a structure that orders society, a part-whole relation (i.e., the relation of a constituent part to the structured whole), and an organic entity that is infused with power.

During DK, the word *Ângkar* seems to have taken on all of these connotations. Both DK ideology and cadres frequently spoke of "the Organization" *(Ângkar),* the "Revolutionary Organization" *(Ângkar bâdevatt),* and the "Upper Organization" *(Ângkar loe).* Sometimes these terms signified the Party Center or Pol Pot himself. In other situations, they might designate the "higher authorities." Thus cadres often told people who were about to be reprimanded, imprisoned, or killed that "Ângkar wants to see you" or "Ângkar wants you to go to a study session." Cadres frequently invoked Ângkar in such ways to deflect responsibility, implying that they were just obeying Ângkar's instructions when they had to take someone away, appropriate property, relocate families, or enact seemingly unreasonable policies. In addition, Ângkar sometimes seemed to refer to all the members of the new society. If a person asked who Ângkar was, for example, he or she might receive the following type of cryptic reply: "Why, the people of course! It is everyone; it is you."[3]

At times these senses converged, as when Ângkar was portrayed as a quasi-divine entity, comprising both the party leadership and the populace, that should be worshiped by everyone. Haing Ngor explained, "Logically, Angka had to be a person or a group of people, but many found it easier to believe that Angka was an all-powerful entity, something like a god."[4] Interestingly, "the Organization" co-opted aspects of Buddhism, a social institution that the Khmer Rouge disbanded both because it was considered "reactionary" and "exploitative" and because, as an alternative center of power and loyalty, it represented a possible source of opposition to the DK regime."[5] Like other Marxist-Leninists, the Khmer Rouge viewed religion as an "opiate of the people." Buddhism was seen as particularly noxious, since it justified social inequalities through the concept of karma. Moreover, Buddhism siphoned off a large proportion of what little money the poor had by tricking them into thinking that they could better their plight in their next life by making religious donations that would increase their merit. Monks, who lived off such offerings and didn't perform "real" labor, were characterized as "bloodsuckers," "parasites," and "intestinal worms" who — like imperialists, capitalists, (neo)colonialists, and other oppressors — corrupted society and impeded class struggle.[6] Accordingly, Buddhism was banned during DK.

Ângkar supplanted Buddhism as the new "religion." Like a deity, Ângkar (and the revolution it stood for) was depicted in hyperbolic, often superhuman terms, sometimes directly adapted from Buddhism.[7] In radio broadcasts, speeches, and everyday discourse, Ângkar was characterized as something to be "believed in," "loved," and "thanked for the good it has done," as an entity that "provided for" the people and was "master of land and earth." Such rhetoric helped make Ângkar seem "omnipotent and omniscient in everyone's mind. Angka blessed us with food, clothing, and purpose. We were to turn to Angka for our every need. . . . [It was like] a new unassailable deity."[8] The totalistic, pervasive, and all-knowing nature of Ângkar was implicit in a common Khmer Rouge warning that "Ângkar has the eyes of a pineapple" (Ângkar mean phnek mnoah).[9] This phrase indicated that, like an enlightened, supernatural being, Ângkar knew what everyone did, so one always had to behave in a proper and obedient manner.

By likening Ângkar to a pineapple, a round fruit, the DK regime was metaphorically depicted as a potent center. The image of the pineapple also implicitly invoked the famous four-faced heads that adorn the towers of the Bayon temple, which Jayavarman VII constructed at the center of his capital, Angkor Thom.[10] The Bayon is a complex cosmogram and mandala symbol, signifying the axis mundi, Mt. Meru, microcosmic-macrocosmic harmony, a galactic polity and world ruler, and an encompassing center. The towering faces, which look in the four cardinal directions, are thought to symbolize both the Bodhisattva Lokesvara and Jayavarman VII, representing, among other things, the radiating compassion of the former and the galactic rule of the latter. The eyes may represent clarity, vision, and power.[11] In Buddhism, this idea of all-pervasive clairvoyance is linked to enlightenment, which is symbolized by one's ability to see what is real and what is illusory. The phrase "Ângkar has the eyes of a pineapple" clearly invokes the conception of a potent center that is all-seeing. Not surprisingly, Ângkar is described elsewhere as "clear-sighted," "brilliant," "alert and intelligent," "clairvoyant," and "enlightened."[12]

Here we find the Khmer Rouge playing upon a direct parallel between Buddhism and Marxism. In both systems of thought, human beings are said to live in a state of ignorance, false consciousness, and suffering. To free oneself from this dismal existence, one must understand certain universal laws (the Four Noble Truths and the Law of Dependent Origination or class oppression and the Laws of Dialectical Materialism) and use certain methods (the Middle Path, meditation, Buddhist logic, moral discipline or revolution, the elimination of capitalism, high-modernist analysis, revolutionary ethics). The enlightened one who clearly understands this situation (the Buddha and monks or Ângkar and the Party Center) can help lead the populace to salvation (nirvana or communism). By portraying Ângkar as an almost divine, "clear-sighted," "enlightened" entity, therefore, the Khmer Rouge were revamping communist ideology in terms of local idioms that ideally would be more meaningful to the population. Like the Buddha, Ângkar was an enlightened and all-knowing center from which power radiated. Like the Bayon, Ângkar was an *axis mundi* that encompassed all the lands, seeing everything with its many eyes. Like Jayavarman VII, Ângkar was a dominant ruler whose power flowed outward, providing comforting shade to the masses it controlled. In a variety of ways, then, the Khmer Rouge Party Center, symbolized by Ângkar, evinced signs of being a potent center that had emerged, enlightened with secret knowledge (Marxist-Leninism), to revitalize a degenerate order.

"The Organization" also appropriated key elements of another traditional Cambodian social structure that was severely undermined during DK — the family.[13] Like Buddhism, "familyism" *(kruosarniyom)* represented a threat to DK because the close bonds between family members constituted an alternative source of loyalty and a potentially "corrupting" influence on the young. In the new communist society, a person's primary loyalty and attachment were supposed to be to Ângkar. As a result, the party attempted to diminish the importance of the family by eliminating its social (private meals, daily interaction, and care-taking) and economic functions (private ownership, production, distribution, and consumption). Family members were isolated from each other by housing restrictions, relocation, illness, communal meetings, long hours, days, or even months in sexually segregated work teams, and death. In accordance with their official policy of egalitarianism and their high valuation of children as the revolution's future,[14] the party also subverted patterns of etiquette that had traditionally governed interactions between family members. Indoctrination sessions informed children that they no longer had to act deferentially toward their parents: mothers, fathers, children, and neighbors were all "comrades" *(mitt)* now.

At the same time as it undermined familial solidarity, the DK regime attempted to co-opt the sentiments associated with these prototypic relationships of personal dependency. Ângkar was idealized through the use of kinship idioms. Thus local party officials might be addressed as "grandfather" *(ta)* or "mother" *(mae)*, and Ângkar was sometimes referred to as the "dad-mom" *(puk-mae)* of its "children." If parents traditionally performed a number of good deeds for their children and created a moral debt that was "heavy like the earth," Ângkar became the new benefactor who cared for, protected, and married off its "children." This relationship of personal dependency was often idealized in songs that played upon familial metaphors:

> Oh, Oh, *ângka* that has loving kindness, the loving kindness
>   of someone great without measure
> for the race and the people, and especially for the children —
> someone who has persevered to train the children, just like
>   a raft trying to cross the water,
> back and forth, so exhausted, it strives until the children
>   have victory.[15]

Like parents who do good deeds for their children, Ângkar's "loving kindness" *(kun)* toward the people was "great without measure." The Khmer Rouge wanted the populace to repay this moral debt by giving Ângkar the same type of loyalty, respect, support, attachment, and obedience that parents and other benefactors had previously commanded.

While the Khmer Rouge idealized this new relationship of personal dependency between Ângkar and the Cambodian masses in general, they focused their ideological indoctrination intensely on the groups that would be most susceptible to its message: the extreme poor and the young, who, as in Maoist China, were likened to a "blank page on which we can write anything we want."[16] In a 1977 speech, for example, Pol Pot glorified the revolutionary potential of the young: "Youth is a period of life in which there are very rapid changes. It is a time when consciousness is most receptive to revolution and when we are in full possession of our strengths. This, then, is a general directive of our Party. It is the youth of today who will take up the revolutionary tasks of tomorrow."[17]

The minds of young children were thought to be particularly "receptive" to revolutionary ideology. In work groups, training camps, and political seminars, children were repeatedly told about the "glorious revolution" and taught that they should be loyal to the party, not to their families. A mother who taught the children of cadres in Phnom Penh reported: "The children's ideological training was intensive. Teaching was organized around the party and the gratitude each one owed it."[18] Similarly, Luong Ung, who was sent to a children's camp and training center during DK, recalled that Khmer Rouge cadres incessantly lectured children about their duty to Ângkar and their preeminent role in the revolution: "Your number one duty is to the Angkar. . . . You are the children of the Angkar! In you lies our future. The Angkar knows you are pure in the heart, uncorrupted by evil influences, still able to learn the ways of the Angkar! That is why the Angkar loves you above all else. That is why the Angkar gives you so much power. You are our saviors."[19] In return for such love, care, power, and protection, children were supposed to be totally loyal to their new parent-like patron, Ângkar — obeying orders without hesitation, spying on others, and reporting on the traitorous activities of enemies, even family members.

The indoctrination of cadres and soldiers was similarly geared to creating a relationship of personal dependency with the DK regime. Ângkar was the parent-patron who did good deeds for cadres and soldiers by giving them rank, prestige, food, and guns. In return, Khmer Rouge were expected to loyally support the party organization and to "cut off their hearts" *(dach chett)* from Ângkar's enemies. Such cadres usually came from impoverished backgrounds and would have had few opportunities to rise in status under the old regime. Many were also young, idealistic, and impressionable, searching for social approval and rewards.[20] A friend of Khel's, who was an "old person" during DK, explained that such people often responded to ideological pronouncements that "Ângkar was the one who had done the greatest kindness *(kun)* for them, not their parents . . . so they should do anything for the revolutionary party. If Ângkar pointed out a traitor, they should dare to destroy that person without hesitation, even if the traitor was their mother or father." Many Cambodians told me how cadres and soldiers who had been successfully indoctrinated actually did kill a parent, spouse, sibling, or relative. Although the Khmer Rouge had some success forging a generalized relationship of personal dependency between Ângkar and its soldiers and cadres, the loyalties of many of these individuals remained divided, split between the Party Center and their more proximate patrons. As we shall see, these alternative loyalties were often perceived by the DK regime as a threat to its power, leading them to purge suspect patronage "strings."

In many respects, then, Ângkar was a blend of the old and the new, a Khmer Rouge symbolic juncture at which high-modernist thought, communist ideology, and local knowledge met. On one level, Ângkar epitomized the high-modernist orientation and aspirations of the Khmer Rouge leadership, which used its "enlightened" and "omniscient" vision to centralize control and implement a program of social engineering that entailed major social transformations — including the attack on institutions that had traditionally been a dominant force and a basis for relationships of personal dependency. The "eye of a pineapple" became a metaphor for the Khmer Rouge panopticon, as Ângkar's authority pervaded all domains of life.

At the same time, the force and significance of the term *Ângkar* was in part due to its appropriation of preexisting, ontologically resonant structures of meaning from the very institutions it attempted to destroy. Thus Ângkar became the new parent-patron of people, idealized in traditional kinship discourses of nurturance, protection, caring, and moral debt. Likewise, the depiction of Ângkar as an omniscient centering force, infused with mana-like energies and bringing order and purity to a situation of chaos and contamination played upon local understandings of the potent center, power, patronage, hierarchical encompassment, millenarianism, and Buddhism. The very association of Ângkar with "enlightenment" constituted a key nexus at which Marxist-Leninist notions of class consciousness, a high-modernist concern with vision and legibility, and the Buddhist focus on clear understanding met. While the use of preexisting knowledge no doubt helped to increase the "take" of this prevalent DK symbol, there was nevertheless "interference" in the way Ângkar was understood and invoked. Thus the term seems to have been used differently by the upper echelons of the party, by cadres, and by the masses at different times and places. Upon hearing this strange term for the first time, many Cambodians no doubt performed "bricolage" as they tried to interpret this word in terms of the local structures of meaning available to them.[21] Still, the symbolic referents of Ângkar clearly illustrate that ideological models are always localized, as the Khmer Rouge mixed the new with the old in order to increase the salience, motivational force, and "take" of these palimpsests.

Ultimately, Ângkar was a multivalent symbol signifying, among other things, that the DK regime was the new potent center. Power was effectively concentrated in the Party Center in general and Pol Pot in particular. By 1978, Pol Pot's picture had appeared in communal dining halls, busts and paintings of Pol Pot began to be produced, and he was described in increasingly exalted terms.[22] Vann Nath, the former Tuol Sleng prisoner, told me that, just before the Vietnamese invasion, there were plans to construct a revolutionary monument in Pol Pot's honor:

> Duch ordered four or five of us to design a revolutionary monument commemorating the history of revolutionary struggle led by Pol Pot. The monument consisted of twenty-five or thirty figures and resembled revolutionary monuments in places like Korea and China. Pol Pot stood in the front, the largest figure of all by far. In his left hand, he held a golden scroll symbolizing the constitution, while his right hand was raised upward, symbolizing greatness. One leg strode forward, contributing to the imposing nature of his statue. Behind Pol Pot stood other figures who had participated in the revolutionary insurrection. Peasants were strung about the memorial, [carrying flags and] grasping knives to symbolize the overthrow of feudalism. Further back were all types of soldiers holding B-40 [rocket launchers]. There were close to thirty figures in all, each having a height of approximately eight meters and constructed out of copper or copper and concrete, depending on what the Party Center decided. Four or five of us designed the monument. After we completed the design, it was sent to the Party Center. If they approved it, the monument was to be built on top of Wat Phnom; the temple complex there was to be leveled. But this was just a plan. The monument was never built because the Vietnamese invaded and defeated [the Khmer Rouge].[23]

Such evidence suggests that, given time, a cult of personality might have emerged around Pol Pot as he finished centralizing power and more openly assumed the role of the DK potent center — distant and all-powerful like an ancient Angkorean king, yet firmly guiding the people as he grasped the "wheel of history" *(kang prâvâttesas)*, to use a Buddhist-inspired metaphor that the Khmer Rouge frequently invoked. Before doing so, however, he had to deal with perceived threats to his authority.

ERADICATING "MICROBES"

There were political errors. We recognize there were errors in going too far to the left. We moved too rapidly. We did not think enough about the organization of the state. We emphasized the political consciousness too much and had too little experience in the management of the state. We did not choose our public servants well and lost some control. Each region constituted a small kingdom. They ran their own affairs.

Ieng Sary, in a 1980 interview with Henry Kamm[24]

During the civil war, the Khmer Rouge fought a decentralized campaign, giving regional zone secretaries great latitude in determining military strategy and the speed of reforms. Moreover, as Ieng Sary notes above, these secretaries were able to develop extensive patronage networks and wielded great authority in the areas they controlled. When the Party Center took power at the war's end, then, they were in a somewhat weak position, lacking a central army or administrative apparatus. Pol Pol and his associates immediately set out to consolidate their control.

Many of the initial sociocultural transformations they implemented were designed not only to create an agrarian communist society but also to undermine old bonds that could potentially threaten party rule.[25] By emptying the cities, for example, the Khmer Rouge were able to disband urban patronage networks they believed might subvert the revolution and to keep the "new people" under surveillance. Likewise, the DK policy of executing or imprisoning high-ranking Lon Nol soldiers, government officials, and police officers had the effect of eliminating the political patrons of the old regime. All over the country, Khmer Rouge cadres loyal to Ângkar assumed positions of power. In addition, as noted in the last section, the Party Center undermined and attempted to co-opt the authority of the family, the village, and Buddhism — socioeconomic institutions that had previously been important centers of social life and commanded strong personal loyalties.

Ultimately, however, Pol Pot and the Party Center felt threatened by the power of senior Khmer Rouge cadres, particularly popular zone secretaries like Sao Phim (Eastern Zone), Koy Thuon (Northern Zone), Nhem Ros (Northwestern Zone), and Ney Sarann (Northeastern Zone) and more moderate intellectuals like Hu Nim, Touch Phoeun, and Hou Youn. Over the next few years, the Party Center secured the allegiance of some officials while annihilating others. During this process, Pol Pot and his close associates became increasingly suspicious, fearing betrayal from within the ranks of the party leadership. After real or imagined coups and plots, this suspicion turned into paranoia, fueling massive purges that resulted in the deaths of tens of thousands of "traitorous" Khmer Rouge cadres and military personnel. Meanwhile, the Party Center continued to centralize power in Phnom Penh, though this polity was infused with patronage ties, some of which included family members of the top Khmer Rouge leaders.

While political purges within the Khmer Rouge ranks occurred in the 1960s, not until the early 1970s did such killings begin to take large numbers of lives.[26] After the Lon Nol coup, for example, over one thousand Cambodians who had received training in North Vietnam since the 1950s returned to help fight the Lon Nol regime. The Party Center distrusted these "Hanoi-trained returnees" because of their close ties to Vietnam, and saw to it that most of them were killed over the next few years, particularly after 1972, when their longtime leader, Son Ngoc Minh, died, and in the wake of the "treacherous" Paris Peace Agreement of January 1973, when the Khmer Rouge began to take an anti-Vietnamese stance.[27] Other Khmer Rouge cadres loyal to Sihanouk, sympathetic to the Vietnamese, or overly lenient on the populace were also eliminated during the pre-DK period.[28]

· · ·

As such purges suggest, the Khmer Rouge were not unified when they entered Phnom Penh in April 1975. In response to this factionalized situation, the Pol Pot–led Party Center took a number of steps to consolidate its power in the months following the liberation of Phnom Penh.[29] It is difficult to assign Khmer Rouge leaders to factions, since the divisions were often fluid, people could switch allegiances, and cadres had multiple, cross-cutting connections to one another. Nevertheless, a cadre's background, relationships of personal dependency, history of association, and political tendencies could serve as an important basis for factional affiliation or, in the context of the purges, perceived treason.[30]

Keeping these caveats in mind, we can still speak of a Pol Pot–led faction of "radicals" (Pol Pot, Nuon Chea, Ieng Sary, Von Vet, Ta Mok, Son Sen, Khieu Samphan, Ieng Thirith, Yun Yat, and Ke Pauk) who were linked by their commitment to, or at least a willingness to support, a radical party line that entailed rapid collectivization, extreme independence and self-sufficiency, a willingness to use brutal force to achieve their goals, and an almost xenophobic nationalism. Some of these radicals had studied in Paris together; others had not. Pol Pot's radicals came to dominate the "Party Center" *(mochchhim bâk)* a multivalent term that was in some ways synonymous with Ângkar and suggested a "potent center." While the term *Party Center* loosely referred to the Standing Committee of the CPK Central Committee (Pol Pot, Nuon Chea, Ieng Sary, Sao Phim, Von Vet, Nhem Ros, Ta Mok, Son Sen, and Khieu Samphan), the phrase might also signify Pol Pot himself, the top leaders of the Standing Committee (Pol Pot, Nuon Chea, Ieng Sary, and Von Vet), or the national officeholders on the Central Committee (Pol Pot, Nuon Chea, Von Vet, Ta Mok, Son Sen, and Khieu Samphan).[31]

After the Khmer Rouge victory, the Party Center took a number of steps to solidify its control over the new national government. Pol Pot's associates assumed key posts on the Central Committee, the army, party and military training schools, the security police, and the cabinet.[32] They were therefore in a position to dictate policy throughout the country, though, as we will see, their directives were not always exactly followed. In keeping with their high-modernist orientation, the Party Center centralized and strictly controlled information and communications. Contact between the zones and even government ministries was limited and regulated.

Perhaps the greatest danger to the Party Center came from the zone secretaries, most of whom were longtime revolutionaries who enjoyed autonomy, power, and popularity in the areas under their control. The Party Center responded by transferring three influential regional chiefs — Northern Zone Secretary Koy Thuon, Northeastern Zone Secretary Ney Sarann, and Region 25 Secretary Non Suon — to Phnom Penh, thereby separating them from their longtime bases of power. One of them, Non Suon, later lamented that at this time he "was worried that the Organization did not trust me, because it had taken me away from my base area."[33] Several of the zones were restructured to dilute regional strength.

Finally, the Party Center established the Revolutionary Army of Kampuchea in July 1975, at a ceremony in which "each zone handed over their armed forces to the Central Committee."[34] Headed by Pol Pot, Son Sen, Ta Mok, Ke Pauk, and Siet Chhe, the Revolutionary Army greatly enhanced the military might of the Party Center, though the zone secretaries retained direct control or at least influence over a substantial number of troops. As Pol Pot noted in a December 1976 speech, the army "[increasingly became] the authoritative instrument of the Party," enabling the Party Center to "increase and expand state power. . . . The Party must, in fact, seize power at every level" while eliminating "spies boring from within."[35] Such statements highlight the fact that, despite the Party Center's countermeasures, the regional chiefs retained a great deal of power. In fact, perhaps out of fear of these alternative power bases, the DK regime at times stationed as many as ten regiments of soldiers in Phnom Penh — almost one soldier for each of the twenty thousand people living in the capital.[36]

As it consolidated control, the Party Center rewarded its most loyal regional clients, such as Mok and Pauk, by increasing their influence.[37] While we do not know exactly how the alliance came about between Pol

Pot's faction and these two regional chiefs, they seem to have been linked by a willingness to impose a radical party "line." Moreover, Mok and Pauk were from the simple peasant background favored by Pol Pot's faction. Mok was given control over the most populated parts of the Southwest Zone, including Non Suon's Region 25. As in the past, Mok placed his "string" of relatives in leading positions throughout the military and political administration of the Southwest Zone and purged Region 25 of cadres loyal to Non Suon. Pauk, the military commander of the Northern Zone, replaced Koy Thuon as zone secretary, eventually becoming the head of the newly formed Central Zone. Like Mok, Pauk appointed relatives to important regional administrative posts over the following year.

Ironically, this type of nepotism was a prominent feature of DK political life, despite the party's explicit antifamily line. It was common for high-ranking cadres in Phnom Penh and the zones to place their relatives in key posts. Laurence Picq, for example, has described how Roeun, the wife of Touch Phoeun, the minister of public works, appointed her relatives to numerous posts in the Ministry of Foreign Affairs after she became Ieng Sary's "right hand." Picq recalls, "Feeling her new-found power, [Roeun] installed people from her clan as team leaders" and other coveted positions, such as head cook.[38] Her entire "string" of relatives was purged in early 1977.

As we have seen, Cambodians often place relatives in key positions in their patronage networks because the ties of personal dependency between relatives, particularly core family members, are usually stronger and more reliable than those linking unrelated patrons and clients. The Khmer Rouge explicitly recognized the potential threat posed by such nepotism: "Up to now in the ranks of our Party it has generally been (a case of) family-ism, sibling-ism, relation-ism. This problem is a very dangerous one because it flouts the Party's criteria. If the Party's criteria are flouted, our Party would not be firm, and so the enemy could come in."[39] Nevertheless, the Party Center had difficulty attacking "sibling-ism" because it was rampant on almost all levels of sociopolitical organization, including the Party Center itself, where Pol Pot allies like Ieng Sary, Mok, Pauk, Nuon Chea, and Son Sen placed family members and relatives in important posts.

During the first year of its rule, the Party Center centralized control by promulgating a constitution, holding elections, initiating radical socioeconomic transformations, and developing a Four-Year Plan. Despite such moves, the initial revolutionary optimism of the Party Center was undermined by events, particularly perceived acts of dissent. Several rebellions are thought to have taken place from mid 1975 to mid 1976, though the details are difficult to confirm.[40] In addition to a possible coup attempt in September 1975, bombs, perhaps dropped by aircraft, exploded in the city of Siem Reap on February 25, 1976. While publicly blaming the CIA, the DK regime suspected that Koy Thuon, who maintained a strong influence in the Northern Zone, might have been responsible for the explosions. Thuon was watched carefully thereafter and eventually arrested. By March 30, the Party Center had issued a directive to "smash (people) inside and outside the ranks" in order to "strengthen our state power."[41]

Of even greater concern to the Party Center was a series of grenade explosions and shots fired in Phnom Penh in the early morning of April 8, 1976, near a secret compound where the top party leaders lived.[42] Several members of Division 170, a former Eastern Zone unit, were arrested and, after being interrogated, implicated their superior, Son Sen's deputy chief-of-staff of the national army, Chan Chakrei, as the leader of the rebellion. In the short term, Chakrei's immediate network of followers in Division 170 was blamed for the attack; in the long term, however, the incident cast suspicion on Chakrei's former superior, Eastern Zone Secretary Sao Phim. The events that followed reveal the escalating cycle of purges that was now set in motion. After his arrest on May 19, 1976, Chakrei was interrogated for over four months and eventually forced to "confess" at Tuol Sleng (also known by its code name, S-21), which was opened around this time under the command of Duch, a former schoolteacher who previously had been in charge of security in the Special Zone.

As David Chandler notes in his groundbreaking study of Tuol Sleng, confessions, which were often written and rewritten multiple times, followed a schematic form — usually including sections on the cadre's life, political history, "traitorous plots," and "strings of traitors."[43] While this structure was strongly influenced by the practices of other communist countries, particularly China and Vietnam, Khmer Rouge confessions blended such models with local understandings of sociopolitical relations, including patronage ties. The "string of traitors" list is particularly salient in this regard. During DK, the Party Center viewed alternative political networks as a serious threat to the regime. Whenever "traitors" like Chakrei were uncovered, it was assumed that they were part of a patronage pyramid, stretching up to their patron and their patron's patron and down to their clients and the clients of their clients.

Everyone in such a "string of traitors" came under suspicion and most of these "microbes," contaminated by association, were eliminated. Tuol Sleng confessions remain fixated on uncovering the development and structure of such (real or perceived) networks — tracing out histories of association, detailing interactions between leaders *(me)* and their "grand-children," and describing secret meetings.

In addition to stating that he had plotted to kill the "upper brothers," Chakrei's 849-page confession asserts that Chakrei had links to the Lon Nol regime and had secretly joined an espionage network with ties to the CIA and Vietnam.[44] In addition, Chakrei "revealed" that he had plotted to kill the "upper brothers" and implicated numerous cadres in Division 170 and the Eastern Zone, many of whom were in turn arrested and interrogated. In fact, over 241 members of this "string of traitors" within Division 170 had been arrested by November 1976, including the unit's deputy secretary (Ly Phen) and a staff member (Ros Phuong).

Based on the confessions of Chakrei and other renegades who had been incarcerated, Duch informed Pol Pot that he had gathered evidence that Sao Phim's Eastern Zone contained espionage rings, including a "rubber plantation network." While Sao Phim was in China receiving medical treatment from May to August of 1976, several of his military and civilian officials were arrested. Ly Phen, the Eastern Zone political commissar, was arrested in June, followed by Sao Phim's trusted protégé and secretary of Region 24, Chhouk, in late August. In September, the Party Center chose Seng Hong (Chan), the recently appointed deputy secretary of the Eastern Zone, to take control of Chhouk's former region. Here we find the Party Center initiating one of its signature political maneuvers: slowly purging the ranks of perceived enemy networks and replacing them with Party Center loyalists. Given the confessions emerging from Tuol Sleng, there was little Sao Phim could do to prevent this erosion of his power base, particularly since he was implicated by many of the confessions.

These confessions provided Duch with evidence from which to diagnose the source of the illness that was supposedly rotting the party from within. As more people arrived at Tuol Sleng, the lists of "strings of traitors" grew longer. Tuol Sleng became the engine of the Party Center's paranoia. Pol Pot's faction suspected treason and was provided with corroborating evidence by the confessions that were manufactured at Tuol Sleng. As the amount of "evidence" increased, the Party Center's paranoia grew accordingly.

. . .

Meanwhile, Duch constructed detailed analyses of the interconnections between these strings, culminating in "The Last Plan."[45] Written in 1978, "The Last Plan" attempts to weave together the important networks in a vast conspiracy, ultimately involving an unlikely alliance between the United States, Vietnam, and the Soviet Union that supposedly had attempted repeatedly to overthrow the Party Center and replace it with a rival party — often called the Workers Party of Kampuchea (WPK) — which had been "buried" within the Khmer Rouge ranks for years. "The Last Plan" argues that Chakrei and Chhouk played a crucial role in the process of sabotage by "placing their agents in order to take over the revolutionary power to occupy ranks and functions in the party and administration . . . in sector 23, and division 170."[46] However, it is crucial not to read Duch's 1978 interpretation of events, produced after hostilities with Vietnam were under way, as a factual account of events in 1976. At that time, Duch was using the confessions of people like Chakrei and Chhouk to imagine more limited and rudimentary espionage networks, although they were still purportedly associated with the CIA, Vietnam, and the WPK.

One of these networks was allegedly run by a group of senior Khmer Rouge cadres who, like Prasith, had joined the Khmer Issarak (Free Khmer) resistance to fight against French colonialism (1946–54). These party veterans had a history of early association with the communist Vietnamese, who had helped them found the Khmer People's Revolutionary Party (KPRP) in 1951. Several of these veteran leftists had established the procommunist Pracheachon Party to contest the 1955 and 1958 postindependence elections, and had held high posts on the Khmer Rouge Central Committee at one time or another, though most had been gradually displaced by Pol Pot loyalists. Because of their seniority, popularity, and long history of revolutionary struggle, these Khmer Rouge veterans constituted a potential threat to the Pol Pot faction. As a 1977 Party Center document later recalled, "They had great influence: they just had to say one word and some others inside the country would listen."[47]

The symbolic struggle between these two groups involved in part a dispute about the foundation date of the party and thus implicitly its historical leadership. While many of the veterans favored the 1951 date, Pol Pot's faction began to insist upon using the September 30, 1960 date of the Party Congress at which, according to Pol Pot's 1977 speech, the party line was approved — thereby establishing Pol Pot's central role in the movement's origins and ignoring an important period of Vietnamese communist influence. This dispute was highlighted by two DK publications, the first of which, the September 1976 issue of *Revolutionary Youth,* contained an article on the upcoming twenty-fifth anniversary of the party. The second publication, a special September–October 1976 issue of *Revolutionary Flags,* explained that the anniversary had been changed to September 30, 1960 because Ângkar had decided to "arrange the history of the party into something clean and perfect, in line with our policies of independence and self-mastery"[48] — a statement implying that those in contact with the Vietnamese prior to 1960 had been contaminated. As this dispute unfolded, several party veterans who had been implicated by Chakrei and Chhouk as part of a "buried" WPK Party were arrested, along with members of their "strings."

On September 20, 1976, Ney Sarann (alias Ya), the secretary of the Northeastern Zone, was arrested. He "confessed" to treasonous activities after being whipped and beaten at Tuol Sleng. Over twenty-five years later, shortly before his death, Pol Pot still claimed that "Comrade Ya" was the head of a Vietnamese-backed conspiracy to overthrow him.[49] Keo Meas, a respected party veteran who had been placed under house arrest after returning from posts in Beijing and Hanoi, was sent to Tuol Sleng five days after Ney Sarann. There he argued that "Keo Meas is No Traitor!"[50] and defended the 1951 date despite harsh interrogation. Non Suon (Chey), the former secretary of Region 25 who was effectively serving as the DK minister of agriculture and was closely linked to Ney Sarann and Keo Meas, was arrested on November 1. Soon thereafter, a string of over two hundred people connected to him, including his family members and those of his followers, was purged. After several weeks of torture, Non Suon plaintively confessed, "I am a termite boring from within . . . and wrecking the Party in every way I can. No matter how the Party has educated and nurtured me, I have not abandoned my dark and dirty intentions."[51] "The Last Plan" later argued that these three men were the chiefs of the "Pracheachon Group," which secretly built up the WPK while recruiting a number of longtime revolutionaries into their fold.

• • •

These purges in the second half of 1976 signaled a turning point in DK history, as Pol Pot and his allies became increasingly paranoid. Besides perceived coup attempts and the supposed existence of espionage rings, the Party Center began to hear reports that people in the countryside were suffering under dire conditions. In mid 1976, Pol Pot sent Ieng Thirith, Ieng Sary's wife and the newly appointed DK minister of social affairs, to investigate these rumors. As she later recounted to the journalist Elizabeth Becker, she found numerous problems:

> Conditions there were very queer. . . . In Battambang I saw they [the cadres] made all the people go to the rice fields. The fields were very far away from the villages. The people had no homes and they were all very ill. . . . I know the directives of the Prime Minister [Pol Pot] were that no old people, pregnant women, women nursing babies, or small children were to work in the fields. But I saw everybody in the open rice fields, in the open air and very hot sun, and many were ill with diarrhea and malaria.[52]

Instead of placing responsibility for these conditions on the extreme policies of the Party Center, Ieng Thirith blamed the problems on internal enemies who had infiltrated the ranks of the Northwestern Zone (headed by another veteran revolutionary, Nhem Ros) and intentionally sabotaged the regime's economic plans. From this point on, economic sabotage became an increasingly prevalent theme in Khmer Rouge discourse and the confessions produced at Tuol Sleng. Convinced of the scientific basis of its high-modernist, revolutionary designs, the Party Center was unwilling to acknowledge the possible shortcomings of its "enlightened" political line.

Some senior cadres, however, may have recognized these failures. At various points prior to and after liberation, more moderate Khmer Rouge, like Hou Yuon, Chhouk, Ney Sarann, Hu Nim, and Koy Thuon, are thought to have questioned the Party Center's radical plans to immediately establish cooperatives, evacuate the cities, abolish money, markets, and religion, and execute the leaders of the Lon Nol regime. In particular, Hou Yuon, an argumentative intellectual who reportedly had disagreements with Pol Pot that dated back to their days together in Paris, is said to have vigorously opposed many of these policies. Because of his dissent, Hou Yuon was labeled a revisionist and executed in 1975, shortly after the beginning of DK. Hu Nim's confession suggests that other high-ranking cadres had problems with the Pol Pot faction's radical line, particularly over the acceptance of foreign aid and the use of technology, which were, in Hu Nim's words, considered to be revisionist "concepts opposed to the basic political line of the party, which is independence — self-reliance — mastery."[53]

Regardless of the extent to which such opposition existed, the Party Center perceived it to be real because of the economic failures, comments made in confessions, and possibly some open dissent over policy. The mood of the Party Center continued to darken. The Four-Year Plan, which had been under discussion since July and was formally introduced at a Party Center meeting on August 21, 1976, was never publicly announced or formally implemented. Mao's death, on September 8, further increased the Party Center's apprehension. And on September 20, Pol Pot briefly resigned as prime minister, a move that may have been intended to draw out his enemies. This announcement coincided with the arrests of Ney Sarann and Keo Meas, the increased use of torture at Tuol Sleng, and the dispute about the birth date of the party. A summary report of a September 30 Party Center meeting triumphantly announced that the party had been "scrubbed clean," that there was now "complete agreement" about the party's Four-Year Plan, and that by adopting a "clean and clear base" by "standing on the line of independence-mastery-self-reliance," the country would have "a very bright future, shining and clear."[54] Nevertheless, the report also cautioned that there were "shortcomings" in the "implementation of the Party line" and the "consciousness of some of our cadres" and that "traitorous networks" and "class enemies" wanted to subvert the revolution and "seize state power"; it concluded with an ominous warning that foreshadowed the December 1976 "microbes" speech: "Let there be no holes at all for the enemy to worm his way into the insides of our Party."

Clearly, the growing wariness of the Party Center must be understood in the context of the historical events delineated above. To fully comprehend the Party Center's paranoia, however, we must also take account of the sociocultural context in which it took root. Earlier I suggested that Cambodian patronage relationships are frequently characterized by mistrust and instability. Imbued with ontological resonance, these relationships of personal dependency are continually being negotiated; power, in turn, is viewed as transient, ebbing and flowing in the course of life. Patrons thus act in a context of uncertainty, often fearing that a disloyal client will switch allegiance or attempt to seize their power.

These patterns were exacerbated during DK, when the Party Center, an extremely secretive organization, attempted to consolidate its control and eliminate all opposition. Everywhere they looked, Pol Pot and his allies began to see signs of betrayal and subversion, ranging from unexplained explosions to economic failures. Tuol Sleng became the fulcrum of their fear, producing confessions that objectified Pol Pot's paranoia about the perfidy of his followers.[55] Guilty by the very fact that the "all-knowing" Ângkar had arrested them, these "traitors" were forced to confess their treason. Confessions were structured to expose plots and "strings of traitors," and entire patron-client pyramids became suspect when a high-ranking patron was suddenly purged. Thus most of Hu Nim's confession is concerned with elucidating plots to "gather forces" to "seize power to rule Kampuchea" and with delineating the membership of these traitorous strings. As more people were brought to Tuol Sleng, their confessions produced additional evidence of subversion, further objectifying Pol Pot's paranoid fantasies and fueling the lethal spiral of action and reaction: mistrust led to arrests, arrests to confessions, confessions to increased suspicion and more arrests. The result was escalating paranoia, terror, and mass death.

· · ·

This process of "genocidal schismogenesis"[56] was further fueled by a dangerous fusion of high-modernist, Marxist-Leninist, Maoist, and Buddhist thought. An article in the September–October 1976 special issue of *Revolutionary Flags*, entitled "Sharpen the Consciousness of the Proletarian Class to be as Keen and Strong as Possible," is revealing in this regard. Probably written by Pol Pot or Nuon Chea, the piece was influenced by Mao's doctrine of permanent revolution, a notion that Pol Pot praised in his September 18, 1976 eulogy for Mao.[57] Like Mao's speech "On the Correct Handling of Contradictions among the People," the tract argues that class struggle is a continual process. To overcome the "life-and-death contradictions" that still plagued Kampuchea, cadres and the masses alike needed to "continually [struggle] to destroy and extirpate the traits specific to the capitalist class and the traits specific to the various oppressing classes."[58] The party provided several mechanisms to help the people "continually struggle" to "build" their political consciousness, including political education, criticism and self-criticism meetings, and work assignments. Even party members, cadres, and soldiers were expected to enthusiastically perform basic labor (farming, construction work, and cleaning), like the masses, to ensure that they didn't become "a separate [class] layer" corrupted by capitalist tendencies such as individualism and the desire for private property.[59]

   This understanding of the lability of political consciousness directly paralleled Cambodian conceptions of thought as transient and difficult to discern, particularly Buddhist notions of impermanence and change.

Sophea Mouth has argued that the Khmer Rouge theory of dialectical materialism *(sâmapheareah bâdechchâsâmobbat)* was a distinct blend of Marxist-Leninist and Buddhist ideas, as suggested by the fact that their translation of this theoretical concept used the word for "dependent origination" *(bâdechchâsâmobbat)*.[60] The *Revolutionary Flags* piece concludes with a discussion of the four laws of dialectical materialism, the first of which is the proposition that "everything is interrelated." Drawing directly on the Buddhist principle of dependent origination, this law argues that "all things always have an influence on one another."[61] In the Khmer Rouge world, this doctrine takes a paranoid twist, since any action may be interpreted as a sign of betrayal, even harming a water buffalo: "If it was done, why? Was it intentional, or was it to oppose the cooperative. . . . The cowherd, what composition is he, what class stand, what political stand, which milieu is his stand in contact with? . . . We follow up."[62] Even more ominous is the arrest of a cadre or suspected counterrevolutionary. No one becomes a spy alone; each person is interrelated to others and must therefore be part of a string of traitors "buried in the revolutionary ranks."

The second law, "Everything undergoes change" (which the article discusses in conjunction with the third law, "Everything undergoes change from quantity to quality"), is also directly adapted from Buddhism, playing upon the doctrine of impermanence *(anicca)*. For the Khmer Rouge, nothing remains "quiet" and "immobile," even the minds of cadres: "If we speak of the personnel in the party, they too are changing. A large fraction have evolved into solid, strong progressives. Another number has evolved not up to the movement and opposed the movement, betrayed the revolution."[63] Like everything else, one's consciousness "always changes," sometimes "progressing" and other times "regressing" into treachery. To prevent traitors from damaging the revolution, it was necessary for the party leadership to remain "wary," carefully "monitoring" the minds and actions of people and "immediately eliminating" those who had "regressed" into something "bad." Here we find an ideological warrant for paranoia, as anyone, even a longtime associate, follower, or ally, might suddenly change and degenerate into an enemy. Even as such traitors were being discovered, new networks were in the making.

These first three laws help generate the fourth law of dialectical materialism, "Everything has contradictions," which, echoing Maoist themes in earlier sections of the tract, holds that things exist in a "permanent state of contradiction." Within DK, there existed ongoing class contradictions and contradictions with invidious external forces, such as imperialism and espionage rings. Human beings contained contradictory elements as well, including contradictory tendencies toward individualism and collectivism. Since everything changes, people progress or regress toward one of these two poles. When a string of "regressive" people gathers in an office or party circle, the severity of the contradiction increases accordingly.[64] Sometimes these "internal contradictions" can be "resolved" by "continuous education."[65] In more serious cases, "life-and-death" or "anti-party contradictions" that are "boring into the revolution . . . cannot be corrected" and must therefore be eliminated.

The Party Center "line" provided the key means of ensuring the demise of these enemies. By taking secrecy "as the base," the line allowed the party to "defend our forces; enemies fail to strike us." Imbued with a high-modernist confidence in the "science of Marxism-Leninism," the Party Center used the laws of dialectical materialism to correctly "monitor," "analyze," and "resolve" the contradictions in society.[66] Those who grasped the "correct view and standpoint" of the "party line" would progress; those who failed to do so would be "purified" through education or death. The paradox, of course, was that only the "enlightened" Party Center knew the correct line. Any problems, dissent, or deviation from this line was, by definition, a sign of a regressive contradiction that needed to be dealt with immediately. These Khmer Rouge ideological palimpsests — fusing high-modernist thought, Maoism, Marxist-Leninism, and ontologically resonant local understandings about impermanence and instability — had the potential to generate considerable uncertainty and even paranoia. For the Khmer Rouge, the mind was capricious. Everyone's political consciousness contained contradictions. Minds changed. People were interrelated. This meant that longtime comrades sometimes "regressed" into enemies whose interconnections suddenly became "strings of traitors."

By the end of 1976, this paranoia was being pushed to its extreme by economic failures, possible dissent, and (real or imagined) plots and coups. Over 1,200 people were arrested and sent to Tuol Sleng during the second half of 1976, and a purge of the Ministry of Foreign Affairs was underway.[67] Laurence Picq, a Frenchwoman who was married to one of Ieng Sary's close associates and who worked as a translator in the Ministry of Foreign Affairs, recalled that everything one said or did became political at this time:

The scope and number of accusations of plots against Angkar was dizzying. The whole family of the accused — brothers, sisters, cousins, nephews, wives, children (even newborns) — were charged with the same crime. In addition, all who had approached these traitors, from near or afar, were considered part of the networks organized by the accused. To have been at a meal or a meeting or even to have smiled while shaking hands was proof of complicity. . . . Angkar congratulated itself on its understanding, audacity, and will to wipe out all the traitors for the good of the people. This provoked laudatory comments from the combatants: "Angkar must truly love the people to turn in cadres it had patiently trained over the years. Long live Angkar, which protects us against foreign plots."[68]

At the ministry, longtime revolutionaries like Sean An, the ambassador to Vietnam, disappeared, only to be condemned by their former colleagues, who lauded Ângkar's "clearheadedness" and attempted to outdo one another in repeating party slogans. Picq's translations were closely examined and critiqued for their subversive connotations. Like many cadres in Phnom Penh and people throughout the country, she lived in terror and feared for her life.

It was in this atmosphere that Pol Pot delivered his December 20, 1976 "microbes" speech. Although the speech describes the glorious achievements of the revolution, it is extremely dark and paranoid in tone. From the onset, Pol Pot bemoans the hidden "sickness inside the Party," warning that unless the "treacherous elements" are located and expelled, these "ugly microbes" could do "real damage" and "rot us from within."[69] In retrospect, 1976 was a year in which the party had "smashed" various "strings of traitors that . . . had been organized secretly during the people's revolution. . . . Many microbes emerged. Many networks came into view." Clearly, the speech references the arrests of Chakrei, Chhouk, and the Pracheachon group, among others. These arrests had produced "documents" (the Tuol Sleng confessions of these "traitors") revealing that "treacherous, secret elements [still seem to be] buried inside the Party" and that "enemies have tried to defeat us using every possible method."[70]

Like the *Revolutionary Flags* tract, the "microbes" speech asserts that these anti-party "contradictions" arose because of deficient political consciousness and failure to follow the party line. Economic problems were blamed on "hidden enemies" who half-heartedly followed party directives and mistreated the people. Nevertheless, there were a number of steps that could be taken to purify the DK regime. As always, secrecy remained crucial "to safeguard the Party and the Party leadership organization." A new generation of pure cadres would be trained. Meanwhile, the party would initiate a process of "verification," carefully examining the backgrounds of both new recruits and old cadres and soldiers at all levels, remaining "wary of life-histories which are entangled with those of our enemies."[71] The party also needed to consolidate its control, "[seizing] power at every level," particularly in the cooperatives and those areas in which enemy networks were "deeply buried." Ultimately, however, the success of the revolution depended on people obeying and reshaping their minds in accordance with the party line: "If we conform to the line of 'struggle and build' according to the correct line laid down by the party, most people will make progress, following the party. But if we fail to conform to the party's correct line, we will stumble and fall into many contradictions. Enemies will [then] seize the occasion to trap us, and to embed themselves in our ranks."[72] Those who were unable or unwilling to conform to the "correct" party line would inevitably "evolve" into antagonistic contradictions, joining the ranks of the hidden microbes against whom the party was already waging a vicious battle.

· · ·

At the beginning of 1977, the Party Center turned against a group of intellectuals who were loosely united by their advocacy of greater democracy — often along the lines of the mass democracy of the Cultural Revolution — and their criticism, albeit usually muted, of the more extreme parts of the Pol Pot faction's radical policies. Many of these cadres, who have been called the "intellectuals," the "cultural revolution group," or the "democracy advocates,"[73] had been teachers and often continued to exert a strong influence within the party. Some, like Hu Nim and Touch Phoeun, had studied with or just after Pol Pot in France or had been active in the Khmer-Chinese Friendship Association during the 1960s. Perhaps the most powerful of these moderate intellectuals, Commerce Secretary Koy Thuon (Khuon), was arrested on January 25, 1977, followed by Touch Phoeun (Phim), the minister of public works, the next day. Two other senior intellectuals, Siet Chhe (Tum), who had taken Chakrei's position in the military, and Minister of Information Hu Nim (Phoas) were sent to Tuol Sleng in April. Deputy Information Minister Tiv Ol (Som), a former teacher who was linked to Koy Thuon and Hu Nim, was incarcerated on June 6. In each of these cases, "strings of traitors" associated with these men were purged en masse.

Koy Thuon, a popular former teacher who had followers in the Ministry of Commerce, the army, and the Northern Zone and strong ties to other senior party figures, was viewed as a particularly strong threat by the Party Center. "The Last Plan" claimed that wherever "traitors" like Koy Thuon went, they "set up their network in clumps," replacing good cadres and soldiers with "bad elements" or converting weak cadres "into traitors" so that their insidious networks could "take power."[74] From February to April 1977, Koy Thuon was interrogated over forty-five times at Tuol Sleng, producing more than six hundred pages of written materials. His confession, given under torture, recounted a "history of treasonous activities" with the CIA and listed hundreds of people in a "string of traitors" that implicated other intellectuals and former followers in the Northern Zone, the army, and the Commerce Ministry.[75] It contained dozens of hand-drawn, columned tables that methodically listed the name, location, position, and miscellaneous information for every person in these strings, including his connections in Region 41.

While it is difficult to know if and how such patronage networks functioned, we can piece together some of the images that drove the Party Center's fears by analyzing these confessions and other Tuol Sleng and party documents. Koy Thuon's supposed treachery, for example, is suggested by his perceived dissent, corrupt activities, and tendency toward individualism. "The Last Plan" condemns Khuon for creating "an atmosphere of pacifism, luxury and excitement entertained by arts, girls, reception and festivities" in the Northern Zone. His womanizing, which may have culminated in the death of a lover's husband, is described in detail in Hu Nim's confession.[76]

Hu Nim's confession also devotes a great deal of space to describing Koy Thuon's hidden network and his own putative links to Koy Thuon, who is depicted as Hu Nim's boss. (It is important to keep in mind that such assertions, like those made in other Khmer Rouge confessions, are a blend of truth, partial truth, and fabrication.) The two men's history of association supposedly dated back to the 1966 elections, when Sreng (Cho Chhan), a follower of Koy Thuon who was based in the Northern Zone district of Prey Totung, helped Hu Nim retain his National Assembly seat. At that time, the confession states, Sreng confided to Hu Nim that he was a member of Koy Thuon's CIA network. Sreng later arranged for Hu Nim and Koy Thuon to meet, whereupon the two men supposedly realized that they were part of the same CIA network and agreed to "gather as many forces as possible in order to overthrow the Communist Party of Kampuchea and take over state power in Kampuchea."[77] Thereafter, Hu

Nim continued to have secret meetings with Koy Thuon or his associate, Tiv Ol, whose job was to "educate intellectuals."

In 1970, Koy Thuon supposedly invited Hu Nim to join his clandestine Workers' Party, which was run by Koy Thuon (secretary) and two clients, Doeun (deputy secretary) and Sreng (member of the Standing Committee). Koy Thuon purportedly explained that after Sihanouk's overthrow, the power of the "Workers' Party" in "the Northern Zone had further expanded, and his traitorous forces in both the administration and the army had expanded also."[78] Hu Nim agreed to join and in the years that followed "completely accepted Khuon's leadership" while continuing to secretly build up forces to oppose the CPK and eventually "seize power." Prior to the revolution, Hu Nim met or interacted with other important cadres who were supposedly in league with Koy Thuon, including Ney Sarann, Chhouk, Sreng, Tiv Ol, Chakrei, Tauch Phoeun, and On. Most of these cadres are named in Koy Thuon's confession and listed as his WPK co-conspirators in "The Last Plan."

When Koy Thuon was transferred to Phnom Penh just after liberation, he continued to have influence in the Northern Zone and various government ministries. Structured to objectify the Party Center's fears about "strings of traitors," Hu Nim's confession describes in detail how Koy Thuon set up his network "in clumps," as he "gathered forces" to "seize power." Toward the end of 1975, Koy Thuon allegedly told Hu Nim,

> We are functioning well because since the liberation the three Ministries of Commerce, Public Works, and Information are connected to one another in one network, and [Euan] and [Soeun's] troops are guarding the northern section of Phnom Penh next to us. [Euan's] division guarding the Information (Ministry) includes a regiment commanded by friend Chet. And along with [Euan's] brigade there is also Suong's. These two brigades are forces that I formed myself. During the liberation of Phnom Penh they were very powerful too. Chhoeun, Mon, Kun, and Sok are already in my Ministry. Doeun is in the Organization's Office and so is Phouk Chhay. In the North, Sreng is helping to run the Zone in my place. Even though Pauk is Secretary of the Zone, I control everything because I have all the Regional Committees. . . . As for the Eastern Zone and the Northwest Zone, I have already met brother Phim and brother Nhim, who have agreed to gather forces.[79]

All of the people named in this passage had been or would be purged, many because of their close links to Koy Thuon. Euan (Sbauv Him) and Soeun (Chea Nuon) were the secretaries of Divisions 310 and 450, respectively, former Northern Zone troops that had been transferred to

Phnom Penh. Hu Nim's confession describes them as being "very slack," since they allowed suspect ministries to carry out their treacherous affairs.

In fact, Euan was born in Romeas, a village located a few kilometers south of Banyan that had long been sympathetic to the Khmer Rouge movement. One veteran revolutionary from Romeas told me that, prior to the civil war, Koy Thuon used to come to the village a couple of times each year, sometimes staying as long as two weeks:

> Koy Thuon was very modest, polite, and honest. Despite his status, he didn't mind living with the peasant class. He wanted us to join the revolution with him and spent a great deal of time giving us instruction. He tried to explain the origins of our poverty, telling us that, as members of the peasant class, we had to learn how to struggle to free ourselves, to move out from under the oppression of the capitalist class. We would become our own masters. Some villagers didn't really get what he was saying, but others, particularly students, understood some of it and followed him into the jungle. Many of them, like Euan, Sey, Saem, Chen, and Hean, later became high-ranking cadres. They were all relatives or friends. Eaun and Saem, for example, were birth siblings. Sey was Euan's cousin and the two had studied together at the temple. Hean and Chen had grown up with them in the village. They all knew each other. But when Koy Thuon was accused of being a traitor, the entire group from Romeas was arrested and later executed, along with their wives and children. Euan and Sey each had a wife and three children. . . . They were all killed, annihilated so that none of the traitors' seed would survive.

Having been "formed" by Koy Thuon, the allegiance and consciousness of such men, their troops, their associates, and even their families became suspect and all were targeted for destruction.

Hu Nim's confession suggests that Koy Thuon continued to "set up his network in clumps" in Phnom Penh, loading the Commerce Ministry with clients, including his deputy Doeun (Suas Va Si), a Northern Zone official and former student. Likewise, Hu Nim describes how Koy Thuon used the slack security to make contact with and place Northern Zone cadres in offices like the Ministry of Information. The Ministry of Information and the Ministry of Public Works, in turn, were closely linked because the ministers, Hu Nim and Tauch Phoeun (Phin), had worked closely together prior to DK (like Koy Thuon and Doeun).[80] Tauch Phoeun supposedly acknowledged to Hu Nim that he had "frequent meetings" with Koy Thuon. These ministers are repeatedly portrayed as corrupting the minds of cadres with whom they had contact both within and outside their ministries.

During his meeting with Hu Nim, Koy Thuon supposedly claimed that he continued to exert strong influence in the Northern Zone through his longtime subordinate and deputy minister of the zone, Sreng, who also had strong ties to Region 41, the home of both Hu Nim and Hou Yuon. Along with Doeun, Sreng was a key member of what Hu Nim sometimes calls "the Khuon-Doeun-Sreng group of the Northern Zone committee." When Koy Thuon was transferred to the Commerce Ministry, Sreng continued to serve as the deputy zone secretary under Pauk, Koy Thuon's rival, who was known for his ruthlessness and his willingness to implement more extreme policies than Koy Thuon would. Pauk quickly moved to undercut Koy Thuon's power, replacing many cadres loyal to Koy Thuon with his own string of followers, particularly in Region 42, where Pauk's wife, nephews, cousins, and in-laws were given top administrative and security posts.[81] Despite this transformation of the Northern Zone political structure, Duch and the Party Center appear to have continued to feel threatened by Koy Thuon's connections in the Northern Zone, particularly in the regional committees.

At the end of his confession, Hu Nim recounts how "comrade Kuoy," a brother-in-law of Nuon Chea who had likely been placed in Hu Nim's ministry to keep an eye on things, informed him that Koy Thuon's entire network had "been arrested by the Organization" while Hu Nim was away in "the West and the Northwest"[82] — a purge that was soon to extend down to Region 41, where many Banyan villagers were living. Of the 1,566 people who were imprisoned at Tuol Sleng between mid February and mid April of 1977, 240 were Commerce Ministry officials, 112 civilians were cadres from the Northern Zone, and almost 400 were Northern Zone military personnel.[83]

Sreng and Doeun were arrested within a week of each other in mid-February 1977. Like Koy Thuon, Sreng eventually produced a confession hundreds of pages long that detailed his patronage ties.[84] His confession is striking for the unusual number of "short-essay" reports he composed tracing his history of contact with members of the Northern Zone network. These reports included some of the following headings: "Please Allow Me to Report about the Contact Euan and I Had while Working to Betray the Party," "Please Allow Me to Report about the Events that Took Place in Siem Reap on February 25, 1976," "The Strings Dispatched to Form CIA Networks in the Military and in the Base of the Northern Zone and Region 106," and "About the Traitorous Activities inside the Northern Zone at Present." The last two reports provide brief narrative summaries of the background, treacherous activities, and patronage connections of dozens of Northern Zone personnel from all administrative levels of Regions 41, 42, 43, and 106. In Region 41, Sreng named, among other cadres and soldiers, the regional secretary, Tang, his deputy and the head of Kompong Siem district, Seuan, and Krauch, the chief of Krala subdistrict, where a number of Banyan villagers resided. Sreng's confession alleges that Seuan ("a member of my string since 1968") had been "building traitorous forces in large numbers in the local government" and lists several of his followers, including Krauch. Krauch, in turn, is accused of supporting local bandits, destroying the rice crop, being slow to implement collective eating, and hiding high-ranking officials from the old regime. The Party Center methodically destroyed most of the Northern Zone personnel named in Koy Thuon and Sreng's confessions.

By May, Euan and Soeun had been sent to Tuol Sleng, where Euan defiantly proclaimed his innocence:

> In my nineteen years of revolutionary life, I have fulfilled assignments as a Communist in which I was ready to sacrifice . . . my life for the cause of the liberation of my class and my nation. Under the Party's leadership I have repeatedly refashioned *[kay pray]* myself. . . . I have nothing to hide from the Party. I have therefore had no thoughts of carrying out a coup d'état against the Party. I find this question preposterous because the thought has never occurred to me. . . . However, it's too late now. I'm shackled in S-21.[85]

Regardless of such protestations, the top officials and hundreds of other soldiers from Euan and Soeun's divisions were purged, resulting in over three hundred confessions and a 1,178-page Tuol Sleng document that traces the interconnections among the Division 310 personnel.[86] These arrests were accompanied by the outright execution of tens of thousands of lower-level cadres, soldiers, and civilians from the Northern Zone whose allegiance to the Party Center was suspect. Top Northern Zone cadres, including the heads or deputies of the zone rubber plantation, agricultural office, transport service, hospital, industry committee, and commerce committee, were arrested and most sent to Tuol Sleng.[87] The secretaries of Regions 41, 42, 43, and 106 were eventually purged, along with many of their followers.

• • •

These events foreshadowed what was to occur in Region 41 and other parts of the new Central Zone. In April or May of 1977, the Party Center began replacing high-ranking cadres linked to Koy Thuon and Sreng with cadres, usually from the Southwest Zone, who were thought to be loyal to the Center. Seuan, Neari's relative who was the head of Kompong Siem district and was implicated in Sreng's confession, and his entire family were executed at this time. Grandmother Yit assumed Seuan's position and began a purge of Seuan's subordinates. Prior to his arrest one month after the Southwest Zone cadre arrived in Kompong Siem, Chi, a subdistrict chief who had been appointed by Seuan, attended a meeting in which Grandmother Yit told local officials that "the cadres who have been working in this area are part of a string of traitors and must be cleaned up." Soon afterward, Chi and several other subdistrict chiefs, most likely including Krauch, Rom's predecessor, were arrested one by one after being sent to help supervise work in a large agricultural project in a nearby district. They were all interrogated after being jailed. Chi recalled that his captors "looked like they were really angry at me. One of them said, 'You are part of a traitorous string. We have already killed your boss and his entire line of traitors.' When I asked why I was a traitor, they didn't respond. I was beaten so severely that I later coughed up blood." To this day, Chi remains unsure why he was later released, while other district and subdistrict chiefs in the prison were killed. The Region 41 purge included the execution or replacement of cadres who had been appointed by Seuan and Sreng, down to the level of village head. The minutes of a July 15, 1977 conference of the Northern Zone explained that these "key personnel" were "reactionaries" who could not be allowed to "continue in their positions."[88]

As in other parts of Cambodia, the conditions for civilians living in the Central Zone became much more difficult. The threat of execution increased dramatically. Since "microbes" existed within the ranks of the cadres and the people living under their control, orders to exterminate civilian "enemies" were sent down to the local level. Teap, a cadre who worked at Rom's subdistrict office, described a letter the office had received from Grandmother Yit's district headquarters in mid 1977: "The letter instructed us to smash internal enemies—Chams, Vietnamese, capitalists, former Lon Nol workers, intellectuals, and CIA agents." Similarly, a newly appointed village head recounted how, during meetings at the subdistrict office, cadres were told that there was "a plan to seek out former soldiers, teachers, doctors, and civil servants from the old regime. They conducted this research and took many people away to be killed." In some cases, the eradication of "microbes" was likened to a public health decision. Teeda Mam, a "new person" who was living in the Chomkar Loe district of Region 41 at this time, recalled, "Leaders justified destruction of 'diseased elements' of the old society. . . . We were told repeatedly that in order to save the country, it was essential to destroy all the contaminated parts. . . . It was essential to cut deep, even to destroy a few good people rather than chance one 'diseased' person escaping eradication."[89]

In order to expedite this "eradication," the Khmer Rouge created a rudimentary but efficient bureaucracy of death. Village heads were required to record the former occupation and family background of everyone living under their jurisdiction. A copy of the book in which they wrote this information was kept at the subdistrict office. Thus, when Pauk ordered Reap to "clean up" parts of Regions 43 and 41, Reap's troops had easy access to a list of suspected "diseased elements" ("new people," reactionaries, and certain ethnic minorities). Reap's troops first killed people locally and then, perhaps to increase efficiency, trucked victims to the Phnom Bros extermination center. Chlat recalled that in August 1977 his village head suddenly announced that a number of villagers — primarily "new people" — were being sent to live in a "new village":

> First we heard that trucks had been coming to take people from neighboring cooperatives to a "new village." Rumors spread that the people were taken to be killed. The trucks arrived at my village without warning. No one had been informed the day before. People began to be taken away at noon. You could see that it was primarily 1975 people, particularly those who were lazy or unable to work hard, who were ordered to go to the "new village." . . . When [my elder brother] Sruon's name wasn't called out — he had been sick and unable to work much lately, so we were worried — he couldn't believe his good fortune. He kept telling me and my father, "I'm really lucky. I must have done good deeds in the past to escape death, because those people are not going to a 'new place,' they're going to be killed and discarded."
>
> Sruon's name still hadn't been called by 8:00 that evening. He had just finished saying, "I'm out of danger. I'm not going to die," when Sieng, the village head, tapped on our door and told Sruon, "Gather your things. The trucks are going to take you to a new village." Sruon stopped speaking and slowly sat down on the bed, terrified, thinking about what he suspected was going to happen to his family. Finally, he said, "So my name is on the list, too." Someone, I suspect it might have been a distant relative of mine who spied for the Khmer Rouge, must have gotten them to replace his name with that of my brother at the last moment. Sruon instructed his wife and children to get ready to go. He told me, "Take care of father and our siblings. As for me, don't believe that they are taking me to a new place.

There isn't one. They are taking us to be killed." Everything was still; no one spoke. All you could hear was the platter of the rain.

The people whose names were called were ordered to gather at a nearby temple. Sruon picked up his youngest child, protecting him from the rain and mud, and took his family there. It was getting late, so the Khmer Rouge ordered everyone to sleep in the temple that night. Guards prevented the people from leaving the premises. Children were crying from hunger because they weren't given food. The next day, at first light, the Khmer Rouge loaded everyone on the trucks and drove off. My brother and his entire family were executed at Phnom Bros. . . . A few days later, clothes were distributed to people in our village. They were the garments of the people who had been loaded into the trucks. I saw them give out my brother's clothes.

Upon arriving at Phnom Bros, Sruon and thousands of other Cambodians were lined up and killed by a blow to the back of the head that was administered by Reap's soldiers. Other extermination centers were in operation throughout Cambodia.

The increase in civilian executions was accompanied by a rise in paranoia and fear. No one could be sure if or for how long he or she would live. Haing Ngor explained, "The terror was always there, deep in our hearts. In the late afternoon, wondering whether the soldiers would choose us as their victims. . . . [At night] lying awake and wondering whether we would see the dawn. Waking up the next day and wondering whether it would be our last."[90] People lived in constant fear of being reported to the authorities by neighbors, fellow workers, or the spies who crept around the village at night listening for subversive talk. Most interpersonal relations were pervaded by distrust, sometimes to the point that parents were afraid to speak in front of their indoctrinated children. Remembering the paranoia in Region 41 at this time, Vong, the Banyan villager who was arrested for stealing two potatoes, recalled the saying, "Ângkar [has] the eyes of a pineapple." He explained, "Everyone was being watched. If you did something, it would be discovered." Such paranoia took a great psychological toll on people, as Teeda Mam has noted: "Suspicion. Distrust. Gut-twisting terror. Each person clutched his thoughts more tightly to himself. Everyone worked harder. We dared not complain. . . . Like walking dead men, we waited our turns in mute silence. Any person or event out of the ordinary filled us with panic."[91]

As this passage indicates, cadres held enormous power over the terrified populace. In fact, Ben Kiernan has suggested that the DK regime "probably exerted more power over its citizens than any state in world history. It controlled and directed their public and private lives more closely than government had ever done."[92] Imbued with a high-modernist authoritarian spirit, the state regulated what and how much people ate, when and where they worked, and even what they should think. Most frightening of all, Ângkar determined who lived and who died. Soldiers and cadres like Grandmother Yit, Rom, Reap, and Boan were the local embodiments of state power and were described accordingly by the populace — as having "despotic power" (amnach phdach kar), "hard power," "potent saliva," and the "rights of power" (setthi amnach). One Banyan villager, who was an "old person" during DK, told me that the Southwest Zone cadres had "hard power. They were strict and dared to kill people. If they told us to do something, we had to do it immediately. That's hard power! . . . I was afraid to even look at a cadre like Phat." He added that such cadres "held despotic power over the people. They were the law and could do as they pleased. We didn't have the right to protest. If anyone spoke out against them, that person would disappear."

Although cadres held power over the populace, they too feared for their lives. Thus Boan could wield enormous control over the civilians living under his jurisdiction, yet end up being executed after coming under suspicion. Like other cadres I spoke with, the man who replaced Boan said that he too was constantly afraid of being purged and was always very careful about what he said around other village heads and the Southwest Zone cadres. Recalling how he was jailed with a Khmer Rouge cadre who had been a longtime revolutionary, Vann Nath, the former Tuol Sleng prisoner, commented, "When he was at his cooperative, he acted like a king. No one dared to look at his face. But now he was shackled by the leg, looking like a monkey. The revolution was always changing [people's fortunes] like this."

• • •

The same could be said of Reap. At one time given power and responsibility by Pauk, who sometimes sent him to arrest suspect cadres, Reap unexpectedly found many members of his faction arrested and himself under suspicion. It was at this point in September 1977 that Reap and some other officers attempted to free their associates and start a revolt by detonating explosives at a munitions warehouse near the Kompong Cham jail. The rebellion failed to materialize, however, and Pauk quickly arrested Reap and his co-conspirators. After being tortured at Tuol Sleng, Reap "confessed" his history of association and plotting with such Northern Zone "traitors" as Koy Thuon, Hu Nim, Sreng, and Euan.[93]

Reap's confession, the importance of which was indicated by the fact that it was carefully typed and summarized in detail, provides insight into the Party Center's imagining of the treachery of Koy Thuon's Northern Zone network. In 1965, at the age of twenty-one, Reap joined the revolution in his native Stoeng Trang district of Kompong Cham. He worked as a messenger and member of a local Khmer Rouge militia until 1970, when he was promoted to the position of deputy of the district militia in Stoeng Trang. At this point, Reap's confession asserts the beginnings of his alleged perfidy, describing how Reap's superior, Toan, "pulled me into betraying the revolution. All the way back in January 1971, he began to instruct me, saying, 'Comrade Reap, you have worked in the revolution for a long time, but you are only a militia guard. Meanwhile, other people who have recently joined the revolution have risen to be subdistrict chiefs and been given new clothes and watches.' "

Toan supposedly began taking Reap to meet Sat, the secretary of Stoeng Trang district, who gradually "pulled me in each time we met." Within a month, Reap had been transformed into a "CIA agent."

In February 1972 . . . Elder Toan called me to come meet with Sat and himself at the district office of Stoeng Trang. When I arrived, Sat and [his deputy] Sim began instructing me on how to join the CIA and fight against the Revolutionary Ângkar. . . . Sat told me, "The big bosses [me] are Ya [Ney Sarann], the secretary of the Northeastern Zone and leader of the group, Khuon [Koy Thuon], the secretary of the Northern Zone who is [Ya's] deputy, and Hou Yuon, who is the group's standing member." But at that time, I had never heard of these three people. Sat went on to say that in the Northern Zone there was also Euan (a member of the Northern Zone committee), Sreng (secretary of Region 30), Hun (secretary of Region 31), Lean (secretary of Kompong Siem district), and Sat himself. . . . Sat told me about this string and I was content to follow.

At that time, which was 8:00 in the morning, Sat began preparing me to join the CIA [with the help of Elder Toan and Sim]. . . . Sat instructed me on how to make my heart determined to serve the CIA and how to secretly hide myself in the revolutionary ranks and be loyal to our secret group without fail. After I made these vows, Sat went on to instruct me about the duties of a CIA agent . . . which are as follows: (1) to subvert the policies of the Revolutionary Ângkar, in matters big and small . . . (2) to obstruct the progress of the revolution and the plans of the revolutionary organization . . . (3) to hide oneself inside the revolution . . . [while] serving the CIA, (4) to maintain the utmost secrecy and not to divulge [that you are CIA or] who the leaders are to anyone even if you are detained . . . and (5) to work hard to build up traitorous forces, looking for whichever forces have hesitations about the Revolutionary Organization, and to be careful about revealing our affairs, knowing who to pull in . . . so that our plans aren't

ruined. After explaining these duties of a CIA agent, Sat dispatched me to
go begin to carry out these activities [in my local district] with Elder Toan.

This passage exemplifies the Party Center's paranoia. Revolutionary consciousness was continuously changing, for better or for worse, in accordance with the situational influences to which a person was exposed. As
the laws of dialectical materialism held, everything was interrelated,
everything changed, and everything contained contradictions. Here we
find Reap's mind being "pulled" in a regressive direction by corrupt
cadres who succeed in transforming him into a CIA agent whose duty is
to "build up forces" by converting other "hesitant" people. In many
ways, these "hidden networks" were the shadow of the revolution, insid-
iously mirroring the party's use of secrecy, its attempt to transform the
revolutionary consciousness of recruits, its economic failures, and its
strategy of "gathering forces" to "seize power."

Much of the rest of Reap's confession tells how he purportedly carried
out these "CIA duties," while also describing the treacherous workings
of Koy Thuon's Northern Zone network. Throughout the confession,
Reap and his associates are represented as trying to subvert the revolution by neglecting their duties, sabotaging Ângkar's military plans, disre-
garding or "spoiling" party policies, demoralizing troops, ruining crops,
and even stealing supplies. These activities are portrayed as continuing
after liberation, thereby attesting to the Northern Zone's treachery and
decadence and explaining away the Party Center's catastrophic economic
policies. As Reap was gradually promoted to higher military positions,
he developed ties to other high-ranking Northern Zone figures, ranging
from Sreng to Reap's later patrons in the military, Veng (the deputy secretary of Division 117) and Sey (Euan's cousin from Romeas, who
became the secretary of Division 117 and later Division 174). "Elder
Pauk" lurked in the background of almost every scene, untainted by and
usually oblivious to the clandestine meetings that took place whenever
his back was turned.

Just after liberation, Pauk promoted Reap to secretary of Battalion
311 (in Regiment 3 of Division 117), under Sim (the head of Regiment 3)
and Veng (now the secretary of Division 117), and reorganized the
Northern Zone troops so that many longtime comrades were sent to
work at different places. Before separating, Veng supposedly called a
meeting of the "CIA string" that had been secretly working together
during the civil war. Reap's confession recounts that Veng purportedly
reminded his followers of their CIA duties, which included: "fighting

against collectivism in order to create privatism because collectivism is really difficult and privatism is easy . . . impeding the progress of the revolutionary society and obstructing Ângkar's plans . . . [and] building traitorous forces by pulling in [those whose minds are hesitant]."

After the meeting, Veng is portrayed as taking on the role of a corrupt patron by throwing a party at which each follower was given milk and five meters of cloth. Reap's confession then lists the thirteen attendees, most of whom were members of his division. Like Sat and Sim, Veng here acts as a corrupter of cadres, pushing their weak minds toward privatism through indoctrination and gifts. Following the meeting, Pauk sent Reap's regiment to cultivate rice around Kompong Cham. Continuing their past activities, the regiment supposedly took the opportunity to engage in decadent pursuits, faking their work, playing cards, and taking moto rides for leisure. Besides ruining the rice crop, these actions supposedly increased the troop's aversion to performing peasant labor, leading them "have a contradiction with collectivism," a "regressive" sentiment exacerbated by Reap's clandestine indoctrination about the merits of privatism.

Sreng is also portrayed in a negative light, further affirming that Koy Thuon had corrupted Northern Zone personnel by encouraging privatism. Reap's confession depicts Sreng as a womanizer who drank liquor, partied with his men, and kept a second wife at the Region 41 office. Sreng is even supposed to have created a group of bandits in Kompong Siem to disrupt activity in the district, an allegation repeated in "The Last Plan" and that appears in the confession of many of Sreng's followers. Reap's confession also devotes attention to imagining the purported machinations and structure of Sreng's patronage string, extending downward to Reap's followers and upward to Koy Thuon and other high-ranking cadres. Sreng's network is initially described when Reap joins the "CIA group" and is subsequently chronicled by a series of secret meetings, which Reap attended or guarded. Even when guarding, Reap learned the details of these meetings from other participants. In each case, Reap's confession carefully lists the names and ranks of those in attendance, providing additional fodder for the Tuol Sleng engine of terror.

The most important series of meetings of "the big traitorous leaders" took place in the middle of 1976, to prepare "to strike the party in September 1976." In April, Sreng supposedly called a meeting at "the water house" of his major clients and allies. Afterward, one of these officials told Reap (who was guarding the path to the water house) that the meeting focused on the preparations of the "leaders on the left side of the Mekong River," who were led by Sreng. Because Reap later attempted to lead a rebellion, the Party Center considered him an important prisoner. His interrogation was supervised and summarized by Pon, who interrogated many of the most important Tuol Sleng prisoners,[94] and reports about his confession were sent to "Ângkar." Pon's twenty-one-page summary of Reap's confession highlights some of the interconnections between members of Sreng's network, including Sey's contact with Euan, his cousin from Romeas, in Phnom Penh.

In the months that followed, a number of high-ranking cadres supposedly came to Kompong Cham to hold clandestine meetings with members of Sreng's network. Hu Nim met with Sey one night in May, while on his way to the Eastern Zone. Afterward, the person who served water to Hu Nim whispered to Reap that Hu Nim favored privatism and had asked him to spy on Pauk. One day in July, Euan and Soeun, the secretaries of Divisions 310 and 450, supposedly drove to Kompong Cham to meet with Sey and other members of "the traitorous cadre in Division 117 of the Northern Zone." After eating lunch together at Sey's house, the officers discussed "the plan to strike the party in September 1977 during the party celebration," their combined troop strength (numbering well over ten thousand soldiers when the Siem Reap division was taken into account), and what to do with their forces after the victory. Before leaving, Euan and Soeun, as high-ranking patrons, were given gifts, including four tins of sugar. Reap's confession goes on to detail how the group's elaborate preparations to seize power were foiled when Pauk suddenly collected most of the division's weaponry, placing it under the watchful eye of his brother-in-law. Such foiled plots were signs that Ângkar was "all-knowing" and "clairvoyant."

In the paranoid world of the Khmer Rouge, new plots emerged as fast as old ones were undone. The Northern Zone was no exception, as secret meetings supposedly continued and Reap was soon informed about the group's new plan to "seize power" on September 10, 1977. When their plan was uncovered by the Party Center, however, the Northern Zone network was dealt a devastating blow: Koy Thuon, Sreng, Veng, and other top leaders in the "string of traitors from the North" were arrested by the middle of 1977. At this point, life became increasingly difficult for the surviving members of the "strings of traitors." Nevertheless, Reap's confession claims that "Elder Hang" (Bou Phat)[95] called a covert meeting of those who had survived the Northern Zone purge to reorganize their network:

Elder Hang said that we had to prepare a new traitorous string in order to strike the party at a later time and gave the new assignments:

Elder Hang	Secretary (Secretary of Region 103)
Sey	Deputy Secretary (Secretary of Division 117)
Chan	Member (Secretary of Region 43)
Sean	Member (Secretary of Industry in Region 42)
Elder Heaun	Member (Secretary of a district in Region 43)

Elder Hang announced that we would seize control of three Northern Zone provinces: Preah Vihear, Kompong Thom, and Kompong Cham, as well as Siem Reap. However, Elder Hang said that we could not yet seize them because our connections were severed. . . . Elder Hang later appointed Li to be the head of the traitorous division, with me as his deputy and Phok [the head of the Kompong Cham security office] as the member. . . . Elder Hang instructed us to be secretive so that the new string wouldn't be revealed to Ângkar. During the meeting, Chan was the most frightened of all and began to cry. Sey hardened him up again.

This passage is striking both for the rapidity with which the Party Center believed that espionage networks were built and rebuilt and for the rare mention of the fear that many Khmer Rouge cadres, like Chan, must have felt as the purges unfolded, moving closer and closer to them. Perhaps Reap was indirectly referencing his own past and present fears in this passage. Soon after this meeting, Pauk sent Reap to help with the arrest of Soth's Siem Reap network.

Reap's confession leaves some doubt about his relationship with Pauk. In many ways, Pauk seems like Reap's patron, entrusting Reap with important tasks and promoting him several times. Perhaps Pauk favored Reap because, like Pauk himself, he was willing to carry out orders, even if it meant killing people. At the end of 1975, for example, Pauk detained thirty Hanoi-trained cadres and ordered Reap to keep them under guard at Phnom Bros. Soon thereafter, he "cleaned up and discarded" (baos somat chaol) these "Hanoi cadres."[96] Likewise, Reap was sent with a squad of soldiers to carry out "security work" (sâkâmmâpheap sântesok) against bandits in the forests who were creating a "contradiction" (tum-noas) in the cooperatives by disrupting work and frightening the people. When purging the Northern Zone and Siem Reap, Pauk ordered Reap to assist him, promoting Reap shortly thereafter. Reap's confession is largely silent on his murderous activities at Phnom Bros. Once in a while there is an ambiguous sentence or two that may reference Reap's brutal deeds, such as when Pauk sends him to "work" in Region 42 after the

Siem Reap uprising. Apparently, the annihilation of thousands of "counterrevolutionary" enemies was a routine matter that was taken for granted, not worthy of mention in a document concerned with the seemingly more important affairs of his "string of traitors."[97]

Having described the organizational structure, treachery, and arrest of top Northern Zone cadres, Reap's confession moves toward closure. More secret meetings took place, new preparations to "strike the party" were made, subversive activities continued, and the "CIA group" continued to build up its forces while other members of their faction were detained. At one point, Reap and his associates allegedly attempted to poison the new chief of Region 41, An, a Southwestern Zone cadre who was related to Grandmother Yit and linked to the Party Center, in order to maintain their dominance in the zone. The influx of new cadres into the zone and Sey's eventual arrest, on August 13, 1977, were the likely catalysts in Reap's decision to raid the Kompong Cham jail, where a number of his comrades were being held, and then flee into the forest. The interrogator's summary explains how their plot went awry:

> Before the explosion, Reap and Sao . . . arrived at the Kompong Cham factory. The first detonation was set off, violently sending debris as far as three hundred meters away. The second bomb then exploded. Afterwards, Li ran from the clock factory shouting that aircraft had dropped bombs on the armory. Their group all yelled, then went to meet in front of the security office. Their group encountered five of Pauk's soldiers who had come to see what was going on. San sent Li to set some cloth on fire on the western wall of the armory. Li did so. The intention was to get the five people to go help extinguish [the blaze] so that we could free the forces inside the security office [using the front entrance]. When the fire was burning, Li yelled for help. But there was only a little fire and other forces came and quickly extinguished the blaze. The preparations didn't work because the bombs had exploded against a stone wall, killing some of the prisoners in the jail. Only thirty people were alive, and guards were everywhere. Sao and Sean told Li to quickly go report to Elder Pauk, who was at the January 1 dam site. Afterward, Sean instructed everyone, "We can't meet together from now on for fear that our plan will be revealed." At midnight, Li returned. Pauk arrived at 2:00 A.M. and called Reap and Sean [to meet] and said, "There wasn't a plane dropping bombs. Li, you were the one who set the fire." So they arrested Li and some of the people from the munitions office. [Two days later,] on September 19, 1977, he arrested Reap. That evening, Reap saw that Chan and Sao had also been arrested.

Soon after his arrest, Reap was sent to Tuol Sleng. Pon's report on Reap's confession states that after being tortured for a day and a night, Reap still wouldn't talk: "I tortured him some more, concentrating on hidden stories. If he was hiding small stories, he was surely hiding big ones as well."[98] Drawing on Sey's replies, Pon then questioned Reap "about the secret water house meeting. I asked Reap, 'What happened at the water house?' At first he acted bewildered, but soon began to speak profusely about the people who came to meet at the water house, including Soeun . . . Bou Phat . . . Hu Nim . . . Euan . . . Soth . . . Ya, and so on." Reap's life had come full circle.

After revealing the "traitorous activities" of the Northern Zone network and listing a string of over a hundred associates in a confession that was over thirty typed pages long, Reap remained at Tuol Sleng for over four more months. His name appears on a list of 162 "prisoners destroyed on March 10, 1978,"[99] comprising a number of Northern Zone personnel, including almost two dozen soldiers from Division 174. Perhaps the Party Center was finally convinced that Koy Thuon's Division 174 string had been completely "smashed" and that there was no reason to keep them any longer. It was one of the busiest days of killing that took place at Tuol Sleng. Reap and the other 161 prisoners were almost certainly executed at Choeng Ek under the supervision of Lor.

· · ·

By the time of Reap's imprisonment, the liquidation of the moderates was largely complete and the severity of the purges abated. Nevertheless, Tuol Sleng continued to uncover plots, real or imagined, thus fueling the Party Center's paranoia. Tensions with Vietnam were escalating dramatically, presaging war and intensifying suspicion of anyone who had a history of association with the Vietnamese. Because most of the senior Khmer Rouge leaders had worked with the Vietnamese communists, anyone could suddenly be accused of being a Vietnamese spy. After its purge of the intellectuals, the Party Center continued to consolidate their power by further undermining the influence of the remaining original zone secretaries, all of whom, except for Mok, were eventually purged.

At this point, the Party Center probably felt most threatened by the two veteran revolutionaries, Nhem Ros (Moul Sambath) and Sao Phim, who were popular, semi-independent zone secretaries connected by marriage. Nhem Ros, a former Issarak fighter who was the secretary of the Northwestern Zone, had been under suspicion since mid 1976, when Ieng Thirith visited the region and attributed the poor condition of the inhabitants to internal enemies: "'Agents had got into our ranks,' she said, 'and they had got into the highest ranks. They had to behave with double faces in order to make as if they were following our line [policies].'"[100] Of all the zones, the Northwest was probably the most devastated by the high-modernist visions of the Khmer Rouge leaders. The Party Center set higher agricultural quotas for the Northwestern Zone, the "rice-bowl" of Cambodia, while relocating tens of thousands of Cambodians — most of them "new people" — to the region to augment the labor force and create new fields for cultivation.

The results on the "front lines" of this economic "battlefield" were often catastrophic, as the regime's high-modernist projects collapsed, rice production quotas were not met, and the masses began to fall ill and starve after rice that should have been set aside for consumption was sent to Phnom Penh by timorous cadres. Not surprisingly, the Party Center agreed with Ieng Thirith's assessment that the suffering of the people was due to the sabotage of "double-faced agents" rather than their own flawed visions. In December, Pol Pot's "microbes" speech would single out the Northwestern Zone for censure for having allowed "soldiers of the old regime and officials [to seep] into the leadership of the cooperatives. . . . The people selected to exercise revolutionary state power must come from the ranks of those vetted by the Party — people with clear life-histories. Don't hand state power over to other kinds of people, no matter how easy it might be to do so."[101] Such comments portrayed the Northwestern Zone as a den of "microbes" with regressive minds, waiting to be uncovered by the Party Center's all-knowing gaze.

Given the problems that his zone faced, Nhem Ros may very well have disagreed with some of the hard-line policies of the Party Center. Hu Nim's confession is interesting in this regard, as it records a secret meeting that he supposedly had with Nhem Ros in March 1976, in which Nhem Ros critiqued the party "line" for overreliance on "labor power" and refusing to accept foreign aid (while, as always, listing alleged strings and plots to "seize power"):

> Brother Nhim said: "The standpoint of the Standing Committee on agricultural construction is basically to rely on labor power. I do not agree with that. In the Northwest, especially in Regions 3, 4, and 5, which are the granary of Kampuchea, there are vast farms kilometers long. In ploughing, harvesting, and threshing, the use of labor power alone has a retarding effect. Tractors and machinery must be used." So brother Nhim's concept was a system of plenty . . . and of not relying on labor power [which were] concepts opposed to the basic political line of the party, which is independence — self-mastery — mastery. . . . And so brother Nim agreed with us, "In order to build up the country rapidly, aid must be

accepted from every country. With foreign aid we can buy many tractors, cars, and machines." This is a revisionist, capitalist line opposed to the line of the [CPK]."[102]

While it is impossible to know if such a conversation ever took place, Nhem Ros may very well have made such critiques of the party line, which placed an enormous burden on the Northwestern Zone. Regardless, when combined with the zone's socioeconomic problems, such comments, real or imagined, were enough for the Party Center to initiate a major purge of the Northwest.[103] Beginning in late 1976 and continuing throughout 1977, Southwest Zone cadres loyal to Mok and the Party Center arrived in the Northwestern Zone, assumed positions of power, and carried out major purges of local cadres, military officers, and suspect elements of the civilian population. Tens of thousands of people were executed at this time. By the end of 1977, all of the zone's regional secretaries and deputy secretaries had been arrested (along with many of lower-level cadres in their "strings") and sent to Tuol Sleng, where many "confessed" their plots, espionage, and economic sabotage.[104] After their power base had been eroded in this manner, Nhem Ros and the remaining members of his patronage circle were finally arrested in June 1978. Mok took over his position as secretary of the Northwestern Zone.

Careful to check the power of even a loyal client like Mok, the Party Center had earlier sent thousands of Western Zone cadres to work in the Northwestern Zone political administration.[105] In fact, the Western Zone had been the site of an earlier purge foreshadowed by Nuon Chea's mid-1977 comment that "enemies and various classes" were in control of some parts of the zone.[106] While some local cadres were purged in 1977, it was not until March 1978 that zone secretary Chou Chet (Si) — another former Issarak and veteran revolutionary who had clashed with Mok and seemed to have doubts about the Party Center's radical line — and members of his string were arrested after allegedly plotting to rebel against the Party Center. Chou Chet's two rivals in the zone, his deputy Pal and military commander Soeung, assumed control. During the next few months, Pal and Soeung, both of whom were loyal to the Party Center, trained thousands of new cadres, many of whom were sent to work in the Northwestern Zone.

Nhem Ros was arrested on June 11, 1978, just eight days after the suicide of his in-law, Eastern Zone secretary Sao Phim. Perhaps the most powerful of the regional chiefs at the beginning of DK, Sao Phim was considered suspect because of his zone's moderate policies, his long association with Vietnam, and the success of Vietnamese military offensives in the zone beginning in October 1977. Perhaps alluding to Sao Phim's network, Pol Pot's 1977 speech warned that there were still "life and death contradictions" within the "new Kampuchean society . . . owing to the presence of enemy agents, who belong to the various spy networks of the imperialists and international reaction[aries] who secretly implant themselves to carry out subversive activities against our revolution."[107]

Sao Phim had initially come under suspicion during the Chakrei affair, when Duch began warning the Party Center about the "the rubber plantation network." In the middle of 1976, several members of this alleged network had been arrested while Phim was in China receiving medical treatment. The Eastern Zone in general and Sao Phim in particular were increasingly implicated in the plots and espionage networks that Duch was "discovering" at Tuol Sleng. Reap's confession, for example, contains a number of references to the Eastern Zone. Likewise, Hu Nim's confession alleges that Sao Phim was opposed to the party line and was conspiring with Koy Thuon and Nhem Ros.

Despite such proliferating accusations, it was not until Sao Phim's power base had been sufficiently eroded, and he went to receive medical treatment in China for a second time in March–April 1978, that Pol Pot and his associates began a major assault on the Eastern Zone.[108] Sao Phim returned to find that hundreds of his officials had been arrested. During the first three weeks of May, Pauk summoned several high-ranking Eastern Zone military officers to "meetings" and had them executed. Pauk then sent two divisions of Central Zone troops to attack the Eastern Zone. Despite receiving additional support from Center and Southwest Zone forces, Pauk met stiff resistance. Sao Phim, who had been summoned to Phnom Penh, committed suicide when he was about to be arrested. Thousands of his soldiers nevertheless continued to resist the Party Center for months before regrouping in Vietnam and forming the core of what was to become the PRK regime.

As the Party Center took control of the Eastern Zone, it conducted a massive purge of local cadres and civilians, executing perhaps 250,000 or more people having "Khmer bodies with Vietnamese minds" *(khluon khmaer khuor kbal yuon)*.[109] Bunhaeng Ung, a "new person" living in the Eastern Zone, witnessed the murder of hundreds of these "impure" Eastern Zone villagers, who, like Chlat's brother, Sruon, had been told they were being relocated. Instead the victims were led to a killing field:

The smell of death hung in the air. Nearby [large] rectangular pits had been dug, and in some half-covered bodies could be seen. Bun was frozen in horror, fear and disbelief. . . . Loudspeakers blared revolutionary songs and music at full volume. A young girl was seized and raped. Others were led to the pits where they were slaughtered like animals by striking the backs of their skulls with hoes or lengths of bamboo. Young children and babies were held by the legs, their heads smashed against palm trees and their broken bodies flung beside their dying mothers in the death pits. Some children were thrown in the air and bayoneted while music drowned their screams. . . . At the place of execution nothing was hidden. The bodies lay in open pits, rotting under the sun and monsoon rain. Some had been carved open and the liver removed to obtain the bile, from which a traditional medicine was made that was supposed to cure fever. Bun believed reports that some soldiers ate human liver in a cannibalistic rite believed to tap the strength and courage of the victim, though he never himself witnessed this.[110]

After observing this horrible scene, Bun fled back to his village, struggling to make sense of the atrocities he had seen. Meanwhile, thousands upon thousands of Eastern Zone cadres and villagers continued to be sent to their deaths.

By the end of the summer of 1978, the purge of the Eastern Zone was complete. Despite having purged almost all of the original zone secretaries and numerous veteran revolutionaries, the Tuol Sleng engine of terror continued to churn, albeit more slowly, moving closer to Pol Pot's inner circle. In November, the deputy prime minister and minister of the economy, Von Vet (Sok Thuok), and his string of followers were purged for supposedly plotting a coup with Sao Phim.[111] Son Sen, who had replaced Sao Phim as the secretary of the Eastern Zone and had close links to Von Vet, also came under suspicion around this time for allegedly plotting a coup; he would likely have been purged if the Vietnamese hadn't toppled the DK regime. Southwestern Zone cadres had also begun to be arrested, suggesting that Mok himself, who was now the secretary of three zones, might have ultimately been purged. While the pace of the purges was abating somewhat, they were certainly not over by the time of the Vietnamese invasion. Continuous revolution required enemies, Tuol Sleng found them, and Pol Pot, the paranoid potent center, was willing to "smash" almost anyone in the name of the revolution.

Throughout the fall of 1978, the war with Vietnam continued to escalate. The Party Center was extremely anti-Vietnamese and had been launching increasingly violent raids into Vietnam since late 1977, ostensibly to regain the part of "lower Cambodia" (Kampuchea Krom) that had been "swallowed" by Vietnam over the centuries. The DK army's failures suggested domestic subversion, and the Eastern Zone, which bordered Vietnam and was the site of most of the fighting, had been an obvious scapegoat. Ultimately, however, the Party Center's assault upon the Eastern Zone and Vietnam proved to be its undoing. Sao Phim's Eastern Zone followers who had escaped the purge enlisted the patronage of the Vietnamese (who were fed up with Khmer Rouge military raids into their territory) to help them overthrow the DK regime. In just a few weeks, 150,000 Vietnamese troops and perhaps 15,000 Cambodian rebels launched a massive assault that was successful in routing the Khmer Rouge army, whose forces had been weakened by the execution of so many experienced military officers and cadres. Phnom Penh was captured on January 7, 1979. By this time, well over one and a half million Cambodians had died.

PART TWO

The Fire without Smoke

Preamble

What happened to Reap after he entered Tuol Sleng? Only traces of his life remain — in the corpses and mass graves left at Phnom Bros, in the memories of those who knew or heard about him, in the multiple drafts of his confession, which concluded with a thumbprint and signature, and in references to him in other Khmer Rouge documents, such as the confessions of his associates and the execution log that registers the day he was killed. Still, we can piece together a rough picture of what happened to Reap and other victims of the DK purges by drawing upon Tuol Sleng documents and information provided by the handful of prisoners who survived incarceration because, as mechanics, carpenters, painters, sculptors, and electricians, they had skills that were useful to Duch, the former high school teacher who was then head of Tuol Sleng. Two of these accounts are described below. The first recounts the experiences of Vann Nath, a painter I interviewed twice who has written a memoir of his ordeal at S-21 and painted a series of murals depicting life at Tuol Sleng. The second account is based on a document written by Ung Pech, a mechanic who later became the first director of the museum. Both men provide disturbing descriptions of what went on at Tuol Sleng, descriptions that ultimately raise larger questions about the mass violence that took place during DK.

TWO PATHS TO TUOL SLENG

Nowadays, when I visit Tuol Sleng, . . . [e]verything comes flooding back: terror and shock, the ghost-like emaciated people, the screams of pain echoing through the prison, the brutality of the guards. The pale faces of the prisoners seem to look at me from every corner, crying, "Help! Please help me . . ."

I never expected to survive this hell. I spent exactly one year in S-21. On January 7, 1978 I was thrust there not knowing why I was arrested. On January 7, 1979, I escaped.

Vann Nath, *A Cambodian Prison Portrait*[1]

One evening in late December 1977, after Vann Nath had worked all day in the rice fields and was preparing to return to the communal dining hall for the evening meal, Comrade Luom, a cadre from his cooperative, rode up to Nath's work group in an ox-cart and asked Nath to help cut rattan in the jungle. Nath, a painter from Cambodia's second-largest city, Battambang, was uneasy because he was being singled out of a group of almost fifty people, but he could not refuse. Comrade Luom told Nath they were going to a distant cooperative to meet up with another work group.

When they arrived at the cooperative, it was late and Comrade Luom told Nath he could go sleep in the dining hall. Just as Nath was drifting off to sleep, he was awoken by Comrade Luom's voice: "Nath, Nath, get up. We need to take another cart ride." Nath rose and had only taken a few steps when he turned and saw the shadow of a man holding a cord. The man told Nath to raise his hands and then tried to bind his arms. A struggle ensued and Nath was able to fend off the man, whom he recognized as Chhreung, the head executioner from the cooperative. Suddenly Comrade Luom yelled out, "Let him tie you up." Nath recounted what happened next: "I asked him with a terrified heart, 'What have I done? What have I done?' Despicable Luom replied, 'I don't know. This is an order from the district office.' I was speechless and stood in a frightened daze . . . letting them tie me up like a pig, thinking my life was finished."

After being shackled for several hours in a wooden house, Nath was led to an ox-cart where he saw his younger cousin sitting in chains next to the chief of Nath's cooperative, Comrade Phean. At one point during the ride that followed, Comrade Phean told Nath, "I saw that you worked really hard, comrade. I don't know why the district office has ordered your arrest." Eventually, they arrived at a district prison, located on the grounds of a temple. Nath and his cousin were shackled in a room with several other people, including one man who had fought for years with the Khmer Rouge and later been appointed the head of a cooperative.

The next evening, around seven o'clock, three people, one carrying an AK-47, entered the temple and ordered Nath to come with them. When they led Nath into the jungle, he thought they were going to shoot him: "I was without hope, knowing in my heart that my life would surely end that night." They led him to a small house that turned out to be a torture chamber. It was equipped with shackles, clubs, plastic bags, and a whip. Fresh blood was splattered on the tile floor. Nath was terrified. One of the men asked Nath to recount his life history and then began interrogating him about why he had been arrested. When Nath claimed he didn't know, the interrogator responded: "No, Ângkar is not stupid and doesn't arrest people who are innocent. Now think hard, comrade. What did you do wrong? . . . Others have reported that you are trying to incite the people to fight against Ângkar. Who are the members of your string [khsae], comrade? Start talking, now." Nath didn't know what the interrogators were talking about but knew the accusations could lead to his execution.

At this point, a cadre walked up and, using a safety pin, stuck a small wire through Nath's shorts so that the metal pressed against the skin of his thigh. He asked, "Do you remember [what you did] or not? Who are the despicable people who joined you in having traitorous thoughts?" When Nath didn't respond immediately, he was given an electric shock: "My entire body began to tremble very hard. . . . I blacked out. As I began to regain consciousness, I faintly heard someone ask, 'How many people are in your group?' I could only respond with two words, 'No, elder,' before fainting again." Upon waking, Nath found himself lying on the floor exhausted and drenched in sweat. His interrogators told him to get up and led him back to the temple. When the other prisoners saw him, their eyes filled with fear. Nath was terrified that he would be tortured again, but the next evening the guards took a different person.

Several days later, Nath and several fellow prisoners were placed in a truck and driven to Tuol Sleng. The ride was extremely painful, since they were not fed and remained shackled the entire time. They arrived at Tuol Sleng in the middle of the night and were immediately photographed and ordered to give their life histories. After being informed of the rules, Nath's group was placed in a cell with many other prisoners, all of whom were shackled. As the days passed, prisoners were taken away and interrogated. Sometimes they came back with blood covering their bodies; other times they didn't return. Because they were given starvation rations, the prisoners became extremely weak: "After living that kind of life for several days my body began to deteriorate. My ribs were poking out. . . . Every four days they gave us a bath. They brought hoses up from downstairs and sprayed everyone from the doorway . . . I lived that way for more than 30 days. I was never released from the shackles, and had to ask permission every time I sat up. If I had to defecate, I asked the guards to bring the bucket over."[2]

After Nath had been at Tuol Sleng for perhaps a month, guards called out his name, and although he could barely walk, they managed to march him to Duch. Duch asked Nath, who had mentioned in his life history that he was formerly an artist, if he could still paint. Nath replied affirmatively and was given the task of painting portraits of Pol Pot. During the year he spent at Tuol Sleng, Nath worked under guard and continued to fear for his life. Slowly, however, he began to understand what happened to the prisoners at S-21. Working from 6 A.M. to midnight with a short break for lunch, Nath saw prisoners being led back and forth morning, afternoon, and evening. As he worked, Nath could

> hear screams of pain from every corner of the prison. I felt a twinge of pain in my body at each scream. . . . I could hear the guards demanding the truth, the acts of betrayal, the names of collaborators. I had undergone this in Battambang, but never here. When would they take me for interrogation again, I wondered. Oh God, please help me avoid such an interrogation! I could not endure it. . . . Prisoners [were] trucked in day and night — sometimes until two o'clock in the morning. . . . When I went upstairs, I would hear them swearing at the prisoners: "You are CIA!" or "You are KGB!" . . . We could hear the interrogators' shouts and threats and the prisoners' screams of pain. These were sounds I heard all the time.[3]

By effectively carrying out his artistic tasks and humbling himself before his guards, Nath managed to survive. Toward the end of 1978, after the Eastern Zone purges had run their course, the pace of torture slackened. Nath finally managed to escape his captors during the Vietnamese invasion. Several months later, he returned to produce the series of paintings depicting Khmer Rouge atrocities that now line the walls of the Tuol Sleng Museum of Genocidal Crimes. At one point, a museum worker showed Nath a document containing his name: "My hands and feet became cold. It was an execution list. My name was there, but underlined in red ink with brackets at the end saying 'keep.' The list was signed by Sous Thy with a note written on the top: 'Request Peng to destroy.' "[4]

· · ·

When the Khmer Rouge took Kompong Som, a port city on the southwest coast of Cambodia, Ung Pech and many other people were happy because they thought the country would again have peace.[5] Like those living in other cities, the inhabitants of Kompong Som were told to evacuate the city and not allowed to return; instead they were put to work cultivating rice and performing other agrarian labor.

Because Pech was a skilled technician, however, the Khmer Rouge later ordered him to return to Kompong Som to repair machinery at the port. He said, "They had us work from 6 A.M. to 11 P.M. with just a short break to eat. If one of us didn't work properly, he or she would be reprimanded, punished, or taken away. We didn't know where they disappeared to." Pech labored like this for a year or so before being told he had just three months to train a group of new workers, most of whom were ten to sixteen years old and illiterate. When Pech protested that completing the training in such a short period would be impossible, "they accused me of being an imperialist who was selfishly withholding my knowledge from others."

A few months later, Pech was arrested. He was tortured for one night and then taken, blindfolded and shackled, to Tuol Sleng. Upon arrival, Pech and another prisoner were led into a room and questioned. Pech recalled, "They asked me, 'Scum, where are you from, you despicable traitor?' A bit later they called my name and asked me to give my life history. At that time, we became the object of great spite and savagery. They told us, 'You, scum, are going to become fertilizer.' I thought in my heart that I hadn't done anything wrong. Why were they accusing me of being a traitor?" Afterward, Pech was photographed and taken to a room full of prisoners where he was made to strip down to his underpants and shackled. He was then informed of the prison regulations: it was forbidden to speak to others and prisoners had to ask permission before doing anything, even sitting up or defecating. Those who violated the rules were often beaten.

At mealtimes, the prisoners were each given a spoon with which to eat their scant rations. Afterward, the utensils had to be returned and were counted. One day, a new prisoner who didn't know the system took two spoons by mistake. When the guards discovered the man had the missing spoon, they accused him of plotting to escape and contacted their supervisor, Peng. The prisoner explained to Peng that he was new and didn't know the rule about the spoons and pleaded for forgiveness. Pech noted, "Despicable Peng didn't listen to his begging. He began to beat the prisoner and kick his head. The guy was bleeding all over. Peng beat him for perhaps an hour. We were all upset, but what could we do?"

In addition to mealtime checks, the guards inspected the prisoners several times each day. Prisoners were allowed to bathe once every three to five days; their few items of clothing were changed infrequently. As a result, they stank and contracted skin diseases, particularly during the hot season. Pech said, "The doctors, who were little kids, would wash out the wounds and give us tiny pills made from trees . . . they couldn't cure skin diseases. They'd say, 'This type of illness won't kill you.' Many of the prisoners had diarrhea or dysentery and died in the prison. Their corpses were left lying there, sometimes until two or three in the morning. We had to sleep with the corpses."

Pech also noticed that prisoners were periodically taken away from Tuol Sleng. After calling out a given prisoner's name from a list, the guards would bind and blindfold the person before releasing his or her legs from the shackles. The guards then jerked the prisoner forward, sometimes beating the person for moving too slowly. Pech commented, "The guards pulled on their bonds as if the prisoners were animals. A few people had been in the prison too long and couldn't walk. They would be dragged along, so that sometimes they fell and were injured. The prisoners were thrown into a waiting vehicle like animals and then driven off." Pech and his fellow inmates eventually realized that, after interrogation, the prisoners were killed.

Almost every prisoner who entered Tuol Sleng died of illness, torture, or execution. Pech and a handful of other prisoners were exceptions. One day, a guard asked the people in Pech's cell if anyone knew how to fix a generator. The other inmates pointed at Pech. Exhausted and barely able to stand, Pech managed to repair the generator. The next day, the guard took him to fix another machine. When he again succeeded, the guards transferred Pech to a different cell, and he began to work as a prison technician under improved conditions.

Because of the nature of his job, Pech worked at different sites around the prison, though always under guard. Both in the silence of the night and when he passed by the interrogation area during the day, Pech "heard loud screaming that would suddenly stop, and the sound of prisoners being struck repeatedly. This gave me goose bumps. Some of the people called out for their mothers and fathers to help their child." Prisoners were interrogated in the morning, afternoon, and evening:

> They had the prisoners sit down on the floor tiles, with both of their hands shackled and their legs chained to the table. One person would sit, waiting to question and write things down. Another person would be holding a stick or a club, waiting to hit. The method of interrogation didn't have anything besides accusing people of working for the CIA or the KGB, or being connected with Vietnam. There were many gentle and honest people who were accidental victims, because they had never done anything. Some didn't answer, so [the Khmer Rouge] would beat them continuously for two or three months. Others, who couldn't endure any more, decided to confess that they were the hands and arms of the CIA or KGB. Then their

group would stop hitting them and have them write down a confession and sign it. Only then would they stop torturing them for a while. Perhaps ten days later, they would take the prisoner away, and he or she would disappear. They were executed. . . . Because the room in which I slept was near the interrogation center, every day and night I would hear the sounds. My ears became exhausted by the suffering of the prisoners. Sometimes they would take an electrical wire and shock [prisoners], knocking them speechless or unconscious. They would stuff fish water into the prisoner's ears or take tweezers and pull off the nails of their fingers and toes and then pour alcohol on them. The sound of their pain would become even louder, sometimes suddenly stopping. They tied the legs of still other prisoners and hung them by the legs, upside down. They would then pour water into the prisoner's noses in order to get them to answer their questions. There was another method in which they would take a cloth and put it over a prisoner's face and pour water until they choked on it. Other times they would take a prisoner's head and pound it on a cement table; sometimes the prisoner would fall unconscious for hours.

While the length of interrogation varied, almost everyone eventually "confessed." Most were later taken by Lor to the Choeng Ek killing field and executed.

The interrogators used a variety of tortures to extract confessions. Interrogators were instructed to "hurt them (only) so that they respond quickly. Another purpose is to break them and make them lose their will."[6] To obtain this information, the executioners tortured the prisoners by administering electrical shocks that would sometimes knock them unconscious; pouring water up their noses and mouths while they were lying on an inclined surface so they would choke; beating them by hand or with a club around which an electrical cord was wound; putting alcohol on fingers or toes after the nails had been removed; suffocating them with plastic bags; burning them with cigarettes; stuffing food down their throats; forcing them to eat excrement or drink urine; hanging them upside down; jabbing them with needles; or making them "pay homage" to the wall, table, chair, or an image of a dog.[7] Reap's confession gives no indication of how he was tortured. Considering how quickly he confessed, however, his torture was likely severe. Im Chan, another survivor of Tuol Sleng, described how brutal interrogation could be:

Tuol Sleng lived up to my fears. I was tortured for 26 days from 6:00 in the morning until 11:00, then from 2:00 to 5:00 and from 6:00 to 11:00 at night. They would put a plastic bag over my head so that I could not breathe and fell unconscious. My torturers put a cloth over my face and then poured water onto it until the water went into my lungs and I started

drowning. They stapled an electric wire attached to a light socket to my leg
and gave me shocks. Every time they would bring me around and ask me
if I was a traitor and I would say I wasn't.[8]

Pech said his "ears became exhausted by the noise of the prisoners' suffering as they were tortured."

Like Nath, Pech had to endure these sounds of misery until the
Vietnamese liberated Phnom Penh in January 1979. The guards then
forced Pech, Nath, and a few other Tuol Sleng survivors to flee with them
to the south. At one point, a Vietnamese tank suddenly appeared, and
everyone ran in different directions. For the first time in almost two
years, Pech was free. Sadly, he discovered that most of his family had
died or been killed by the Khmer Rouge.

· · ·

These chilling narratives emphasize several interrelated issues that are at
the heart of this book. First, both Nath and Pech's narratives involve
political identity, highlighting the process by which a "normal" person
is suddenly transformed into an enemy. Second, their stories raise questions about the structure and function of Tuol Sleng. Why were people
like them taken to Tuol Sleng? Why was the prison structured in the
way that it was? Third, both Nath and Pech emphasize the brutality of
the guards. Why were the prisoners treated so badly? What motivated
the guards to perform acts of cruelty that often exceeded their direct
orders?

When interviewing perpetrators and victims, I was repeatedly told
that one of the reasons Khmer Rouge cadres were willing to "destroy"
their enemies was to gain face and honor. Nath, for example, has
described how the prisoners treated the guards and prison officials with
enormous deference, a pattern that also characterized the treatment of
Khmer Rouge cadres and soldiers in the countryside. Likewise, Lor told
me that many of his peers and subordinates were quite willing to brutalize prisoners in order to gain "face and rank." At first glance, such comments might seem strange, since the Khmer Rouge revamped the social
order and proclaimed everyone equal. However, despite such assertions,
DK society retained hierarchical elements that blended the old and the
new.

The second part of this book, then, also asks how, when, and why it
became honorable to participate in genocide. To answer such questions,

we need to examine the DK social order, the sorts of "genocidal brico-lage" that perpetrators performed as they drew upon different blends of cultural and ideological knowledge, the ways in which difference was manufactured during DK, notions of face and honor, and perpetrator motivation.

CHAPTER FOUR

The DK Social Order

I first asked the enemy *(khmang)* about his *(vea)* life and
associations. When I had done this, I spoke of the discipline
of the office [S-21], and I told him that his body, tied up with
fetters and handcuffs, was worth less than garbage. I had him
pay respect *(korop)* to me. I told him that if I asked him *(brey)*
to say a single word to me; he had to say it. I made him pay
homage *(sâmpeah)* to the image of a dog [a common torture,
involving an image of a dog with the head of Ho Chi Minh].
I beat him and interrogated him until he said that he had once
been CIA. After I beat him some more, he admitted that he
had joined the CIA in 1969.

 Once he had confessed, I didn't have to beat him to obtain
the rest of his story, but when he hesitated or came to weak
points in his story I beat him, and I also beat him to clarify
the points in his story where the information about important
matters was confused.

Vaen Kheuan's summary
of his interrogation of prisoner Oum Chhan[1]

Like other Tuol Sleng documents, the disturbing passage cited above —
an August 1978 interrogator's description of how he tortured Oum
Chhan, the former head of a mobile work team in the Eastern Zone —
reveals much about the dynamics of violence at Tuol Sleng and other DK
"spaces of death." It is impossible to know exactly what happened in
Oum Chhan's interrogation cell; one can only imagine the pain and suffering he and other prisoners endured. Nevertheless, such texts do help
us understand the pattern of violence at places like Tuol Sleng, what
might have been going through the minds of perpetrators, and some of
the wider processes at work during DK. This chapter argues that, to
understand the dynamics of such acts of violence, we must unpack the

local frames of knowledge that gave such acts shape and meaning, particularly Cambodian conceptions of status, dyadic interactions, hierarchy, and social order.

Broadly, this passage is full of hierarchical language that conveys the utter dehumanization of Oum Chhan. Like Reap's interrogator, Oum Chhan's interrogator, Vaen Kheuan, repeatedly refers to Oum Chhan using the derogatory third-person pronoun *vea*. In contrast to English, the Khmer language contains an enormous number of hierarchical expressions, including vulgar, familiar, and formal terms of address, whose usage varies depending on the context.[2] For example, there is no single Khmer equivalent of the English all-purpose term "you"; the term used depends on the situation and the speaker's assessment of and relationship to the person being addressed.

The pronoun *vea* can be translated as "he, she, they" or "it" but is specifically used to refer to people younger than the speaker (particularly children), people of a subordinate or lowly social status *(thnak)*, animals, and objects; in fact, in the past *vea* denoted a type of male slave, perhaps accounting for the term's pejorative connotations.[3] *Vea* belongs to a larger group of "vulgar" forms of speech that tend to be used for animals, objects, those to whom one doesn't need to show much respect (such as children), and those one holds in contempt.[4]

John Marston has argued that these vulgar usages are more marked and have an "objectifying self-orientation," in the sense that they may connote nonrelatedness, informality, self-specificity, indifferent superiority, or outright hostility (anger, condescension, disdain, insult).[5] In addition to *vea,* this register includes the first-person pronoun *ânh,* the second-person pronoun *âhaeng,* the diminutive prefixes *a-* and *mi-,* and vulgar verbs for eating *(si),* sleeping *(dek),* and dying *(ngoap).* Thus a rice farmer usually refers to his oxen as *vea* and uses terms like *si, dek,* and *ngoap* when they eat, sleep, or die. Likewise, the author of the *Island of Peace* article about Suen of the Earth described him as *a-* ("despicable little") to indicate his anger and contempt toward Suen for killing Chan Dara. People also commonly refer to Pol Pot as *a-Pot.*

These vulgar, self-objectifying terms may be broadly distinguished from the formal and familiar registers, which Marston calls "otherworldly respect" and "relationship/reciprocity," respectively.[6] The otherworldly respect register also tends to be marked and connotes deference and respect toward powerful figures. It is used in more formal, public contexts, particularly when speaking to high-status individuals. A variety of titles are included in this category, ranging from the somewhat formal expressions *lok* and *neak* (roughly analogous to *Sir* and *Madam,* though they are also used more formally to address teachers and monks) to more deferential terms like *aekodâm* ("Your Excellency") and, most exalted of all, the often elaborate titles given to high-ranking monks, officials, and royalty. In fact, people are expected to use special pronouns and vocabularies when speaking to monks and royalty. If a child or animal eats *(si),* monks *chan* and kings *saoy* their food.

The more ordinary "relationship/reciprocity" register is a very broad "default" category of less marked terms that are loosely united by their signification of interdependence and connection.[7] It includes familiar personal pronouns *(khnhom, yoeng, knea, koat),* personal names, and kinship terms. While sex and age are both linguistically distinguished in the Khmer bilateral kinship system, relative age is particularly salient, reflecting a larger pattern of social organization in which status and authority are associated with age. Within the family, for example, siblings refer to and address one another based on age, with younger siblings called *b'aun* and elders *bâng.* As soon as they are able to speak, children are taught to call people by the appropriate pronoun. Because such terms connote a sense of mutual support, obligation, and connection, they are often extended to dyadic relationships formed outside the family in contexts of familiarity, interdependence, and affinity.

Besides its use of the term *vea,* the interrogator's summary of Oum Chhan's confession references two acts that are directly linked to Cambodian conceptions of hierarchy. First, the summary uses the word *korop* twice, as in the phrase "I had him pay respect *(korop)* to me." In Cambodia, dyadic interactions, particularly in contexts of "otherworldly respect" and personal dependency, are usually structured by an assumption that the parties involved are unequal and by a publicly idealized expectation that those who are subordinate will *korop,* or "respect, honor, and obey," their superiors. This term is difficult to gloss in English but connotes deferential behaviors such as "bowing before someone, behaving in a humble and polite manner, bowing to show respect, a bearing that shows respect in accordance with one's awe of someone else, a bearing that trusts."[8] *Korop* thus implies a prostrating reverence, often tinged with awe and fear, that leads a subordinate to respect, honor, and obey an imposing person or institution. While we don't know exactly how Oum Chhan's interrogator made him "pay respect," then, it seems likely that this terse statement referenced bodily abuse, since to *korop* someone often entails some sort of bodily prostration.

From these various strands, we begin to get a picture of Cambodian conceptions of hierarchy, status, and social order. The term *hierarchy* is etymologically derived from the Greek word *hierarches,* meaning "high priest" or "president of sacred rites."[9] This religious connotation was later extended to refer to "an organized body of priests or clergy in successive orders or grades," from which it came to have its more general modern sense of a system or "body of persons or things ranked in grades, orders, or classes, one above another." Drawing on this modern sense, I define *hierarchy* broadly as a system of ranked difference enacted on the basis of cultural understandings of rank and status, or relative social standing — recognizing that religions often provide some of the most salient moral principles for determining relative social standing and thus generating systems of ranked difference. Notions of hierarchy and status, then, are a crucial part of the social order, a broader category that includes both hierarchical and nonhierarchical structural positionings.

While Khmer does not have a single word that would serve as a direct translation of *hierarchy,* it does have a number of terms associated with ranked difference. The *Khmer Dictionary* definition of *vea,* for example, states that the term is used to refer to those of a lesser *thnak,* which means "level," "class," or "stratum," as in "high/low class" or an educational grade level.[10] Likewise, Khmer includes terms like *sâkti* ("authority, rank, grade, power"), *bon sâkti* (literally "merit rank"), *vonnah* ("social class/rank"), *than* ("place, station"), and perhaps the words closest to *hierarchy* — *lumdap sâkti* ("order of ranks") and *thânanukram* ("arrangement/order by rank"). Moreover, Buddhism provides a number of principles that help generate a system of ranked difference, as I discuss below.[11]

Linguistically, the relative (in-)equality of dyadic interactions is indexed and negotiated by the selection of speech registers. Cambodian villagers, for example, use terms of "otherworldly respect" when interacting with powerful figures. In their casual, everyday conversations, though, they are more likely to select terms of "relationship reciprocity" that, while highlighting relative age, stress interdependence and greater equality. Similarly, in contexts of familiarity and ease, two friends or classmates might refer to one another through the reciprocal use of terms from the "objectifying self-orientation" register.[12] Finally, I should note that there has recently been a proliferation of discourses about "equality" *(pheap smaoe knea)* and "human rights" *(setthi monuss)* that are broadly tied to Cambodia's encounter with modernity and more proximately linked to the ideological influence of foreign governments, Khmer refugees and expatriates, the United Nations (particularly during and after the UNTAC period), NGOs (especially human rights organization), and government officials who want to show that they have "modern" values — often speaking of "human rights" and "equality" in tandem with other modern tropes of "the rule of law," "development," "progress," and "civil society."

Nevertheless, one should not underestimate the salience of hierarchy in Cambodia. Even in nonformal, familiar contexts, people remain aware of status differences, which are calculated from an assessment of a person's age, gender, familial background, ethnicity, birth order, occupation, political influence, power, education, benevolence, religious piety, and personal character. Dyadic relationships are negotiated and structured on the basis of such knowledge, as illustrated by each person's choice of verbal and nonverbal patterns of behavior. Moreover, it would be a mistake to simply project Western liberal democratic egalitarian ideals onto the Cambodian landscape and assume that people view hierarchy negatively, as a form of domination opposed to their "natural" desire for equality. While Cambodians sometimes resent or resist having to defer to people of higher status, they often value relationships of personal dependency, which provide protection, order, and the possibility of improving one's station.

Moreover, the idea that ranked difference is "natural" has enormous ontological resonance for many Cambodians. Buddhism, for example, provides a highly salient ontological foundation for Khmer conceptions of hierarchy and social order, particularly the Buddhist principles of dependent origination and karma, which I described in Chapter 2. Structurally, Buddhism generates a moral hierarchy, since each being is viewed as having a different store of merit that determines their place in the social order.[13]

At the same time as it posits a structural hierarchy, however, Buddhism also allows for the possibility of social mobility. The Buddha explicitly rejected the Brahmanic link between status and birth, arguing that one's station is determined through individual action. Each person chooses to act in more or less mindful ways, thereby leading to a rise or decline in cosmic rank. Moreover, a person's store of merit may not be immediately manifest (or, according to many lay practitioners, it may change over this lifetime as one performs meritorious acts). A man may suddenly rise in status when joining the monastic order. Or, a peasant child might one day become a high-ranking official, as was the case with one man from Banyan village. This model of structural mobility, combined with the great stress that is placed on social prestige in Cambodian society, strongly motivates many people to increase their social status.

Such cultural models of hierarchy also gain resonance from embodied practices. As a number of scholars have noted, the body is a self-implicating template upon which cultural knowledge is inscribed. Some of our earliest understandings are derived from the experience of having bodies that move, bend, feel, and breathe. As we develop, these sensorimotor schemas become part of the scaffolding out of which increasingly complex cultural models are built, helping to provide them with emotion-laden, self-implicating meaning and motivational force. All human beings, for example, have some sort of elementary notion of verticality associated with the perception of high and low, the experience of bodies and limbs that move up and down, and life in an environment structured by gravity and filled with beings and objects that rise and fall.[14] If all human beings share such elementary embodied experiences, each society shapes and elaborates them to a different extent and in culturally distinct ways, often through a process of metaphorical mapping. Because they are such a salient part of early sensorimotor experience, then, some of these elementary schemas may structure knowledge in a wide variety of cultural domains, perhaps contributing to the sense of cultural ethos.[15] In Cambodia, center-periphery and verticality imagery is widespread, providing an ontologically salient metaphorical basis for verbal and nonverbal conceptions of status, hierarchy, and power.

As we saw earlier, to *korop,* or to "respect, honor, and obey" someone, is literally defined as "to bow" *(lumot)* or "bend" *(lumot lumaon)* oneself before them, though the term figuratively connotes respect, humbleness, modesty, and a fearful or awesome reverence. Not surprisingly, in Cambodia there are a number of semiformal to formal social contexts in which one is expected to physically bend one's body *(aon, lumaon, aon lumton)* when passing in front of those of a higher status. The cultural model of a social subordinate giving honor, respect, and obedience to his or her social superior is reflected in a number of idealized nonverbal behaviors: a subordinate should sit lower than a superior, not stare at a superior's face, allow superiors to walk first, not touch superiors, and get out of their way as they pass. Like linguistic registers, these embodied hierarchical practices are learned at an early age and later performed regularly and often without conscious reflection.

A somewhat more formal way of bending down to pay homage to social superiors is to *thvay bângkum.* This more ritualized form of prostration involves kneeling down, pressing the palms together and then touching the hands (less respectful) or upper arms and head (more respectful) to the floor.[16] A person typically pays homage in this manner when interacting with "mana-filled" beings who deserve "otherworldly respect," such as monks, Buddha images, or royalty. Thus, when entering or leaving the presence of a monk or Buddha image, a person will *thvay bângkum* three times, a symbolically loaded number in Buddhist cosmology.

In less formal interactions, a person may evince deference through a polite greeting *(chumreap suor)* that includes a nonverbal salutation *(sâmpeah)*. This salutation involves pressing the hands together at the chest, with the fingers extending upward and the head bent slightly forward.[17] The status of the person being greeted is indexed by the level of the hands, which may be raised to the chest (slight deference), mouth (moderate deference), or eyebrows (strong deference). The importance of this polite salutation is illustrated by the emphasis placed on it during the socialization process. Many Cambodian parents begin to teach their infants to politely greet visitors and family elders even before the child can walk. To prefigure some of my discussion below, I should also note that, in his summary of Oum Chhan's confession, the interrogator briefly states that he forced Oum Chhan to "*sâmpeah* the image of a dog" with Ho Chi Minh's head on it, a torture used at Tuol Sleng.[18]

By enacting codes of knowledge inscribing rank, these embodied practices serve as a form of social memory and as an ontologically resonant "choreography of hierarchy."[19] One literally molds one's body into a icon of ranked difference, experiencing, feeling, and performing the relative "height" of one's social "standing." Not surprisingly, metaphors of verticality also appear frequently in speech.

THE DK SOCIAL ORDER

Unless there is a view and an analytical standpoint
according to the science of Marxist-Leninism following
dialectical materialism, only then will that analysis be
correct as a base; and if analysis is valid as a base it will
lead to . . . similarly valid basic measures.

Revolutionary Flags[20]

In keeping with their desire to eliminate traditional forms of inequality while creating an egalitarian, peasant-based communist society, the Khmer Rouge attempted to suppress most linguistic registers and nonverbal behaviors that connoted hierarchical difference.[21] The strongly marked titles, terms of address, and special vocabularies in the "otherworldly respect" register were banned,[22] a transformation fostered by collectivism and the elimination of the monarchy, Buddhism, and the old civilian and military order. When one man addressed a Khmer Rouge soldier with the title *lok* ("sir") just after liberation, the soldier replied: "Don't call me sir, call me comrade. . . . No one is called sir after the revolution. We have been fighting to get rid of these words."[23]

Likewise, because they could imply nonrelatedness, condescension, anger, and self-specificity, most terms from the "objectifying self-orientation" also dropped from usage, particularly in the context of everyday collective life.[24] Many connotations of this register were opposed to the core values of the new DK society, where the people were expected to work in a spirit of cooperation and equality. Moreover, instead of *vea,* Cambodians were supposed to use the mid-level personal pronoun *koat* when referring to children, who were glorified by the Khmer Rouge regime.[25] More generally, the "self-orientation" of this register conflicted with a core value of this ethos: the subordination of the individual to the collective interest. Even the use of the first-person personal pronoun *khnhom* ("I") was often discouraged in favor of expressions such as *yoeng khnhom* ("we/I") or *yoeng* ("we"), which emphasized the primacy of the collective. This tendency was taken to its extreme among the party elite in Phnom Penh, where, as Laurence Picq recalled, *khnhom* "disappeared from the spoken language. . . . One would speak or act only in the name of the group: *we* do this, *we* think that."[26] High-modernist regimes thrive on such imagined homogeneity, as a population of "individuals" is leveled into a "collective" mass, divisible into a limited set of "compositions" *(sâmasâpheap)* that are more legible and conducive to manipulation from above.

As the decreased use of *khnhom* suggests, the "relationship/reciprocity" register, with its relatively greater emphasis on interdependence, connection, and equality, was also modified in accordance with Khmer Rouge ideology.[27] While people continued to use kinship terms in some contexts (for example, in secrecy at home), Cambodians most frequently called each other by the title *mitt* ("comrade friend"), though sometimes this title was combined with a kinship term to broadly mark a difference of age. In keeping with their veneration of children and their attempt to co-opt family sentiment, the Khmer Rouge encouraged children to refer to their parents as "comrade" or to extend the use of the more rural terms for "mother" *(puk)* and "father" *(mae)* to older adults in general.

More broadly, the Khmer Rouge promoted the use of such rural terms because the regime glorified the peasantry, with its more egalitarian ethos and less "corrupt" way of life. A number of words associated with urban areas — now regarded as vile centers of capitalism, corruption, imperialism, and class oppression — dropped out of usage. If, for example, a person showed knowledge of a foreign language, he or she was immediately suspect, since this indicated an impure class background. During DK, Cambodians most commonly used the rural words for such activities as eating and sleeping *(houp* and *sâmrak* as opposed to *nham* and *keng)*. Seng, a Kompong Cham civil servant who was an "old person" during DK, recalled:

> The Khmer Rouge created a new order of life and a new morality that was based on the peasant class. For example, their style of dress didn't have color; it was [modeled after] the plain black clothes that farmers wore when working in the fields. . . . They also governed our speech and created new ways of talking. For example, city people used to say words like *keng* ("sleep"), *nham* ("to eat"), and so forth. The Khmer Rouge replaced *nham* with [the peasant class word] *houp* and *keng* with [the peasant class word] *sâmrak*. Everyone slept/rested *(sâmrak)* and ate *(houp)*, "big people," "little people," those having rank *(bon sâkti)*. In addition, we learned that we were expected to boast about and praise the goodness of the Revolutionary Organization and Communist Party of Kampuchea. Ângkar did things because it was clairvoyant, was alert and intelligent, had a brilliant party line, and [guided us with its] correct leadership. Thus the people had to speak [Ângkar's] language fluently. This was the way in which they controlled our consciousness *(sâtiarâmma)* and minds.

Seng's comments illustrate how the Khmer Rouge transformed linguistic registers in accordance with their communist ideology and exaltation of the peasant class. More broadly, these changes were part of the DK plan to transform the consciousness of the population.

The DK attack on the old hierarchy took place on other fronts as well. Nonverbal behaviors connoting hierarchical difference, such as bending down, prostration, and politely greeting others, were largely abandoned during DK. Still, as Oum Chhan's confession suggests, verbal and nonverbal expressions of hierarchical difference remained in use in some contexts. In more public settings, a person's status might be acknowledged through modest forms of deference, such as averting one's eyes, slightly lowering one's head or body, or using a moderately deferential term of address. For example, a person might call a village chief or a high-ranking cadre "elder" *(bâng)* or "grandfather" *(ta)*. Even Pol Pot was sometimes referred to as "elder brother number one" *(bâng ti muoy)*. In less public social spaces, a relatively greater degree of deference might be shown. Haing Ngor, for example, recalls how, after he gained the patronage of Youen, a village chief, he and his wife began to do a variety of tasks for Youen's family and showed them great respect: "Whenever I walked past anyone in Youen's family I bent over to keep my head lower than theirs. Even if they were sitting down, I tried to stay lower than them. In Cambodia this is the normal deference shown to masters by their servants."[28]

Tuol Sleng provides another interesting illustration of this point. A telephone directory for the prison staff lists cadres in three tiers: by full name (Vaen Kheuan's name appears in this category), by the title *mitt* ("comrade-friend"), and by the title *bâng* ("elder brother").[29] Nine high-ranking cadres, including Lor and Duch, were listed by the last title, though Duch was occasionally referred to as *ta* ("grandfather") in documents. According to Vann Nath, the prison staff treated Duch with deference. When guards brought him before Duch, who was seated on a couch, Vann Nath immediately noticed that they treated him "with a lot of respect. . . . His words seemed so powerful and his bodyguards appeared like mice cowering in front of a cat."[30]

The interactions between prisoners and guards are also revealing. Both Vann Nath and Ung Pech recalled that S-21 personnel referred to the prisoners using terms from the "objectifying self-orientation" register (for example, *ânh, âhaeng, a-/mi, vea, si*) that connoted their animosity, superiority, condescension, and contempt. These terms, which largely dropped from use in the context of everyday social life among the masses, were considered appropriate when referring to "enemies" and "traitors" who were excluded from this revolutionary community of equals. Moreover, their ostracism and dehumanization symbolically asserted the superiority and dominance of the DK regime over the countries with whom these "traitors" were allied. Not surprisingly, Khmer Rouge publications, speeches, and documents frequently refer to "enemies" using the vulgar pronoun *vea*.

By marking its enemies in this dehumanizing manner, the DK regime helped to morally legitimate violence against them. Vann Nath recalled the disdain with which cadres usually treated prisoners:

> We were worth less than an animal to them. They'd yell, threaten, and order us around. They'd just say one or two words and if we didn't do what they said they would come and beat us. They didn't treat us like people. . . . I was really scared of them. . . . They were "bigger" and "higher" than us by far. We'd bend down *(aon lumton)* before them. They didn't

respond to us, in turn . . . We called them "elder" *(bâng)*, never "younger
sibling" or "cousin." Always "elder." If we wanted to do anything, we'd
have to ask their permission. . . . Lor was particularly brutal. I didn't dare
look at his face. Once he walked up to me while I was painting and
knocked my shoulder. He glared at me and asked, "Do you *(aeng)* know
who I *(ânh)* am?" We were really afraid of him. I bent down *(aon)* before
him and replied, "Elder *(bâng)*, I don't know you." Then he laughed.

Vann Nath's comments highlight the relationship of extreme domination
that existed between prisoners and guards at S-21. The prisoners
expressed deference and respect toward the guards (calling the cadres
"elder," bending down before them, not daring to look at their faces),
who usually responded with disdain (ignoring the prisoners, speaking to
them in vulgar or hostile terms, intimidating them). When angered, cadres
might hit a prisoner on the head with their hands or shoes, another nonverbal behavior of superiority since the head is a symbol of a person's status and touching the head may signify contempt or domination.

As this example illustrates, Cambodians continued to strategically
negotiate hierarchical difference during DK, in part through the use of
linguistic registers and nonverbal registers, though the social landscapes
in which they acted had changed. While the DK regime exerted structural
pressures to use language in ways that accorded with their revolutionary
goals, people operated within these constraints, strategically choosing
when and how to speak to others. If Haing Ngor used "proper" revolutionary discourse most of the time, he might invoke ostensibly banned
registers when interacting with his wife or Youen's family. Similarly,
cadres like Lor and Vaen Kheuan altered their speech registers when
addressing prisoners, their peers, or superiors like Duch.

Despite Khmer Rouge claims to the contrary, then, new elites emerged
and were given high social status during DK. To many Cambodians, the
new DK society seemed to be characterized by a series of structural reversals. Haing Ngor remarked upon this when discussing his relationship
with Youen: "It was amazing, really, what had happened to us. In Phnom
Penh, as a doctor, I would never have stooped before an illiterate farmer
like Youen. He would have lowered himself in front of me. Now everything was reversed. I offered him water with my eyes downcast, the cup
held in both hands."[31]

DK society was characterized by a number of status reversals, as the
rural poor came to dominate the urban rich. Thus "new people" (which
included peasants who had sought refuge in the cities during the civil
war) were distinguished from "base/old people." Likewise, the Khmer

Rouge frequently contrasted the "corrupt" cities from "pure" rural areas and used a tripartite classification system to categorize people into those having "full rights," "candidates," and "depositees." Urbanites were placed in the lowest rungs of this new social order (becoming "new people" and "depositees") and were last in line for party membership.

But there were other structural shifts as well. Status differences between men and women (like those between the young and the old) were supposed to be eliminated in the new egalitarian society. Article 13 of the DK constitution stated: "There must be complete equality among all Kampuchean people. . . . Men and women are equal in every respect." Whereas a woman's honor had formerly been linked to the industriousness, comportment, orderly household, and sexual purity of "the perfectly virtuous woman" *(srey kruap leak)*,[32] it was now judged, like the honor of a man, by her revolutionary zeal. Men and women performed many of the same arduous tasks, and women like Grandmother Yit, Rom, and Phat were given positions of authority that would have usually gone to men in earlier times. Nevertheless, aside from the wives of Pol Pot, Ieng Sary, and Son Sen, women were largely absent from the highest echelons of the DK regime.

Another interesting aspect of DK gender ideology, partly inspired by Maoist China, was its erasure of many outward differences between men and women. Women cut their hair short, dressed in the same black garb as men, worked like men, avoided wearing markers of gender like jewelry and perfume, and used the same revolutionary idioms as men. Moreover, the collectivization of economic production, consumption, and sometimes even caretaking undermined the traditional role of women in the household. Sexual relations also became more infrequent because of forced separation, state-arranged marriages, malnutrition, and exhaustion. This ethos of gender homogenization, in which women tended to exhibit traditionally masculine behaviors, was symbolically reflected by transformations in song and dance, which had been highly gendered. While there was still variation, male and female performers now tended to dress similarly and move with the same stylized (and often more traditionally masculine) motions and gestures.[33] The leveling of status and gender difference between men and women also reflects the DK regime's high-modernist orientation, as it sought to create and manipulate a homogenous population of revolutionaries.

DK social status in general was closely linked to this project of social engineering, which was often idealized through metaphors of construction. These metaphors of construction were among the most salient tropes in Khmer Rouge ideology and took a number of forms. Khmer Rouge discourse exhorted the population to "build" *(kâsang)* the country, the revolution, socialism, the collectivist economy, one's worldview, and themselves. From their high-modernist vantage, the DK regime envisioned the revolutionary society as an edifice to be constructed. To be successful, this structure required an appropriate design, which the Party Center as social engineer provided through its party "line" *(meakea)*, formulated on the basis of the high-modernist "science of Marxist-Leninism." Like an engineer's blueprint, Khmer Rouge discourse about this "line" is full of structural and spatial metaphors: "lines," "borders," "bases," "stands," "standpoints," and "dividing lines."

More broadly, the DK party "line" delineated the proper way to build a "base" *(moulâdthan)* upon which the revolution could "stand" *(chhor, chhor loe)*. Specifically, the base required a certain organization and people with a proper revolutionary consciousness, notions that were adapted from Leninist and Maoist thought.[34] The September–October 1976 issue of *Revolutionary Flags,* for example, argued that both of these "basic measures" *(viteanâkar moulâdthan)*, elsewhere referred to as "stands" *(chumhor)* or "standpoints" *(kol chumhor)*, were crucial to the elimination of private property. In terms of "organization" or "management" *(karchattang)*, the Khmer Rouge undermined private property through the elimination of markets and money and the implementation of socioeconomic collectivization: "Live collectively, manage collectively, work collectively, lead collectively. . . . By organizing the collectives this way, we are the masters. Assault private property, keep on pushing private property. It will not have time to breathe."[35] With this organization base, even those "compositions" who were not used to collectivism would be won over as they became accustomed to it and saw "the self-sustaining nature of the collective regime; eating is easy; working is effective; raising children is easy; security is assured."[36]

Perhaps the most significant aspect of the party "line," however, was "political consciousness," an emphasis that was taken from Leninist voluntarism and the Maoist notion that revolutionary will, spirit, and morality (as opposed to an "advanced" stage of economic development) could propel an agrarian state to make a "great leap forward" toward communism. An October 1976 issue of *Revolutionary Young Men and Women* proclaimed, "From the very beginning, the Party determined to take the work of political consciousness *(sâtiarâmma)* as the most important work of all."[37] The Khmer Rouge most often discussed political "consciousness" using the term *sâtiarâmma.* Cambodians sometimes use *arâmma* broadly to refer to emotions or moods, but *arâmma* also has the more specific Buddhist connotation of a "perception" or "object of mind" that is generated when something attracts the senses.[38] In Buddhism, one of the ways in which one begins to overcome suffering is by learning to understand and control *arâmma* through mindfulness, or *sâti*.

Sâtiarâmma can be glossed as "mindful" consciousness in the sense that one remembers, recollects, recognizes, thinks, and acts in a lucid, attentive, and aware manner.[39] According to the Buddhist monk Phra Prayudh Payutto, the basic function of *sâti* is:

> to prevent the mind from becoming unfocused; it does not allow day-dreaming nor aimlessly drifting along with the flow of mind-objects. It focuses the mind's eye of attention on each passing impression that comes into consciousness, and it turns our gaze on the flow of thought. When we wish to concentrate on a particular object, it fixes our attention on it, not allowing the object to drift away or disappear. . . . [It] can be compared to a gatekeeper, because it guards over the various sense-doors through which impressions pass, checking everything that happens. . . . [M]indfulness is the overseer and inspector of the stream of consciousness and all thought and action, ensuring that they remain within determined bounds and stay with the designated mind-objects.[40]

The Khmer Rouge term *sâtiarâmma*, then, may be translated as "revolutionary consciousness" but implies that one "mindfully" assesses, monitors, and focuses upon objects of consciousness. Just as, in Buddhism, mindfulness is based on an understanding of *dhamma*, for the Khmer Rouge *sâtiarâmma* required comprehension of the DK party "line," and ultimately Marxist-Leninism. In both cases, proper action follows from this mindful understanding.

The article in the September–October 1976 special issue of *Revolutionary Flags* that I have discussed is entitled "Sharpen the Consciousness [*sâtiarâmma*] of the Proletarian Class to be as Keen and Strong as Possible," and it is explicitly concerned with explaining the principles that would enable revolutionaries to think and behave in such a "mindful" manner.[41] Much of the document focuses on basic class analysis, which the author (probably Pol Pot or Nuon Chea) attempts to convey through simple theoretical explanations, concrete examples, concise summaries, revolutionary slogans, and repetition. The most difficult section is the brief concluding "Review of Dialectical Materialism."

If revolutionaries "absorbed" the principles relating to class struggle, class division, class traits, class contradiction, and "building" an appropriate "standpoint," they would be able to mindfully "scrutinize" the thoughts and actions of themselves and others. In a subsection entitled "What Must We Struggle to Eliminate and What Must We Struggle to Build On?" for example, the article discusses the qualities that each person must seek to eliminate and "build upon": "We must rid in each party member, each cadre, everything that is of the oppressor class, of private property, of stance, view, sentiment, custom, literature, art . . . which exists in ourselves, no matter how much or how little. As for construction, it is just the same: we must build a proletarian class worldview, proletarian class life; build a proletarian class stand regarding thinking, in living habits, in morality, in sentiment, etc."[42] The tract goes on to argue that this process had to be guided by comprehension of the "clear dividing line between private property and collective property; private stand and collective stand." With this understanding, each person would be able to act mindfully, carefully evaluating their thoughts and feelings:

> If we stand on collectivism, even if some objective attracts us, we will have the time to consider. Having thought about it, we realize that we are about to slide into the private; we run back immediately to the collective. . . .
>
> Therefore, we must hasten to stand on collectivism immediately. And do not stand on the dividing line. Stand deeply on collectivism. Get ourselves ready, immediately sit on collectivism's chair. Scrutinize each problem. We must scrutinize ourselves; is there a stand on collectivism yet? Sometimes we say we are already standing on collectivism, but the result of solving the problem affects collectivism. There, this stand is not yet correct; our line of solving is not yet valid. We must reevaluate our stand.
>
> Morality is the same. For example, if we are living with a woman. As time goes on, the material atmosphere leads to the development of sentiment. If we stand on the collective, we must manage the solution immediately. But if we just expand and strengthen the management, remaining attached to this woman, this is a strong private stand. A strong private stand by a certain point will have affected morality. . . .
>
> And say that someone offered the private chair to us to sit in. No one gave it to us. Because the private chair is everywhere around us. We must look for the collective chair and grasp it tightly.

This passage is revealing about *sâtiarâmma* and suggests another way in which Khmer Rouge ideology drew directly on Buddhist thought. (It also suggests why the Khmer Rouge viewed interpersonal sentiment, outside of attachment to the party, as a threat: it led to a "private stand" that was opposed to collectivism.) From moment to moment, each person's consciousness is attracted to and focused on given "mind-objects." A person's response to these mental formations may be based on ignorance, conditioned by the impure dispositions and traits that are linked to a person's past experience and that ultimately lead to suffering. Two examples of this are given in the above tracts: being drawn to a "private stand" and becoming attracted to a member of the opposite sex, leading to mental and moral defilement. If a cadre comprehends the party line and its "collective stand," however, he or she may mindfully evaluate these mental formations and respond accordingly, resulting in mental and moral purity. Thus the passage urges cadres to "scrutinize" and "consider" things mindfully, making sure that they do not "slide into the private" but continue to build the "proper socialist traits" that would supposedly alleviate social suffering.

This line of thinking about revolutionary consciousness directly parallels Buddhist thought, with the "Party line" and "collective stand" being substituted for *dhamma*. In Buddhism, mindfulness enables one to see the true nature of things and act in a proper and aware manner, while ignorance leads to craving and attachment, and ultimately suffering. Moral purity is linked to mindful evaluation and action; moral defilement is a consequence of ignorance and corrupt tendencies. One could certainly push this argument further, contending that the Khmer Rouge attempted to assume the monk's traditional role as moral instructor (teaching their new brand of "mindfulness") and that the DK regime's glorification of asceticism, detachment, the elimination of attachment and desire, renunciation (of material goods and personal behaviors, sentiments, and attitudes), and purity paralleled prominent Buddhist themes that were geared toward helping a person attain greater mindfulness.[43] For the Khmer Rouge, the construction of such traits was essential to building a proper revolutionary consciousness — just as monks sought to cultivate a mindfulness that would enable them to reach nirvana *(nibanna)*. Yet again, we encounter a strange Khmer Rouge ideological palimpsest blending high-modernist, Marxist-Leninist, Maoist, and local Buddhist thought.

If the Khmer Rouge deemphasized the individual, they nevertheless viewed the cultivation of *sâtiarâmma* as something that each person should diligently pursue and that they obtained to different degrees, somewhat like merit. Because "everything always changes" *(brae bruol chea nich)* and everyone had been exposed to the corrupt old society, even the most loyal of cadres might come to "sit in the private chair" and betray the revolution. Thus everyone had to continually struggle to eliminate "everything that is of the oppressor class, of private property, of stance, view, sentiment, custom, literature, art . . . which exists in ourselves, no matter how much or how little," while building the opposite proletarian traits. To help both cadres and the masses "build" their political consciousness, the Khmer Rouge employed a number of mechanisms: "There are meetings, listening to radio broadcasts, studying short documents, by word of mouth itself, by documents from the Regions or the Sectors. The study can be a half day, one day or two to three days depending on the concrete situation."[44]

The DK regime supplemented such propaganda with structural practices — many of which were modeled after other communist movements — designed to help people "build" their consciousness. First, consciousness could be constructed through the alteration of one's everyday environment and habits in accordance with the "collective stand." Collectivization undermined the pernicious influence of money, trade, and private property. Ideally, everyone would renounce their private possessions and sentiments and throw themselves into collective tasks. Even suspect groups, like "new people," might eventually be redeemed by performing types of manual labor associated with the "worker-peasant" class. The virtue of education through hard work was extolled through slogans, many adapted from Maoist discourse, such as "Our school is our farm. The land is our paper. The plow is our pen."[45]

This type of "thought-reform," which was heavily influenced by Maoism and had high-modernist and Buddhist overtones, was supplemented by criticism and self-criticism sessions and biographical questionnaires that were supposed to enable a person to learn how to regularly "scrutinize" his or her thoughts and behaviors. Thus, during DK, a senior aide to Foreign Minister Ieng Sary kept a notebook in which he summarized the self-criticism of "Comrade Dean," who admitted to shortcomings in his consciousness, such as feeling attachment to family members ("still misses family and children"), having tendencies toward a "private stand" ("wants enough property," has a "middle-class standpoint," and exhibits "private ownership in terms of power and orders"), and behaving in ways that reflected improper attitudes (not instructing comrades constantly or behaving "impolitely" or "badly" toward others). [46] Of course, such remarks, whether made by oneself or by others, were dangerous, since they might suggest "regression" or even espionage.

Like criticism and self-criticism sessions, the practice of constructing autobiographies took place in the cooperatives, where it was used not just to help people build their consciousness but also to extract basic information about class background.[47] Among cadres, the writing of autobiographies was more formal and crucial to one's career. When someone became a member of the party or joined the secret police, for example, he or she was required to complete an eleven-page biographical questionnaire.[48] The questionnaire was divided into seven sections, which asked for information about the respondent and his or her spouse, children, parents, in-laws, siblings, and "close friends and social environment."

As illustrated by Lor's autobiography, the questions were designed to ascertain a person's class status, history of associations, and state of consciousness. After asking basic information about a person's name, place and date of birth, sex, ethnicity, and marital status, the first section of the questionnaire, "About Yourself," attempted to determine a person's class status by inquiring about the respondents' "occupation and original class." Lor's autobiography states that his family were vegetable farmers of the "mid-level middle class," an assertion that is supported by a detailed description of his family's land holdings (seven plots of various sizes), crop yields (primarily corn and green beans used for subsistence), material possessions (two oxen, an ox-cart, a rake, a plow, a bike, and a radio), and house (7 × 5 meters with a bamboo floor, wooden walls, and concrete stilts). Other questions attempt to fix the respondents' revolutionary status by inquiring about such things as their length of revolutionary service (Lor joined the army in 1972), membership in revolutionary organizations (he belonged to the Communist Youth League of Kampuchea), educational background (he had three years of schooling and was literate), positions and rank (he had risen from mere combatant to deputy commander of the S-21 guards), and history of revolutionary activity (though he didn't mention it in his autobiography, Lor had twice been wounded in battle, which would have given him additional status).

Yet another set of questions were concerned with tracing a person's history of connections. The questions inquire about the dates the respondent joined the revolution or various revolutionary organizations, asking: "Where? Who brought you to join?" Lor joined the revolution on October 2, 1972, shortly after Khmer Rouge troops "liberated" his village in Kandal province, under the patronage of the village chief. Such information might prove lethal, as these conjunctions of patronage and association could be viewed as moments of betrayal. The confessions of Reap and Oum Chhan provide a clear illustration of this point, since they eventually "confessed" that their patrons enticed them to "join the CIA," often with a promise of material rewards that signified regression into a "private stand." Similarly, Lor became nervous when a former commander who had "brought him to join" the Communist Youth

League of Kampuchea was incarcerated at Tuol Sleng, and when coworkers at S-21 were arrested and interrogated.

The biographical questionnaire also sought information about a
respondent's connections in other ways, inquiring about the names, occupations, class, and revolutionary background of his or her spouse, children, parents, in-laws, siblings, and "close friends." In each case, the
respondent was asked about how much influence *(etthipol)* these friends
and relatives had over the respondent and vice versa. For instance, Lor
provided basic information about his parents (mid-level middle peasants
who were not directly involved in politics) and siblings (two of whom
had joined the Khmer Rouge, one as an S-21 guard). He acknowledged
that his parents had influence over him, but in a positive manner: "[My
parents] have influence over me. They instructed me to love the revolution and [taught] me absolutely not to deviate from the Party line." As a
high-ranking revolutionary, Lor had "some influence on [my parents]. I
instructed them to join a cooperative in order to serve the collectivity."
Because he was the eldest child, Lor could also claim that he helped his
siblings build their revolutionary consciousness: "Each of my younger
siblings has no influence on me. For me, I have influence on them. [I tell]
them to strive to build *(kâsang)* themselves and to strive to fulfill the revolutionary duties for the Party." In reality, Lor had little or no contact
with his family during DK.

Lor's replies to this question about "influence" highlight a key issue in
the questionnaire: revolutionary consciousness. On the one hand, the
purity of a respondent's revolutionary consciousness was suggested by
class background, interpersonal associations, organizational affiliations,
history of revolutionary activity, political education (Lor had attended
political education seminars four times and had prepared his autobiography three times previously), and "reasons for joining the revolution"
or membership in revolutionary organizations. Lor, for example, asserts
the "progressive" nature of his consciousness when describing his motivation to join the revolution and the Communist League of Kampuchea:

> Reasons for joining the revolution: came from my "painful anger" *(chheu
> chap)* toward colonialists, old and new, capitalists, feudalists, reactionar-
> ies, and imperialists who oppressed, invaded, and harmed the people. For
> these reasons, we/I *(yoeng khnhom)* had the spirit and awareness to come
> join the revolutionary ranks, serve the revolution, to fight American impe-
> rialism [in order to] liberate the [oppressed] classes and people.
>   Reasons for joining the Communist League of Kampuchea: I had been
> instructed, educated, and indoctrinated about [revolutionary] politics, con-
> sciousness *(sâtiarâmma)*, standpoint *(kol chumhor)*, and organization *(kar-*

chattang). Since then, we/I *(yoeng khnhom)* have striven to fulfill [my] duties and tried hard to build *(kâsang)* myself further. Ângkar entered me in the organization, the Communist League of Kampuchea.

In many ways, such assertions, like so much DK discourse, were performative. Cadres listened to DK pronouncements about the "party line" and attempted to display the verbal and behavioral cues that signified proper consciousness — regardless of the degree to which they supported the revolution — because the public display and evaluation of one's consciousness determined one's social standing and odds of survival.

On the other hand, the questionnaire was intended to help cadres learn to "build" their revolutionary consciousness through self-scrutiny. Of particular importance in this regard was a question that asked, "How clearly do you know your character? To what level? How well do you know your strengths and weaknesses? How have you changed your non-revolutionary character and weaknesses? What is the result?" In their autobiographies, most cadres, including Lor and Vaen Kheuan, answered this question about revolutionary consciousness in the greatest detail (usually followed by fairly lengthy responses to the questions concerning their class background and history of revolutionary activities). The responses to this question were usually divided into a list of prerevolutionary and revolutionary "strengths" *(kunsâmbâtte)*, "weaknesses" *(kunvibâtte),* and "directions for change." Lor's autobiography states:

MY CHARACTER IN THE OLD SOCIETY

Strengths: Helped parents and siblings with [various] work. Talked politely with seniors.

Weaknesses: Talked impolitely with siblings; irritable, quick to anger, and strong tempered; liked to tease [others] a lot; watched movie dramas; danced; liked to listen to the radio; stole vegetables and fruits from neighbors but just in small amounts for eating.

Consciousness (sâtiarâmma): Loved a girl named Sim Leang Suy, but never violated/touched her body. Never talked with her. Just secretly fell in love with her.

MY CHARACTER IN THE REVOLUTIONARY SOCIETY

Strengths: Strive to fulfill my duties, big and small, which the party assigns, without hesitation or argument. As for my duties, even if these duties are in some way difficult, cause suffering, or are complicated, [I] strive hard to overcome [these difficulties] and fulfill these duties for the party until they are completed.

Weaknesses: Speak impolitely to comrades; tease [others] a lot; irritable,

quick to anger, and strong-tempered. In leadership, [I] was not careful,
leading the people to guard carelessly so that an enemy escaped and an
enemy seized a gun [from the guard] and killed itself *(vea)*. In analyzing
and investigating the people, not arresting those close [to me]. In investigating the activity of the enemy, [I] don't yet do it vigorously enough.
[I] underestimated the enemy's activities. In fulfilling my future duties,
[I am] still too loose and not yet wise. In carrying out my work and
fulfilling my duties, [I] don't draw on experience often enough. If there
is a problem, I'm too slack. Until the level above gives directions, I'm
slow [and lack the] stand *(chumhor)* and intelligence to lead the people.

Directions for change: After seeing my failures, I am determined to change
my attitudes and behaviors that have a nonrevolutionary character,
to make myself clean and resolute. And I will strive to build *(kâsang)*
myself and build the revolutionary stand *(chumhor)* of the proletarian
class and of the party firmly and resolutely.

Structurally, Lor's response illustrates the mental dialectics of Khmer
Rouge thought, which had Buddhist overtones. Everything changes,
including the perceptions, feelings, and thoughts that enter one's mind.
Because of past experience, many of these thoughts may be "regressive"
and deviate from the party line. Through practice, one cultivates a proper
understanding, which enables one to mindfully scrutinize one's thoughts
and appropriately focus one's revolutionary consciousness.

Even seasoned cadres might slip into a "private stand" due to
unwholesome tendencies they had developed in the old society. Lor, for
example, recounts how, during prerevolutionary times, he fell in love
with a girl. As we saw above in a passage from the special issue of
Revolutionary Flags, for the Khmer Rouge, such attachments constituted
"a strong private stand" that at a "certain point will have affected morality." Lor is careful to note that he never "violated" the woman, thereby
asserting that his morality remained pure even if his thoughts did not.
Elsewhere, Lor analyzes other aspects of his revolutionary consciousness, including his concentration, perseverance, implementation, and
understanding of the party line. Although Lor always worked hard to
"fulfill my duties, big and small, . . . without hesitation," he sometimes
lost focus and was "careless." These shortcomings led to problems. Thus
a prisoner was once able to seize a gun and commit suicide. Even as Lor
admits that he is "too loose and not yet wise . . . [and lacks the] stand
and intelligence to lead the people," he nevertheless vows to "to change
my attitudes and behaviors that have a nonrevolutionary character, to
make myself clean and resolute."

Ultimately, writing one's autobiography, like participating in criticism and self-criticism sessions, was a dangerous, performative practice. One had to carefully balance one's "strengths" and "weaknesses," while ultimately asserting the potential of one's revolutionary consciousness. No doubt many cadres believed in what they were doing, as Laurence Picq's description of life among the Khmer Rouge elite in Phnom Penh suggests. In some situations, a cadre's responses might be clichéd, a parroting back of slogans that he or she had heard but did not understand. Thus one finds a great deal of redundancy when comparing the autobiographies of cadres like Lor and Vaen Kheuan. Both claim to be "irritable," "quick to anger," "impolite" at times, and so forth. These almost rote responses are mixed with real events. Lor loses focus and enables a prisoner to seize a gun; Vaen Kheuan loses concentration and "sometimes beats prisoners to death."

Interestingly, Vaen Kheuan's horrific admission occurs in a longer subsection of his autobiography entitled "The Execution of the Party Line." Vaen Kheuan begins the discussion of his "strengths" by asserting: "From the time I joined the revolution, I have understood a large part of the party line." He goes on to analyze his character and interrogation behavior in terms of *sâtiarâmma*, his "stand," "construction," "mastery," and "duty." Like Lor and other cadres, he attempts to demonstrate that he can recognize and distinguish wholesome and unwholesome thoughts and behaviors, a capacity of mindfulness that, in the Khmer Rouge worldview, could ultimately lead to an enlightened state of pure revolutionary consciousness.

Theoretically, anyone could attain this state of Khmer Rouge "enlightenment." But, as we have seen, the Khmer Rouge believed that one's capacity for change was strongly influenced by one's class background and history of associations, since one's mental tendencies were highly structured by past experience. Khmer Rouge social structure followed from this premise. In accordance with their high-modernist orientation, the Khmer Rouge parsed and sorted the population into a set of class-based categories, each having a given "essence" *(khloemsar)* or "composition" *(sâmasâpheap)* and characterized by certain "elemental traits" *(theatu)* and a given degree of mental contamination, particularly with regard to their relative leaning toward a "private" or "collective stand."

The "Sharpen the Consciousness" article devotes a great deal of space to discussing the "traits" of each social class. At one point, the article condenses its class analysis into a chart ranking the "private stand" of various classes:[49]

		1. Capitalist	
PRIVATE	I.	2. Landlord	10%
PROPERTY		3. Rich Peasant	

		Upper Bourgeoisie	4%
	II.	4. Upper-Middle Peasant	
		Upper Peddler	

		Lower Bourgeoisie	
		Middle Bourgeoisie	Receive
	III.	Poor and Lower-Middle Peasants	Influence
		Worker-Coolies	

According to the tract, the first three groups "base themselves on private property as their foundation."[50] Capitalists, in particular, "stand on the base of private property," which has become part of their "soul" and "oppresses" lower classes while seeking "profit" — the motive that also drove "feudal-landlords" (who participated in "exchange, usury, and land rent"), rich peasants ("semi-capitalists"), and the upper bourgeoisie ("big and small peddlers in the markets" and "upper-middle peasants"). Even the lower classes, ranging from petty bourgeoisie to poor peasants, had been influenced by the capitalist regime under which they lived, so that their "dealing, living and working habits are in the framework of private property. Therefore their dealings seek to obtain individual wealth, to live individually, work individually, and make merit individually." Ultimately, however, workers and peasants were much more "at ease" with collectivization because they had been oppressed. The private stand of the "capitalist, landlord and rich peasants classes," in contrast, remained "thick," and this "trait" was directly opposed to the collectivist "base" upon which the new revolutionary society "stood."

In the DK social order, then, group status was directly linked to revolutionary consciousness. Each class varied in its "composition" and "traits," resulting in behavioral and mental tendencies that more or less predisposed it toward the party line. The greater the potential to "absorb" this "line," and therefore to develop a proper revolutionary consciousness, the higher the group's status. Again we meet the theme of reversals, as the old social order in which the capitalists classes dominated (categories I, II, III in the above list) was inverted (III, II, I). Thus, "old people" were accorded much higher status than "new people," who had lived in the cities, the bastions of capitalism, and were therefore strongly predisposed toward a "private stand." In the DK regime's plans for social engineering, these "old people" would form the "base" upon which the revolution would "stand" — thus their alternative designation as "base people." Similarly, the young, who supposedly hadn't had time to develop many unwholesome tendencies, were viewed as having the greatest potential for developing a revolutionary consciousness, though the children of "old people" tended to be viewed as more pure than those of "new people." In fact, the Khmer Rouge sometimes called children the "central supporting column of the country."[51]

From their high-modernist perspective, the Khmer Rouge leadership devised a blueprint for revitalization in which those groups with the greatest potential for developing a pure revolutionary consciousness would form the "base" of the new society. Regardless of the structural axis upon which groups were divided in DK — capitalists versus the worker-peasant class, rich versus poor, "new people" versus "old people," urbanites versus the rural population, "depositees" versus "candidates" and "full rights" people — those who formed the foundation of the DK regime's project of social engineering were accorded much higher status than those who had "regressive traits." Since "all things change," even those low-status groups with a "thick" private stand could theoretically be transformed into revolutionary "worker-peasants."[52] Those making "small mistakes must be straightened out by political-consciousness, by warnings, criticism, and education," though transforming oneself was "not easy."

Ultimately, the DK regime faced economic failures and internal subversion, suggesting that many members of these suspect groups had been unable to transform their consciousness. A passage from "Sharpen the Consciousness" states, "For a number of them, we have had results correcting them. A number of them *(vea)* cannot be corrected. The latter *(vea)* continuously seek occasions to oppose the revolution." These incorrigible "enemies," who remained mired in a "private stand," created "class contradictions" that threatened to subvert the revolution and therefore had to be eradicated: "We must eliminate the aspect that opposes, that breaks from the worker-peasant, that affects the worker-peasants."[53] Here we find a warrant for genocide, as the DK regime calls for cadres to "purify out the enemy among the people."

On the local level, such pronouncements contributed to the suspicion, devaluation, and annihilation of low-status groups whose supposedly corrupt minds threatened the revolution. While both "old" and "new

people" experienced great difficulty, "new people" typically received less
food, were allocated worse housing, were subject to more difficult relocation demands, and perhaps most importantly, were given harsher punishments. With luck, an "old person" like Vong might get off with a
warning if caught stealing potatoes; a "new person" might be killed for
doing so. Such discrimination was directly linked to the DK party line. At
one point, the tract in the 1976 special issue of *Revolutionary Flags*
instructs cadres to develop "the analytical habit" of investigating such
"problems."[54] Thus, if a buffalo's leg was injured, cadres were to determine whether the act was intentional by considering the cowherd's
"composition," "class stand," "political stand," and "milieu." Such ideological messages were often "absorbed" by local cadres in an essentialized form. Rom, for example, instructed a village head: "If someone
doesn't work hard, breaks a plow or harrow, or steals, he or she may be
considered an enemy. . . . In such cases, the guilt of an 'old person' is low,
but that of a 'new person' is heavy enough for them to be killed."

Even groups of people who ostensibly could be classified as "worker-
peasants," such as the largely rural, ethnic Muslim Cham population,
might need to be purified.[55] Most of Cambodia's Chams resided in villages located on the banks of waterways, where they subsisted on fishing
and practiced a distinct way of life. Chams spoke their own language (as
well as Khmer), had their own schools, and worshipped in local
mosques. Although Marxist-Leninist theory does not inexorably result in
the abuse of such ethnic groups, it does contain a strong essentializing
impulse that can lead to discrimination and, in the extreme, genocide.[56]
Theoretically, anyone can become a revolutionary. A person's background, however, increases or decreases the likelihood that they will do
so readily, since each group is characterized by a given set of tendencies.
In addition, diversity implicitly constitutes a threat to a communist
regime's goal of creating a homogenous, classless society. In practice,
then, communist regimes have tended to ruthlessly crush minority
groups, especially those suspected of opposing state policies.

Cambodia's Chams were no exception. As the DK regime began reor-
ganizing society in accordance with its "collective stand," it demanded
that Chams abandon most of their customs and live like the rest of the
revolutionary masses. The Khmer Rouge required Cham women to cut
their long hair short and made both sexes stop wearing traditional dress.
All Chams were expected to stop using their "foreign" language and
renounce their religion. Like temples, Cham mosques were often dese-
crated and destroyed. The DK regime also compelled Chams to work

and eat collectively, even if this meant consuming pork. Many Cham communities were also dispersed.

When Chams began to protest and sometimes rebel against these changes, the Khmer Rouge quickly quashed their dissent, interpreting it as an indication of the group's "regressive" traits. Like "new people," Chams would have difficulty developing a proper revolutionary consciousness because of their revisionist "private stand" — their strong personal attachment to religion and private property and their corrupt "worldview," ranging from sentiment to custom. The DK regime responded with a policy of forced assimilation and outright murder. Ben Kiernan, who has conducted extensive research on the genocide of the Chams during DK, interviewed two men who stated they saw a 1978 party document that said Chams would not be spared "because if spared they will resist, [and produce] revisionism. It said that the Cham race is not to be spared because it has a history of resisting the socialist revolution. . . . The document said that 'now, they must be smashed to pieces.'"[57]

As this document suggests, Chams, despite their predominantly rural origins, fell at the bottom of the DK social structure. Like "new people," they were often discriminated against and singled out for execution. In some respects, the local-level treatment of the Chams was even harsher than that of "new people" because of traditional Khmer fear, suspicion, and prejudice against this minority group. If given the option of killing "new people" or Chams, local cadres often chose to execute Chams. A local official who was friendly with the parents of one Banyan villager gave the following explanation for why all fifty Cham families in Ta Khong village were killed (as opposed to only two Khmer families), "It's really difficult because they give me orders to kill Khmer. But I can't cut off my heart and do so. So we take Chams instead, though there aren't many of them."

Overall, approximately 90,000 of Cambodia's 250,000 Chams — over a third of the Cham population (compared to a quarter of the urban Khmer population) — perished during DK.[58] The death toll was particularly brutal in Kompong Siem district (Region 41 of the Central Zone), where Banyan is located. Two PRK documents allege that almost every Cham in the district was executed (estimates range from two thousand families to twenty thousand people).[59] Sim, a Banyan peasant who lived in Kompong Siem at the time, recalled the devastation: "I never saw anyone being killed, but I did see corpses and I saw [the Khmer Rouge] taking away a string of ten Chams who had been arrested. They looked

pale and scared. The subdistrict head was in charge and his men had axes
and knives. Phat was there as well. They killed all the Chams, perhaps
sixty families. None of them survived." Sadly, his comments were typical
of the accounts I heard about the annihilation of Kompong Siem's Cham
population.

As the plight of the Chams illustrates, social status during DK did not
simply follow from class background, though this was the key variable in
the DK social structure, which established new parameters within which
Cambodians negotiated their lives. In the DK social calculus, a variety of
factors influenced a person's status, most of which were related to their
level of political consciousness. Both the biographical questionnaire and
the "Sharpen the Consciousness" tract illustrate that, in addition to
"class composition," social status was related to an individual's history
of revolutionary service, interpersonal associations, morality, and record
of self-construction.

If the autobiographies of Lor and Vaen Kheuan effectively assert the
author's claims to status, the confessions of prisoners are often structured
in an opposite manner to highlight their highly "regressive" political
consciousness. In contrast to Lor's autobiography, for example, Reap's
confession glosses over his class background (most likely mid- or low-
level peasant) and describes his history of treasonous service (he joins the
CIA and attempts to build up a secret network of followers, just as he
probably did when he joined the Khmer Rouge), his membership in corrupt "strings" (his links to the Northern Zone network), his immoral
behavior (sabotaging crops, getting drunk, womanizing, working with
bandits, corrupting others, lack of discipline and renunciation, enjoy-
ment of private property), and minimal self-construction (he "builds"
forces rather than himself). The confessions of Oum Chhan and numerous other cadres are similarly structured to demonstrate their regressive
political consciousness, which allegedly leads them to take a "private"
stance, carry out treasonous activities, and engage in acts of agricultural
sabotage that rationalized the DK regime's economic failures.

Given the above criteria, the status of some people discussed in this
book might be roughly categorized as follows (keeping in mind that we
have limited data and that individual status could change over time),
from highest to lowest:

- Lor: very high status (mid-level middle peasant class background;
  joined revolution at young age; injured in battle; high rank;
  exhibits revolutionary morality and renunciation; engages in
  self-construction)

- Reap: very high status falling to very low status (probably peasant background, long revolutionary service; high rank; initially clean associations turn dirty; "betrays" the revolution and allegedly engages in "immoral," nonrevolutionary behaviors illustrating his strong "private stand")

- Vaen Kheuan: very high status (lower-level middle peasant class background; joined revolution at young age; moderately high rank; asserts revolutionary morality and renunciation; engages in self-construction)

- Grandmother Yit: very high status (peasant background; high rank; clean associations)

- Khel: very high status falling to medium status, then rising again to very high status (peasant background; high rank; clean and dirty associations — required to do agricultural work because his father was a "new person" and drove an orange juice truck)

- Rom: very high status (peasant background; relatively high rank; clean associations)

- Oum Chhan: high status falling to very low status (worker-peasant background; fairly high rank as head of mobile brigade; initially clean associations turn dirty; "betrays" the revolution and allegedly engages in "immoral," nonrevolutionary behaviors illustrating his strong "private stand"; he confesses to uniting with his associates to "make the people have a contradiction with Ângkar's line and destroy the crop yields")

- Vong: moderately high status falling to moderately low status ("1973 person"; peasant background; relatively good associations; status falls after he steals potatoes)

- Neari: moderately low status falling to very low status ("new person/depositee"; rural origins, but family flees to Kompong Cham city during war; father is an "intellectual"; clean and dirty associations — initially protected by Seuan, who is then purged; Khel and Chuon are friends of family)

- Chlat: low status ("new person/depositee"; educated/student; upper-level peasant origins but moves to Phnom Penh; clean and dirty associations — peasant relatives but brothers are a "capitalist" and a Lon Nol soldier who was killed during the civil war)

- Vann Nath: low status falling to very low status ("new person/ depositee"; peasant roots but moves to Battambang and becomes

"petty bourgeoisie"; "betrays" revolution and incarcerated at
Tuol Sleng)

DK social status, then, was strongly correlated with political consciousness: those individuals and groups who had a high, or at least potentially
high, level of revolutionary consciousness usually had high status; low
status in turn reflected a low level of revolutionary consciousness.

Ultimately, the attainment of a pure revolutionary consciousness was
an individual matter, just as in Buddhism each person must learn to cultivate mindfulness. Even if a "new person" could theoretically develop
such a proper revolutionary consciousness over time, the Khmer Rouge
unfortunately grew increasingly paranoid and convinced that at least
some members of these low status groups were incorrigible and therefore
had to be annihilated to prevent the new revolutionary society from
being contaminated. As we will see in the next chapter, identifying enemies was often not easy.

CHAPTER FIVE

Manufacturing Difference

It is necessary to draw a clear line between us and the enemy
and stand on our side to make the revolution. First of all, let
us determine who we are. "We" means our nation, people,
worker-peasant class, revolution, collective system of the
proletariat, cooperatives, trade unions, Revolutionary Army
and KCP. The "enemy" includes imperialist aggressors and
lackeys of all stripes; the enemy has the intention of annexing
and swallowing our territory; the enemy which is planted
within our revolutionary ranks; the enemy in the for[m]
of the feudal-capitalist and landowner classes and other
oppressor classes; the enemy in the form of private and
individualist system; and particularly, the expansionist,
annexationist Vietnamese enemy.

> Khmer Rouge radio broadcast, "Who Are 'We'?"[1]

As this Khmer Rouge broadcast suggests, constructions of belonging and
exclusion lie at the center of genocide. Genocidal regimes manufacture
difference in a number of important and interrelated ways, including the
crystallization, marking, organization, bodily inscription, and mimetics
of difference. First, genocidal regimes construct, essentialize, and propagate sociopolitical categories, crystallizing what are normally more complex, fluid, and contextually variable forms of identity. This "crystallization of difference" is often associated with socioeconomic upheaval — as
illustrated by the tumultuous events that took place prior the emergence
of genocidal regimes in Bosnia, Rwanda, and Nazi Germany — and leads
to the dehumanization of victim groups, who are singled out and stereotyped (what I refer to in the conclusion as the "marking of difference").

Because crystallized group identities are so rigid (and, like crystal,
prone to cracks and breaks), genocidal regimes must find ways to impose
and maintain these social divisions. Perpetrators, however, often find it

difficult to distinguish between themselves and enemy "others," thereby inserting a fundamental condition of uncertainty and anxiety into the murderous process.[2] For it is frequently difficult to distinguish between Hutu and Tutsi, Nazi German and Jew, Bosnian Serb and Muslim, revolutionary and counterrevolutionary, and so forth. Moreover, even when such differences are found, they may not support the dehumanizing stereotypes that murderous ideologies assert. As a result, genocidal perpetrators often manufacture difference by transforming their victims into caricatures of these dehumanizing images.

One way of accomplishing this is to revamp sociopolitical organization so those who have been placed in one of these crystallized categories of belonging live under conditions that (re)produce their essentialized identity. Dehumanized groups are particularly brutalized and constrained by this organization of difference, as illustrated by Nazi policy toward Jews. And because identity remains somewhat fluid even in these circumstances, genocidal regimes often develop institutional mechanisms for imprinting the characteristics of the crystallized group identities on the bodies of their subjects.[3] In many contexts, this bodily inscription of difference is institutionalized at centers of death like the Nazi concentration camps and Tuol Sleng.

The most infamous instance of this lethal process of manufacturing difference occurred in Nazi Germany. Drawing on everything from archaeological evidence to theories of race, the Nazis divided the population into a hierarchy of biosocial types with the Aryan race at the peak. Jews, in contrast, were placed at the bottom of the hierarchy and viewed as a dangerous source of contamination. The Nazis propagated a number of discriminatory policies against the Jews and other devalued groups. Concentration camps became the ultimate institution for manufacturing difference, as Jews were stripped of the last vestiges of their humanity (clothing, hair, names, free will), treated like animals (beaten, verbally abused, and made to perform dehumanizing acts), and forced to live in horrendous conditions that led to starvation, disease, stealing to survive, and death. By subjecting Jews to such circumstances, the Nazis attempted to turn them into beings who were, as Nazi anti-Semitic propaganda proclaimed, like a "disease," "bacilli," "thieves," "lice," "subhumans," "parasites," and "alien bodies."[4] And once such difference had been manufactured, genocide was made to seem like a justifiable "purification" process necessary for the protection of the health of the German national body.

An analogous process of manufacturing difference may be seen in most modern genocides, including the one that took place in Cambodia. The "Who are 'We'?" speech, for example, was broadcast by Phnom Penh domestic radio in April 1978, as the Khmer Rouge purges were in full swing and border tensions with Vietnam were escalating. Like other Khmer Rouge documents, this speech attempts to manufacture difference by crystallizing the "clear line" between "us and the enemy." The broadcast constructs the following oppositions in group membership and group traits.

"US"	"THE ENEMY"
"our" people/army/party	enemy planted within our revolutionary ranks
worker-peasant class	feudal-capitalist/landowning class
"our" nation	imperialist aggressors and lackeys
	expansionist, annexationist Vietnamese
CPK	antinational and counterrevolutionary sham party

"OUR" TRAITS	"ENEMY" TRAITS
collective system	private and individualist system
patriotism	treason
love for the nation	betrayal of the nation
revolution	counterrevolution
collective proletarian system	private antiproletarian system

Ultimately, the broadcast differentiates "us" and "the enemy" in terms of "political, ideological, organizational, sentimental and traditional views and politics." Friends and enemies are distinguished by political consciousness, or the degree to which a person is "mindful" of the party "line" and "standpoint." Group traits follow from this premise. "Enemy" groups, ranging from imperialist lackeys to the "feudal-capitalist/landowning class," are those having a strong "private stand."

On the surface, identifying these enemies was relatively easy. When cadres received orders to purify the cooperative by killing members of the "feudal-capitalist/landowning class," they could check local registers and see who belonged to this crystallized category of difference. Party documents and speeches defined each of these classes roughly as follows: feudalists (royalty, former ministers, provincial governors, high-ranking Lon Nol military officials), capitalists (businessmen, particularly those with foreign trading connections), petty capitalists (high civil servants, "intellectuals," teachers, hairdressers, tailors, craftsmen, small businessmen, low-ranking civil servants, employees, clergy), landowners (rich peasants who used modern equipment and employed laborers and upper-middle peasants who hired laborers to do over 60 percent of their work).[5]

In practice, however, the identification of "enemies" was more difficult. For, given their premise that everything changes, the DK regime allowed for the possibility that some of these former enemies might transform themselves and become revolutionaries. Therefore, cadres were instructed to examine the extent to which people exhibited "antiproletarian" sentiments and traits. While the "Who Are 'We'?" broadcast did not go into detail about what these traits were, the "Sharpen the Consciousness" tract did. A key trait of an enemy was a strong private stand, which was reflected in "worldview, life-view, economy, morality," and "living and working habits."[6] Those having this private stand were drawn to private property, thought primarily of themselves and their families, followed "personal sentiments," tried to oppress others, yearned for the old society, or opposed the party's collective line.

The "we" that belonged in DK society exhibited opposing traits on the collectivist side of the "dividing line" — a "proletarian class worldview," collective stand, the renunciation of private property and personal attachments, enthusiasm for the new society, and revolutionary sentiments. The 1978 radio broadcast also explained that a person who "sharpened and clarified" this collective stand would come to feel "a constantly seething hatred for the enemy; a profound revolutionary sentiment toward the oppressed classes; a powerful love for the nation, revolution, collective system and party. These three emotions constitute the basis of the daily fighting spirit."

Such sentiments were a crucial part of the political identity idealized by the Khmer Rouge. By political identity, I mean a set of characteristics that make one recognizable as a member of a political group. Political identities are relational (marked by contrasts with the characteristics of other political groups), self-implicating (giving us a sense of who we are), and communal (providing a sense of belonging and solidarity with those sharing our political identity).[7] The "Who are 'We'?" broadcast touches on all of these aspects of political identity, defining the characteristics of a revolutionary, establishing a "dividing line" between "us" and "the enemy," asserting certain ways of thinking and feeling, and glorifying the shared spirit of revolutionary patriots. Ideally, those who exhibited such a political consciousness would follow the dictates of the DK regime without question, even if it meant killing other human beings. For those revolutionaries who had fully "absorbed" Khmer Rouge ideology and strongly identified with the DK "us," then, killing "enemies" became an honorable thing to do, a way of fulfilling one's solemn duty of "building and defending" the revolution by eradicating impure "elements."

In many ways, this DK political identity played upon Khmer nationalist themes, some of which date back to the French colonial era and continue to be invoked in contemporary partisan politics.[8] With their "discovery" of Angkor Wat, French scholars provided the Khmer with an enduring ethnohistorical past, culminating in the Angkorean empire. During the "decline" that followed this period of grandeur, Khmer were portrayed as continuously threatened by evil others who schemed to "swallow" Cambodian land and destroy the country and its people. These "others" were constructed as the binary opposites of the Khmer — "dirty," "treacherous," "greedy," "mendacious" beings (often Vietnamese, Thai, or Chinese) who contrasted sharply with the essential goodness and moral purity of the Khmer.[9] Such imagery constitutes both a crucial part of the orientalist myth of Cambodia as a "gentle land" of "smiling," peaceful Buddhists and an ontologically resonant basis for Khmer nationalist political identity, providing a sense of self and community ("we" the pure Khmer) and a set of relational characteristics of belonging (an essential moral purity contrasting with the various negative qualities of the evil "other"). For the Khmer Rouge, "imperialists," "capitalists," and later, the "expansionist, annexationist Vietnamese" were constructed as the evil, invading "other."

Traditionally, Khmer nationalists portrayed the Vietnamese (and, to a much lesser extent, ethnic Chinese) as the quintessentially evil "other." Part of this image was co-opted from French colonial portraits of the "mendacious, dirty, thieving" Vietnamese national character (with the Chinese depicted as "wily, greedy, heartless").[10] The "true" nature of the Vietnamese was highlighted in French historical reconstructions, Khmer royal chronicles, and the local oral tradition. While both the Thai and the Vietnamese had "swallowed" Cambodian lands, the Vietnamese were perceived as particularly dangerous because of their historical "march to the south," their annexation of Prey Nokor (which they renamed Saigon) and "lower Cambodia" (Kampuchea Krom), their incessant meddling in Khmer politics, their attempt to "Vietnamize" Cambodia in 1835–40, and most recently, their perceived attempt to take over Cambodia during the PRK period.[11] Most Cambodians were also quite familiar with the legend of the "Master's Tea," a variant of which was put forth in the 1978 Democratic Kampuchea document, *Black Paper:*

> In order to maintain their vigilance, Kampuchea's people have kept alive two phrases in their mind. The first one says: "Be careful not to spill the master's tea!" It recalls the barbarous crime committed by the "Yuon" in 1813 during the digging of Vinh Te canal. The Yuons buried alive the Khmer people up to their necks and used the latter's heads as a stand for a wood stove to boil water for their master's tea. As they burned and suffered, the victims shook their heads. At that moment, the Yuon torturers said to them, "Be careful not to spill the master's tea."[12]

This legend embodies a number of the aforementioned Khmer nationalist themes regarding the Vietnamese: their evil nature (sadistically burning and inflicting incredible suffering upon the helpless victims), their attitude toward Cambodians (scorn, superiority, lack of sympathy), their "energy" (versus the immobilized/"lazy" Khmer slaves), their desire to destroy Cambodia and its people (the slaughter of Khmer slaves), and their treachery (using slaves as stands for the stove). It also symbolizes the Khmer's historical loss of "face" (the abuse of the victims' heads, bodily symbols of hierarchy and respect), Cambodia's constrictive geographical location (being buried up to the neck in the sand), Cambodia's victim status (being enslaved and abused), and the emotional "heat" that these conditions generated (writhing in the flames, an embodied metaphor for shame and anger).

The *Black Paper* passage scornfully refers to the Vietnamese as *Yuon,* a term that the tract asserts has historically meant "savage." Regardless of whether this etymology is correct, many Cambodians use this colloquial term for the Vietnamese in a similar manner, often enunciating the term in ways that stress their contempt, anger, and hatred of the Vietnamese. The strong anti-Vietnamese sentiment that many Cambodians feel was revealed to me all too clearly during an interview with Chlat, when this highly intelligent and thoughtful man suddenly began to speak passionately about his hatred of the Vietnamese. "I hate them. I don't have words to tell you how much I hate them," he said. When I asked why, he explained, "History and their actions clearly show that the *Yuon* have repeatedly done bad things in Cambodia. They learn the tricks of thieves. They steal from [our] economy. They start many fights. They have come to live in Cambodia, but they don't respect the rights of the Khmer. And their biggest professions are stealing and prostitution. Even the *Yuon* women are thieves." Chlat's diatribe continued for several minutes, punctuated by various anecdotes about Vietnamese prostitutes and "savage" Vietnamese soldiers who "looked down upon" the Khmer.[13]

Not all Khmer harbor such animosity toward the Vietnamese; in fact, Khmer human rights workers have risked their lives defending ethnic Vietnamese who were being attacked and persecuted in Cambodia. Nevertheless, many Khmer continue to have racist attitudes toward the Vietnamese, providing nationalist politicians with an emotionally charged theme to tap into, particularly during times of socioeconomic upheaval when people seek a scapegoat for their problems.

Lon Nol's anti-Vietnamese rhetoric and policy provide an extreme illustration of this point: shortly after the March 1970 coup, he began to drum up popular support for his Buddhist holy war against the Vietnamese "infidels," who supposedly were responsible for Cambodia's woes. Lon Nol's actions provide yet another illustration of the crystallization of difference, as more fluid divisions between Khmer and ethnic Vietnamese became increasingly rigid; extreme ethnonationalist government propaganda, disseminated through speeches, the media, rallies, military indoctrination, and official publications, suggested that *all* Vietnamese, even those who had been living in Cambodia for decades and were strongly anticommunist, were a threat to the racial purity and survival of the Khmer.

In the months that followed the coup, Lon Nol supporters periodically intimidated, discriminated against, robbed, and attacked ethnic Vietnamese, some of whom were relocated to detention centers.[14] Thousands of ethnic Vietnamese were massacred, many by Lon Nol military troops, who sometimes tossed their bodies into the Mekong River, where they floated toward Vietnam. This brutal practice illustrates the bodily inscription of violence, as Khmer soldiers transformed the bodies of the "disordering" ethnic Vietnamese into an impurity (grotesque, water-logged corpses) that was "cleansed" (by being killed, plunged into water, and expunged from Cambodia) and "reordered" (by being sent back to the "true" place where they belonged, Vietnam).[15] Roughly 310,000 of Cambodia's 450,000 ethnic Vietnamese are thought to have fled Cambodia by August 1970.[16] The DK regime dealt with the remainder.

The ebb and flow in the crystallization of difference is illustrated by the post-DK history of Cambodian relations with the Vietnamese. When Vietnamese troops helped overthrow the DK regime, many Khmer felt a sense of gratitude toward the Vietnamese, a feeling that was strongly encouraged by PRK government propaganda. While there was some tension and resentment toward Vietnamese military personnel in Cambodia, ethnic Khmer and ethnic Vietnamese generally got along well during this period.

During the UNTAC period, however, difference began to crystallize, as political factions attempted to attract support by outdoing one another in racist diatribes. Cambodian politicians once again portrayed the Vietnamese as a dangerously evil "other," which was inundating Cambodia with prostitutes, thieves, and spies, which was responsible for the country's problems, and which ultimately threatened the very survival of Cambodia and its people.[17] This rhetoric was most virulent in the propaganda disseminated by the Khmer Rouge political arm during the UNTAC period, the Party of Democratic Kampuchea (PDK), which was responsible for attacks that resulted in the death or serious injury of some two hundred ethnic Vietnamese.[18]

Such ethnonationalist rhetoric bears a strong similarity to the Khmer Rouge obsession with "hidden enemies burrowing from within" (khmang bângkap si roung phtai knong). While the DK regime applied this term to a wide range of "enemies," it took on increasingly racist overtones when used in reference to the Vietnamese. By 1978, when the "Who are 'We'?" speech was broadcast and the Black Paper was published, such discourse was being taken to the extreme as the military conflict between Vietnam and Democratic Kampuchea intensified. Even before DK, however, the Khmer Rouge viewed the Vietnamese with suspicion, as shown by skirmishes between Khmer Rouge and communist Vietnamese military units, sporadic massacres of ethnic Vietnamese living in Khmer Rouge zones, and the purge of the Hanoi Khmer.

The roots of this distrust and the eventual military conflict between Cambodia and Vietnam are complex, linked both to specific historical events and to Khmer conceptions of the Vietnamese as the archetypal evil, invading other.[19] In particular, many Khmer Rouge leaders felt that they had been mistreated and betrayed by their Vietnamese communist allies. The Black Paper focuses on these themes, repeatedly complaining about the "arrogance" of the Vietnamese, who frequently ignored their wishes, initially discouraged them from engaging in armed struggle, abandoned them at the international negotiating table, and didn't respect Cambodian territorial rights. Almost immediately after the DK regime came to power, the Khmer Rouge began skirmishing with Vietnam over disputed coastal islands and arguing over the timing of the departure of Vietnamese troops from Cambodia. Such events played into Khmer ethnonationalist suspicions, suggesting that the Vietnamese didn't respect the DK party line of "independence, sovereignty, and self-reliance" and secretly desired to "swallow" Cambodia.

As the Khmer Rouge purges got underway and the military conflict with Vietnam escalated, the DK regime increasingly elaborated these doubts into conspiracy theories exemplified by alleged coups, assassination plots, and secret alliances outlined in documents such as "The Last Plan," the *Black Paper,* and confessions. Like the CIA, the Vietnamese were portrayed as having attempted to "infiltrate," "sabotage," and "destroy" the Cambodian revolutionary movement. The *Black Paper* traced this treachery back to the Indochina Communist Party, when the Vietnamese allegedly began building up "secret networks" that eventually came to include an alternative state apparatus headed by veteran revolutionaries of the "Pracheachon group" and Eastern Zone personnel. Even before the purges began, ethnic Vietnamese were singled out for persecution. By September 1975, the DK regime had expelled approximately 150,000 of the country's remaining ethnic Vietnamese. The *Black Paper* later claimed that this ethnic cleansing was necessary because "Vietnamese nationals secretly infiltrated into Kampuchea and [were] living in hiding [among] the population."[20]

The ten thousand or more ethnic Vietnamese who remained in Cambodia — many because they wanted to remain with Khmer spouses — initially faced discrimination. By mid 1977, when the purges were fully underway (producing confessions that "proved" the treachery of the Vietnamese) and the military conflict with Vietnam was escalating, the Party Center had launched a campaign to eradicate the remaining Vietnamese.[21] Several former cadres who worked in Region 41 described how ethnic Vietnamese were singled out for execution in the area. Teap, the cadre who worked at the subdistrict office under Rom recalled that, during political training sessions and meetings, cadres would "always talk about CIA and KGB 'enemies' . . . later on, though, they stopped talking as much about the CIA and Lon Nol regime and began speaking about the 'arms and legs of the Yuon' and 'Yuon strings.' . . . If a person was ethnic Vietnamese, it was certain that they wouldn't survive. Once they were discovered, that was it." Several Banyan villagers confirmed that all of the Vietnamese living in their villages in Region 41 had been killed. This genocidal pattern was repeated throughout Cambodia, resulting in the annihilation of almost all of the ethnic Vietnamese in the country.

Under the DK regime, then, we find yet another situation in which a set of more fluid differences became increasingly crystallized. Theoreti-

cally, anyone, even an ethnic Vietnamese, could develop a proper revolutionary consciousness. As economic failures, purges, and political and
military tensions with Vietnam intensified, however, the Khmer Rouge
increasingly portrayed the Vietnamese as an "evil," invading other. While
the Vietnamese could be accused of having a "regressive" political consciousness (due to their violation of the DK party line of "independence-
sovereignty and self-reliance" and a dependency on foreign powers that
suggested privatism), they were demonized publicly in traditional racist
terms. Ultimately, this situation facilitated genocide and the almost
unique situation of two communist re˘ ˌimes and former allies going to
war. By manufacturing difference ι̇. this manner, the Khmer Rouge
asserted a political identity that, as the "Who are 'We'?" speech exemplifies, "drew a clear line" between Khmer and Vietnamese. "We," the
pure, revolutionary Khmer, were contrasted with a Vietnamese "other"
who supposedly embodied the inverse characteristics of the Khmer (a
regressive political line, an "evil" and "perfidious" nature, deceptiveness
and treachery, and so forth). It is one of the most vexing problems of our
time that imagined sociopolitical identities are so often forged out of
hatred toward contrasting others.

Of course, the Vietnamese were one of a number of "enemies burrowing from within" whom the Khmer Rouge attempted to exclude
from the DK political community. If it was easier to identify an ethnic
Vietnamese or Cham because of their language and habits, even devoted
revolutionaries often found it difficult to spot the other enemies, particularly those whose minds had "regressed." Discerning the enemy
involved "mindful" analysis: one had to examine the degree to which a
person's actions and remarks accorded with the party line. A June 1977
edition of *Revolutionary Flags* explained, "To distinguish between good
and bad compositions, those who are enemies and those who are not
enemies, we must examine the application of the Party line. How does a
composition execute the political line of the Party, the Party's line on consciousness, and the organizational line of the Party? How do they implement the line of defending the Party, of revolutionary socialism, of building Socialism?"[22] Cadres looking for more specific criteria could examine
the many examples that Khmer Rouge tracts and speeches provided.

Given this ideology, genocidal practice became a semiotic enterprise
and an interpretive act, as cadres set out to identify enemies through the
reading of signs. Everyday life became increasingly performative; everything one said or did served as an index of political consciousness. This
tendency was taken to an extreme in Phnom Penh, where everyone strove,

to evince thoughts and behaviors that accorded with the party line while constantly assessing the political consciousness of other cadres. Criticism and self-criticism sessions became the ultimate performative arena in this regard, as Picq explained:

> Criticism sessions intensified at the rate of two nights per week. During these meetings, it seemed that each person's past, far from being a tapestry of complex motives, could be reduced to a straight line pointing inevitably toward either service to the party or treason.
>
> The most harmless facts now assumed high political significance. A lack of speed in executing a task demonstrated a sabotage mentality. Zeal was an undeniable sign of longing for power.
>
> Thoughts had as much value as action. To be on the right track, one had to imbue oneself with the ideas of the party in such a way that the mind was perpetually mobilized to the party's service, without hesitation and without wasting time, like a machine.
>
> "In terms of discipline, I have some shortcomings," one heard. "I didn't listen to the radio transmissions with all the required concentration." (Listening to the radio had become obligatory; each of us had to pay close attention to the broadcasts so as to be able to comment on them later.) Or, "I urinated outside the manure bin. . . ."
>
> . . . Listening to these accounts of facts and signals, people searched for signs of weakness. Language was analyzed and psychoanalyzed. Each of the "mistaken actions" underwent interpretation. One bulletin badly stapled, printed, or typed became an indicator — if not actual proof — of secret conspiracies.[23]

On the local level, cadres followed a trail of signs indicating a regressive consciousness: an oppressor class background (suggesting a "thick private stand"), soft hands or a lack of knowledge about agricultural work (suggesting that one was educated and had avoided manual labor), glasses (suggesting vanity and education), the use of foreign words (suggesting imperialist leanings), complaints or lack of enthusiasm (suggesting that one did not support the new regime), dwelling on the past (suggesting that one retained capitalist attitudes), sickness or laziness (suggesting a bad attitude toward collective work), close familial ties (suggesting that one had private sentiments), sexual affairs (suggesting corrupt morality), or hiding one's personal possessions or stealing food (suggesting that one remained attached to private property).

A "progressive" consciousness was indicated by many of the opposite qualities: peasant origins, familiarity with farming, a lack of formal education, a peasant accent, revolutionary zeal, hard work, renunciation, unquestioning obedience, persistent self-construction, hatred of the enemy, and as the 1978 radio broadcast announced, staying "alert in your efforts to weed out and exterminate the enemy planted within the cooperatives." The Khmer Rouge sometimes likened the ideal revolutionary to a water buffalo. Pin Yathay recalled:

> The perfect revolutionary was submissive to Angkar, should not experience any feeling, was forbidden to talk about spouse or children, could not love. In addition, he rejected all reactionary beliefs. . . . In an often-heard Khmer Rouge parable, the individual was compared to an ox: 'You see the ox, comrades. Admire him! He eats where we command him to eat. If we let him graze on this field, he eats. . . . He cannot move about, he is supervised. When we tell him to pull the plough, he pulls it. He never thinks of his wife or his children.' Often during the meetings, the Khmer Rouge spoke about 'Comrade Ox' as the ideal revolutionary. . . . Comrade Ox never refused to work. Comrade Ox was obedient. Comrade Ox did not complain. Comrade Ox did not object when his family was killed.[24]

Immersed in this world of fear and terror, many Cambodians attempted to "plant a kapok tree," or to remain mute, following a Buddhist prophesy foretelling that during a time of infidels only those who were deaf and dumb would survive. Teeda Mam recalled, "Though talkative and friendly by nature, I had become wary and silent. . . . I mentally reviewed everything before I spoke. It was best to play dumb. I tried never to stand out except by working extra hard. I never volunteered for anything or complained. . . . I took no initiative. Whenever I was asked a question, I answered, 'I don't know.' "[25]

Those who exhibited "regressive" signs were often told that they had a "sick consciousness" (chhoeu sâtiarâmma), a condition that, if severe and persistent, usually led to execution. One Phnom Penh monk recalled, "In the Pol Pot period they used the term 'sick consciousness.' . . . If they sent a person to dig earth, dig canals, transplant rice, harvest [crops], and that person replied, 'I am not able to go because I'm sick,' the Pol Pot people would say, 'You are not sick, you have a sick consciousness.' " He explained that this phrase "meant that a person who didn't fulfill their work for Pol Pot was not satisfied with the regime's leadership. A person who didn't join in the collective work was not truly sick, only sick in spirit (smarâti) and unhappy. They didn't like the new system. Sâtiaramma meant that one did not focus one's mind on the work that the Pol Pot people assigned." Ultimately, the goal of the Khmer Rouge was, as one Khmer Rouge saying held, to "completely annihilate diseases of consciousness" [26] and create a society of pure revolutionaries.

The search for "hidden enemies" and those with a "sick consciousness" was facilitated by the organization of difference. Earlier I discussed how the DK regime revamped Cambodian society by creating a new sociopolitical order defined in terms of a person's class origins, revolutionary activity, and state of consciousness. The members of various groups were given different rights and statuses, with devalued groups like "new people" often forced to live and work in comparatively much more degrading circumstances. Potentially "impure" groups were forced to act within a set of organizational constraints and circumstances that disempowered and dehumanized them. The conditions of life transformed the bodies of these victim groups, making them seem more like the degrading caricatures that the DK regime discussed. A gaunt, emaciated "new person" who stank thus embodied the "impurity" of political consciousness that Khmer Rouge ideology asserted—in contrast to "old people" and cadres, who were given more food and accorded more rights. Bodily difference might be inscribed in others ways, as when a "new person" was forced to plow like an oxen, thereby becoming equated symbolically with a passive and obedient animal, or when a person was executed in "the wild."

TUOL SLENG AND THE PRODUCTION OF DIFFERENCE

1. It is absolutely prohibited to talk to each
   other;
2. Before doing anything you [must] have
   authorization from the guard;
3. It is absolutely prohibited to make any noise;
4. At the entrance of the guard or somebody else
   you must lie down.

Tuol Sleng prison regulations

The process of manufacturing difference during DK is exemplified by Tuol Sleng, a liminal site at which uncertain political identities were diagnosed, stabilized, and transformed. Oum Chhan's interrogation and confession, for example, may be read as a single, horrible episode epitomizing the Party Center's attempt to manufacture difference. It also brings us back to the questions I posed earlier regarding why perpetrators at places like Tuol Sleng were so brutal to their victims and how it could even become honorable for them to participate in genocidal violence. While historical, economic, and political factors are crucial to our comprehension of the origins and operations of institutions of terror like Tuol Sleng, such spaces of death cannot be fully understood without an examination of the processes that give them impetus, structure, and form.

As we have seen, despite the Khmer Rouge attempt to crystallize difference and eradicate enemies, DK was plagued by chronic suspicion and a deep unease about political identity because of the difficulty of determining whether or not a person had a "regressive" consciousness. Consciousness had to be read from signs — a lost cow, poor crop yields, laziness, class background, personal and political associations, and so forth. The uncertainty was deepened by the fact that a longtime revolutionary or former comrade could suddenly be accused of being an enemy. Since the party was "all-knowing," arrest signified guilt; interrogation in turn produced the evidence that retrospectively proved the claim. Like the latent content of a dream, the "true" state of a person's consciousness could be revealed through confessions, which, at Tuol Sleng, were written and rewritten until the prisoner had it "just right."[27]

Given this broader context, what do the confessions of people like Oum Chhan tell us about the nature of "spaces of death" like Tuol Sleng? First, such institutions are organized to produce differences that have been crystallized by state discourse. At Tuol Sleng, prisoners often arrived bound and gagged in a truck, sometimes after having been interrogated in a provincial prison. The prisoners were then blindfolded and ushered (sometimes while being kicked and beaten) into a room where they were photographed and required to give biographical information. Guards eventually took the prisoners to a room where they were informed of the prison regulations (listed above), forced to remove their revolutionary garb, and shackled in a cell.[28] A few of the highest-ranking prisoners, like Koy Thuon, were incarcerated in a "special prison" area.[29] Those undergoing extensive interrogation — including, quite possibly, Reap — were shackled alone in small (2 × 0.8 meters) cinder-block cubicles. The remainder of the prisoners, including Vann Nath, were placed in larger, sexually segregated rooms and chained by the legs to opposite sides of a long iron bar. Most prisoners were incarcerated for two to four months, though important prisoners might be held for much longer. Some of the prisoners arrived with their spouses and children, who were often executed within days of arriving at Tuol Sleng.

The prisoners were immobilized most of the time and not allowed even to sit up without permission. Ung Pech recalled that prison regulations forbade speaking and required prisoners to ask guards for permission before doing even the most basic of bodily acts: "If any of us urinated, slept on our side, sat up, or defecated without permission from the guards, they would come and beat us until blood flowed from our wounds." Inspections took place several times a day, and the prisoners were bathed once every four days and given starvation rations. If prisoners violated the rules, they might be beaten. As a result of these conditions, prisoners quickly became emaciated and foul-smelling, often contracting skin and intestinal diseases. Vann Nath's ears eventually began to ring, and he became hard of hearing. He described his condition after several weeks of incarceration: "I didn't know what day of the week or month it was. . . . My body was like that of a seventy-year-old grandfather. The mop of hair on my head was like the root of a bamboo stalk and had become a lice nest. I itched all over. My mind and spirit were gone. I knew only thirst and hunger." Some prisoners died in their cells or during interrogation; others were executed at Choeng Ek by Lor and his men.

In a variety of ways, then, prisoners like Oum Chhan underwent a lethal rite of passage,[30] moving from their previous status as "revolutionary" to a liminal space at Tuol Sleng where their identity was uncertain. The need to manufacture difference at Tuol Sleng was exacerbated by the fact that most of the prisoners resembled their captors in terms of youth, rural origins, social class, ethnicity, and revolutionary origins.[31] (Some "new people" and "class enemies" were incarcerated at Tuol Sleng, particularly during the early operation of the prison, but most of these individuals were jailed or executed on the local, district, and regional levels). In fact, some prisoners were former coworkers or associates of Tuol Sleng cadres. The "separation" of such prisoners began with arrest and was typically followed by a long, uncomfortable journey to Tuol Sleng. Upon their arrival, their "structurally dead" position, to use Victor Turner's term, was signified by their loss of previous markers of human identity, such as revolutionary garb and physiological capacity (for example, the freedom to eat, drink, see, move, sleep, bathe, and even defecate). As uncertain, marginal beings, they were polluting, a condition mimed by their stench and disease. Even as they entered this liminal space, their new status began to be inscribed on their bodies, for their filth marked their difference, suggesting that they were precisely the type of "contradiction" or "microbe" that, as Party Center discourse often warned, was "burrowing from within" and threatened to "rot society, rot the Party, rot the army."[32] Until the exact nature of this "sickness" could be diagnosed, it had to be contained through confinement and shackles. Diagnosis, and the fixing of identity, began with interrogation.

This was likely the condition in which Oum Chhan — a twenty-nine-

year-old ethnic Khmer who was married and came from a rural background — arrived in his interrogation room, roughly two weeks after his
August 2, 1978 arrest at a cooperative in the Eastern Zone, which was in
the last stages of a massive purge. Bound and shackled, gaunt and reeking,
Oum Chhan was informed that he was "worth less than garbage," an
assertion that mimed his physical condition and status-in-the-making. The
first word of the interrogator's summary states the political identity that
was eventually manufactured for Oum Chhan — "enemy" *(khmang)* —
and describes how his "true" allegiance to the CIA was revealed through
beatings and torture.

The interrogation process may be read partly as an institutional
attempt to organize and crystallize difference on politically uncertain
bodies. It is literally a project of "drawing a clear line between us and the
enemy" through the etching of words, bodily surfaces and interiors, and
pain. If Oum Chhan's guilt was assumed, his interrogator, Vaen Kheuan,
still had to retrospectively construct the signs of his regressive consciousness. He had to be made to evince the characteristics of "the enemy" —
privatism, treason, betrayal, counterrevolutionary activities, and so
forth. This was done in two ways. First, interrogators produced a confession containing the appropriate signs. Thus Oum Chhan eventually
"confessed" to such deeds as joining the CIA, being a part of traitorous
"strings," hiding and secretly supplying the Vietnamese, helping to
"build forces" to fight against the revolution, fomenting popular dissatisfaction with the party line, serving as a messenger, carrying out acts of
economic sabotage (for example, destroying rice crops, bags of salt, and
a rice mill), fighting against communal dining, and participating in an
Eastern Zone plot to overthrow the DK regime. Such alleged activities
were clear signs of an "enemy," thereby shifting Oum Chhan from the
unstable position of longtime revolutionary to the other side of the
"dividing line" — an "enemy planted within."

Second, the interrogator inscribed this enemy status on Oum Chhan's
body. The bodily inscription of difference in such situations was facilitated
by the organization of difference: Oum Chhan arrived in the interrogation
cell in an already dehumanized and impure state. A person who stinks, has
skin diseases and lice, and is emaciated is marked as different and doesn't
appear quite human. According to Vaen Kheuan's description, the interrogation process proceeded along these lines. Throughout the summary, Vaen
Kheuan uses hierarchical idioms that convey Oum Chhan's dehumanization. He refers to Oum Chhan using the derogatory pronoun *vea* nineteen
times in the ten-line passage. By using this term, Vaen Kheuan likened

Oum Chhan to an object or animal, one that could be used and abused at will. His bound and fettered body was "worth less than garbage."

Vaen Kheuan treated Oum Chhan accordingly. He beat and abused Oum Chhan at will, asserting his and the Party Center's total domination over the "lowly" prisoner. This bodily inscription of difference often took on a cultural patterning, which was partly informed by the onto-logically resonant cultural models of hierarchy and status that I discussed earlier. Thus Vaen Kheuan reports that he forced Oum Chhan to "pay homage" *(korop)* to him, an embodied cultural behavior that likely involved some sort of abusive prostration.

The manner in which cultural knowledge helps structure the bodily inscription of violence is dramatically illustrated by a torture Vaen Kheuan inflicted upon Oum Chhan: forcing him to *sâmpeah* (the torture was also described using the term *thvay bângkum*), or "pay homage to the image of a dog."[33] This painful torture, which may have been loosely adapted from the "airplane" torture used during China's Cultural Revolu-tion, is thought to have involved assuming an extremely degrading and uncomfortable pose before a picture of Ho Chi Minh or, by 1978, Lyndon Johnson, sometimes repeatedly or for a prolonged period of time.[34] While we do not know exactly how this torture was implemented, it is men-tioned briefly in the notebooks of three interrogators, Tuy, Pon, and Chan, who attended a political meeting on May 28, 1978, a few months before Oum Chhan was incarcerated:[35]

> We test them by getting them to pay homage to two dogs. Dogs have polit-ical meaning. The first dog is America. The second is Vietnam. When they salute them, they acknowledge that they support these two.
>
> From the standpoint of ideology, we cast [the prisoners] aside, and no longer allow them to stay with us.
>
> From the organizational standpoint, we force them to honor *santebal* ["the security police"]. We have achieved good results from this already. (Tuy and Pon)
>
> We force them to salute the images of two dogs. This is a kind of interro-gation. The dogs have political significance.
>
> First dog: American imperialism.
>
> Second dog: Vietnamese consumers of [our] territory.
>
> We have them pay homage so as to hold them firmly. Because when they are arrested, 90 percent of them [still] consider themselves revolu-tionaries. After they have paid homage to the dogs, they will realize that they are traitors.
>
> From an ideological standpoint, we reject their ideology.
>
> From an organizational standpoint: do they respect *santebal*, or not?
>
> Procedures: Say what you can to make them change their minds and

obey "older brother." If they argue, don't beat them yet, but wait for a minute before making them say that they served these two dogs: from what year? in what organization? Be careful: they may say that the CIA has no venom [real strength?]. (Chan)

What is perhaps most striking about the passage is the transformation in the prisoners' consciousness that supposedly took place after they endured this torture. Apparently, roughly nine out of ten prisoners proclaimed their innocence at the onset of interrogation. Their identity was uncertain, not yet fixed into an appropriate and contained political category. By forcing prisoners to "pay homage to the image of the dog," interrogators manufactured a new political identity, removing the prisoners from their state of liminality as they were transformed into tokens of the enemy "other." They physically assumed a form of bodily prostration that indexed their inferiority and "true" state of mind—someone who really served the enemy. As the first notebook entry states, "We cast [the prisoners] aside, and no longer allow them to stay with us." This metaphor parallels the "Who are 'We'?" speech, signifying the prisoners' placement on the enemy side of the "dividing line."

Interestingly, the interrogator notebooks reference this effect, stating that after enduring the torture, prisoners "acknowledge that they support these two [America and Vietnam]" and "realize that they are traitors." The true regressive state of the prisoners' minds had already been proven by their arrest. The problem was to diagnose exactly what their crime was (and to force them to reveal their traitorous strings). By making the prisoners "pay homage" to their true "masters," this hidden state of consciousness was both revealed and realized by the victim, who began to confess. The prisoners' dehumanized status was also symbolically asserted, since they were bowing to an image of a dog. The bodies of the prisoners thus became icons on which their torturers inscribed their "regressive" characteristics and enemy status. Oum Chhan may have been forced to prostrate himself before an image of Lyndon Johnson or Ho Chi Minh, since his confession details both his supposed entry into the CIA and his secret ties to the Vietnamese (he came from a region bordering Vietnam).

When their political identity as an "enemy" was fixed, prisoners like Oum Chhan lost their "Khmerness." Bodily violence helped construct them into the "evil other" of Khmer ethnonationalist discourse. In his

1977 speech, Pol Pot warned, "We do not consider these traitors, these counterrevolutionary elements, to be part of the people."[36] When tensions with Vietnam escalated, such enemies were increasingly referred to as people having "Khmer bodies and Vietnamese minds." Through the organization and bodily inscription of difference, then, Tuol Sleng served to manufacture new political beings, whose identity accorded with their sudden arrest and the categories of difference the DK regime was crystallizing. By manufacturing difference in this manner, the interrogators also asserted the dominance and superiority of the Party Center, the institution of Tuol Sleng, the security police, and themselves in a culturally meaningful manner by forcing the prisoners to enact an embodied practice of subordination. Such emotionally salient models of hierarchy and status gave motivational impetus to and helped pattern the violence that took place at Tuol Sleng, providing a culturally salient way of objectifying the prisoners, highlighting their total dehumanization, and asserting their complete lack of worth.

Tuol Sleng was also a key institution in the attempt to diagnose, reorder, and purify the regime. Longtime revolutionaries with a consciousness that had "regressed" were particularly contaminating and disordering, since they held important positions within the new regime. Tuol Sleng "reordered" these threatening beings, confining their movements and manufacturing their "impurity" through dehumanizing practices that turned them into tokens of impurity: they stank, they were diseased, they wore rags, their confined bodies didn't move in "normal" ways, and their emaciated bodies made them look nonhuman.

This process of diagnosing, ordering, and ultimately eliminating "microbes" that were "burrowing from within," was epitomized in the torture chamber, where disordering beings were reordered, both through bodily techniques of pain and discipline, such as "paying homage to the image of a dog," and through the process of constructing a confession that revealed the true state of their minds. Such tortures also affirmed their contaminating states. (As noted earlier, prisoners were sometimes forced to eat their own feces or drink their own urine, a horrible mimetic act whereby impure beings ingested impure substances that had emerged from their impure bodies.) Ultimately, these contaminating beings were eradicated in a desolate field, clubbed on the back of the head with an iron bar and dumped into a ditch that was eventually covered over — the final step in the reordering and containment of these dangerous, and now dead, bodies.

PERPETRATOR EXCESS: AN EXISTENTIAL APPROACH

Sometimes we go blind with rage, and this causes us to·
lose mastery.

Tuol Sleng interrogators' notebook[37]

If Tuol Sleng served to manufacture difference, stabilize uncertain identities, produce "proof" that confirmed the suspicions of the Party Center,
and eradicate dangerous sources of impurity, how did perpetrators like
Vaen Kheuan feel about what they were doing? This is a difficult question to answer, and requires speculation. As we have seen, when they are
asked about their deeds, most perpetrators simply claim that they were
"just following orders." This "banal" explanation, to use Hannah
Arendt's term,[38] provides some insight into mass violence. While we do
not know how Vaen Kheuan came to be an interrogator (Was he
assigned to this task? Did he actively seek it out?), he had to achieve certain results within a specific institutional structure. Had he not interrogated and extracted an acceptable confession from his victims, Vaen
Kheuan would probably have been arrested and killed.

Like many cadres at Tuol Sleng, including Lor, Vaen Kheuan was a
"low-level middle peasant" from Region 25 in Kandal province, a key
base of support for the Khmer Rouge. According to his life history, Vaen
Kheuan joined the revolution in March 1975, less than a month before
the end of the civil war, because the party had taught him to see how the
"feudalists, capitalists, reactionaries, and the American imperialist
invaders of our land" had oppressed "workers, peasants, and the
poor."[39] He initially received "more than ten days of political education" at a local office and then "more than a month of military training"
at the Division 12 (later renamed Division 703) technical school. In fact,
a large number of Tuol Sleng cadres had belonged to Division 703,
including Ho and Peng, two of Duch's top-ranking deputies, and Lor.
Vaen Kheuan began serving in Division 703 in May 1975.

In December 1975, Vaen Kheuan, who was around eighteen at the
time, was sent for more than five months of additional training at a
"technical school" in Ta Khmau where many Tuol Sleng cadres were
trained. Vaen Kheuan received military and political training, which
would have included composing a life history, performing manual labor
tasks, attending political seminars, memorizing revolutionary slogans
and songs, and participating in criticism sessions.[40] This indoctrination
was intensified by exhaustion, sleep deprivation, and hunger, all aimed at

producing recruits who would have a proper revolutionary consciousness and be completely loyal to the DK regime. Tuol Sleng personnel continued to perform these practices, particularly the criticism sessions and
political seminars. Beginning in May 1976, Vaen Kheuan began working
as a "messenger" *(nirosa)* at Tuol Sleng. Many of these "messengers" or
"catchers" participated in the arrest and transport of suspected traitors
in Phnom Penh and the countryside; in fact, Lor gained renown while
working in this unit.[41]

Aside from the top administrators, most people worked in one of five
capacities at Tuol Sleng: as interrogators, documentation workers,
guards, messengers, or support personnel.[42] Discipline was strict. One
surviving circular, for example, provides precise rules about guard duty
(for example, not leaning on walls, not fraternizing with or learning the
names of prisoners, making four checks of the prisoners every twenty-
four hours, not allowing prisoners to undress themselves), the use of
locks, chains, and shackles (including instructions on how to chain the
arms and legs of prisoners who were being brought to defecate), and
other "measures" (for example, the proper handling of weapons).[43] Low-
ranking cadres often feared their superiors, who may have yelled at or
beaten them when they made mistakes.[44]

Two months after he arrived at Tuol Sleng, in July 1976, Vaen Kheuan
became an interrogator, eventually serving in the "hot" *(kdav)* division of
interrogators, who were permitted to use torture. By the middle of 1977,
prisoners were sometimes interrogated by three-person teams (in other
instances they were interrogated by a single cadre) that included a chief
and an annotator, and almost all interrogations involved "hot" tactics, or
torture.[45] Like the guards, interrogators were required to follow specific
rules, which were discussed repeatedly in political meetings. Many of
these are laid out in a fifty-two-page interrogator's notebook containing
notes taken by a cadre during training sessions in 1976. Interrogators
were supposed to use a combination of "doing politics" *(tvoe noryabay)*
and "torture" *(tearunakâm)*, as illustrated by the following rules for
interrogation:

1. First, extract information from them *(vea)*.
2. Next, assemble as many points as possible to pin them down and
   prevent them from not answering the questions.
3. Pressure them with political propaganda.
4. Press on with questions and insults.
5. Torture.

6. Review and analyze the answers for additional questions.
7. Review and analyze the answers for documentation.
8. Prevent them *(vea)* from dying *(ngoap)* or communicating with each other.
9. Keep things secret.[46]

Even more chilling were a series of "tactical" suggestions for breaking down a prisoner's resolve, including: "making them *(vea)* see that the Party was not confused when arresting them," "making them think about their wife and children," making them realize that "nobody is going to help them," "reassuring them by giving them something to eat . . . that the Party will be giving them back their posts," "terrifying them," and "making them uncertain about whether they will live or die so that they will continue to hope that they may survive."[47] Ultimately, the goal was to "keep prisoners alive a long time in order to extract answers that could be offered to the Party."

· · ·

One can only imagine the terror such tactics inspired in prisoners like Reap and Oum Chhan. From the moment they arrived at Tuol Sleng, their bodies were transformed and regulated by the state; they had lost their freedom to move, bathe, eat, drink, and defecate. Some had already been beaten or had their heads smacked by guards, to whom they had to show verbal and nonverbal behaviors of respect. When their names were finally called, most probably felt like Vann Nath: "My hands and feet turned cold, realizing that it was my turn now. All the other prisoners turned to stare at me. . . . I tried to control my heart so that my tears wouldn't flow. I was so weak I could barely stand up."[48] The rules of interrogation were written on small chalkboards kept in some of the cells:

1. You must answer [in accordance with] my questions. Do not turn them away.
2. Do not try to hide the facts by making pretexts of this and that. You are strictly prohibited to contest me.
3. Do not be a fool for you are a chap who dares to thwart the revolution.
4. You must immediately answer my questions without wasting time to reflect.
5. Do not tell me either about your immoralities or the revolution.

6. While getting lashes or electrification you must not cry at all.

7. Do nothing. Sit and wait for my orders. If there is no order, keep quiet. When I ask you to do something[, you] must do it right away without protesting.

8. Do not make pretexts about Kampuchea Krom in order to hide your jaw of traitor.

9. If you do not follow all the above rules, you shall get many lashes of electric wire.

10. If you disobey any point of my regulations you shall get either ten lashes or five shocks of electric discharge.[49]

The horror of those who had already been tortured was more intense, for they knew what awaited them as they were led to their interrogation sessions, which were held morning, afternoon, and night. They often returned to their cells bruised, bloodied, and battered, and dreading the next round, which was only hours away.

What did they experience in the interrogation room, as they found themselves chained before interrogators in a room filled with instruments of torture that might have included truncheons, electric wire, plastic bags, whips, shackles, pliers, needles, tanks of water, ropes and pulleys, and pictures of a dog with the face of Ho Chi Minh or Lyndon Johnson? When they looked around, they might have seen blood stains (their own? someone else's?) splattered on furniture, an instrument of torture, or the floor. Then the ordeal began, with an ebb and flow of questions, accusations, humiliations, threats, beatings, and torture until finally they produced an adequate confession that could be "offered to the Party." Some prisoners rapidly confessed to anything to shorten their ordeal; others required prolonged interrogation and torture. For example, in the hundreds of pages of his confession, Sreng, the deputy secretary of the Northern Zone, was forced to respond to the question: "Why do you think that they shouldn't beat [you]?" His two-page response noted that he hadn't been beaten up to this point because he was "reporting things to Ângkar continuously." Indeed, he provided detailed lists of his "strings." Another document begins with the heading: "The answers Cho Chhan, alias Sreng, confessed in order to not be tortured."[50]

Based on the interrogator's notebook and other documentation, we know that the prisoners were emotionally manipulated and made to feel abandoned, to think of their loved ones, and to hold onto a glimmer of hope that they might survive. The resulting mixture of hope, despair, and confusion is evident in a rare memorandum written on May 8, 1977 by Siet Chhe, a high-ranking Khmer Rouge official who was interrogated and tortured for more than five months. He states, "My state of mind has been unstable in a way that I cannot describe. I can't see any road to the future," while lamenting that "from the evening of 4 May until [today] I underwent all kinds of torture according to *santebal's* procedures. *Santebal's* perception [so far] has been that I am a 100 percent traitor and that there is no way at all that I am not a traitor. So, given their stance, the level of torture has gradually been increased so that as I face this situation my feelings fluctuate wildly. I do not see any way to get out."[51] At the same time that he emphasizes his longtime connections to the party and close relationship with Pol Pot, Siet Chhe laments that death may be "the best way out . . . sudden death to escape the pain. . . . But there is no possibility of sudden death. Again, no way out. . . . I fear torture and death."

Such harrowing words exemplify the fear, confusion, and disorientation that so many prisoners must have experienced under interrogation.[52] Most immediately, Siet Chhe searches desperately for an end to the suffering, whether from "sudden death to escape the pain" or through a miraculous intervention by "the Organization" that would "kindly delay my torture." With his "feelings fluctuating wildly," Siet Chhe does "not see any way to get out" at the same time as he invokes patronage idioms ("I beg the Party to show pity on its child") and pleads with "the Organization" (and, indirectly, his former patron, Pol Pot) to miraculously intervene and exonerate him.

· · ·

What motivated the interrogators to brutalize human beings in this manner? It is true that they were given orders to interrogate their prisoners. The interrogators worked in a highly structured environment in which they had to follow specific rules and guidelines. Ultimately, they had to extract acceptable confessions. Nevertheless, Vaen Kheuan and other perpetrators had leeway to act within these constraints. As David Chandler has pointed out, the line between "doing politics" and "imposing torture" was not clearly defined, and interrogators had choices in how to go about obtaining the confession — including when, in what manner, and to what degree to use torture.[53] Many Khmer Rouge perpetrators seem to have used torture with abandon, and an explanation based on obedience to authority cannot fully account for these excesses.

Already, by 1976, interrogators seem to have been readily using torture. The 1976 interrogator's notebook contains a number of references to this problem, cautioning, "Our experience in the past has been that our interrogators for the most part tended to fall on the torture side. They emphasized torture over propaganda." The notebook also warns:

> The purpose of administering torture is to get answers from them *(vea)*, not for our own happiness. Thus we must make them *(vea)* hurt so that they *(vea)* will answer quickly. Another purpose is to break them *(vea)* through fear and terror. It's not something that we do out of individual anger or self-satisfaction. Therefore, beat them to make them *(vea)* afraid but absolutely not to kill *(ngoap)* them. When torturing, we must examine their health before turning to the whip. Don't try to selfishly kill them, thereby failing to obtain documents.[54]

As the references to torturing for personal "happiness" and "self-satisfaction" suggest, some interrogators appear to have at times tortured with an almost sadistic zeal. One former interrogator who had been arrested, Ma Meng Kheang, recalled an incident that illustrates how brutal the interrogations could be:

> Noeun, Sreng, and I were taking a break on the top floor of the canteen [at S-21]. At that time, Noeun said, "In [interrogation] group 1, all you hear everywhere is the sound of beatings, and [people] asking [prisoners] if they are 'C' [i.e., CIA] or not. . . . With a question like that what can anyone answer, if some of them don't even know what 'C' stands for? You never hear [people in] Group 1 'doing politics' at all, all they think of is beating, and when all they think of is beating, the enemies answer confusingly, accusing this one, accusing that one. This is the weak point of Group 1." The one named Saeng said that it was the same near where he was: all you ever heard were thuds and crashes and people screaming, 'C or not C?' when they don't know 'C' chicken from 'C' duck.[55]

Not surprisingly, Tuol Sleng documents are replete with references to all sorts of brutal excesses, ranging from everyday acts of unnecessary cruelty (for example, refusing to allow prisoners to defecate, removing the shirt of a shackled prisoner to allow mosquitoes to bite him all night) to extreme acts, such as torture, sexual violence, and beating prisoners to death. In fact, Vaen Kheuan admitted to killing several prisoners before he had obtained their confessions.[56] Many of these deeds are reported in a matter-of-fact manner in documents, highlighting how commonplace extreme acts of violence had become at Tuol Sleng.

While excessive brutality seems to have been frequent at Tuol Sleng, we should be wary of assuming that this abuse was the result of the sadistic personalities of perpetrators who were predisposed in a straightforward manner to gain pleasure from dominating and harming other human beings. It is quite possible that a small number of cadres could be accurately characterized as "sadistic." For example, one interrogator who was later arrested, But Heng, confessed to performing a series of chilling deeds, including the sexual mutilation of a female prisoner and beating prisoners to death.[57] Pathologizing all of the perpetrators in this manner, however, explains away their actions, constructing them as deviant others. Moreover, such an explanation may lead us to overlook the processes by which ordinary people are transformed into perpetrators and how these individuals may derive pleasure from domination, violence, and torture.

All human beings, including those who become perpetrators, belong to social groups in which they positively affiliate with others and internalize prohibitions against harming people. In Cambodia, great emphasis is placed upon "having friendly relations with others" *(roap an knea, reak teak)* within a social and moral community. Similarly, Buddhism discourages violence in most contexts and includes an injunction against killing among its basic moral precepts. Those who transgress such norms are subject to public censure through gossip, avoidance, shame *(khmas ke)*, loss of face *(mukh)*, and the threat of incarceration.

Not surprisingly, many perpetrators have shown at least an initial reluctance to harm other human beings in a variety of contexts, ranging from soldiers in the trenches of World War I to Hitler's reserve police battalions and Greek torturers.[58] To overcome this psychic conflict between the requirement to perpetrate violence against another human being and the often deeply internalized prohibitions against doing so — what I called in the introduction "psychosocial dissonance" (PSD)[59] — a person must usually make a series of psychological moves, such as changing their understanding of what they are doing, altering their behavioral norms, or learning new cognitive models for action. The state may facilitate this conversion process through political training and indoctrination by promoting an ideology of hate, diminishing the legal and moral inhibitions against violence, normalizing violence, and creating new contexts in which violence against the "the enemy" is legitimated. Thus killing tends to become easier when perpetrators are desensitized to violence, internalize violent ideologies, dehumanize their victims, undergo moral restructuring so that violence becomes morally justified, use euphemistic language that masks their deeds, and displace responsibility onto figures of authority.[60]

The specific inputs required to turn someone into a perpetrator vary depending on that individual's life history. One, several, or all of the aforementioned PSD reduction strategies may be pivotal in creating people who can commit horrible atrocities. State training and indoctrination help to generate this response. Such cognitive restructuring involves a dialectic in which complex processes interact to push the individual along a "continuum of destructiveness."[61] The exclusion and devaluation of a group of individuals sets them outside a given community. Dehumanization morally justifies harming them. By using euphemisms and deflecting responsibility onto authority figures, any remaining culpability can be diffused. As victims are harmed, the perpetrators become acclimated to violence. Desensitization makes the dehumanization of victims seem more normal.

Some Tuol Sleng cadres seem to have had an initial reluctance to brutalize prisoners. At a meeting on February 18, 1976, Duch told his staff, "You must rid yourselves of the view that beating the prisoners is cruel. Kindness is misplaced [in such cases]. You must beat [them] for national reasons, class reasons, and international reasons."[62] The DK regime facilitated the conversion process in a number of ways. Structurally, Tuol Sleng was designed to strongly dehumanize the prisoners and ensure compliance through the various institutional disciplines, including the routines, regulations, habits, practices, verbal and nonverbal cues, and sanctions discussed above and the very design of the prison (with its cells, barriers, fences, interrogation rooms, instruments of violence and torture, and so forth).[63] Discipline was strict. Duties were often exhausting. Cadres were required to attend frequent political meetings and self-criticism sessions. Recruits were isolated from their families and informed that their primary loyalty should be to Ângkar. Such isolation, discipline, and exhaustion — combined with a sense of fear and anxiety — were designed to increase a cadre's openness to the party's political message.

While there is little specific information on how Tuol Sleng interrogators were specifically trained, we do know some things about their broader political training and indoctrination, which was frequent and intensive. The interrogator's notebook, for example, illustrates some of the ideological messages that decreased perpetrator inhibitions and facilitated violence. Throughout the notebook, prisoners are dehumanized through linguistic strategies. They are called "enemies" *(khmang)* and "traitors" *(kbot)*, referred to using the vulgar pronoun *vea*, and described as objects to be manipulated and abused. Everyday moral norms did not apply to these "enemies"; in fact, the interrogators had a "duty" *(pheareakech)* to interrogate and torture them. This moral restructuring was coupled with a displacement of responsibility. Interrogation and torture were carried out in order to "get answers for the party. This is our glorious duty."[64] In fact, both within institutions of violence like Tuol Sleng and throughout the countryside, perpetrators often acted in the name of Ângkar, sending people to "see Ângkar" or telling victims that Ângkar had arrested or was punishing them. Lor told me that if a person he arrested protested, he would say, "If you want to know [why you have been arrested], wait until we arrive and you can ask Ângkar." The interrogators also refer to acts of violence using euphemisms; thus interrogation becomes "doing politics," "class-struggle work," "defending the country," or "getting answers."

Over time, most Tuol Sleng cadres probably lost their moral inhibitions and became desensitized as a result of living in this highly structured institution of violence, being exposed to intense political indoctrination and training, and regularly observing or participating in the abuse of prisoners. Vaen Kheuan fits this profile. He had already been interrogating prisoners for two years by the time Oum Chhan was incarcerated and was likely highly desensitized to his victim's pain. In his summary of Oum Chhan's confession, Vaen Kheuan's word choice suggests that his conversion had been facilitated by Tuol Sleng disciplines and Khmer Rouge ideology. The confession is generated within a set of prescribed institutional practices (working in specific kinds of spaces, occupying a certain role and status, participating in given routines of interrogation and torture). His ten-line interrogator's summary dehumanizes Oum Chhan by labeling him an "enemy," referring to him as *vea*, and informing him that his body was "worth less than garbage." Elsewhere, Vaen Kheuan employs euphemisms (for example, making Oum Chhan "pay respect" or "pay homage to the image of a dog"), morally justifies his violent actions (for example, by calling Oum Chhan an "enemy" and proving that Oum Chhan was a "traitor" by getting him to produce a confession admitting he was CIA), and displaces responsibility for his actions (since Oum Chhan's confession is ultimately "offered to Ângkar").

. . .

There is no doubt that Vaen Kheuan operated in a highly structured and constraining environment. However, while coercion, the violent institutional structure of the prison, and the conversion process of perpetrators in part explain the psychology of perpetrators like Vaen Kheuan, these factors are less helpful in explicating the violent excesses that took place at Tuol Sleng. To return to my earlier question: Why did some interrogators beat prisoners with abandon and sometimes to death? Why was it necessary for interrogators to be warned that torture was not supposed to be done "out of individual anger or self-satisfaction?"

We can only speculate about this issue, shifting to a more intrapersonal and dyadic level of analysis and weaving anthropological and psychological analysis into something along the lines of an "existential anthropology" that may help to explain at least some of the sadistic excesses committed at Tuol Sleng and, perhaps, other genocidal spaces of death. In particular, I want to suggest that the brutality of many cadres and soldiers at Tuol Sleng might be partly related to the atmosphere of fear and anxiety that pervaded DK in general and Tuol Sleng in particular.

As we have seen, life in DK was uncertain both for the general populace and for Khmer Rouge cadres. Driven by an authoritarian high-modernist desire to thoroughly control and manipulate social life, the "all-knowing" Party Center attempted to extend its gaze into the most private of spatial, corporeal, and mental spaces. The DK regime sought to regulate almost every aspect of people's lives, from what they ate and thought to whom they married. Terror was used to ensure the success of these plans for revitalization. Fearful of being accused of being "counterrevolutionaries" or "traitors," many Cambodians withdrew into themselves, silently carrying out the regime's orders as they shied away from most interpersonal relations.

If DK life was broadly characterized by atomization, fear, and terror, these tendencies were taken to an extreme at Tuol Sleng, especially for the prisoners whose bodies and minds were isolated, controlled, regulated, and manipulated. While being careful not to rationalize the horrible deeds Tuol Sleng cadres carried out, however, we must be willing to examine the environment in which they acted in order to better comprehend their actions. Evidence suggests that they too experienced atomization and fear. When asked if cadres were friendly with and trusted one another, Lor replied:

> No, each person knew only about their own work, that's it. They just knew that at 11:00 they would go sit at the table and eat with one another. After eating, they would leave the mess hall. They didn't let us have contact with each other, they just had each person do their work. . . . We were always afraid. Most of all, we were scared that we'd say something wrong. Or, if they arrested a big boss and brought them there [and you were con-

nected to their string], you might be imprisoned too when they gave names. Thus each person just thought about themselves. If you were told to do something, you would do it so you would escape [arrest and death] for another day.

Lor's comments, which echo those of other former Tuol Sleng personnel, highlight several aspects of the atmosphere at Tuol Sleng.[65] Cadres were isolated. Each person was expected to perform his or her duties and follow the extensive prison regulations, which included restrictions on social interaction. Those who failed to do so could be accused of treason and killed. Personal relationships were subordinated to politics, since DK ideology emphasized that each person's primary loyalty should be to the party. Lor recalled that he was taught: "Don't think about your mother and father; don't be attached to your brothers and sisters. Just work hard to serve the state." Tuol Sleng cadres were not permitted to return to their homes and were expected to support the arrest of friends and relatives who came under suspicion.

Interpersonal relations were dangerous. Tuol Sleng cadres were told that enemies were everywhere, even within their ranks. If a person was associated with someone who was later arrested, he or she might come under suspicion. Cadres were expected to watch each other for signs of treason and knew that they were being observed in turn. Everything a person said was political, so cadres lived in fear that their comments would be misinterpreted. Criticism and self-criticism sessions were particularly dangerous in this regard, since cadres were supposed to reveal and were critiqued by others for their "weak points." Thim, a former nurse at S-21, told Meng-Try Ea: "During the livelihood meeting, Sok [his superior] always talked about how late I was in getting up and how lazy I was. I was afraid of everyone, especially Sok. I did not trust anyone. Everyone tried their best to search for one another's faults. I was working and living in fear and horror. I kept trying to work harder and harder, and I kept my mouth shut all the time."[66] Here we find many of the same themes that appear in Lor's remarks: distrust, isolation, silence, uncertainty, and fear. These sentiments were justified, since many cadres were arrested after making a "mistake" or because of their associations. Sometimes coworkers simply disappeared.

Interrogators worked in an atmosphere that was particularly charged politically. Although interrogators were accorded honor for carrying out duties viewed as integral to the success of the revolution, they nevertheless worried constantly about whether the confession they were extract-

ing was "correct" and would satisfy their superiors. Dozens of interrogators failed at this task and were themselves incarcerated. In his confession, interrogator Ma Meng Kheang described some of the problems
interrogators confronted: "It's difficult to think so much. You get so tired
[at S-21] and you get headaches, and besides, it's a political place, it's not
easy to work there. . . . You never know when the day is finished. You
never know if you are 'correct.' With farming, on the other hand, you
either have a crop or you don't, in a factory a machine starts up or it
doesn't."[67] According to Ma Meng Kheang, interrogation was an
exhausting and uncertain job that could result in somatic symptoms like
headaches — though obviously their bodily discomfort was insignificant
in comparison with that of prisoners. Moreover, an interrogator's fear of
arrest was likely stronger than that of other Tuol Sleng cadres, for they
knew all too clearly the pain and violence that soon followed.

For Tuol Sleng cadres, then, life at Tuol Sleng was pervaded by fear,
isolation, and anxiety. In many ways, this situation resembles Hannah
Arendt's description of totalitarianism, in which people are increasingly
atomized as their liberties, privacy, and individuality are diminished; they
become homogenous units performing tasks for the state, which legitimates its radical program of social engineering in the name of the generic
masses.[68] Fear and terror are used to enforce this ideological vision,
which legitimates state control over almost every aspect of life. Formerly
private spaces are rendered increasingly public. As individuality is erased,
each person becomes more and more isolated, wary, and lonely. The paradox, of course, is that everyone is watched: the overseer is overseen and
the dominator dominated. The eyes of the pineapple peer everywhere,
including back at themselves.

. . .

How did perpetrators respond to this atmosphere of fear and uncertainty? A number of existential philosophers and psychologists, ranging
from Søren Kierkegaard to Rollo May, have argued that anxiety — a feeling of apprehension generated by uncertain threats to our meaningful
understandings and very being — is a fundamental condition of human
existence.[69] Anxiety, while closely related to fear, is distinguished by its
lack of a definite object: a person fears something concrete, but the
source of anxiety is difficult to ascertain. In Khmer, "anxiety" and "fear"
can be very loosely glossed by terms like *kângval, kar barom, kar pruoy
barom*, and *kar khlach*,[70] though these emotions are also implicit in the

Buddhist concept of suffering *(tukkha)*. For many existentialists, the greatest source of anxiety is the threat of nonbeing, the sense that our life is somehow in danger, that our self-identity is under attack, and that we don't know what happens when we die. However, anxiety is also associated with the meaninglessness that emerges when our most fundamental beliefs are threatened or do not provide an adequate explanation for what we are experiencing.

These emotions have strong ontological resonance, involving mind, body, and one's very sense of being. In terms of evolution, they are associated with situations that are crucial to our existence.[71] Fear and anxiety are responses to circumstances that potentially threaten our well-being. As anthropologists often point out, human beings are meaning-seeking creatures. We develop cognitive schemas, including cultural models, that enable us to make sense of and survive in the world. Anxiety may emerge in situations in which these understandings are threatened or break down, and we then feel apprehensive and overwhelmed. These self-implicating feelings are deeply embodied, involving autonomic arousal and physical symptoms. Among Cambodians, anxiety is often interpreted and expressed through idioms of "wind" dysfunction and related somatic complaints (for example, headaches, heart palpitations, shortness of breath, dizziness, fever, diarrhea, vomiting, muscle tension).[72]

Living and working in a context of enormous uncertainty, atomization, and danger, many cadres likely experienced a great deal of anxiety at Tuol Sleng. A cadre's consciousness could suddenly "regress." Suspicion was prevalent. Enemies were everywhere. Surveillance was constant. Former comrades disappeared. Cadres worked in an institution of pain and death. And at any moment, they might be arrested. Such anxiety was likely even more intense for interrogators, who, while inflicting horrible pain upon others, confronted nonbeing on a daily basis, an existential reality that may have been all the more difficult to deal with given the ideological renunciation of Buddhism and other forms of religious worship. Of all the Tuol Sleng cadres, they had the most reason to be fearful and anxious, for they knew exactly what happened to people after arrest. Ma Meng Kheang's comment about his frequent headaches and exhaustion can be better understood in this light.

Perpetrators are not to be pitied or excused, but some of their brutality may be explained in terms of fear and anxiety. While human beings have a number of ways of coping with stressful emotions, several of these psychosocial responses have the potential to motivate violence. *Being* is a broad term that overlaps with the concept of *self*, which I define as a sense of being that is continuously being generated from a variable mix of overlapping conscious and unconscious processes, including one's perceptual existence in relation to the environment (the I/me that sees, smells, feels, hears, and moves in the world), interpersonal relations (the I/me that interacts with others), private experiences (the I/me that has a distinct past), and conceptual memories and schemas (the I/me that identifies with and acts on the basis of meaningful moral values, social roles, fundamental beliefs, and personal goals).[73] Anxiety is a particularly stressful emotion insofar as it signals an uncertain threat to these processual foundations of the self. Thus meaninglessness, uncertainty, and danger — conditions that may generate considerable fear and anxiety — not only threaten one's continued being but also undermine the self-concepts that give us a sense of identity and structure the ways in which we interpret experience and act in the world.

People may respond to this existential dilemma by attempting to inflate their diminished and fragmented sense of self, often by seeking out and identifying with a new set of concepts.[74] These ideas tend to be grandiose, inflating the self through association with something that seems transcendent, eternal, and powerful (for example, a cause, a charismatic leader, an institution, a religious worldview, a nation, or an ideology). Moreover, such beliefs may be internalized, at least initially, in a highly schematized, narrow, and rigid manner; this cognitive "constriction" may provide a person with a feeling of greater existential security, since it allows these new self-concepts to be defended more easily and provides straightforward cognitive maps for acting in and making sense of a world that seems overwhelming.[75] It is precisely at such moments that people may be drawn to ideological messages that crystallize difference, simplifying what are otherwise more complex and fluid categories. Such self-inflation and cognitive constriction are involved in many types of fanaticism, as converts are drawn to an essentialist ideology that divides the world into black and white, erasing gray zones — everything and everyone is either "right" or "wrong."

Revitalization movements sometimes attract followers by combining such a Manichean vision with a blueprint for sociopolitical renewal. Such fear and anxiety likely played a part in drawing recruits to the Khmer Rouge. In the midst of civil war, when bombs ravaged the countryside and villages became battlefields, many Cambodians likely experienced fear and anxiety as a result of the threat of death, a growing sense of meaninglessness, and the atmosphere of uncertainty. These feelings would have heightened the appeal of DK ideology, as some recruits were drawn to a simplified message that identified the source of their woes (class exploitation) and hinted at the wonderful new society that would be established after victory. Moreover, recruits gained a sense of being a part of something much larger than themselves. They fought in the name of communism (against capitalism), nationalism (against foreign invaders), and righteousness (for equality and the end of oppression). Even more, they belonged to a revolutionary movement that seemed destined to attain communism more rapidly than any other country. This sense of belonging was symbolized by Ângkar, the god-like entity that was referred to in grandiose terms, as "all-knowing," "pure," "alert," "intelligent," "correct," "clear" and "enlightened."[76] Ultimately, each cadre was encompassed by Ângkar, partaking of its essence while ideally serving it with complete loyalty and obedience.

For many cadres, then, Khmer Rouge ideology, often in a constricted form, became an important part of their sense of self and being. Tuol Sleng was a particularly stressful and politicized institution. Cadres were exposed to constant indoctrination while working in an atmosphere of isolation, fear, and anxiety. As one former guard recalled, "I think we became crazy at that time, because of the Khmer Rouge indoctrination. We believed what they said. We did what they ordered us to do. We tried to forget what they told us to forget. We did not think about our families; instead, we only tried to work hard to serve the Khmer Rouge revolution."[77]

Given these circumstances, it seems possible that some interrogators, who dealt directly with pain and violence on a daily basis, may have responded to the existential threats they faced through enormous self-investment in the Khmer Rouge belief system. This type of narcissistic identification, in which a self under siege attempts to defend and fortify itself through grandiose inflation, can contribute to violence in at least two important ways.[78] First, it may dull one's empathy for others who, in comparison with the inflated self, seem relatively insignificant. And second, such an identification can lead to outbursts of rage when the self-image is threatened or undermined.

The brutality of the interrogators, then, may be partially explained by the combination of a lack of empathy for their victims and the fact that these prisoners enraged the interrogators both by their very existence (since their "treachery" implied the desirability of an alternative system of belief, thereby diminishing the grandeur of Khmer Rouge ideology, and therefore the perpetrator's sense of self) and through their "lies" and protestations (which suggested that the omnipotent Ângkar, and thus, through identification, they themselves, had either made a mistake or was being challenged by supposedly inferior beings). Perhaps this is why so many prisoners were beaten and tortured after proclaiming their innocence. Perhaps it was partly because their inflated sense of self was perceived to be under attack that perpetrators beat their prisoners in a rage, leading to Ma Meng Kheang's comment that "all [the interrogators] think of is beating." In fact, Vaen Kheuan's autobiography recounts how his revolutionary consciousness *(sâtiarâmma)* sometimes broke down when he was "quick to anger with prisoners," and he began to focus on raw power *(amnach)* so much that his hands shook when he wrote.

Because people are different and their motives shift across time and place, however, the brutal excesses perpetrated at Tuol Sleng may be explained in other ways as well. One of the most basic means by which the human mind processes information is through categorization, as we parse, typologize, and distinguish the world, often through the use of binary contrasts. When human beings are sorted in this manner, the ensuing categorizations are mediated by sociocultural knowledge, including ideology. Thus, we saw the DK radio broadcast distinguish between an "us" and a "them." In an atmosphere of uncertainty, when it is difficult to distinguish "us" from "them," violent regimes strive to manufacture difference by attempting to transform their victims into images that accord with the category to which they allegedly belong. Our current problematic arises from the fact that if perpetrators like Vaen Kheuan were merely automatons who carried out the ideological dictates of the state, then they would have carried out their orders in a more dispassionate manner — and we have seen that this does not seem to have been the case at Tuol Sleng. In other words, an explanation of human action that only invokes ideological discourse is a partial one that has difficulty explaining violent excess and the passion with which difference is manufactured.

Victor Turner's theory of symbolism provides a bridge linking the process of manufacturing difference to the insights of object relations theorists on projection. Turner argued that symbols have three important qualities: "condensation," the "unification of disparate significata," and the "polarization of meaning."[79] Because of its generality, a single symbol may represent a larger number of phenomena (condensation) that are connected because of local associations or their analogous qualities (unification of disparate significata).[80] Each symbol has two poles of meaning. The ideological pole encompasses those "arrangements of norms and values that guide and control persons as members of social groups and categories," while the sensory pole involves "natural and physiological phenomena and processes . . . that may be expected to arouse desires and feelings."[81]

Turner's ideas provide another way of looking at manufacturing difference, which is centered around one of the most general symbolic containers of meaning, a being. While there are many ways of parsing such beings, the "Who are 'We'?" radio broadcast, echoing Khmer Rouge ideology more broadly, attempted to divide them into two types: an "us" and an enemy "them." This discourse, which categorized social beings in specific ways, provided an important ideological pole of meaning that guided Tuol Sleng cadres in their understanding and treatment of prisoners. However, it tells us less about the sensory pole of meaning of these symbolic beings, who had bodies, perceptual abilities, physiological functions, cognitive capacities, and so forth. These sensory associations had a strong mimetic resonance for the perpetrators because of their own embodied experience.

There are, however, ways to connect the ideological and sensory poles of meaning that are nonreductive and nuanced. In object relations theory, for example, the human propensity to use binary discriminations is referred to as "splitting."[82] In addition to this cognitive-perceptual function, splitting is used as a psychological defense, as people sometimes "split off" unwanted thoughts and feelings and "project" them onto other beings. These senses of "splitting" are interrelated, since binary opposites are separate yet inextricably bound: one cannot have "hot" without "cold," "good" without "bad," or an "us" without a "them." Moreover, there is always someone who is "better" or who exemplifies "us" better than we do, thereby implying that we contain an element of the opposite quality.

Ideological discourses thrive on binary contrasts, valorizing one set of categories while denigrating and demonizing their opposites. Because ideologies play upon our psychosocial propensity to split and project, they may have greater appeal, particularly during times of stress. Ideologies offer ideas that can be used to inflate weakened selves (which strongly identify with an idealized "us") and a target onto which uncomfortable thoughts and feelings can be projected and "contained" ("others" placed in the "them" category). More broadly, splitting and projection provide a means of connecting Turner's two poles of meaning, since they constitute a psychosocial process through which symbols come to be invested with ideological and sensory force. In particular, these processes suggest why one person may brutalize another being, in that the victim becomes a symbolic container for thoughts and feelings that are highly salient to the perpetrator.

Manufacturing difference thus involves more than the ideological construction of "enemies." For Tuol Sleng cadres, each encounter with a prisoner was self-implicating on a variety of levels. Living in an atmosphere of enormous stress and uncertainty, many cadres identified strongly with Khmer Rouge ideology, inflating their weakened sense of self through projective identification with a larger cause. Not surprisingly, the first association of "us" in the DK radio broadcast is with "nation," thereby asserting the encompassment of the self by the nation. By manufacturing difference, these interrogators were also indirectly constructing an inflated self-image, for by implication (since binary contrasts are antagonistically linked), they contained the opposite qualities of these enemies. Whereas ideology provided a conceptual structure that could be projected onto the prisoners, the sensory meaning of these symbolic beings arose from their mimetic qualities, particularly their capacity to be manufactured into an icon that inversely mirrored the self-image of the perpetrators.

The motivational force of these projections came from other sources as well. Since each side of a binary contrast contains the potentiality of its opposite, ideological identifications are often problematic: we always potentially contain aspects of the "other." Through projection, a person is able to translocate into a symbolic container these undesirable qualities, which can thereby be disavowed and expelled, temporarily buttressing a fragile sense of self. From this perspective, violence and torture can be viewed in part as an attack on these rejected and hated self-images, which undermine a person's self-identity. Similarly, projection may be used to split off aspects of our self-experience that we find unpleasant. As we have seen, fear and anxiety tend to arise in situations in which our existential being is threatened. Anxiety is particularly disturbing, because the source of the threat is uncertain. Splitting and projective identification provide a means of dealing with such feelings, which are translocated onto a being who can "contain" them. The source of one's anxiety is found; one's fears are projected into another place. Projection may also be used to control such uncomfortable thoughts and feelings by providing a way of entering into, exploring, and dominating a being who symbolically contains them. All of these forms of projection ultimately serve to inflate the self and provide one with a sense that the threat of nonbeing has been diminished.

Such projections provide an emotionally salient motivational basis for at least some forms of violent excess, including the types of brutality that occurred at Tuol Sleng. While it is impossible to know what was going on in Vaen Kheuan's mind as he interrogated and tortured Oum Chhan, we can speculate on some of the motivations that led interrogators like him to brutalize prisoners. When prisoners entered an interrogation cell, they were liminal beings awaiting transformation. DK discourse provided a set of ideological categories that gave structure and meaning to this process of manufacturing difference. On a more sensory level, the prisoners could symbolically contain the projections of perpetrators because of their mimetic potentialities as fellow beings. As mimes, however, these liminal beings functioned as a psychosocial camera obscura, inverting and distorting the projected thoughts and feelings of the perpetrators.

Inversion is linked to splitting, since binary contrasts create sets of oppositions. Ideology accentuates this categorical separation while privileging one side over another. Because they are antagonistically bound, however, each part of a binary opposition inflects the other. The identity of the prisoner, which is manufactured out of such ideological oppositions, therefore inversely mimes the identity of the perpetrator. By asserting that Oum Chhan was an "enemy," "worth less than garbage," a *vea,* and an agent of the CIA, Vaen Kheuan was also revealing something about his own self-image — that he belonged to an "us" that contained the inverse qualities of this "them." For such a person, manufacturing difference is both an ideological and a self-implicating act, which is given meaning in the ritual transformation of a mimetic being.

This transformation may involve distortion in the sense that thoughts and feelings of the perpetrator may be "twisted apart" through projective identification. By projecting negative qualities onto prisoners like Oum Chhan, Vaen Kheuan was disavowing them in himself, placing these attributes into a symbolic container where they could be hated and destroyed. Fear and anxiety increase the tendency toward splitting and projective identification, as a person attempts to cope with these feelings by projecting them onto a new location. In the uncertain atmosphere of Tuol Sleng, where the threat of treachery and death abounded, perpetrators may have projected their uncomfortable feelings onto the liminal beings they were interrogating. These evil and feared "others" became the imagined source of the perpetrator's existential discomfort, threatening both the regime with which they strongly identified and their own sense of meaning and being. Thus a perpetrator's fear of annihilation could be temporarily denied and obliterated by striking out at the beings who, through projection, now symbolically contained these feelings.

Besides this attempt to destroy their projected fears and anxieties, perpetrators could also cope with such feelings through mastery.[83] From this perspective, the interrogation and torture process may be viewed in several ways. First, the interrogators attempt to control their own feelings of fear and anxiety by dominating the symbolic others onto whom these feelings have been projected. In this fashion, Oum Chhan is constructed into an enemy who threatens both Vaen Kheuan and the DK regime. By dominating Oum Chhan, Vaen Kheuan is able to master this projection. Moreover, each of these acts is a ritual display of the dominance of the DK regime with which the perpetrators have self-identified. In this context, the DK slogan glorifying "mastery" *(mâchaskar)* takes a sinister twist.

On another level, such domination enables a person experiencing an existential threat to strengthen his or her fragile sense of self by controlling another being. Torture is one of the most extreme manifestations of mastery, since the torturer violates the boundaries of the victim's flesh with fists, kicks, and instruments of horror. With each grunt, plea, scream, and loss of consciousness that these acts of violence produce, as the victim comes closer to death, the perpetrator's sense of self expands into the space of being that is negated, achieving a precarious and momentary form of sovereignty. Perhaps perpetrators also develop a voyeuristic fascination with their brutal deeds, as they are allowed to watch things that are normally out of sight: another being's pain, terror, and journey toward death.

Here we find another connection between the sensory and ideological poles of meaning, since these acts of domination are partly expressed in terms of cultural forms. From this perspective, Vaen Kheuan's summary of Oum Chhan's confession reads like a eulogy to his domination of Oum Chhan, who is labeled an "enemy," described with the pronoun *vea,* told that he is "worth less than garbage," forced to "pay respect" to the DK regime and "pay homage to the image of the dog," and ultimately tortured into confessing. When invoked in such ritual acts of violence, these culturally salient forms of knowledge comprise an important part of the ideological poles of meaning, providing norms and values associated with social order. For a person like Vaen Kheuan, the sensory pole of meaning is linked to the mimetic properties of his victim, who symbolically reflects Vaen Kheuan's own sense of being in ontologically resonant ways through the bodily inscription of violence.

It is partly because of this sensory pole of meaning that perpetrators may be motivated to brutalize their victims in excessive ways: their violence cannot simply be explained as "obeying orders" or blindly following ideological dictates. A person like Vaen Kheuan, while operating within a set of constraints, has latitude in choosing how to perpetrate violence. He decides if and when to make Oum Chhan "pay homage to the image of a dog" and has psychosocial motivations for doing so. Such attempts to completely control another being bring us back to the issue of sadism and suggest that we must also be careful to not simply pathologize perpetrators. Rather than being the result of sexual pathology, the sadistic "pleasure" people sometimes experience when perpetrating violent acts seems to be linked to the sensory pole of meaning, which makes brutality "desirable" insofar as it provides a means for them to cope with existential uncertainty, deal with feelings of fear, anxiety, and isolation, and inflate a self that is threatened with disintegration.

To conclude, I should note that I have attempted to phrase my discussion so as to parallel Buddhist theory, which overlaps in interesting ways with the existential tradition and object relations theory.[84] In Buddhism, the self is viewed as an illusory sense of enduring being that arises from the momentary coalescence of the "five aggregates" *(khântha)*: form/body *(roupâkhântha)*, feeling/sensation *(vetoneakhântha)*, perception *(sânhnhakhânta)*, mental formation *(sângkharâkhântha)*, and consciousness *(vinhnheanâkhântha)*.[85] Our bodily senses make contact with objects in the material world, generating sensations and feelings that have pleasant, unpleasant, or neutral valences. When we perceive these sensations and feelings, we react to them with desire, aversion, or neutrality, impulses conditioned by our mental predispositions. Consciousness is the gestalt-like experience of this mental process, which disappears and begins anew each time we make contact with another object.

Suffering arises from ignorance and desire, as people mistakenly crave, and believe there is a permanence to, consciousness. This illusory sense of self is partly rooted in our mental formations — which resemble what some cognitive scientists call "self-schemas" — or a set of cognitive, emotional, and behavioral predispositions that mediate our experience. Because our past actions have consequences and leave traces that condition the present *(kâmm)*, we develop a craving *(tânha)* for and attachment *(upadana)* to certain things, which lead us to react with passion, aversion, or neutrality to the objects with which our senses make contact. The paradox is that all things that give us a sense of self are impermanent and changing. An ignorant *(avijja)* person therefore lives in a state of fear and anxiety, dreading annihilation and desperately seeking out and defending attachments that provide an illusory foundation for the self.[86]

Like existentialism, then, Buddhism argues that most human beings experience fear and anxiety. Like object relations theory, Buddhism holds that a self that is threatened with fragmentation will seek ways to inflate itself. These two theories also assert that the sense of self is maintained by something akin to projective identification, as people respond to, identify with, and react to objects to which are attached self-implicating thoughts and emotions. And, Buddhism maintains that these psychosocial dispositions may lead people to perpetrate acts of violence. Clearly, there are differences between Buddhism, existentialism, and object relations theory (for example, regarding the reality and nature of the "self"). Nonetheless, the similarities provide additional support for the above explanation of some of the violent excesses perpetrated within the Tuol Sleng "space of death."

CHAPTER SIX

The Dark Side
of Face and Honor

Face is the mask of status and dignity that Asians show to
others, who are all wearing masks of their own. It is what
makes Cambodia such a polite society in normal times: I
respect your face, you respect mine, and we keep our real
feelings about each other hidden. In our language, to insult
someone publicly is, in the literal meaning, to "break his
face."

Haing Ngor, *Cambodian Odyssey*

After 1975 . . . [v]iolence became a virtue. Waging war
became prestigious. So did smashing enemies of the party.

David Chandler, *The Tragedy of Cambodian History*

To more fully comprehend the violence perpetrated at Tuol Sleng and
elsewhere in DK, we need to consider yet another level of analysis, the
dynamics of group-level interactions. Vaen Kheuan did not interrogate
Oum Chhan in isolation; he was a member of a larger unit of interrogators. Similarly, when Lor went to Choeung Ek and killed "one or two
people," he did so in a group context. While the motivations of perpetrators are complex, they, like all human beings, are influenced by their
location in specific social settings.

In Cambodia, one of the key dynamics informing group interactions is
"face" *(mukh, mukh moat)*, an embodied metaphor for relative social
standing. Face is the self-image one asserts in given contexts, depending
on the evaluations of and esteem accorded by self and others. Because it
is directly related to the positive and negative evaluations of others, face
is loosely correlated with honor and shame. The Khmer noun *mukh* lit-

erally refers to a person's "face" or the "front" of something, but it includes among its many secondary meanings the notions of "reputation" and "place, position, rank, title."[1] Face therefore reflects one's place in the social order, a position that is strategically negotiated during social interactions, particularly with regard to the extent to which others *korop*, or respect, honor, and obey the person. As a Cambodian man told me, "Having face means that we have honor, that wherever we go others are friendly with us. When they see our face, they may be scared of and *korop* us, but they also may admire and praise us. . . . [It has to do with the way] people evaluate us." The importance of "face" in Cambodian social life is illustrated by the large number of compound phrases involving *mukh*. Thus a powerful and respected person is not just said to "have face" *(mean mukh)*, but also to have a "full face" *(penh mukh)*, a "big face" *(thum mukh)*, "high face" *(khpuas mukh)*, or "face and voice" *(mukh moat)*.

Several aspects of this concept deserve emphasis. First, face is predicated on the evaluations of others. One often hears Cambodians discuss their assessment of the "value" *(veay/aoy tâmlei)* of different people. Most people are constantly concerned with how others evaluate them and thus carefully consider the social implications of any action. Second, face is performative. Because each person holds a certain position in the social order that is subject to negotiation and evaluation, he or she feels pressure to perform given duties and roles in accordance with social expectations. Lurking in the background of any public interaction is fear of the exposure and shame that results when others do not respond in accordance with the "line," to use Erving Goffman's term, that a person is asserting.[2] At such times, Cambodians say a person is "shamefaced" *(mukh khmas)*, has a "little face" *(tauch mukh)*, "loses face" *(amas mukh, ap mukh)*, or, as Haing Ngor notes above, has their face "broken" *(bambak mukh)*.

A third key dimension of face concerns contextual variation: the extent to which face is at stake differs according to the social situation. In any given interaction, the degree to which one fears exposure and shame depends upon a consideration of who is present, the familiarity and social distance between the actors, and the type of social situation involved. The stereotype of Cambodians as "gentle" people emerged in part because most foreigners interacted with Cambodians in more formal situations, in which politeness and smiles are the expected norm. Obviously, Cambodians, like people throughout the world, engage in violent behaviors in some contexts. Finally, individual variation exists in

face sensitivity. While most people act in accordance with social expectations, some lack sensitivity to issues of face, honor, and shame, and therefore are said to have a "thick face" *(mukh kras)*.

Social interactions are structured to buffer people from losing face.
First, there is an expectation that people will act in accordance with preexisting rules of etiquette and respect. Therefore, as mentioned, when
two nonintimates interact in a formal situation, the subordinate person is
expected to honor his or her social superior by employing the appropriate speech registers, assuming the proper body position and mannerisms,
and generally acting in a polite and reverent manner. The subordinate
person receives honor by behaving in this way and through his or her
superior's positive response.

When two people interact in this orderly manner, social relations
remain smooth and friendly, and no one loses face. Cambodians value
"order" *(sântap thnoap, riep roy, mean robiep)* in many aspects of their
lives. A wife who keeps her household in proper order (for example,
keeping her home clean, taking care of the family wealth, not arguing
with her husband, and properly receiving guests) gains honor. Likewise,
a political leader who runs the government in an orderly manner receives
respect from the populace.

By enabling interactions to flow smoothly, the orderly performance of
social roles and norms of etiquette helps people observe an important
social principle: mutual face-saving.[3] People protect the face of others,
who return the favor. Since one can lose face both through one's own
performance and through one's treatment by others, this principle lends
predictability to social encounters.

In addition to being respectful and polite, interactions are characterized by indirect speech, circumlocution, and the avoidance of conflict or
sensitive topics. A person who wants to express displeasure (although
such feelings are frequently kept to oneself) usually does so through
slight changes in posture, facial expression, eye contact, gesture, and
tone of voice, shifts that are often almost imperceptible to a foreigner.
Moreover, if a potentially discordant topic must be broached, Cambodians sometimes use an intermediary or address a third party.[4]

Given its centrality to social interaction, it is not surprising that face
has deep ontological resonance for most Cambodians. Face is self-implicating on a number of levels; we must be careful not to assume that face
is just an artificial "mask" used to hide a person's true feelings.[5] If, as
Haing Ngor states in the epigraph that began this chapter, face is in some
sense a "mask," it is not an "artificial" mask but rather reflects a per-

son's self-image and identity. The "lines" we take and the self-images we assert are an important part of who we are. One is polite and gives respect to one's superior not just because it is necessary and expected, but also because such face norms have been internalized and constitute a key element of a person's sense of self. Moreover, face is directly related to duty, since a person gains or maintains face by properly carrying out his or her status tasks. In Western discourses, duty is often conceptualized as an external constraint, as something that is artificial and opposed to individual autonomy.[6] Although similar discourses exist in Cambodia, duty is more often regarded as something positive, a reflection of who the person is and how they fit in local group obligations (including patronage ties) and the larger social order in which all things have a place.

Face is also an embodied metaphor that analogically links social standing to a specific part of the body. Our physical face is central to our sense of being, serving as the primary locus through which we communicate with other human beings and they respond to us. This communicative function has an adaptive basis in that our species has evolved complex facial expressions to convey or dissemble intention, signal emotion, and regulate interpersonal interaction.[7] The face includes a nose that smells, eyes that gaze and cry, cheeks that flush and pale, skin folds that mark age and activity, ears that hear, hair and facial adornments (earrings, makeup, moustaches, hairstyles) asserting gender and status, and a mouth that speaks, smiles, and eats. To lose one's facial functions — through paralysis, neurological disorders, or disfigurement — is to lose one of our most fundamental ways of being in the world.[8] When a jealous wife carries out an acid attack against their husband's lover, for example, she strikes at the very foundation of the lover's social "face" and being, ruining her beauty, crushing her social status, and impairing her very capacity for social interaction. If the face is the most visible part of the body, the metaphor of "face" refers to a social standing that is determined by the way one is "seen" by others. It is a metaphor for one's relative social "visibility."

Face is also self-implicating in an emotional sense. It is directly associated with shame and pride, emotions centering on the negative and positive evaluations of self and others. In all societies, human beings internalize norms and values for behavior and evaluate themselves and others accordingly. Shame, in particular, serves as a strong mechanism of social control, since most people feel anxious about the potentially negative social evaluations that will occur if they violate these behavioral codes. Such negative evaluations, which are a common topic of conversation and gossip in Cambodia, undermine and diminish one's self-image, leading to the shame that almost always accompanies a loss of face. Perhaps the closest Khmer word that can be glossed as "shame" is *khmas*. This term, which can also be used to refer to the genitals, is most frequently used in the expression *khmas ke* ("shamed before others") or in the compound *ien khmas* (which ranges in meaning from "shy and embarrassed" to "crestfallen and shamed").[9] Emotions like shame and pride motivate people by providing goals (to avoid/gain negative/positive evaluations) and are embodied in the sense that they have physiological correlates — a diminished or "lowered" bearing (for example, an averted gaze, a shrunken and stooped posture, blushing, the desire to escape) — that mime the loss of social standing.[10]

Face is ontologically resonant in another physiological sense. As we have seen, Khmer ethnophysiology is largely centered around the notion of equilibrium and proper flow, particularly with regard to the "wind" and blood that course through small vessels *(sârsai)* in the body. When a person is in distress, the circulation may become impaired, leading to various somatic symptoms and ailments.[11] At such times, Cambodians may say that they "have pain/hurt" *(chheu)* or that their bodies are not at ease *(min sruol khluon)*. To restore physiological balance, Cambodians often use local treatments that remove inner blockages or release excess wind, such as "coining" (firmly scraping the skin with the edge of a coin), pinching or massaging key spots on the body, "cupping" the skin with a heated cup so that wind is suctioned out, or rubbing in a wind-releasing oil. This ethnophysiology, while strongly related to the Ayurvedic tradition, has also been influenced by the Buddhist emphasis on spiritual and bodily equilibrium.

Balance, then, is a strongly resonant theme in Cambodian society. Social interactions are ideally structured in a smooth and orderly manner that protects each person's face. If the social equilibrium is upset, a person's "face" is likely to suffer, a condition that often manifests itself somatically. Thus social equilibrium and bodily balance are intertwined in Cambodia, thereby heightening the emotional and physiological resonance of face.

Two further dimensions of face are important to note. First, there are situations in which a person interacts with others but does not feel constrained by face norms. Such "anomic behavior"[12] sometimes occurs when a person ventures outside his or her known community and feels uninhibited. Anyone who traveled Cambodia's roads in the mid 1990s would be familiar with the reckless driving style that sometimes resulted in loss of life due to the implicit rule that whoever is bigger and more daring has the right of way. In the extreme, anomic behavior may involve total callousness toward others. For example, in 1995 a newspaper reported how, after hitting a man with their armored personnel carrier, a group of soldiers simply moved his body to the side of the road and continued on.[13] This type of "heartless behavior"[14] is characteristic of situations in which a person acts as an anonymous member of a larger group. War is an obvious example, since soldiers are fighting a generic sociopolitical enemy whom they are expected to kill without hesitation. Moreover, if a person acts in a disrespectful manner that makes one lose face (thus violating norms of mutual face-saving), one will be more likely to disregard face norms when interacting with that person in the future.

Finally, face is strategically negotiated and at times competitively structured, particularly insofar as it is bound up with *ketteyos*. Although the word *ketteyos* can be roughly translated as "honor,"[15] the term carries a strong sociocentric connotation that the English word does not capture. Thus the *Khmer Dictionary* defines *ketteyos* as "glory and fame that is well-known, splendid reputation."[16] While the English word *honor* is similarly defined as "high respect, esteem, or reverence accorded to exalted worth or rank . . . glory, renown, fame," it carries the connotation of an "elevation of character, 'nobleness of mind' . . . a fine sense of and strict allegiance to what is due or right."[17] This sense of honor as a characteristic of the self that leads one to act in a moral manner is less emphasized by the Khmer term. *Ketteyos* may be gained through proper moral behavior, but it is largely focused on the external recognition and evaluation of one's glory, prestige, and reputation. Face and *ketteyos* are therefore closely linked, since both involve one's self-image and are highly dependent on evaluations of one's relative social standing. In fact, Cambodians sometimes use these words interchangeably, and the loss of either typically leads to shame.

Since everyone has the potential to rise or fall in stature, many Cambodians are strongly motivated to increase their status — to be "higher" than others, to be the "big person" who is respected rather than the little person who is looked down upon. One gains face and honor by being given respect, acting in a proper and dignified manner (dressing well, behaving politely, fulfilling one's duty), and raising one's social status (increasing one's educational level, occupation, wealth). Since social standing is relative, Cambodians frequently evaluate, compare themselves to, and compete with other people for honor. Such "honor competition" *(brânang, brâlang, brâkuot ketteyos)* often centers around a discourse of victory and defeat, as one person "vanquishes" *(chneah)* or "loses" *(chanh)* to another.[18]

FACE AND HONOR DURING DK

Although the DK regime asserted that "face *(mukh moat)*, rank *(bon sâkti)*, [and] duty positions" were regressive "manifestations of private property,"[19] this official discourse often diverged from on-the-ground realities, in which face and honor continued to influence interpersonal interactions. The criteria by which people were evaluated, the contexts in which face and honor were at stake, and the signs of status had simply changed.

Social evaluation during DK was almost constant. While Cambodian society had always been very public, life in DK was more extreme in this regard, since the boundary of the public realm was pushed far into what had previously been private spaces (and therefore contexts in which face had been less directly at stake). In the countryside, people were rarely alone due to long work hours, sexually segregated work teams, communal dining, and frequent meetings. Parents even had to be careful about what they whispered at home because of spies and because the Khmer Rouge encouraged children to report on "traitors" of the revolution. The stakes in DK were also much higher than before. If a person failed to perform according to expectations, he or she would not just lose face, but would also quite possibly be put in prison or even executed. Positive evaluations, in turn, could result in procuring a better position, additional food, or other advantages.

For the masses and especially those groups devalued during DK, the face and honor of cadres was closely linked to their enormous power and authority. DK was viewed as a time of reversals, when the poor and uneducated had gained ascendancy over the rich. Even though "face, rank, and boastfulness" were "manifestations of private property," members of these new elites often could not resist exhibiting their high status. Sometimes these displays were overt: cadres might receive better food rations, ride on bikes or in motorized vehicles, carry machetes and guns, have bodyguards, live in larger homes, or wear new clothes, watches, and pens. In other situations, their status was marked in less obvious ways, such as when cadres gave speeches at meetings, commanded soldiers, held positions of power, made life-and-death decisions, or were respected and feared by the people.

When discussing the face and honor of cadres, Banyan villagers often commented on these signs of status. Vong, for example, said that Boan, the village head who arrested him for stealing potatoes,

> had honor *(ketteyos)* during [DK]. The people were scared of those who worked in higher levels, like the village head. . . . No one dared to cause trouble with them. Because they were the village heads, they could eat any-thing they wanted at their homes. Boan was full every day and had strength. If [a cadre like him] wanted food, they would go scoop up rice from the granary and take it home to cook. . . . No one dared make trou-ble around Boan for fear he would have them taken away to be killed. Boan could order us around as he pleased. Sometimes he said that we were lazy or that we didn't want to work. He would blame us for things. Meanwhile, we went hungry, while he ate his fill. . . . He had enormous power. . . . We didn't dare look at the faces [of cadres like him]. . . . Boan was also partial to his neighbors and relatives (even though many of them had worked for the Lon Nol regime!). Before he was arrested, they had face *(mean mukh)*, enormous face. But when [soldiers] came and took Boan away to be killed, they lost their face and voice *(mukh moat)* and became quiet.

Similarly, another man from Banyan stated that such Khmer Rouge cadres had honor "because we had to do whatever they said. They were the law and held total power over the populace. Everyone feared and honored them. The common people didn't have much honor; we just thought about work and death."

If members of the populace often continued to assess a cadre's face and honor in terms of their possessions and power, Khmer Rouge ideol-ogy provided a key new criterion for evaluating people: the state of their revolutionary consciousness. From this perspective, a cadre's face and honor were determined by many of the factors discussed earlier: their class background, history of revolutionary service, associations, devotion to the party, position in the new regime, and mindful thought and behav-ior. Thus, in some contexts, cadres could take the "line" of a progressive revolutionary, which would give them face and honor in the new regime. In Phnom Penh, the quality of a cadre's consciousness, and thus his or her status, was signified in ways that paralleled status on the local level — housing accommodations, bodyguards, clothing, position, vehicles, authority, public recognition, retinues, special food and clothing, and for the highest-ranking cadres, sometimes even imported luxury goods.[20] High-ranking cadres had enormous face and were treated in an almost reverent manner.

Ultimately, revolutionary consciousness was evinced through behav-ior. Face and revolutionary consciousness converged in social performance, as people publicly asserted a "line" about themselves that was read, interpreted, and assessed by others. The claim to face and honor could be competitively structured, as cadres attempted to display their relatively more progressive state of mindfulness."[21] Underlying such actions was a desire to prove beyond a doubt that one was loyal to and willing to fulfill any duty for the DK regime. In many contexts, this proof consisted of a demonstrated willingness to kill. The head of a Cambodian Buddhist association noted how the Khmer Rouge linked loyalty and killing:

> Let me tell you about Pol Pot's method of indoctrination. They'd instruct people repeatedly until they believed [their ideology]. . . . It was like a religion. Pol Pot said that if a person was truly loyal *(smah trang)* they would dare to kill their father. Some children dared to do this because they believed in [the Khmer Rouge]. If a father did something wrong, they'd have his child kill him in order to demonstrate that this child was truly loyal *(smah trang)*. This was the way they indoctrinated people. If a person dared to kill, obeyed their orders to the point of killing, that person was considered good. In the despicable Pol Pot period, people were evaluated in this manner.

This comment echoes a question I posed earlier: how could it become honorable to brutalize and execute other human beings during DK? Part of the answer to this question lies in DK ideological conceptions of honor, loyalty, and duty, which were all bound up with revolutionary consciousness. For example, an article in the May 1977 issue of *Revolutionary Young Men and Women* was devoted to the topic of "true loyalty" *(smah trang)*.

The preamble of the tract exhorts the revolutionary youths to "unconditionally love, *korop,* and be completely loyal *(smah trang)* to the Party, Revolution, and People," while praising them for having "renounced *(leah bang)* everything — mind and body, sentiment, parents, siblings, home, rice and vegetable fields — to join [the] revolutionary movement . . . [,] carrying out every sort of revolutionary duty *(phearokech)*, big and small, while joining to strike and crush the American imperialists and their lackeys, traitorous groups, and the various oppressor classes."[22] The next section of the article, entitled "But What Does Being Truly Loyal Mean?" goes on to delineate the four key qualities of a loyal revolutionary:

> True loyalty is not just words, resolution, ideology, consciousness, or thought alone. True loyalty means having fully absorbed [these things so that one's] standpoint and execution are clear and correct all the time. . . .

1. One must be completely loyal to every aspect of the Party's political line, consciousness line, and organizational line, all the time. . . .

2. One must always execute every aspect of the Party line accurately. . . .

3. One must struggle to defend the Party line so that it is always accurate and pure *(l'a bâresot)*. Thus, the Revolutionary Young Men and Women must not only work hard to execute [the line] accurately, but also to always observe and obey *(tam dan)* the application of the Party's line at every place. . . .

4. One must struggle to clean up *(boas somat)* hidden enemies burrowing from within and to purify various bad compositions so that they are completely gone, cleansed from inside the ranks of our revolution, Party, and revolutionary youth. Any place in which there are hidden enemies burrowing or various bad compositions in the ranks of the Party, revolutionary young men and women, revolution, and people, we aren't able to defend the Party line so that it is pure *(l'a bâresot)*, because all of these compositions, they *(vea)* subvert the Party line and continuously do activities that destroy the Party, revolution, nation, and our Kampuchean people. . . . Thus, it is necessary for our revolutionary young men and women to join together to struggle to clean up *(boas somat)* hidden enemies burrowing from within and various groups whose composition isn't good in order to completely cleanse them from inside the ranks of our Party, our revolutionary young men and women, our revolution, our people.

For the Khmer Rouge, being truly loyal required the constant display of a set of behaviors demonstrating that one was a progressive revolutionary, a status that accorded great honor.

Such a person had to be "mindful" in ways that would follow from their having "fully absorbed" the party "stand." When Khmer Rouge ideology had been fully absorbed, a cadre would be "completely loyal to every aspect" of the DK party line, would "always execute every aspect of the Party line accurately," and would relentlessly "struggle to defend the Party line so that it is always accurate and pure." Perhaps the most overt way in which a person could display his or her revolutionary consciousness was a demonstrated willingness to "clean up hidden enemies burrowing from within and to purify various bad compositions." To ensure that the party line remained "pure," these subversive enemies — who had allegedly infiltrated the ranks of the party, the people, and even the revolutionary youth — had to be "cleaned up" and annihilated so that they were "completely gone." A "truly loyal" revolutionary, in other words, would be ready to commit acts of genocide in order to "defend" the purity of new social order.

A willingness to kill was linked to another theme in DK ideology: renunciation *(leah bang)*. The DK regime glorified those who had "renounced everything — mind and body, sentiment, parents, siblings, home, rice and vegetable fields — to join the revolutionary movement." As noted earlier, DK "mindfulness" involved renunciation of these and other "private" inclinations, an idealized state of mind that resonated ontologically with preexisting Buddhist conceptions of the elimination of attachment and desire. This Khmer Rouge ideological palimpsest was sometimes portrayed in terms of metaphors of separation. The term *leah,* for example, carries the connotation of cutting apart, as in cutting branches off a tree or splitting bamboo.[23] *Leah bang,* in turn, refers to a disconnection from something, as in abandoning one's studies.

The Khmer Rouge also spoke frequently about cutting off one's sentiment and thought *(dach chett, chett dach, bdechnha chet, pdach/leng manosânhchetâna)*, a notion that was also implicit in a common DK ideological refrain that exhorted cadres to carry out their revolutionary duties with "firm resolution" or "without fail" *(dach khat)*. The word *dach* may be defined as "detached" or "separated," as when the electricity is suddenly "cut off." *Chett* broadly refers to the "psychological heart," though it implies an awareness that is animating and reactive (to sensory information), generating feelings, impulses, and a disposition to act.[24] This cluster of terms *(phdach/leng manosânhchetâna* has almost the same meaning as *dach chett* and the terms were often used interchangeably) therefore connotes an intellectual and emotional separation that enables one to act in a dispassionate and determined manner.

Many former cadres mentioned this Khmer Rouge ideological model of detachment. For example, Teap, the cadre who worked with Rom at the subdistrict office, recalled that when he was sent to a regional school for political education, his instructors not only instructed cadres to be on guard for agents of the CIA, the KGB, and the Vietnamese who had infiltrated the country, but also emphasized the importance of cutting off one's heart:

> They sent us to be indoctrinated with their ideology, saying that whatever we did, we had to always be dispassionate and resolute *(dach chett)*. They didn't allow sentiment between a child and his or her mother and father. They didn't let us know them. If we expressed feelings for our parents, they'd say we [were building] the garden of the individual *(suon tuo)* and were at fault. Their ideology was the hardest and strictest of all. They didn't allow us to recognize our siblings! Their slogan was "Anything for the Party!" . . . They asked us, "Comrade, if your mother or father was such a traitor, would you dare to kill them? Could you cut off your feeling *(dach khat)* toward them? Would you act with firm deter-

mination *(bdechnha chett)*?" . . . None of us could say no. We had to answer that we would dare to do so without hesitation.

For Teap, Grandmother Yit exemplified this attitude because she lacked compassion and had supposedly executed her husband: "She shot her husband! Grandmother Yit killed him herself, saying that her husband had joined a string of traitors. . . . She was really *dach chett!* Grandmother Yit lacked pity and . . . didn't laugh or play much with children, either. . . . It was said that she had been a revolutionary since the age of eighteen . . . and she didn't have any children of her own."

Lor recalled receiving indoctrination that was similar to Teap's. He said, "When I was in the army, they taught us to cut off our feeling for the enemy, even if it was our parents. At Tuol Sleng, they reinforced this training even more, telling us that we had to become resolute *(dach khat)* and kill whoever was at fault. Even if someone had been our friend before, we couldn't recognize them once they had become an enemy." When I asked him what the term *dach khat* meant, Lor explained, "This meant that we had to renounce *(leah bang)* our sentiment *(manosân-hchetâna)* [toward others]." Interestingly, the term *dach chett* is also directly related to Buddhist "mindfulness." A person who is meditating attempts to "cut off" attachments as he or she practices focusing the mind — another example of how the Khmer Rouge drew upon Buddhist terms to localize their ideological concepts.

Because the family had been the cornerstone of Khmer social life, the Khmer Rouge strove to sever this bond and co-opt the sentiments it evoked. To highlight how awful the Khmer Rouge were, many Cambodians recount some variation of an anecdote in which a cadre, imbued with this ideology, arrested, beat, or killed a parent or spouse, an almost unimaginable act prior to or after DK. Chlat told me a story about a female cadre who arrested her husband after discovering he had been stealing extra food. When the man asked his wife how she could execute her own husband, she replied, "I'm not killing my husband, I'm killing the enemy." Chlat explained, "She had been brainwashed to love and be loyal only to the Party."

Such acts of violence, although chilling, made sense within the logic of Khmer Rouge ideology, which made it honorable to kill. Those who had a progressive revolutionary consciousness were given face and honor. Revolutionary consciousness was discerned by displaying signs of one's "mindfulness," particularly the aforementioned characteristics of a "truly loyal" cadre. Ultimately, one of the strongest signs of loyalty, and therefore of a progressive state of consciousness, was a willingness to kill enemies for the party. The closer the tie between the perpetrator and the victim, the more significant was the display of one's loyalty to Ângkar and the demonstration that one had eliminated the "garden of the individual." Enormous honor was therefore bestowed upon those who were willing to kill any enemy, even a parent, sibling, relative, patron, or friend.

Of course, the stakes were high for cadres who took the "line" of a progressive revolutionary. When successful, a cadre gained honor and possibly rank. If one failed to prove one's loyalty to the regime, however, the consequences could be fatal. This insight can help us understand the actions of Khmer Rouge killers like Lor. When Lor told his boss, Duch, that he had never killed anyone, Duch questioned whether Lor could "cut off his heart" from the enemy. Within the paranoid atmosphere that pervaded DK, questions about a person's loyalty to the party could result in an accusation that he or she was an enemy. Had Lor failed to kill in such a situation, he could have been accused of being a traitor — thus his statement that he "couldn't refuse." As Lor explained, "I was afraid they would suspect me until they saw me kill with their own eyes, until they saw that I could cut off my heart."

If the DK regime idealized these ideological models of loyalty and detachment, it also tried to facilitate killing by transforming the interactions between perpetrators and "enemies." Prior to DK, one encountered sociopolitical enemies in certain specified contexts, such as politics, law enforcement, or war. Under the Khmer Rouge, however, one might discover hidden enemies anywhere, since they were "burrowing from within" the ranks of the party, army, revolutionary youth, and people. Violence against these enemies was legitimated even in everyday communal interaction, since one might be working with and eating beside an enemy. One could suddenly discover that one's friends or family members really stood on the opposite side of the DK "dividing line." Anyone could abruptly be labeled an "enemy." Vann Nath commented on the "enormous power" of this "one word. . . . It could make a child stop recognizing his or her mother, father, and siblings. Upon hearing the word 'enemy,' everyone became nervous." Once a person was labeled an "enemy," everyday social norms no longer applied to them. They became a *vea*, an object that could be abused and no longer deserved cordiality, let alone face and honor.

The DK regime recognized that, despite their efforts to crystallize difference into rigid us-versus-them categories, some cadres might still have hesitations about killing people. To help cadres overcome this psychosocial dissonance, the Khmer Rouge also attempted to structure the killing process so that perpetrator-victim relations would be as anomic as possible. While there was variation in the manner in which executions took place, they tended to be carried out in an anonymous manner that made it easier for perpetrators to cut off their hearts from the "enemy."

As we have seen, the Khmer Rouge established a rudimentary but efficient bureaucratic system for mass murder. Former village heads were required to maintain two ledgers listing the names, ages, and former occupations of the people in their village. One was kept in the village; the other was given to the subdistrict office. Orders were often passed down the Khmer Rouge chain of command instructing village and district officials to round up those people on the lists who had suspect backgrounds (intellectuals, "new people," capitalists, ethnic Vietnamese and Chams, and former Lon Nol soldiers, police, and officials) and inform them that they were to be "taken to a new village."

Sometimes the victims were then transported to extermination centers like Phnom Bros, where they were killed en masse by Khmer Rouge soldiers who didn't know them. Seng, an "old person" who lived in the area, explained, "The executioners would be told, 'Today you will destroy enemies that the Party has captured.' When they saw their victims arrive, they didn't think, 'Oh, this person is gentle and honest' because the Party had told them that they were enemies. Therefore, the person had to be killed." In other situations, the victims were arrested by people they knew and then taken to a subdistrict or district office to be interrogated. Vann Nath's incarceration followed this pattern: a cadre told him that his arrest had been ordered by the district chief. He was then taken to a district prison and interrogated and tortured by people he had never seen before.

Such anomic behavior against "the enemy" was also characteristic of local-level executions. While there are certainly exceptions, life in areas run by cadres with local ties seems to have been generally better than life in places governed by strangers, particularly for "old people." In Region 41, for example, the frequency of killings dramatically increased when cadres like Grandmother Yit, Phat, and Rom from the Southwest Zone replaced officials who had ties to the area. The Khmer Rouge seem to have recognized this pattern and, to prevent enemies from escaping, often placed cadres and soldiers without local ties in positions of power. Even if some of the cadres were locals, the ones who did the killings were likely to come from the district office and be rotated periodically. Teap, the cadre who worked with Rom, told me:

During the Pol Pot period, the Khmer Rouge switched people from area to area. . . . This was really important because they wanted [the soldiers and cadres] to cut off their sentiment *(phdach manosânhchetâna)* so that they wouldn't know anyone and it would be easier for them to do their work. . . . The executioners killed in the area for fifteen days at most. They changed them for fear that if they worked in one place too long, they would develop attachments there. . . . They executed people like we kill fish. . . . They killed at night and didn't have any responsibilities during the day. They just rested and ate well, much better than the people. . . . Their work began near dusk, when the soldiers would begin to sharpen their knives and axes. They'd roll up their pant legs and sleeves, put a scarf *(krama)* on their head and disappear. [After rounding up their victims] . . . the soldiers would lead the prisoners forward while their superior gave orders from behind. . . . When they returned, they would sometimes have blood stains on their clothes or even spots of blood on their faces. They went and bathed by [Rom's] house, where I was guarding nearby and could overhear them. Sometimes they would return happy, laughing and shouting things like "That despicable one jumped well [when he was killed], did you see him?" or "That despicable one fainted before he even reached the ditch" or "There was another one who pissed so much that he completely soaked himself and even got you wet!" . . . When they looked at their victims, they didn't think they were killing fellow Khmer, just enemies.

Teap's description is chilling, but the executioners' actions can partly be understood in terms of the preceding analysis. On the one hand, the interactions between perpetrators and their victims were typically anomic. As Teap notes, the executioners might be rotated in and be unfamiliar with their victims, making it easier to treat them in a "heartless" manner. Even if the perpetrators knew their victims, the killings usually took place in liminal contexts in which their difference could be manufactured. Like many other Khmer Rouge perpetrators, the executioners from Rom's subdistrict office worked at night and in the wild, a place that is associated in Cambodia with the amoral, uncivilized, and disordered.[25] Similarly, Vann Nath was tortured in a small brick house located in the forest, away from the district prison. Phnom Bros and Choeung Ek (where Lor worked) were also liminal sites used to inscribe and fix the identity of the "enemies" who died there. In addition to providing secrecy, such "wild," anonymous settings were appropriate for the anomic behaviors that took place as people like Lor and Reap executed enemies to whom normal everyday communal norms no longer applied.

On the other hand, perpetrators also worked in a group context, in which they were enacting an identity, proving their loyalty, and competing for honor. As we have seen, cadres were required to display signs of their progressive revolutionary consciousness and complete loyalty to the regime. This meant properly executing and "defending" the party line, renouncing attachments, cutting off one's heart, and crushing enemies of the revolution. If a person refused to execute an enemy, they would immediately come under suspicion as someone who was not "truly loyal," not one of "us."

It is crucial to bear in mind that cadres were not just "carrying out orders" in response to this negative constraint; they had positive motivations for participating in genocide. Like Lor and Vaen Kheuan, many of the perpetrators were adolescents or young men who tended to be idealistic and malleable as they sought to establish a sense of identity.[26] This is an age when Cambodian youths often become particularly sensitive to the evaluations of others and desire to gain face and honor. An ideology that provides a set of simplified, relational contrasts (of "us" versus the enemy) often appeals to such youths — particularly during times of socioeconomic upheaval, when there is a tendency toward cognitive constriction — since it gives them an accessible and appealing foundation for constructing this identity.

Khmer Rouge ideology revolved around just such a set of crystallized categories of difference and glorified the revolutionaries, as illustrated in the preamble to "But What Does Being Truly Loyal Mean?" Such discourses frequently played upon the image of "struggle" *(tâ sou)*, a notion that resonated with the powerful cultural image of the heroic warrior *(neak tâ sou)* who struggles against adversity and defeats powerful foes. Like the heroes of Cambodian legend, young revolutionaries were portrayed as struggling valiantly first to help win the civil war and later to defeat invidious "hidden enemies burrowing from within." Violence was glorified in the name of the revolution.[27] Blood sacrifice was a frequent theme in political speeches, revolutionary songs and slogans, and even the national anthem, which began with these verses: "Bright red blood that covers towns and plains/Of Kampuchea, our Motherland,/Sublime blood of workers and peasants,/Sublime blood of revolutionary men and women fighters!/The blood changing into unrelenting hatred/And resolute struggle."[28] A valiant revolutionary was expected to be ready to sacrifice his or her life in order to defend the country by seeking out and destroying internal enemies, even if the traitor was a parent, spouse, or relative.

In accordance with doctrine asserting that violence against the enemy was a virtue, these revolutionaries were also glorified for "carrying out every sort of revolutionary duty *(phearokech)*, big and small." If cadre had previously fulfilled their duty by "joining to strike and crush the

American imperialists and their lackeys, traitorous groups, and the various oppressor classes," they now did so by killing internal enemies. In Cambodia, "duty" *(katâppakech, phearokech, kech)* does not have the negative connotations of the English term. By properly carrying out one's duty, one enacts one's place in the social order and affirms one's face, since status is dependent on performative competence and the positive evaluations of others. Interestingly, duty and the tasks it entails are sometimes called one's "face work" *(mukh ngear)*.

During DK, the way one performed one's duty was particularly salient, since one was displaying signs of a proper revolutionary consciousness. One of the best ways to demonstrate the right attitude was to perform one's duties in an enthusiastic, wholehearted, and unquestioning manner. George DeVos has called this type of extreme commitment to and identification with one's duty "role narcissism,"[29] a notion that seems highly appropriate to DK, given the enormous investment many cadres made in the Khmer Rouge belief system in a context of existential uncertainty. To carry out one's duty by killing was, in a sense, to affirm one's sense of self and identity, both on an existential and a group level, and to avoid shame. Perhaps this is why Haing Ngor thought that his cooperative leader, Chev, "killed to feel good about himself. If he purged enough enemies, he satisfied his conscience. He had done his duty to Angka . . . to the ever-smiling Chev, the act of killing was routine. Just part of the job. Not even worth a second thought."[30] Similarly, while Lor later claimed to have had reservations about executing people, he acknowledged that he did so because it was his duty and because he wanted "to demonstrate that I was truly loyal *(smah trang)* to Ângkar." For the executioners Teap observed working at Rom's office, killing was likely viewed in a similar manner. The cadres sharpened their knives and axes and then set out to fulfill their duty of killing enemies of the regime, an action that would affirm their status as pure revolutionaries and demonstrate that they were completely devoted to the DK party line.

In addition to serving as a symbolic enactment of a perpetrator's revolutionary status, carrying out duties such as executing enemies allowed cadres to negotiate their relative standing in the DK social order. Although the criteria by which status was evaluated had changed, many people continued to desire face and honor. Aside from evincing the qualities of a progressive revolutionary, perhaps the primary means of increasing one's face and honor during DK was to rise in political rank. For example, a DK village head from the Banyan area recalled that Boan would do almost anything to increase his status:

> Boan was a person who wanted to gain face *(yok mukh moat)*. His level of culture and understanding was the lowest of all. He'd report on people about all sorts of matters. . . . He wanted to gain face and rise in rank. . . . At that time, if you arrested people you rose in rank. He was also skilled at gaining the good graces *(aep âp)* and winning the favor [of his superiors].

Most Cambodians I interviewed complained about people like Boan, both out of resentment of the privileges they enjoyed and out of anger that their means of rising in rank often involved the abuse of others. Thus Vong lamented that Boan was always reporting on people, sometimes even giving false information: "Boan barely knew how to write, but he could write down names and report on people. He was responsible for the deaths of perhaps thirty people. They just disappeared, usually at night. Some of these people hadn't done anything at all—I remember them clearly: Yin, Samaen, Tali, Tavun, Run—but despicable Boan reported that they had been soldiers." Chlat explained, "The mindset of many Khmer Rouge was such that they thought only about rank *(bon sâkti)*. So they would kill or report on others about some matter. The people would suffer, but they could rise in rank. . . . They might rise to become the head or deputy head of a group, a village, the subdistrict, or even the district. . . . If they killed people, Ângkar would love them and trust them."

Despite their resentment, the populace still feared and respected such cadres and had to acknowledge their high status in public settings. This might mean averting their eyes or acting deferentially toward these sociopolitical superiors, whom they were expected to honor and obey. In general, both "new" and "old people" lived in fear of insulting their superiors and thus had to be vigilant about face work. One Banyan villager told me that when people encountered Phat, the head of the local subdistrict office, "We were really frightened, too scared to speak with her. We were afraid that if we said something wrong, she would notice and take us to be killed."

Public meetings constituted another context in which status was displayed, as the populace was expected to praise the revolution and, by implication, its local representatives, in an unqualified manner. In addition to singing revolutionary songs and reciting slogans, one "old person" told me that the assembly would listen to cadres repeatedly "praise the kindness and power of the Revolutionary Organization through whose victory and leadership the construction of the country was progressing rapidly." Even if people were exhausted and bored, they were expected to applaud enthusiastically and respond affirmatively to all that was said, thereby symbolically accepting the status line established by the cadres and publicly giving them face. If they did not, the party and its officials would lose face and the offending person might be accused of being one of the "enemies" against whom the speakers spent a great deal of time haranguing.

Within the ranks of the Khmer Rouge, there were other contexts in which cadres negotiated their status, such as in the composition of a life history or participation in criticism and self-criticism sessions. At the same time as cadres illustrated their mindfulness and standing as progressive revolutionaries, they were also making a statement about their entitlement to a certain degree of face and honor. Not surprisingly, life histories and criticism and self-criticism sessions touched on topics discussed in this chapter, such as carrying out one's duty and devotion to the DK party line. In fact, Vaen Kheuan's life history includes a subsection entitled "Execution of the Party Line," which discusses a key characteristic that showed whether someone was "truly loyal" to the DK regime. One could fashion and refashion a life history, but the stakes were higher during criticism and self-criticism sessions, since people never knew what might be said about them or how what they said would be received. Although a "mindful" person recognized his or her faults, strong criticism could lead to shame and a loss of face.[31]

Status could also be negotiated in the context of killing, as perpetrators attempted to gain honor in a group situation. Earlier I noted that during indoctrination sessions and political meetings, Khmer Rouge were repeatedly asked if they would "dare" *(hean)* to "cut off their hearts" and kill an enemy, even if the person was a parent, sibling, spouse, or relative. Such propaganda played upon a male ethos of bravery, which held that, like the heroes of Cambodian lore, those who courageously struggle *(tâ sou)* gain face, while cowards who do not dare are shamed. The Khmer Rouge used this discourse of bravery to facilitate killing, which usually was done in front of a perpetrator's peers or superiors.

Within this structured setting, the killers attempted to gain honor through the positive evaluations of others. Those who excelled at killing were considered to have "defeated" and to be superior to those who showed hesitation, cowardice, or incompetence in this duty. One of my research assistants explained that at a place like the Phnom Bros extermination center, the executioners had to

> act bravely like everyone else in the group. If just one person was not daring, he or she would be considered a coward, the most inferior person in the group, the one who had lost to the others and was looked down upon. Such people would lose face and honor, and their superior would stop

trusting and giving power to them. The person who loses in such a situation loses face because they are unable to struggle *(tâ sou)* to fulfill their duty. Those who carry out their tasks, in contrast, gain honor. Ângkar would trust them more and raise them further in rank.

Similarly, local-level Khmer Rouge like the cadre observed by Teap might compete to prove their complete loyalty to the party by daring to kill people. If they discovered and executed enough enemies, they would gain honor and maybe even "defeat" their peers and be promoted. Perhaps bravado and competition were partly behind the chilling comments made by Rom's executioners, as they tried to display enthusiasm for what they had done.

While Lor no doubt engaged in such formal honor competition in some contexts, the incident mentioned at the beginning of this book is an example of a more defensive type of honor competition. By asking Lor if he had "ever dared to kill" and questioning whether he could "cut off his heart," Duch was effectively challenging Lor's honor and loyalty to the party. If Lor had tried to avoid killing the person, he would have lost face and probably would have subsequently been labeled a traitor. Influenced by Khmer Rouge ideology, which glorified violence and daring, Lor picked up the iron bar and killed "one or two" people. In doing so, Lor defended his honor and demonstrated his loyalty, bravery, and detachment from the enemy. Considering the paranoid atmosphere of DK, it seems likely that Khmer Rouge cadres and soldiers throughout Cambodia, like Lor, were at times forced to defend their honor by killing people.

As we have seen, DK was characterized by frequent attempts to seize power and authority (and the honor associated with higher status) from others, or more offensive honor competitions. For example, a former cadre from Romeas, the village near Banyan that Koy Thuon used to visit, told me that when the Southwest Zone cadres arrived in Region 41,

> they began to kill the string of old warriors *(neak tâ sou)*. . . . The old and the new cadres were competing for authority. The Southwest faction wanted to seize total power, so they would have the old cadres followed and carefully watched. Their soldiers would go to our homes and eavesdrop on us. If we said something wrong or made even a little mistake, the Southwest cadres would accuse us of being a traitor and immediately have us arrested. Some people were arrested for no reason at all. The Southwest cadres wanted to seize power and rank *(bon sâkti)*.

A great deal of tension existed between the Southwest faction and Reap's soldiers, who were stationed around Phnom Bros. Ultimately, Reap attempted to start a rebellion in Kompong Cham city after members of his faction had been jailed and he realized that his power in the area was being usurped by the Southwest cadres. This tension continued with Chuon. According to Khel, after Chuon helped Neari and her sister, Grandmother Yit reported to Pauk, the head of the Central Zone, that Chuon had helped the two woman escape and was "going against" him. Chuon, however, managed to deny the accusation. In fact, reporting on one's rivals was a common strategy in offensive honor competitions; it was encouraged by the DK regime and contributed to the Party Center's paranoia and the purges that ensued. As Bros, my research assistant, explained, Khmer Rouge like "the Southwestern cadre would report to Ângkar that their rivals were traitors in the hope that Ângkar would drop or kill the accused individual. The Southwestern cadre would gain honor and be praised by Ângkar, who might even raise their rank." When cadres won such honor competitions, their status and power within the DK social order rose.

· · ·

How, then, might Vaen Kheuan and his subordinates have been influenced by these group dynamics when they interrogated prisoners like Oum Chhan? At such times, each cadre was performing an identity and asserting a "line" that, if confirmed by his or her peers, gave him or her face and honor. To demonstrate that they were progressive revolutionaries, cadres had to evince given characteristics, particularly mindfulness and complete loyalty to the DK regime. While they did so, the eyes of their coworkers were on them, constantly assessing their actions. By enthusiastically and effectively interrogating Oum Chhan, Vaen Kheuan was making a claim that he had "renounced everything" and was heroically struggling to carry out "every sort of revolutionary duty, big and small" for the party. To show the slightest hesitation or pity toward a prisoner suggested one could not "cut off one's heart" and had not "fully absorbed" the party line. Thus, in his summary report of Oum Chhan's confession, Vaen Kheuan highlights his detachment from Oum Chhan by immediately labeling him an "enemy," telling Oum Chhan that he is "worth less than garbage," and torturing Oum Chhan effectively to extract a confession. We know from Vaen Kheuan's life history that he was concerned with executing the party line, and both during the interrogation itself and in documents like the summary confession, he asserts his progressive revolutionary consciousness. Vaen Kheuan is fulfilling his duty as an interrogator and playing a key role in the "struggle to clean up hidden enemies burrowing from within."

The interactions of Vaen Kheuan and his men are likely to have been competitively structured, since the public display of a progressive consciousness provided a means of rising in rank. Lor recalled that some Tuol Sleng cadres "were diligent in their tasks and tried to gain the good graces *(aep ap)* of their superiors so that they could rise in rank. They wanted to be seen by big cadres who might increase their rank . . . like despicable Phal, who was the head of my group." He explained, "Even if there was just a little problem, Phal would report it in order to gain face *(yok mukh moat)* and rank *(bon sâkti)*. . . . He did this so that he could work big." Given that Lor rose high in the Tuol Sleng hierarchy, he may very well have been adept at getting in the good graces of his superiors by carrying out his tasks diligently or perhaps even reporting on others.

Interestingly, a number of Tuol Sleng confessions refer to cadres who were motivated by the desire to rise in rank. But Heng, a notoriously brutal Tuol Sleng interrogator who was eventually arrested, stated in his confession that the weak point of one of his subordinates was that the cadre wanted to have "face and rank" *(mukh moat bon sâkti)* and often used flattery to gain favor.[32] Elsewhere, But Heng alludes to honor competition, asserting that when he began to work with a group of interrogators under the command of "Comrade Chhin," he failed to help them and often placed them in complicated situations: "I would then go report that Comrade Chhin's group couldn't do the work well and that they couldn't interrogate effectively. The goal of my activity was to ruin Comrade Chhin's reputation so it would be bad and I would seem good."

Prisoners often confessed that they had betrayed the revolution to gain promotion and increase their status. The Tuol Sleng confession of a soldier named Min Rin provides a typical example: his superior supposedly told Min Rin that he should have been promoted long ago and promised that if Min Rin joined the CIA, he would have "face *(mean mukh moat)* and rank *(bon sâkti)* before others . . . and live happily."[33] Afterward, Min Rin confessed that his "consciousness *(sâti)* became angry with the revolution, which I was thereafter against." The invocation of *sâti* in this negative manner constructs Min Rin as regressive. Given that promotion was an important way in which patrons maintained the loyalty of clients, such remarks construct the confessor as a member of a traitorous string. Loyalty is another theme that appears in the confessions, as prisoners direct toward their traitorous patrons the complete loyalty that should have been given to the party. Euan's confession, for example, includes a subsection on *smah trang* [complete loyalty] in which he describes how Koy Thuon "pulled my sentiment *(manosânhchetâna)* . . . [making] me really love [him]."[34]

Given such comments and the preceding discussion, it seems likely that there were competitive dynamics among Tuol Sleng cadres, including those working in the same interrogation unit. As the interrogation proceeded, each cadre likely made a series of strategic calculations as they negotiated their relative status and attempted to gain a sort of "dark honor." While cadres performed their tasks, they competed to display revolutionary fervor by brutalizing enemies like Oum Chhan. Those who displayed the greatest resolution and daring or extracted key pieces of information in some sense "defeated" his or her coworkers. Perhaps the striking language in Vaen Kheuan's summary of Oum Chhan's interrogation can in part be explained in terms of such competitiveness, as he sought to demonstrate the quality and effectiveness of his interrogation skills (in comparison with those of other interrogators), an excellence that might enable him to rise in rank. If Vaen Kheuan or one of his men showed any hesitation in administering torture, however, their peers would have evaluated them negatively and the person would have lost face. Lor seems to have found himself in just such a defensive honor competition. These interpersonal dynamics provide yet another possible motive for perpetrator excess, as cadres could sometimes gain this "dark honor" by brutalizing prisoners, who were constructed as their mimetic opposites.

Finally, we must bear in mind that, even in the radically transformed context of DK, face and honor continued to have ontological resonance. Face remained a self-implicating, embodied locus of social visibility, communication, and public standing. If the criteria of evaluation had changed, people still asserted a "line" that was assessed by their peers, a "line" that was a crucial component of a cadre's political identity as a progressive revolutionary. Many Tuol Sleng cadres may have been heavily invested in this identity, both because of their youth and because of the context of enormous uncertainty in which they worked.

Shame may also help to turn such narcissistic identification into outbursts of rage, as an already vulnerable sense of self is threatened and diminished in a given social context. In response, the shamed individual may suddenly become enraged, attempting to attack a perceived (real or symbolic) source of danger and to regain a sense of grandeur and domination through expansion into the space of another object or being. In the context of an interrogation, then, shame was likely an ontologically resonant undercurrent of interpersonal interactions that motivated violence in at least two ways: first, by pressuring cadres who wanted to avoid shame to dare to cut off their hearts and torture the enemy; and, second, by moving cadres who had lost face to perpetrate brutal excesses against prisoners like Oum Chhan (who were symbolic containers for their projective identifications). Perhaps it was at just such a moment of shame and imbalance that a perpetrator like Vaen Kheuan would beat a prisoner to death.

In response to the existential anxiety that contexts of enormous uncertainty like Tuol Sleng can generate, people may also be more strongly motivated to seek social approval, which provides a self-inflating sense of grandeur and of belonging to a larger community. Praise, of course, is closely bound up with face, honor, and shame, all of which resonate ontologically with Cambodian socialization practices. By excelling in their violent duties, then, interrogators could potentially gain the praise of their peers, thereby ameliorating their own existential anxiety.

Prisoners, in turn, could serve as projective containers for the assertion of rank insofar as they represented, as low-status individuals lacking face, the inverse qualities of the interrogator's relatively high status. The very act of brutalizing the prisoners enacted the perpetrator's social worth even as it diminished that of their victims. Once again, Gregory Bateson's notion of schismogenesis seems relevant: the torturer/victim relationship is one of complementary schismogenesis, as the perpetrator's relative dominance and the victim's relative subordination both increase through violent interaction. Bateson notes that such relationships are normally regulated and balanced by internal mechanisms. Although perpetrators are somewhat constrained in the torture chamber, these constraints are often minimal, thereby enabling the relationship to spiral toward the most extreme form of violent domination, the eradication of the other.

Why People Kill

I had to obey the orders of my superiors. If they ordered me to
do something, I would do it. If we didn't obey, we would have
been killed.

Lor, on why he executed "one or two people"

At the 1979 People's Revolutionary Tribunal in Phnom Penh, which convicted Pol Pot and his cronies in absentia for genocide, Denise Affonço
provided gruesome but detailed testimony about an episode of liver-eating that she observed in an area of Battambang province that was suffering from great famine:

> One day a young fellow named Touch was arrested for digging up a few
> cassava roots. On learning this, Ta Ling simply said: "Take him to the
> western forest" (where a special spot had been cleared for such jobs). The
> condemned man was accompanied by three executioners: Ta Sok, who was
> in charge of manure collection, a bloodthirsty fellow coming from
> Kambaul; Ta Doeung, also bloodthirsty and also from Kambaul; and Ta
> Chea, a "new person" like us from Phnom Penh but who had turned
> proud and arrogant when he became Ta Ling's aide. . . .
>
> Out of curiosity, I followed the men at a distance without letting them
> see me. When I got to the spot, I hid in a thicket from which I could watch
> the "ceremony" without being seen. But I was so horrified by what I saw
> that I nearly fainted. The condemned man was tied to a tree, his chest bare
> and a blindfold over his eyes. Ta Sok, the executioner, using a large knife,
> made a long cut in the stomach of the poor man.
>
> In pain, the man screamed like a wild beast. Even today his cries still
> ring in my ears. Blood rushed out everywhere, his insides were all laid bare,
> and Ta Sok cut out the liver and cooked it on a little stove that Ta Chea
> had just heated up. A strange fact to mention is that the human liver, cook
> ing on the stove, made little jerks like frying pancakes. They divided up the

liver among them and ate it hungrily. After they buried the body, they left looking satisfied. I did not dare leave my hiding place until they had gone far away, because if they found out that I knew about their bloody deeds, it would be all over for me. That night I could not sleep, because I was haunted by the horrors of the day.[1]

How do people come to commit such brutal acts? This question has been a key focus of this book, which has examined a variety of "spaces of death," including Lor's execution of "one or two people" in the killing field of Choeung Ek, the extermination center at Phnom Bros, Oum Chhan's torture at Tuol Sleng, and the local-level executions of people like Touch.

When asked after the fact why they committed such abuses during DK, many former Khmer Rouge cadres, like genocidal perpetrators all over the world, have claimed that they were just "following orders." Lor invoked this excuse to explain why he had killed "one or two people." Likewise, when I asked what he would say if he met one of his former prisoners on the street, Lor responded, "I would tell them, 'Don't be angry with me. When I worked at that place, I had to obey the orders of others. I am not mean and savage. I didn't do anything to anyone. If they had me arrest someone, I would go arrest the person. If they ordered me to do something, I would do it.'" It is precisely this type of response that victims find so unsatisfying, since it absolves the perpetrator of responsibility and the need to personally express remorse. Their outrage is magnified when such an assertion comes from high-ranking cadre like "Grandfather" Pauk, the secretary of the Central Zone, who portrayed himself as a passive instrument of the Party Center, explaining that "an order is an order — [if] the top leader[s] ordered us to do things, we [had to] do it . . . people at the low level just carried out the orders."[2] A similar excuse would likely be given by Ta Ling's henchmen.

More broadly, such assertions invoke obedience as an explanation for their lethal deeds. To obey someone is "to comply with, or perform, the bidding of; to do what one is commanded by (a person); to submit to the rule or authority of, to be obedient to," a meaning that is etymologically derived from the Latin word *oboedire,* meaning "to listen to."[3] Obedience, "the action or practice of obeying," thus implies fulfillment of duty, "submission to the rule or authority of another; compliance with or performance of a command, law, or the like; the action of doing what one is bidden."[4]

The Khmer glosses for *obedience* have a similar range of meaning, though they do not necessarily have the negative connotations that the

English terms often carry, in part because of the Cambodian valuation of hierarchy and proper order. Obedience is connoted by *korop,* the Khmer term for a prostrating reverence tinged with awe and fear that leads one to respect, honor, and obey a person or institution. While the Khmer terms *tveu tam* (to follow, to obey) and *stap* (to listen to, to obey) are the other words most easily translated as "to obey," the notion of obedience is also captured by the passive use of *aoy* (to have someone do something), *braoe* (to be "used" or commanded to obey), *bângkoap* (to be commanded), and *bânhchea* (to be ordered).[5] Thus, in the passage above, Lor uses *stap* and *aoy* to explain that he had to "obey the orders of others" *(stap bânhchea ke)* and that if "they had *(ke aoy)* me do something, I would do it."

In both English and Khmer, then, obedience involves acts performed in a context of situational constraint, as one carries out the tasks, duties, and orders given by some authority. The power of these contextual pressures is vividly illustrated by a series of experiments conducted by Stanley Milgram in the 1960s.[6] Milgram asked his test subjects to assume the role of a "teacher" and to administer increasingly strong shocks to a "learner" (who was really an actor) when he or she answered a question incorrectly. Milgram found that the majority of the subjects, who were ordinary residents of the New Haven, Connecticut area, would obey the experimenter's commands to keep shocking a "learner," even when the subject could clearly see that the voltage designation read "Danger — Severe Shock." Afterward, many subjects explained that they were "only doing as I was told."

Milgram suggested that this psychosocial process, in which people come to view themselves as a vehicle for carrying out the demands of authority figures, occurred in a wide range of contexts, including the Holocaust. Thus, while the historical conditions varied, the actions of a Nazi bureaucrat like Eichmann strongly resembled those of the "teachers" who continued to shock the "learners"; in each case, "ordinary people, simply doing their jobs, and without any particular hostility on their part, can become agents in a terrible destructive process."[7] Milgram found himself largely agreeing with Arendt that, in contexts of strong situational constraint, extremely evil acts may be perpetrated in a "banal" manner. This is exactly how perpetrators like Lor, Pauk, and Eichmann wish to portray themselves — as passive subjects whose murderous deeds were ultimately the responsibility of others — when they explain that they were "only following orders." As we will see, this explanation is only a partial one.

The "obedience to authority" explanation highlights a key dynamic involved in genocide. In some situations, like Tuol Sleng, perpetrators are heavily pressured (for example, by the threat of punitive sanctions, including death, or by shame) to obey orders. And for most people, killing is easier when it is authorized by another person or institution. Responsibility is displaced onto that authority and moral inhibitions that might apply are mitigated by the authorization.

Nevertheless, as Milgram notes, this explanatory paradigm has trouble accounting for other dimensions of genocidal violence, such as the intense rage and hatred that so often accompany it. Why, for example, do perpetrators so often brutalize their victims in a manner that exceeds their "orders"? A second problem with the obedience explanation is that it does not provide insight into the pattern of violence. If, in the example above, Ta Sok, Ta Doeung, and Ta Chea obeyed Ta Ling's order to take Touch "to the forest of the west," they carried out this command in a particular manner — extracting and consuming Touch's liver. A similar point could be made about torture at Tuol Sleng, where the interrogators obeyed their orders to extract information, but had leeway in choosing how to do so (for example, whether or not to make the prisoner "pay homage to the image of a dog").

Third, by itself, the obedience explanation provides a very thin description of subjectivity. People may have multiple motivations for carrying out their orders to kill, including the desire to please their superiors, to take revenge, to fulfill their duties, to gain face, or to rise in rank. In a given "space of death," perpetrators negotiate and remake their subjectivities through genocidal bricolage. Both the patterning of violence and the production of subjectivities are key cultural dimensions of genocide, as I discuss below. Fourth, there is variation in the degree of pressure and constraint across time and place. Thus Lor was much more highly constrained in obeying Duch's orders than were Ta Sok, Ta Doeung, and Ta Chea. Fifth, obedience may be of greater or lesser relevance for a perpetrator, depending on a person's life history (for example, their relative desensitization to killing) and personality. It is likely that Lor had more difficulty the first time he killed someone than he did after killing "one or two people" at Tuol Sleng. Finally, the obedience explanation is decontextualized: it needs to be accompanied by an account of the historical processes that generate a genocidal context in which orders for mass murder are given and obeyed. This brings us back to the first of the two key questions that my study addresses: how does genocidal violence come to take place? After discussing this issue, I will turn to my second question — what motivates perpetrators to kill? — and attempt to provide a more nuanced account of perpetrator motivation that moves us beyond the obedience explanation, which is often invoked in a monocausal fashion and provides perpetrators with a means of explaining away their actions. In doing so, I will return to the issue of human liver-eating.

· · ·

How does genocide come to take place? In his seminal work on the origins of genocide, Leo Kuper emphasized the importance of viewing genocide as a process — not as a uniform, teleological phenomenon — that is generated by a variety of factors and has diverse outcomes.[8] One way to think about this process is through metaphors of priming and heat, what I have elsewhere called "genocidal priming."[9] To "prime" something is to "to make [it] ready" for operation, as in preparing a gun to fire "by inserting a charge of gunpowder or a primer" or by "pouring water into a pump or gasoline into a carburetor."[10] The intransitive form of the verb means "to prepare someone or something for future action or operation," and, like the transitive verb, implies that which comes first. We can call each of the subprocesses that contribute to a "discharge" — such as adding gunpowder and cocking the trigger — a "prime."

Genocidal priming, then, refers to the process(es) by which various primes coalesce, making genocide more or less likely, though by no means an inevitable outcome, in given historical situations.[11] A metaphor of heat is useful for considering the relative likelihood of genocide: those situations in which a number of primes are operative in an intense form can be thought of as "hot" and volatile; in "warm" or "cool" cases, the primes will be fewer and less extreme. Moreover, the degree of heat is never stagnant, but rather changes as domestic and international events unfold. Yet another way to conceptualize genocidal priming is to think of a circuit board containing a large number of nodules (representing "primes"), each of which may glow from a dim to an intense red (representing the "heat" of a situation).[12] While some of these nodules may be involved in most genocides, the particular constellation (and relative degree of "glow" in each nodule) will vary from situation to situation.[13]

Even in an extremely "hot" situation, genocide is by no means preordained. Such violence almost always involves some sort of "genocidal activation" — a series of direct and indirect, more or less organized pushes from above — that triggers the "charge" that has been primed.[14]

Sometimes this process of activation is precipitous. Thus, in Rwanda, after a long process of priming, the activation process was quickly set in motion when President Habyarimana's plane was shot down: well-organized and trained Hutu extremists, often getting their orders to kill over the radio, rapidly began to annihilate political moderates and Tutsis. In other situations, such as Nazi Germany, Cambodia, and the former Yugoslavia, the activation was more gradual.

Discerning these primes and assessing the "heat" of a situation is therefore of crucial importance to understanding the origins of and preventing genocide. While each genocide has a distinct etiology that resists reduction to a uniform pattern, many are broadly characterized by a set of primes that make the social context in question increasingly "hot," including socioeconomic upheaval, deep structural divisions and an identifiable target group, structural change, effective ideological manipulation, a breakdown in moral restraints, discriminatory political changes, and an apathetic response from the international community.[15]

As these and other facilitating processes unfold, genocide becomes increasingly possible. Not every "hot" situation, however, results in mass violence. International pressure, local moral restraints, political and religious mechanisms, or a lack of ideological "take" may hold potential perpetrator regimes in check and, in the long run, facilitate a cooling of tensions. In other situations, the process of genocidal priming may never be more than "lukewarm."[16] However, when the priming is "hot" and genocide does take place, there is almost always some sort of genocidal activation that ignites the "charge" that has been primed. Barbara Harff and Ted Gurr have identified a number of "accelerators" that may rapidly increase the "heat" in a situation, often initiating a spiral of action and reaction.[17]

Such processual approaches have been of enormous importance to our understanding of how genocides take place. Most importantly, they provide a basis for monitoring "hot" situations, predicting when genocide is about to occur, and with luck, preventing mass murder from taking place.[18] Because of their broad focus, however, many of these approaches do not fully account for the local-level dynamics that are essential to genocidal priming and activation. For genocidal priming and activation to occur, there must be a synergy between state-level initiatives and local-level responses. If this synergy is not taken into account, perpetrators will simply be portrayed as generic automatons who are motivated by genocidal ideology in a straightforward manner — a depiction, I have argued, that is too narrow. In what follows, I suggest a way of describing the process of genocidal priming and activation that incorporates both macrolevel and microlevel dynamics, and therefore can account for this synergy.

Almost all genocides are associated with some type of socioeconomic or political upheaval.[19] Genocides have taken place in the wake of decolonization, civil war, international conflict, economic collapse, and political strife. Such events upset the status quo, destabilize previous understandings and people's sense of well-being, contribute to unemployment and hunger, intensify group divisions, force people to take sides, undermine social structures that promote cohesion and solidarity, and create a sense of threat and danger. Colonial regimes, for example, may contribute to such upheaval by leaving a power vacuum and a legacy of structural underdevelopment and dependency, of overreliance on a few crops and resources subject to the whims of global markets and weather patterns (leaving agriculture vulnerable to droughts and floods), and of "modern" ideologies that construct the locals in new and often overly essentialized ways. All of these factors contributed to the violence that occurred in Rwanda and Burundi after independence.

War and economic turmoil also increase the "heat" of a situation, as illustrated by the murder of Armenians during World War I, the annihilation of the kulaks after the Russian Revolution, "ethnic cleansing" in the former Yugoslavia, and the Nazi atrocities that occurred in the aftermath of a devastating combination of Germany's defeat in World War I, the humiliating Treaty of Versailles, worldwide depression, and later, the onset of World War II. In places like Nigeria, Indonesia, Pakistan, Rwanda, and Burundi, coup attempts, election results, and assassinations have also contributed to political strife.

Cambodia fits this pattern. The Khmer Rouge came to power after a period of extreme socioeconomic upheaval: the economy broke down in the wake of the Vietnam War; the United States intensively bombed parts of the Cambodian countryside, killing thousands, destroying homes, and inciting youths to join the antigovernment movement; foreign troops moved at will through strategic areas; Prince Sihanouk was overthrown in a coup headed by pro-U.S. elements; and the country was rocked by a civil war in which up to six hundred thousand people died. As their lives were torn apart, tens of thousands of Cambodian peasants — particularly the extremely poor and the young — joined the Khmer Rouge in order to restore their king to power, to seek vengeance against the corrupt "oppressors" who were responsible for their impoverishment and for the bombing of their homes, and to find meaning in a chaotic and violent world.

As I suggested in Chapter 1, it is precisely at such moments that people are drawn to movements and ideologies that promise renewal.[20] Upheaval exacerbates existential anxiety and meaninglessness, contributes to cognitive constriction, and increases the appeal of more simplified schemas for thought and behavior. Genocidal ideologies tap into this anxiety, discontent, and meaninglessness by promoting a blueprint that will lead to a more satisfactory way of life — including the elimination of elements of the population portrayed as the cause of social woes or as a threat to this new social order. Charismatic leaders are often central to this process, because they espouse a certainty and purpose to which their followers are drawn and with which they want and need to identify.[21] Not all modern genocides are full-fledged revitalization movements, but most contain the notion that the annihilation of a threatening or impure group will help create the preconditions for a better life.

This process of envisioning difference is a second key genocidal prime: a state or group of leaders who hold power develops a vision of a better society, scapegoats certain types of beings, excludes them from the new collectivity, and implicitly or explicitly calls for their annihilation. Thus the Nazis, under the leadership of the charismatic Hitler, promised to lead the country out of its steep decline through the creation of a German folk community *(volkgemeinschaft)* of Aryans. The annihilation of Jews and other "impure" groups was justified as necessary to ensure the health of this community. Similarly, the Khmer Rouge "line" held that, in order to achieve a "super great leap forward" into a "clean and just" utopia, Cambodian society needed to be completely revamped. For this project of social engineering to succeed, a new type of "mindful" revolutionary had to be "built"; those incorrigibles, "impure components," and "hidden enemies burrowing from within" who were unwilling or unable to construct this progressive revolutionary consciousness constituted a contaminant that had to be eradicated.

With this vision set in place, genocidal regimes begin to manufacture difference. Distinctions between "us" and "them" become more rigid and pronounced as the perpetrator regime propagates the essentialized sociopolitical categories of difference it has envisioned, crystallizing more fluid forms of identity. Germans are distinguished from Jews, Hutus from Tutsis, Turks from Armenians, Bosnian Serbs from Muslims, the "civilized" from indigenous "savages," and so forth. This crystallization of difference often accentuates preexisting structural divisions based on ethnicity, race, religion, nationality, political affiliation, class, and other imagined communities of belonging. While all societies have a degree of pluralism, structural divisions crystallize more readily in situations in which the cleavages between groups cut across a number of domains, involve domination, exploitation, and inequality, are linked to a history of tension and conflict, or are reflected by political polarizations.[22] Thus, as the "Who are 'We'?" speech illustrates, the Khmer Rouge attempted to crystallize differences along a variety of axes related to political consciousness: "new people" versus "old people," revolutionaries versus reactionary enemies "hidden within," "full rights" people versus "depositees," and the "worker-peasant class" versus the oppressor "feudal-capitalist/landowning class." Such categorization strips individuals of their personal histories, identifying them primarily on the basis of their imagined membership in an abstract, socially constructed grouping.[23] This is a hallmark of genocide: each person is assessed not on the basis of his or her individual characteristics, but in terms of his or her membership in an abstract category that is essentialized, stigmatized, and targeted for elimination.

If the crystallization of difference involves essentialization, the "marking of difference," a second dimension of manufacturing difference, is concerned with the processes through which the victim groups are stigmatized. This ideological marking, which follows the contours of the crystallized differences, further sets "them" apart from the larger social community through devaluation. As less than fully human beings, these "others" are depicted as legitimate targets of violence whose execution should not pose a moral dilemma. Killing them is not murder, but rather like the slaughter of a lowly animal. Haing Ngor captured this sense of dehumanization during DK when he explained why his commune leader, Comrade Chev, killed and ordered the execution of so many people: "We weren't quite people. We were lower forms of life, because we were enemies. Killing us was like swatting flies, a way to get rid of undesirables."[24]

Khmer Rouge ideology demonized the "oppressor classes" and its other "enemies," likening them to an impurity that threatened the well-being of the revolutionary society. In fact, the marking of difference is frequently characterized by metaphors of purity and contamination depicting "them" as permeating the boundaries that have been envisioned and crystallized by the genocidal regime — as an invasion that infects "us." Like the human body, which is endangered by "microbes" or spirits crossing within, the sociopolitical body is threatened by "them." Such beings are, to use Mary Douglas's phrase, "matter out of place," a dangerous source of pollution that needs to be eliminated.[25]

This imagery was prevalent in Khmer Rouge ideology, which incessantly spoke of the need to "clean up" and "crush" various "diseased elements" and "hidden enemies burrowing from within." Similarly, Nazi ideology portrayed Jews as "vermin," "alien bodies," "eternal bloodsuckers," "parasites," "bacteria," "a disease," "an infection," and "a plague" that threatened to destroy the German *volk* community.[26] Comparable themes can be found in most genocides, ranging from the destruction of indigenous "savages" to the eradication of Tutsi "cockroaches." By marking difference in such a manner, genocidal ideologies further "heat up" a situation, making the annihilation of the impure seem critical to the renewal and very survival of the body politic.

Ideological imperatives alone, however, are not enough to activate genocide. Genocide is almost always preceded by structural transformations that alter the ways in which people interact and bodies are disciplined.[27] Throughout this book, I have noted how the DK regime completely revamped Cambodian society by evacuating the cities, dismantling the old government structures, banning Buddhism, undermining familial solidarity and attachment, creating cooperatives in which economic production and consumption were collectivized, restricting communication and travel, and abolishing money, courts, market exchange, and formal education. Traditional hierarchies were inverted, as the young and the poor were elevated in status over the old and the wealthy, who were suspected of being enemies and having a regressive consciousness. Besides establishing the basis for a new communist society, these structural changes had the more lethal effect of undermining traditional prosocial norms, moral restraints, and legal prohibitions.[28]

These structural transformations also involve the organization of difference, a third process by which genocidal regimes manufacture the differences they have envisioned. To facilitate violence against their newly marked enemies, perpetrator regimes usually initiate a series of institutional, legal, social, and political changes that transform the conditions under which the targeted victim groups live and, ultimately, perish. The structural changes that underlie this organization of difference create mechanisms, disciplines, and social spaces for distinguishing, dividing, confining, and regulating the target group, such as the Nazi Nuremberg Laws, racial courts, ghettos and concentration camps, propaganda outlets, and secret police. During DK, the Khmer Rouge organized difference by establishing new print and radio forums to disseminate their messages of hate, instituting new practices that defined backgrounds (for example, criticism and self-criticism sessions, political meetings, and life histories), differentially allocating food, shelter, medical care, and other resources, constructing interrogation centers, prisons, and killing fields, and establishing a spy network and centralized command structure through which genocidal edicts against political and ethnic "counterrevolutionaries" could be carried out. Interactions were reorganized to create contexts like Tuol Sleng, Phnom Bros, and the "forest of the West" (where Touch was taken) in which individuals occupied given identity positions and were differentially constrained and enabled to kill those who had been marked as "enemies."

Because the crystallization of difference reduces complex on-the-ground realities to a set of rigid, abstract categories, it inevitably produces uncertainty about identity. One way perpetrator regimes deal with this situation is to continually discuss how to distinguish "us" from "them," as illustrated by the "Who are 'We'?" speech. Another response is to organize difference by creating mechanisms for sorting and institutions for confining people in spaces that demarcate and affirm alleged identities by "their" very location in a space like a ghetto, death march, concentration camp, or interrogation center. This reorganization of difference establishes institutional contexts in which uncertainty is dealt with by transforming victims' bodies into the tokens for which they are supposed to stand. A "new person" placed into a context in which he or she was given less food, fewer rights, less medical care, harsher punishments, and worse shelter than an "old person," for example, often began to resemble the dehumanized images advanced by Khmer Rouge ideology. As I described in Chapter 5, this bodily inscription of difference was especially pronounced in formal contexts such as Tuol Sleng, where prisoners like Oum Chhan and Reap were transformed through harsh living conditions, strict regulations, and brutal modes of interrogation and torture into icons of difference. As I will discuss shortly, this process was also a factor in the mutilation of Touch's body.

· · ·

What motivates perpetrators to kill? While the process of genocidal priming that I have described to this point goes a long way toward providing the contextual background that is necessary to understand why people obey orders to kill, it does not provide a "thick description"[29] of local motivation. Many accounts of genocide that focus on the macrolevel implicitly assume that, given a set of primes like the ones I have discussed, genocide is ready to be activated. As these primes become "hotter," the likelihood of genocide greatly increases. Even in a context of enormous upheaval, however, a regime's blueprint for "renewal," ideology of hate, projects of social engineering, and structural transformations alone do not lead to genocide in a straightforward manner.

To motivate people to commit the mass murder that it has envisioned, a genocidal regime must localize its ideological pronouncements so that they make sense, are compelling, and "take" among its followers. This priming process of effective ideological localization and "take," a key cultural dimension of genocide, has been underexamined or oversimplified in much of the literature on genocide, which often presupposes the "fax-like" model of ideological internalization that I discussed in the Introduction. Much of this study has been geared toward demonstrating the complexities of this prime.

Regardless of the extent to which they have been influenced by global and regional flows of ideas, genocidal leaders must localize their ideologies in order to make them appeal to their followers. The resulting ideological palimpsests are both transforming and transformed, blending the old and the new. Thus, if Pol Pot and his colleagues were strongly influenced by Marxist-Leninist and Maoist ideas, they had to adapt these notions to the local Cambodian context in order to gain recruits, many of whom were poor peasants with little education.

In this study, I have described a number of these ideological palimpsests, ranging from the Khmer Rouge use of Buddhist terms like "mindfulness," "renunciation," and "dependent origination" to translate key Marxist-Leninist concepts to the invocation of Ângkar, a multivalent symbol with high-modernist, Buddhist, and local valences. In particular, I have argued that a number of these ideological models were explicitly formulated to encourage mass violence, as illustrated in my discussion of the Khmer Rouge call for the destruction of "strings" of traitors, for "cutting off one's heart," for demonstrating one's "true loyalty" by killing "hidden enemies burrowing within," for carrying out one's "duty," and for disproportionate revenge.

By drawing upon preexisting, emotionally salient local knowledge, perpetrator regimes increase the "take" of their ideologies by increasing their comprehensibility and making them more compelling to their followers. Another key theme of this study has been to describe some of the ways in which Khmer Rouge ideological models had ontological resonance for perpetrators. Thus the desire for revenge gained motivational salience through its association with reciprocity and exchange, imbalance, "painful anger," heat, and rage. Patronage idioms, in turn, tapped into feelings of personal dependency and moral debt learned at an early age in the family, as well as local notions of potency and power. And Khmer Rouge notions of status were linked to one's sense of self and social "balance," to the pride and shame associated with face, and to the desire for honor. Such ontological resonances increase the potential "take" of ideological palimpsests by steeping them with emotional and existential salience.

Even if it moves us closer to perpetrator psychology, the process of ideological localization and "take" still does not give us a complete picture of why people kill. There is always "interference" in the manner in which these ideological models are received, and a strictly "top-down" account cannot adequately depict the ways in which subjectivities are remade on the ground. In the Introduction, I suggested that variation is generated by the dialectical duality of cultural knowledge, which may generate differences in the internalization, motivational force, contextual salience, and distribution of these ideological amalgams.

Moreover, we need to remember that perpetrator motivation can change through time. Even in a context like DK, many perpetrators who killed for the first time likely experienced psychosocial dissonance when strong moral prohibitions against harming other human beings clashed with Khmer Rouge pronouncements that glorified violence against Ângkar's enemies. The Milgram experiments demonstrate the enormous tension that such predicaments can generate, as the "teachers" began to sweat, shift uncomfortably, seek reassurance, and complain. Many of the "teachers" performed psychological maneuvers to alleviate this tension, including a narrowing of focus, displacing responsibility, devaluing the victim, and reemphasizing their legitimating belief that the shocks were ultimately promoting a larger social good — scientific advancement.

Genocidal perpetrators seem to engage in similar cognitive shifts, as they overcome moral prohibitions against killing by dehumanizing their victims, displacing responsibility, and morally justifying what they have done (by diminishing the negative effects while placing greater emphasis on ideological beliefs that legitimate their actions). One among many striking parallels with the Milgram experiments is the manner in which the harming of other human beings in DK was legitimated in the name of social progress. Genocidal regimes facilitate the process of killing in many of the ways described above, such as by instituting structural changes that undermine moral restraints, promoting a dehumanizing ideology of hate, and creating contexts in which violence may legitimately be perpetrated. Like some of the Milgram "teachers" who continued to

shock after an initial bout of psychosocial dissonance, genocidal perpetrators usually become increasingly desensitized as they move along what
Ervin Staub has called the "continuum of destructiveness"[30] and are converted into agents of death. By the time we arrive at a situation like the
interrogation of Oum Chhan, the killing fields of Chhoeung Ek, or the
extraction of Touch's liver, the perpetrators involved, who had likely
been performing violent acts for some time and were fairly desensitized,
may not have experienced much psychosocial dissonance, though this
could vary depending on the individual's personality and life history.

Moreover, even when perpetrators become desensitized, their murderous deeds are usually not carried out in a mechanical, generic manner
devoid of passion. Like all human beings, genocidal perpetrators are
active meaning-makers, for whom the act of killing is often highly symbolic, ontologically resonant, and suffused with meaning. They are
"genocidal bricoleurs" who draw on a large " toolkit" of personal and
cultural knowledge to carry out the task at hand, often asserting their
identity in the process. Quite frequently, they bring to bear the meanings
invoked by state ideology, which constructs "enemies" in a certain fashion and provides a variety of reasons why they should be killed. Their
actions, however, are motivated by more than ideological discourses that
have "taken." To illustrate this point, I want to return to the incident of
liver-eating that Denise Affonço observed, an act that cannot be
explained in terms of ideology alone, since Khmer Rouge discourse did
not directly call for its followers to extract the livers of the regime's
enemies.

Human liver-eating is a brutal, troubling, and seemingly bizarre form
of violence that must be understood within a particular cultural and historical context. The consumption of human liver, gallbladder, and bile is
known to take place *infrequently* in Cambodia and some other Asian
societies,[31] and has occurred in earlier historical periods in Cambodia.[32]
In the contemporary period, liver and gallbladder consumption was
practiced by anticolonial Khmer Issarak, Sihanouk, and Lon Nol soldiers, as well as Khmer Rouge prior to DK,[33] and is reported to have
occurred in the early 1990s at "Black Tree," a secret government military
detention center in Battambang province and after the July 1997 coup.[34]

The Khmer Dictionary defines "liver" *(thlaoem)* as "a part of human
and animal bodies that is grouped with the gallbladder and heart. A 'big
liver' *(thlaoem thom)* means a 'big heart' *(chett thom),* great insolence or
rudeness, as in 'Now I [contemptuous prefix] have a big liver and am not
in awe of or scared of anyone.' "[35] As the second part of this definition

implies, the liver has a figurative connotation somewhat like the English terms "spirit" or "heart," in the sense that the liver is a vitalizing organ that initiates action and emboldens a person. If English speakers refer to a person as "having a lot of heart," Cambodians may characterize a brave or daring individual as "having [a lot of] liver" *(mean thlaoem)*. In fact, the liver is often portrayed as a "seat of courage."[36]

Because it is a source of individual initiative, however, one's liver may lead one to transgress norms of propriety or to have too much desire and craving (in the Buddhist sense). Accordingly, some Khmer terms and phrases associated with the liver have an extremely negative connotation, often of excess. A person with an evil or bad character is sometimes said to have a "black liver" *(thlaoem khmav)*. Pol Pot has been described in this way. Alternatively, as the *Khmer Dictionary* highlights, people who act in an aggressively rude, arrogant, or insolent manner or who don't fear the potential repercussions of excessive behavior are characterized as having a "big liver" *(thlaoem thom)*. The liver is also associated with drinking, an activity that may lead to excessive emotions or behaviors. Cambodians sometimes say that "drinking raises the liver" *(phoek loek thlaoem)*. While this phrase may be employed to reference the desire to maximize the good feelings of being among one's drinking companions, it also expresses the potential for extreme and sometimes even violent behaviors. Occasionally, the connection between the liver and violence is made directly during arguments when one person tells an adversary, "I am so angry I will eat your liver" *(khoeng si thlaoem)*. While this threat is rarely acted upon in normal Cambodian life, liver-eating does occur in extreme contexts, such as military operations and warfare, violent demonstrations, and DK executions, to which I now return.

How may we explain horrific acts like the extraction and consumption of Touch's liver? This question brings us back to the issues of manufacturing difference and perpetrator motivation. As we have seen, during DK, there was enormous uncertainty about the identities of others because the state of a person's political consciousness had to be interpreted from signs. In this case, Ta Ling gives orders for Touch to be "taken to the forest of the West" because he had stolen some cassava roots. Given that such an act would have been considered a minor offense in earlier historical periods, we may plausibly conjecture that even "bloodthirsty" individuals like Ta Sok, Ta Doeung, and Ta Chea might have entertained some doubts about Touch's "enemy" status, for, just prior to his arrest, he had been considered a member of their community.

Within this context of uncertainty, then, the extraction of Touch's liver may in one sense be understood as the perpetrators' attempt to transform their victim into the political token he was accused of being. This process of manufacturing difference, like that to which Oum Chhan and other Tuol Sleng prisoners were subjected, resembled a rite of passage. Thus Touch is separated from his former social position and taken to a liminal space, "the forest of the West." In Cambodia, the "forest" is often associated with the wild and uncivilized,[37] while "the West" represents the direction of death in Buddhist cosmology.[38] Ta Ling's short command is thus symbolically loaded: it tells the three executioners to take Touch to a liminal space in which death and transgressive acts may take place.

Touch, deprived of markers of human identity, such as his shirt and his physiological ability to eat, drink, see, and move his body, occupies a "structurally dead"[39] position at this liminal locale. He becomes a text upon which difference is inscribed by violence — in this case by Ta Sok's "large knife." By cutting into Touch's abdomen, Ta Sok violates a fundamental human barrier, the "social skin,"[40] and, through the resulting disfigurement and death, thoroughly dehumanizes Touch. As if to confirm this loss of humanity, Touch's last act before death is to scream in agony, producing sounds that are no longer human, but rather like those of "a wild beast." Ta Sok continues to violate what's left of Touch's human status as he gropes for his liver, the organ of vitality. In a sense, the process of disembowelment mimes the search for "hidden enemies" and the DK regime's high-modernist attempt to render everything visible and thus subject to state control. Touch looks and seems like everyone else; however, his stealing demonstrates that he is secretly an "enemy." Just as such secret identities must be uncovered and revealed — these local cadres had no doubt received orders to find enemies who were "burrowing from within" — so too is Touch's body opened up and a hidden organ removed from a place of internal invisibility in which it was "burrowed" to one of external visibility.

After removing Touch's liver, Ta Sok and his comrades slice, fry, and consume it. In doing so, the perpetrators perform another horrifying mimesis. If Touch has violated the community by extracting and consuming its food, he is punished by a bodily violation in which his liver is removed and eaten by representatives of the collective. This mimesis resonates with Buddhist conceptions of purgatory, in which, as I noted in Chapter 1, those who have sinned are reborn in hells in which the punishment mirrors their deeds, sometimes involving being physically hacked, mutilated, burned, or even consumed. On some level, Ta Sok and his cronies may thus be acting as symbolic guardians of hell who righteously carry out the verdict of the Party Organization, or Ângkar — the new Yama, or Buddhist Lord of Death — in a manner that involves a type of bodily mutilation that mirrors the "sin" (extracting Touch's liver, just has Touch had extracted food from the collective). Perhaps by frying Touch's liver, a key source of individual vitality, Ta Sok and the others were symbolically burning him in the flames of the new hell.

The act of communal eating provides a symbolic means of decontamination, as it moves the perpetrators — who themselves have been defiled by committing violent transgressions and through contact with an "enemy" and violator of the collective — from the realm of the impure (killing) to the pure (sociality and communal consumption). The process of decontamination is symbolized by the frying of Touch's liver, which is purified through the heat of the flames and transformed into a "cooked" food object that may be jointly consumed in the "civilized" social context into which Ta Sok and his fellow cronies are reintegrated. Moreover, the cooking of the liver may also be seen as signifying the purification of the collective, which had been violated by Touch's stealing. Touch, for his part, is symbolically reincorporated into the collective in a cooked, or "civilized" and "purified" form.[41]

On another level, this act of liver-eating manufactures Touch's status as an enemy. As illustrated by the Khmer phrase "I'm so angry I will eat your liver," liver-eating is performed in extreme contexts, such as when a person is irate and strongly desires revenge. By eating Touch's liver, Ta Sok, Ta Doeung, and Ta Chea affirm Touch's newly inscribed and dehumanized status as an enemy, since one consumes the liver of those one hates. Moreover, the flames of the fire that are used to cook Touch's liver could also symbolize the "burning rage" that proper revolutionaries were supposed to feel toward such "enemies." In ambiguous situations, then, liver-eating provides one way for perpetrators to express their extreme anger toward their victims and assert certainty about the identities of alleged "enemies."

Liver-eating also serves other purposes. On the one hand, people often believe they are able to incorporate qualities associated with the liver by eating this organ. (The great potency and vitality of human liver may be indexed by the fact that it supposedly jumps around in a frying pan, unlike the livers of animals.) When I asked why people sometimes ate human liver during the Pol Pot period, I often received a response along the lines of that given by Saruon, a resident of Kompong Cham city:

People sometimes say that if one eats human liver, one's heart becomes detached *(chett dach)*, that one's heart becomes audacious *(chett mut)* . . . . Having an audacious heart is doing something one has to do. For example, if one decides to kill, it means one kills without thinking about it. You see, if they tell you, 'Kill these two people,' it means that — 'Bang!' — they would be killed at once. If one doesn't eat liver, one's heart doesn't become detached. And when they eat liver, they say (I've never seen it, but I've heard others talk about it) that after eating liver one's eyes become red. When one's eyes become redder, one's heart is really detached. So, if a group of perpetrators is killing many people in some situation, perhaps they really do eat human liver in order to make their hearts detached. . . . I believe that human liver really is eaten in order to make the heart detached, to prevent them from thinking. If the order to kill comes, they kill.

Similarly, Khel explained that "people eat human liver at times when they are way too irate, such as when they hold a grudge. . . . When they eat human liver, it makes their heart dare *(chett hean)*, as if 'there is no one like me [prefix of superiority], there is only I' [prefix of superiority], as if they have taken some potent power *(etthipol)*." Like many other people I interviewed, Saruon and Khel portray human liver-eating as an act that transforms a perpetrator's state of mind and potentially their character in general. To consume a person's liver, their "seat of courage," is to appropriate their courage. As a result, the perpetrator becomes extremely audacious and bold, someone who "dares" to engage in transgressive acts, like those who have "big livers." The incorporation of liver therefore may have a cumulative effect, as it symbolically "adds" to the size of one's own liver.

Moreover, since the liver is an organ that initiates action, one may increase one's ability to act by eating it. Like Saruon, many of my informants mentioned that human liver-eating enables people to "cut off their heart" toward something or someone or to become dispassionate and resolute when dealing with a matter. Killing a human being like Touch, even if a "hated enemy," is an act that causes most people, particularly those who are not yet fully desensitized, to have some qualms. Eating human liver, then, may help perpetrators overcome this psychosocial dissonance: they incorporate qualities that enable them to become audacious, brave, dispassionate, and resolved enough to commit the most transgressive of acts, killing another human being. Like a person who is extremely inebriated, a liver-eater is able to act without hesitation or forethought. As one person observed, "If they are told to kill, they will kill. That person wouldn't think much. They eat liver in order to be able to kill." The very act of cutting out the liver is a gruesome mimesis of the

perpetrator's mental state of "detached" resolve (mirroring the separation of the liver from the body) and transgressive daring (mirroring the
cutting out of the "seat of courage" and initiative).

On the other hand, liver-eating also provides a means of expressing
power and intimidating others. As the above quotations suggest, cutting
out and consuming an enemy's liver represents an extreme assertion of
power, as it implies that perpetrators can do whatever they want without
fearing the consequences. Further, the removal of a victim's liver marks —
both physically and symbolically — the victim's inferiority, powerlessness,
and dehumanized status, as he or she is incapacitated and stripped of an
organ of vitality and agency crucial to human life. Human liver-eating
may also be seen as a twisted display of power, a violent show of force
intended to instill fear and obedience in others. One Kompong Cham city
resident told me that, in contexts like DK, people sometimes eat human
liver "to become braver and to gain renown through their actions. When
others know that a person has eaten human liver, they will bend down
before them, not dare to go near them."[42]

The Khmer Rouge practice of consuming human liver, then, suggests
that, when perpetrators kill, much more is going on than simple obedience or ideological fanaticism. If people like Ta Sok, Ta Doeung, and Ta
Chea were simple automatons, they would have carried out their murderous deeds in a straightforward manner. To account for their actions,
we must examine a number of motivational dynamics. More broadly,
such perpetrators are heavily influenced by state-level initiatives.
Genocidal regimes institute structural transformations and reorganize
difference in a manner that lessens moral inhibitions and produces contexts in which mass annihilation may take place. And, through a variety
of forums and practices, genocidal regimes disseminate a message of hate
that envisions and manufactures difference, legitimating violence against
a dehumanized "enemy."

Assuming that the regime's ideological manipulation is effective, perpetrators will "take" these ideological messages, though in a variable
manner, since there is always "interference" in their reception and internalization. This process of "take" establishes various "channels" that
perpetrators "tune" into when killing. Due to the frequency with which
certain ideological models are invoked (for example, the constant Khmer
Rouge refrain to be "resolute" and "smash" "strings of traitors" and
"enemies burrowing from within" who did not have a proper "revolutionary consciousness" and "stand"), many or most perpetrators may
"take" them, though their personal understandings of these models may

vary. While it is impossible to know exactly what went on in the minds of Ta Sok, Ta Doeung, and Ta Chea (no doubt they varied somewhat in their motivations), they did share an understanding that they were supposed to kill a "hidden enemy burrowing from within" who had been discovered. Moreover, their actions suggest that they were influenced by Khmer Rouge discourses about maintaining a "burning rage" and "cutting off their hearts" toward such enemies.

Nevertheless, these ideological discourses, even if they are effectively localized and "taken" by many cadres, are not sufficient to explain perpetrator motivation. Nor can we explain killing simply in terms of obedience to authority. Both factors are a piece in the puzzle of why people kill, but neither completely accounts for the patterning or intensity of the violence. Neither can fully explain why a practice like human-liver eating takes place. Although the liver was occasionally mentioned in Khmer Rouge discourses, such as in the song about Baribo village that lamented that the "the hated enemy killed my friend," who died with "chest and stomach asunder, liver and spleen gone" (see Chapter 1), Khmer Rouge ideology did not directly call for its followers to extract and consume the livers of its enemies. Instead, it was a local-level initiative, one that illustrates how perpetrators perform genocidal bricolage while carrying out their deeds. In particular, Khmer Rouge perpetrators combined salient ideological messages (for example, the need to maintain burning rage toward, seek vengeance against, and uncover "hidden enemies burrowing from within") with local knowledge about how the consumption of liver is done to those whom one hates and to whom one is "tied in malice," and how it raises the "heat" in one's body, increases one's daring, and enables one to "cut off the heart" and carry out orders.

Perpetrators like Ta Sok, Ta Doeung, and Ta Chea are also motivated by group-level dynamics. Like Lor, each of these men was asserting through their actions an identity that was evaluated by their peers. By "cutting off their hearts" and killing "enemies," these men were making a claim that they were "truly loyal" to Ângkar and had a progressive political consciousness. When this "line" was affirmed, a perpetrator gained face and might even rise in rank. Had they failed to carry out their "duty," the perpetrators would have been shamed and perhaps even killed—for it would indicate that they, like the enemy, had a regressive consciousness. Moreover, by killing and then consuming the liver of their victims, the perpetrators affirmed their bond to one another and their membership in a larger social collective that was distinct from the impure and evil "other." Both these group-level dynamics and genocidal brico-

lage are mediated by ideological discourses, but neither can be fully
explained by them.

The same point can be made about the "mimetics of difference,"
which brings us back to Turner's "two poles of meaning." As I noted in
Chapter 5, the bodies of victims serve as symbolic templates through
which their subjectivity and that of the perpetrator may be manufactured. On the one hand, the victim's state of being mimes that of the perpetrator, albeit in inverse fashion. Located in a liminal space, Touch's
body is marked and mutilated, transforming him into a contaminated
being who is no longer fully human. He no longer speaks, but can only
make sounds like those of an animal before he dies. Touch's diminish-
ment inversely mimes the inflation of his killers, who split off and project
the negative qualities of the bad, impure "enemy" onto him. As Touch
takes on these qualities, his killers remake themselves into their binary
opposite (bad versus good, them versus us, enemy versus comrade,
impure versus pure, regressive versus progressive, and so forth). In the
face of the enormous uncertainty and anxiety many Khmer Rouge perpetrators experienced, these mimetics of difference also served to narcis-
sistically inflate their sense of self, to affirm the ideological ideas in which
they were invested, and to annihilate their own fears of annihilation (represented by the dangerous and impure "enemy" they killed). And finally,
the liver itself became a symbol that mimed the perpetrator's desired
state of consciousness, one of daring, resolve, clarity (through the extraction of this "hidden" object that was "burrowing from within"), and
purity (through the liver's transformation from a "raw" to a "cooked"
state).

One could argue that there is a great deal of difference between
killings "in the wild" and the execution of "one or two people" carried
out by Lor at Choeung Ek under the gaze of Duch. However, even in a
highly structured context, genocidal perpetrators are motivated by a similarly wide range of factors. Thus I argued that people like Lor and Vaen
Kheuan were not just obeying orders, but were likely motivated by those
ideological "channels" into which they were "tuning," by group-level
dynamics (such as the desire to gain face and demonstrate one's loyalty to
the party), and by the self-inflation that was achieved through the mimetics of difference. While operating in a constrained environment, perpetrators have leeway to act and make choices that have profound consequences for their victims.

Their behaviors are also influenced by distanciation and intimacy. The
motivational dynamics for a highly educated party leader like Pol Pot no

doubt differed from those of a person like Lor. For Pol Pot, the annihilation of difference was envisioned as part of a high-modernist project of social engineering that would lead society to a revitalized future. Human beings were conceptualized in abstract terms, as units with which to "build" the new revolutionary society. Since some of these units were regressive and threatened to subvert social progress (as suggested by food shortages, perceived coups, and supposed betrayal), they had to be eliminated. Even at a distance from the actual killing, Pol Pot's actions were motivated by local understandings of patronage, the ideological doctrine he had helped to formulate, the atmosphere of suspicion and anxiety he had helped to create, his group interactions with others, and the narcissistic inflation he achieved through the destruction of impure enemies "burrowing from within."

· · ·

Is evil banal? Even for the most bureaucratically distanced and highly constrained of perpetrators, like Eichmann and Lor, killing is never completely banal. We are all enabled and compelled by the contexts in which we live. We all have multiple motivations. And we all invest psychologically in what we do. Though we might despise them, genocidal perpetrators are meaning-making beings with complex motivations that cannot simply be explained away in terms of ideological fanaticism or obedience to authority. These two motivations play an important role in genocide, but neither leads us to an understanding of the complexity of human action, including those brutal deeds carried out by perpetrators like Pol Pot, Vaen Kheuan, Reap, Ta Sok, and Lor.

In conclusion, this book has argued that, if we are to answer the most pressing questions about the origins of genocide — why it takes place and what motivates perpetrators to kill — we must take a processual approach that weaves together the warp and woof of various levels of analysis. Because of the lack of research on the cultural dimensions of genocide, which are so crucial to answering the above questions, much of this text has examined how ontologically resonant local knowledge makes ideological palimpsests more motivationally compelling and helps give violence its distinct pattern and form. Nevertheless, cultural factors cannot fully explain genocide.

As my discussion of genocidal priming highlights, a more comprehensive explanation must move from macro-level historical process to local-level sociocultural dynamics to psychological mimetics, with the understanding that all of these levels of analysis are linked and cannot be understood in isolation. For some people, it perhaps may be easier and more satisfying to explain genocide as simply the result of obedience or some type of cultural proclivity, like anti-Semitism. Unfortunately, such explanations always fall short, since they fail to account for the complexities of human behavior.

To this end, I have offered a number of concepts — including genocidal priming and activation, manufacturing difference, ideological "take" and "interference," ontological resonance, genocidal bricolage, local motivation, and the mimetics of difference — that provide a means of beginning to tackle this complexity in a manner that emphasizes the "thick description" of local level dynamics yet lays the basis for a comparative analysis of genocidal process.

In Buddhism, such understanding is viewed as a step-by-step process. Maha Ghosananda explains, "In Cambodia, we say, 'A journey of 10,000 miles begins with a single step.' Slowly, slowly, step by step. Each step is a meditation. Each step is a prayer."[43] In this spirit, this book is meant as one small step toward understanding the shadow of genocide that has devastated Cambodia and so many other lands, in particular the reasons why people kill.

A Note on Transliteration: Franco-Khmer Transcription

CONSONANTS		TRANSCRIPTION	VOWELS	TRANSCRIPTION	
1st	2nd			1st	2nd
ñ	ñ	k	- -	â	o
ə	ឈ	kh	- :̣	a	ua
	ង	ng	-ា-	a	ea
ច	ឆ	ch	-ា:̣	a	oa/ea[d]
ឈ	ឈ	chh/ch[a]	:̊	e	i
	ឈ	nh	:̊	ey	i
ដ	ឌ	d	:̊	oe	eu
ឋ	ឍ	th	:̊	oeu	eu
ណ		n	:̣	o	u
ត	ទ	t	:̣	au	ou
ថ	ធ	th	:̣	uo	uo
	ន	n	ើ-	aoe	oe
ប		b[b]	ឿ-	eua	eua
ឋ	ព	p	ៀ-	ie	ie
ផ	ភ	ph	េ-	e	e
	ម	m	ែ-	ae	e
	យ	y	ៃ-	ai	ei
	រ	r	ោ-	ao	o
	ល	l	ៅ-	av	ov
	វ	v	ុំ	om	um
ស		s	ំ	am	um
ហ		h	ាំ	aın	oam
ឡ		l	ាំង	ang	eang
អ		Ø/'[c]	:̣	ah	eah

[a]When followed by another consonant, as in *chnam* [year].

[b]Final ប is written *p*.

[c]When subscript to another consonant, as in *s'at* [clean].

[d]Before a velar final, as in *neak* [person].

Note: Transcriptions in this book are based upon the Franco-Khmer transcription system developed by Franklin E. Huffman in 1983. Although Huffman's system is similar to that used in many French-language works on Cambodia, additional diacritics were added to distinguish all of the various vowel sounds. Only one of those diacritics (â) is retained in this text.

Notes

1. Youk Chhang (2000:1).
2. All transliterations are based on Franklin E. Huffman's Franco-Khmer translation system as reproduced in Heder and Ledgerwood (1996a:xvii).
3. In what follows, I use pseudonyms for the people I interviewed and quote in this study. I employ the real names of the Tuol Sleng survivors who have written about their experiences using their own names, major public figures, and the DK cadres and soldiers named in documents and in my interviews.
4. The 1948 U.N. Convention defines genocide as "the intent to destroy, in whole or in part, a national, ethnical, racial or religious group." From an anthropological perspective, this definition is highly problematic because it privileges certain social categories — race, ethnicity, religion, and nationality — over others. While the marking of social difference is a human universal, the categories into which we parse the world are culturally constructed. Thus, as we move from place to place, we find people being classified in a myriad of ways, ranging from totemistic groups and castes to categories based on sexual orientation and alternative genders. Surely there is a need to take account of such emic social categories, as opposed to simply assuming that the categories highly salient in "modern" societies are universal. Accordingly, many scholars use a broader definition, such as the one proposed by Helen Fein: "Genocide is sustained purposeful action by a perpetrator to physically destroy a collectivity directly or indirectly, through interdiction of the biological and social reproduction of group members, sustained regardless of the surrender or lack of threat offered by the victim" (1990:24). For a discussion of how the Cambodian case fits both the more strict and broader definitions of genocide, see Kiernan (1996). See also Hinton (2002b, 2002c, 2004).

5. Lemkin (1944, italics his).

6. Quoted in Power (2002:29).

7. Power (2002:42).

8. Bauman (1989); Bowen (1996); Eller (1999).

9. Bauman (1989); Horkheimer and Adorno (1944). See also Hinton (2002b, 2002c, 2002d, 2004); Kaye and Strath (2000).

10. Milgram (1974); See also Scheper-Hughes (2002); Nagengast (2002).

11. Power (2002).

12. The label "the Pol Pot regime" was promoted by the People's Republic of Kampuchea (PRK), the regime that overthrew the Khmer Rouge. Many members of this new government were former Khmer Rouge who had fled brutal purges. By focusing blame on Pol Pot and his "clique," these government officials were able to deflect attention from their own roles during DK.

13. See Naranhkiri Tith (1998); Ledgerwood (1998b); and country profiles by the CIA, IMF, and World Bank. See also French (1994) on the plight of mine victims.

14. Caldwell and Tan (1973:383–90, 393). On the personal attacks on Sihanouk and his response, see Becker (1998:114f.); Chandler (1991:201); Corfield (1994); Shawcross (1987:125).

15. For descriptions and analyses of U.S. bombing in Cambodia, see Chandler (1991:225); Kiernan (1989, 1996:16f.); and Shawcross (1987).

16. U.S. Foreign Broadcast Information Services, Asia and Pacific (hereafter FBIS) (5/12/75:H5–6).

17. For detailed discussion of the parallels between Khmer Rouge policy and foreign models, see Burgler (1990); Chandler (1991, 1999a, 1999b); Kiernan (1996); Jackson (1989a).

18. "The Party's Four-Year Plan to Build Socialism in All Fields, 1977–1980" (hereafter Four-Year Plan), in Chandler, Kiernan, and Boua (1988:45–46).

19. Ebihara (1968, 1990).

20. "Four-Year Plan," in Chandler, Kiernan, and Boua (1988:51).

21. Burgler (1990:75); Ponchaud (1978:91f.); Twining (1989:127f.).

22. Pol Pot (1977:61). For detailed analyses of the Khmer Rouge's use of military metaphors, see Marston (1994); and Ponchaud (1978).

23. Haing Ngor (1987:197).

24. See Chandler (1991:270–71).

25. "Report of Activities of the Party Center According to the General Political Tasks of 1976" (hereafter "Report of Activities"), in Chandler, Kiernan, and Boua (1988:207).

26. "Report of Activities," in Chandler, Kiernan, and Boua (1988:188).

27. On the domestic and international problems the PRK regime initially confronted and general historical information about the PRK period, see Ablin and Hood (1990); Chandler (2000); Becker (1998); Gottesman (2002); Martin (1994); Shawcross (1985); and Vickery (1986). My description of recent Cambodian history loosely follows Chandler's (2000) account.

28. On the Paris Agreement and the UNTAC period, see Brown and Zasloff (1998); Chandler (2000:239); Gottesman (2002); Kamm (1998); Heder and Ledgerwood (1996a); Shawcross (1994).

29. My description of post-UNTAC events is based on Becker (1998); Brown and Zasloff (1998); Chandler (1999b, 2000); Marston (1999), and relevant issues of the *Phnom Penh Post*.

30. Thayer (1997a:1).

31. Thayer (1997b:16–17).

32. I made several archival trips to Cornell University and Yale University. In the summer of 2000 (and again in July 2003), I returned to Cambodia to do follow-up research for a month, splitting my time between Kompong Cham and Phnom Penh. I was able to interview several former Khmer Rouge cadres, and Lor for a second time. In addition, I spent much of my time perusing thousands of pages of documentation at the DC-CAM archive, which had just begun operation during my 1994–95 fieldwork. Such materials, along with some new books and articles, particularly David Chandler's (1999) groundbreaking study of Tuol Sleng, have proven invaluable to the completion of this project.

33. For a review of this anthropological literature and a discussion of some of the reasons for the anthropological silence about genocide, see Hinton (2002b, 2002c, 2002d). For a review of the anthropological literature on political violence and war, see Ferguson (2003); Ferguson and Faragher (1988); Nagengast (1994); Simons (1999).

34. See, for example, Appadurai (1998); Aretxaga (1995); Besteman (2002); Feldman (1991); Kapferer (1988); Kleinman, Das, and Lock (1997); Taussig (1987); Taylor (1999); Whitehead (2002).

35. See, in particular, Becker (1998); Chandler (1991, 1999a, 1999b, 2000), Heder and Tittemore (2001); Kiernan (1985a, 1996), Other important analyses of DK include: Ablin and Hood (1990); Burgler (1990); Carney (1977); Chanda (1986); Chandler (1996); Chandler, Kiernan, and Boua (1988); Etcheson (1984); Frieson (1991); Heder (1980; 1997); Jackson (1989c); Kiernan (1993, 1997); Kiernan and Boua (1982); Martin (1994); Ponchaud (1978, 1989); Quinn (1976, 1989b); Shawcross (1987); Thion (1993); Vickery (1984).

36. Ebihara (1990, 1993a, 1993b, 2002), Ledgerwood (1990a, 1997, 2002); Marston (1985, 1994, 2002, 2003). See also Ebihara and Ledgerwood (2002); French (1994); Smith (1989).

37. Quinn (1989a:240).

38. Goldhagen (1996). For an anthropological critique of Goldhagen's argument, see Hinton (1998c). See also Finkelstein and Birn (1998) and Shandley (1998).

39. Goldhagen (1996:470, 33, 46).

40. Barth (1995); Borofsky (1994); Ortner (1999); Rodseth (1998).

41. See Barth (1990, 1993); Hannerz (1992); Rodseth (1998); Schwartz (1978); Sperber (1985).

42. See Bloch (1998); D'Andrade (1995); D'Andrade and Strauss (1992); Holland and Quinn (1987); Nuckolls (1996); Shore (1996, 1998); Strauss and Quinn (1997). The term "local knowledge" is from Geertz (2000).

43. Shore (1996, 1998). See also Shweder (1991); Sperber (1996); Strauss and Quinn (1997).

44. Hinton (1998a). See also Chigas (2000).

45. Giddens (1984).

46. The terms "conventional mental models" and "personal mental models" are from Shore (1996:46).

47. See Barth (1990); Obeyesekere (1981).

48. See, for example, Ortner (1989) or Sahlins (1981).

49. Strauss (1992).

50. Spiro (1987). See also D'Andrade (1995) and Strauss and Quinn (1997).

51. On the use of early sensorimotor schemas as "scaffolding" for later experience, see Piaget (1932); and Vygotsky (1978). On embodiment and motivation, see Lakoff (1987); and Johnson (1987). On the motivational force of symbols, see Turner (1967). On cultural models and motivational force, see also D'Andrade and Straus (1992); Nuckolls (1996); Shore (1996, 1998); and Strauss and Quinn (1997).

52. I loosely follow Bruce Kapferer's definition of ontology as "the fundamental principles of a being in the world and the orientation of such a being toward the horizons of its experiences" (1988:79). See also Taylor (1999).

53. Schwartz (1978:425). See also Rodseth (1998:58).

54. See Appadurai (1996); Hannerz (1996).

55. Lakoff (1987).

56. See Quinn and Holland (1987:13).

57. Hinton (1996).

58. Levi-Strauss (1966).

59. Levi-Strauss (1966:17).

PART I PREAMBLE

1. On the feelings of horror experienced by a person who was about to be executed in a similar manner, see Yimsut (1997:187–93). See also Him (1997:147f.).

2. Ke Pauk was allowed to defect to the Cambodian government in March 1998 (Thayer 1998a:24). Like several other senior Khmer Rouge leaders, Ke Pauk remained immune from prosecution — despite being strongly implicated in the Cambodian genocide — until his death in 2002. In addition to overseeing the 1977 purges of local leaders in the Central Zone, Ke Pauk led the 1978 Eastern Zone massacres, in which tens of thousands of people were killed. If he had lived long enough, Ke Pauk would likely have been convicted by an international tribunal (see Heder and Tittemore 2001).

3. Tuol Sleng confession of Re Sim (Reap), Cornell Microfilm Reel (CMR) 126.20.

CHAPTER I

1. *Phnom Penh Post* Staff (1999a:1).

2. Sainsbury and Chea Sotheacheath (2000:8).

3. Of course, alternative models of more disproportionate revenge also exist in the Judeo-Christian tradition, as a reading of the Old Testament or Greek tragedy illustrates.

4. Hawk (n.d.)

5. Kiernan (1996:248).
6. Scott (1998).
7. Pol Pot (1977:19).
8. See Becker (1998); Chandler (1991, 1999b); Kiernan (1985a).
9. Sainsbury and Chea Sotheacheath (2000:8).
10. See Chandler (1991, 1996).
11. Pol Pot (1977:23).
12. Haing Ngor (1987:197). See also Ponchaud (1978:72f.).
13. "Four-Year Plan," in Chandler, Kiernan, and Boua (1988:47).
14. Pol Pot (1977:28).
15. Pol Pot (1977:29).
16. Chandler (1991); Kiernan (1985a); Kiernan and Boua (1982); Martin (1994).
17. Kiernan and Boua (1982:173).
18. Pol Pot (1977:38).
19. Pol Pot (1977:27).
20. Willmott (1981). See also Summers (1987).
21. Khieu Samphan (1979:24–25, 30f.).
22. Khieu Samphan (1979:39–40); Willmott (1981:214).
23. Khieu Samphan (1979:40).
24. Delvert (1961); Kiernan and Boua (1982); Willmott (1967, 1981).
25. Kiernan (1996).
26. See Kiernan (1996:288f., 458).
27. Ebihara (1968:579–80). See also Edwards (1996).
28. Delvert (1961:519).
29. Ebihara (1968:332).
30. Ebihara (1968:333).
31. Willmott (1981:214f.).
32. Delvert (1961:495). See also Willmott (1981:218).
33. Delvert (1961:470–74, 495).
34. Delvert (1961:470–72).
35. Pol Pot (1977:26).
36. Delvert (1961). See also Frieson (1991:24); Willmott (1981:214f.).
37. Ebihara (1968, 1990).
38. Ebihara (1990:17).
39. Ebihara (1990:17, 1968:196).
40. Ebihara (1993a:161, 1968:194–95).
41. Kiernan (1985a); Kiernan and Boua (1982).
42. Kiernan (1996:7).
43. Kiernan (1996). See also Shawcross (1987).
44. FBIS (4/17/70:H4).
45. See, for example, *Revolutionary Young Men and Women,* in Carney (1977:30).
46. *Khmer Dictionary* (1968:282, 284, 1263); Headley et al. (1977:240–41, 259, 1040). See also Chandler (1991:242).
47. Reynolds and Reynolds (1982:75). See also Mahasi Sayadaw (1996:36–38).

48. Ebihara (1968:389).
49. Maha Ghosananda (1992:58).
50. See, for example, Chigas (2000); Hansen (1999).
51. See Headley et al. (1977).
52. Headley et al. (1977:408); *Khmer Dictionary* (1967:479); Rhys Davids and Stede (1992:331–32).
53. *Khmer Dictionary* (1967:123).
54. Lazarus (1991:217f.).
55. On metaphors of anger and heat in the Euro-American tradition, see Lakoff (1987).
56. See Eisenbruch (1992); D. Hinton, Khin Um, and Phalnarith Ba (2001a, 2001b); Marcucci (1986, 1994); Sargent, Marcucci, and Elliston (1983); White (1996).
57. D. Hinton, Khin Um, and Phalnarith Ba (2001a, 2001b); Marcucci (1986).
58. Rice (1994). See also Hansen (1988); Sargent, Marcucci, and Elliston (1983); White (1996).
59. Sargent, Marcucci, and Elliston (1983:76). See also Hansen (1988:34f.); Rice (1994:53); White (1996:90f).
60. See D. Hinton, Khin Um, and Phalnarith Ba (2001a, 2001b).
61. Ebihara (1968); Hinton (1997). See also Hollan (1988).
62. *Khmer Dictionary* (1967;170). See also Headley et al. (1977:133).
63. *Khmer Dictionary* (1967:170).
64. *Khmer Dictionary* (1967: 217, 308); Headley et al (1977: 175, 266); Ledgerwood (1997:91).
65. *Khmer Dictionary* (1967:308).
66. Headley et al. (1977:1039). See also *Khmer Dictionary* (1967:1262).
67. Ebihara (1968). See also Delvert (1961); Martel (1975); Sedara Kim (2001).
68. See Marston (1997:100); Smith-Hefner (1999:166).
69. See Marston (1997).
70. *Khmer Dictionary* (1967:1263, 171). See also Headley et al. (1977:1039, 134). I would like to thank Sophea Mouth for his comments on this translation.
71. See Hinton (1998a).
72. *Khmer Dictionary* (1967:729). See also Headley et al. (1977:614).
73. Bun Chân Mol (1973:180–81).
74. *Phnom Penh Post* Staff (1999b:1, 3). See also Lon Nara and Phelim Kyne (2000); Lon Nara (2001:2).
75. See Fisher-Nguyen (1994).
76. Thion (1993:197).
77. See Headley et al. (1977:659); *Khmer Dictionary* (1967:759)
78. Bun Chân Mol (1973). See also Burgler (1990:313n16); Um (1990:285).
79. Hinton (1998a).
80. Barber and Chaumeau (1997:3).
81. Barber (1997:7).
82. Levy (1998).
83. Quoted in Levy (1998).

84. Hinton (1998a).

85. My modeling of Cambodian disproportionate revenge is loosely adapted, for purposes of comparison, from Johnson's (1993:48) schematization of the Biblical tradition of "an eye for an eye" revenge—though we should keep in mind that there exist alternative models of revenge in both cases.

86. Jackson (1989c:262).

87. Quoted in Kiernan (1985a:231–32).

88. "The Communist Party of Kampuchea and the Problem of Khmer Young Men and Women," in Carney (1977:30).

89. Carney (1977:32).

90. Ith Sarin, in Carney (1977:39).

91. Ith Sarin (1973:68); Carney (1977:52).

92. Ith Sarin (1973:63); see also Carney (1977:51).

93. Ith Sarin (1973).

94. Carney (1977:31).

95. Cited in Kiernan (1996:422).

96. Ebihara (1968:186, 348, 579).

97. Ebihara (1968:584).

98. Ebihara (1968:562).

99. Ebihara (1968:569).

100. FBIS, May 12, 1975, H5–6.

101. FBIS, May 15, 1975, H4–5.

102. Tooze (1962:90). See also Kiernan (1996:5).

103. Soth Polin (1980:44).

104. Chandler, Kiernan, and Lim (1976:2, 9).

105. CMR 12.25, quoted in Heder and Tittemore (2001:31).

106. Ponchaud (1978:29). On the roundup and execution of the Khmer Rouge leadership in Phnom Penh, see also Becker (1998:192–93); and Pin Yathay (1987:16).

107. Ponchaud (1978:28).

108. See Ponchaud (1978:40f.). See also De Nike, Quigley, and Robinson (2000:219–221); Ponchaud (1978:41–3).

109. Thion (1993:166).

110. One of eight key components of the Party Center's plan that was allegedly discussed by Pol Pot at a conference on May 20, 1975 (Kiernan 1996:55).

111. *Revolutionary Flags* (1977:21–22). See also FBIS (4/14/78:H5).

112. Ben Kiernan (1996:62) interview with Ouch Bun Chhoeun.

113. FBIS (1/20/76:H1). See also FBIS (1/20/76) on how oppression "fired the anger of our poor brothers and sisters"; and McIntyre (1996) on the Khmer Rouge construction of the urban/rural divide.

114. FBIS (3/31/76:H2–3) and (4/16/76:H8).

115. FBIS (1/16/76:H3).

116. Haing Ngor (1987:140). On Khmer Rouge song and dance, see Locard (1998); Shapiro-Phim (2002).

117. FBIS (10/4/77:H25).

118. This translation by Chandler is from Chandler, Kiernan, and Lim (1976:14); and Locard (1998:324–26).

119. Haing Ngor (1987:159).

120. Haing Ngor (1987:202).

121. Someth May (1986:165).

122. See Haing Ngor (1987:165f.); Stuart-Fox (1985:60); Szymusiak (1986:147).

123. Moyer (1991:123).

124. "Decisions of the Central Committee on a Variety of Questions" (hereafter "Decisions"), in Chandler, Kiernan, and Boua (1988:3).

125. See Heder and Tittemore (2001:42f.).

126. CMR 12.25, translated in Heder and Tittemore (2001:94n425; see also 2001:95).

127. See Locard (1996:55).

128. See Eisenbruch (1992:286).

129. On some historical precedents for decapitation in Cambodia, see Becker (1998:3); Chandler (1996:119f., 2000:37); Tauch Chhuong (1994:49–50). On decapitation in other Southeast Asian contexts, see George (1996) and Rosaldo (1980).

130. See www.dccam.org.

CHAPTER 2

1. "Report of Activities," in Chandler, Kiernan, and Boua (1988:183–4).

2. For an excellent description of the important parallels and differences between the Khmer Rouge purges and those that took place in other communist regimes, see Chandler (1999a).

3. See Ang (1987); Ebihara (1968); Keyes (1995); Mabbett and Chandler (1995).

4. On "men of prowess," see Wolters (1999). On *broleung* and related conceptions of the vital essence, see Keyes (1995); Kirsch (1973); Hanks (1964); Phya Anuman Rajadhon (1946); Thompson (1996).

5. Wolters (1999:22, 111, 226).

6. Heine-Geldern (1942). See also Geertz (1980); and Mabbett and Chandler (1995).

7. Rhys Davids and Stede (1992:335). See also Conze (1975:92).

8. Headley et al. (1977:425); *Khmer Dictionary* (1967:499).

9. Coomaraswamy (1964:13–4).

10. See Mouth (n.d.b); Swearer (1995).

11. See Reynolds and Reynolds (1982); Tambiah (1985). See also Phra Prayudh Payutto (1995:275).

12. Rhys-Davids and Stede (1992). On *etthipol,* see the *Khmer Dictionary* (1967:1796); and Headley et al. (1977:1451). See also Tambiah (1976, 1985).

13. *Khmer Dictionary* (1967:1744); Headley et al. (1977:1403). On *amnach,* see the *Khmer Dictionary* (1967:1878); and Headley et al. (1977:1438).

14. The former Cambodian minister of justice, Chem Snguon, described the Cambodian judicial process as follows: "The judge prepares his decision before

the trial opens. Before the case opens, he already has a model. During the trial, issues may be brought up that modify the judge's decision. If the responses to questioning are slightly different than expected, the judge will modify the decision for ten or fifteen minutes at the end of the trial. If the events during the trial are very different, he must suspend the trial until a later date. At that time, he will look at additional evidence and make a decision. Judges always make a map of their decision after looking at the [pre-trial] evidence" (Pape 1997:13). Such Cambodian judiciary practices are based on the Vietnamese model of socialist law in which, as Fernando and Wickremasinghe (1997) argue in a response to Snguon's comments, the trial presentation of evidence is not emphasized and the courts lack independence from the executive branch of government.

15. Grainger (1995:3).

16. Rizzi and Chea Sotheacheath (1995:1).

17. At that time, a *Phnom Penh Post* article described Suen as having "a fearsome reputation for violence, but also of generosity [to his followers] and loyalty [to his superiors]. Standing only about 160 cm tall, he is tattooed from the ears down and wears amulets said to be priceless for [their] power. 'He eats glass and can see everything around him,' swore an acquaintance who declined to be named. 'With weaker magic, bullets go around people. With him the guns jam' " (Scroggins 1998:3). Despite losing his official rank and guns, Suen continued to live in a luxurious new villa in Kompong Cham that "sports meticulously manicured gardens, artificial waterfalls and two tigers from Rattanakiri. He has two 1998-model cars—a 500 series Mercedes and a Lexus Land Cruiser—and a two-hundred-horsepower speedboat that purportedly reaches Phnom Penh in less than fifty minutes. He exhibits fierce loyalty to the [prime minister], generally wearing a Hun Sen lapel pin and always wearing a massive five-*damleng* gold bracelet engraved with '7 January 1979—Hun Sen' " (ibid). When I returned to Cambodia in the summer of 2000, however, I heard that Suen was trying to sell his house because of gambling debts.

18. Ang (1986:157f.); Ledgerwood (1990a:54f.). See also Marcucci (1986:155f.).

19. Ledgerwood (1990a:61); see also Ebihara (1968).

20. Headley et al. (1977:658). See also *Khmer Dictionary* (1967:795). For an interesting description of the skilled efficacy of Cambodian dancers, see Shapiro (1994).

21. Headley et al. (1977:23).

22. Ledgerwood (1990a).

23. On karma and merit, see Keyes (1983); Keyes and Daniel (1983); Hanks (1962); Spiro (1982).

24. Reynolds (1972).

25. On "signs of power," see Anderson (1990) and Tambiah (1985). On Cambodian regalia, see Chandler (1996); and Heine-Geldern (1942).

26. See Ebihara (1968:200).

27. See also Tannenbaum (1995).

28. See Chandler (1996); Mabbett and Chandler (1995); and Martel (1975) on this Cambodian distinction between the "wild" forest/jungle *(brei)* and "civilized" domesticated lands *(srok)*.

29. See Smith-Hefner (1999:56). On religious hierarchical registers, see Marston (1997). See also Tannenbaum (1995).

30. The following general description of Southeast Asian patron-client ties draws on the important work of Hanks (1964, 1975) and Scott (1977). For descriptions of contemporary Cambodian and Khmer American patronage practices, see: Ashley (1998); Breckon (1999); French (1994); Hughes (2003); Ledgerwood (1990a, 1990b); Ledgerwood and Vijghen (2002); Marston (1997); Peang-Meth (1991); Shapiro (1994); and Thion (1993). John Marston (1997) has recently emphasized that Cambodian patronage ties diverge somewhat from Scott's model because they often involve more negotiation and flux. Ledgerwood and Vijghen (2002) have made a similar point about village-level patronage ties in contemporary Cambodia, noting the ways in which these ties are negotiated, relatively flexible, frequently kinship-centered, and often linked to moral authority.

31. Scott (1977:127). See also Anderson (1990); Hanks (1962, 1975).

32. See Marston (1997:182f.) for an analysis of *khsae royeak* and other patronage terms as depicted in Cambodian satirical cartoons.

33. Hinton (1997, 2000).

34. Weber (1964). As Weber readily notes, legal, traditional, and charismatic authority are ideal types: few pure cases can be found in the world and many mixed systems of authority exist or have existed — as illustrated by the fact that Cambodian patronage networks often operate in the context of an institutional bureaucracy (see also Eames 1997 for a Nigerian analog).

35. Scott (1977:126).

36. This Cambodian cultural idiom bears similarity to the ontology of encompassment that Bruce Kapferer (1988) has argued is at the root of much Sinhalese Buddhist nationalist discourse. Kapferer's analysis has served as an inspiration for parts of my discussion of hierarchical encompassment.

37. Skidmore (1997).

38. See Ledgerwood (1996).

39. Samreth Sopha and Moorthy (1998:5).

40. Chandler (2000:59, 75). See also Mouth (n.d.b:2).

41. Ebihara (1968). See also Smith-Hefner (1999).

42. See Headley et al. (1977); *Khmer Dictionary* (1967).

43. Ledgerwood (1992:117). See also Ledgerwood (1996). The Khmer gender ideal of maternal nurturance stands in contrast to common male gender norms, which stress strength, potency, and the accumulation of secular wealth and prestige (Ledgerwood 1990a, 1992, 1996). See also Keyes (1984, 1995); Kirsch (1985); Mulder (1994).

44. On the positive valences of relationships of personal dependency and for an interesting description of how *peung* and *ang* are used in Cambodian political satire, see Marston (1997:206). The positive connotations of personal dependency among Cambodians contrasts with the ideals of self-reliance and independence that tend to be strongly emphasized in the United States.

45. Headley et al. (1977:760). See also *Khmer Dictionary* (1967:930); and Ledgerwood (1990a:289).

46. Scott (1977). See also Eisenstadt and Roniger (1984); Roniger (1990).

47. See also Marston (1996, 1997).

48. Marston (1997:70). On the unequal and instrumental dimensions of patronage, see Eisenstadt and Roniger (1984); Roniger (1990); Scott (1977).

49. See also Ayres (2000:174).

50. On the negotiation and fluidity of patronage ties, see Hanks (1962, 1975); Marston (1997).

51. See Maha Ghosananda (1992); Phra Anuman Rajadhon (1995); Spiro (1982); Tannenbaum (1995).

52. See Maha Ghosananda (1992:44). See also Hansen (1999); Phra Prayudh Payutto (1995); Reynolds (1985).

53. Maha Ghosananda (1992:45).

54. See Keyes (1983); Phra Prayudh Payutto (1995); Spiro (1982).

55. Ledgerwood (1998a); Reynolds (1985); Reynolds and Clifford (1980); Tambiah (1976).

56. Anderson (1990); Chandler (1996, 2000); Collins (1998); Keyes (1977, 1995).

57. Fisher-Nguyen (1994:96).

58. Fisher-Nguyen (1994:96–100).

59. See Ebihara (1968:186). See also Hanks (1962, 1975); Marston (1997).

60. Hanks (1962:1255); Marston (1997:73, 81); Roniger (1990:192).

61. Ebihara (1968, 1986); Ledgerwood (1995).

62. See Thion (1993).

63. For a discussion of ancient and more contemporary examples of how Cambodians political dynamics are often characterized by suspicion, see Hinton (2000).

CHAPTER 3

1. Scott (1998).

2. Rhys Davids and Stede (1992:6); Headley (1977:1314). The definition of *ângkar* given below is from the *Khmer Dictionary* (1967:1601). On the term *Ângkar,* see also Marston (1994, 2002); and Ponchaud (1978).

3. Criddle and Mam (1987:153).

4. Haing Ngor (1987:199). On Ângkar's co-opting of some aspects of Buddhism, see Ponchaud (1989).

5. Ponchaud (1989).

6. See Locard (1996). On the banning of Buddhism during DK, see Boua (1991); Ebihara (1990); Keyes (1994); Ponchaud (1989).

7. See Locard (1996); Ponchaud (1978, 1989).

8. Criddle and Mam (1987:70–1).

9. For an interesting analysis of this term, see Marston (1994:106). See also Locard (1996:88).

10. Marston (1994:108–9). On the symbolism of the Bayon, see Chandler (2000); Coedès (1969); Jessup and Zephir (1997); Mabbett and Chandler (1995).

11. See Mabbett and Chandler (1995:208).

12. Locard (1996); Picq (1989); Ponchaud (1989).

13. Ebihara (1990, 1993).

14. See Ebihara (1990); Ponchaud (1989).

15. Cited in Marston (1994:110). See also Kiernan (1996:247) and S. Shapiro (1996:2).

16. Cited in Picq (1989:60).

17. Pol Pot (1977:48-9).

18. Picq (1989:122).

19. Luong Ung (2000:129-30, 132).

20. See Chandler (1999b:33f.).

21. See, for example, Haing Ngor (1987:82).

22. See Chandler (1999a:40; 1999b:148f.). See also Vann Nath (1998) on the production of busts and paintings of Pol Pot at Tuol Sleng; and Picq (1989) on how a cult of personality began to form around Ieng Sary within the Foreign Ministry.

23. See also David Ashley's interview with Nath, cited in Chandler (1999b:149-50), and Vann Nath (1998:82, 86).

24. Kamm (1998:137).

25. Chandler (1991, 1999b); Kiernan (1996). See also Picq (1989).

26. Chandler (1991, 1999a, 1999b); Kiernan (1985a, 1996). The following description of the Khmer Rouge purges draws on the important work of Chandler and Kiernan, as well as that of other scholars, such as Becker (1998); Burgler (1990); Etcheson (1984); Heder (1997); Jackson (1989c); Thion (1993); Vickery (1984).

27. See Becker (1998); Burgler (1990); Kiernan (1985a).

28. On the 1974 purge of the faction led by Prasith, an ethnic Thai who had fought against French colonialism and at the time was ranked seventh in the CPK Central Committee, see Kiernan (1996:68f.).

29. Becker (1998); Burgler (1990); Chandler (1991, 1999a, 1999b); Kiernan (1996).

30. On Khmer Rouge factions, see Burgler (1990); Chandler (1999a); Etcheson (1984); Kiernan (1996); Stuart-Fox (1985); Vickery (1984). On the fluidity of Khmer Rouge factions and the difficulty of characterizing them, see Burgler (1990); Heder (1997).

31. See Kiernan (1993:13-15). Even within the Standing Committee, zone secretaries Nhem Ros and Sao Phim resided far from Phnom Penh and were often unable to attend CPK Standing Committee meetings, thereby significantly reducing their influence on policy made by the Party Center (see Kiernan 1996:324).

32. Burgler (1990:100).

33. Non Suon confession, cited in Kiernan (1985a:418).

34. Democratic Kampuchea (1978:75). The Khmer Rouge later claimed that a Northern Zone fighter had tried but failed to assassinate Pol Pot and his close associates during this ceremony (ibid). On the formation of the Revolutionary Army, see Becker (1998:175); Kiernan (1996:94); Kiernan and Boua (1982:223f.).

35. "Report of Activities," in Chandler, Kiernan, and Boua (1988:208, 210).

36. Kiernan (1996:323).

37. Burgler (1990); Kiernan (1985a, 1996); Vickery (1984).

38. Picq (1989:66, 90).

39. "Summary of the Results of the 1976 Study Session," in Chandler, Kiernan, and Boua (1988:176). On "sibling-ism" in the DK political hierarchy, see Kiernan (1996); Martin (1994:206f.); Picq (1989); Thion (1993:129f.).

40. See Chandler (1999a:46–47); Kiernan (1996:316–19).

41. "Decisions," in Chandler, Kiernan, and Boua (1988:3). See also Chandler (1999a:51).

42. On the Phnom Penh explosions and subsequent arrest of Chan Chakrei, see Chandler (1999a:46, 52f.); Jackson (1989c:299); Kiernan (1996:321f.).

43. Chandler (1999a:89). On Tuol Sleng, see also Barnett, Kiernan, and Boua (1980); Hawk (1986); Heder (1997); Kiernan (1996).

44. Chakrei confession, CMR 11.7; Chandler (1999a:52–3). On the arrests of Chakrei's faction and the "rubber plantation network," see Chandler (1999a:52f.); De Nike, Quigley, and Robinson (2000:397); Kiernan (1996:322f.).

45. CMR 99.13. "The Last Plan" is translated in Jackson (1989c:299–314). See also Chandler (1999a:22).

46. Jackson (1989c:300).

47. "Abbreviated Lesson on the History of the Kampuchean Revolutionary Movement Led by the Communist Party of Kampuchea," in Chandler, Kiernan, and Boua (1988:219).

48. *Revolutionary Flags,* translated in Chandler (1996:217). On the dispute over the birthdate of the party and the purge of the party veterans, see Burgler (1990:111); Chandler (1996:215f., 1999a:59f., 1999b:122–23); Kiernan (1985a:364–68, 1996:350f.).

49. Thayer (1997b:16).

50. Heder (1991:8).

51. CMR 12.28, translated in Chandler (1999a:60). On the arrest of Nuon Suon's string, see Kiernan (1996:335).

52. Becker (1998:236).

53. "Planning the Past: The Forced Confessions of Hu Nim" (hereafter "Hu Nim Confession"), in Chandler, Kiernan, Boua (1988:290). See also Burgler (1990:120f.); Kiernan (1985a:328, 416).

54. "Summary of the Results of the 1976 Study Session," in Chandler, Kiernan, and Boua (1988:168f.).

55. See Chandler (1999a:50, 107).

56. The term *schismogenesis* is from Bateson (1958, 1972), who argues that when two groups (or individuals) interact over time, their given behavioral norms will become progressively differentiated in either symmetrical or complementary fashion. Symmetrical differentiation consists of a scenario in which members of a group respond to the behavior of another group in a like manner (for example, increasing armament in the nuclear arms war). Complementary differentiation occurs when the members of a group respond in an opposite manner to the actions of another group (for example, submission in response to assertiveness in feudalism). If these two types of social relations are not culturally restrained, differentiation will increase to the point that hostility breaks out or the system collapses. Bateson calls the cycle of progressive differentiation "schismogenesis."

57. Chandler (1999a:41, 56). See also Kiernan (1985b); Schram (1976:301f.).

58. "Sharpen the Consciousness of the Proletarian Class to Be As Keen and Strong As Possible" (hereafter "Sharpen the Consciousness"), in Jackson (1989c:269f.). I would like to thank Youk Chhang and the staff at DC-Cam for providing me with a copy of the original text of this document.

59. "Sharpen the Consciousness," in Jackson (1989c:288).

60. Mouth (n.d.a). See also Jatava (1968).

61. "Sharpen the Consciousness," in Jackson (1989c:287).

62. Ibid:288.

63. Ibid:289.

64. From a Tuol Sleng cadre notebook, cited in Mouth (n.d.a:8).

65. This and the quotations below are taken from "Sharpen the Consciousness," in Jackson (1989c:279, 280).

66. Ibid:287.

67. Kiernan (1996:225). See also Chandler (1999a:61).

68. Picq (1989:97–98).

69. "Report of Activities," in Chandler, Kiernan, and Boua (1988:183–4). For an analysis of the full text, see Chandler (1996).

70. "Report of Activities," in Chandler, Kiernan, and Boua (1988:185, 204).

71. Ibid:203, 211.

72. Ibid:208.

73. Burgler (1990:20f.); Chandler (1999a:61f.); Etcheson (1984:164f.); Heder (1997:126); Kiernan (1996:352); Stuart-Fox (1985). "The Last Plan" refers to this group as "the intellectuals," which included CIA operatives who "pretended to be progressive and infiltrated the revolution to gather information" (Jackson 1989c:302).

74. "The Last Plan," in Jackson (1989c:300–1).

75. Chandler (1999a:61f., 180n59); and DC-Cam documents J00918–J00921. See also Kiernan (1996:314, 337f.).

76. "The Last Plan," in Jackson (1989c:307). "Hu Nim confession," in Chandler, Kiernan, and Boua (1988:266, 293f.).

77. "Hu Nim confession," in Chandler, Kiernan, and Boua (1988:244f.).

78. Ibid:252.

79. "Hu Nim confession," in Chandler, Kiernan, and Boua (1988:281).

80. See "Hu Nim Confession," in Chandler, Kiernan, and Boua (1988:281).

81. Kiernan (1996:338); Vickery (1984:130).

82. "Hu Nim Confession," in Chandler, Kiernan, and Boua (1988:316).

83. Kiernan (1996:339, 350). See also Chandler (1999a:61f.); De Nike, Quigley, and Robinson (2000:297f.).

84. Sreng confession, Tuol Sleng confession C-120 and DC-Cam files.

85. Sbauv Him confession (CMR 140.12), translated by Steven Heder and quoted in Chandler (1999a:79).

86. Chandler (1999a:62).

87. De Nike, Quigley, and Robinson (2000:402); Kiernan (1996:338).

88. De Nike, Quigley, and Robinson (2000:410).

89. Criddle and Mam (1987:153–54).

90. Haing Ngor (1987:289).

91. Criddle and Mam (1987:151).

92. Kiernan (1996:464).

93. The following material on Reap (Re Sim) is drawn from his Tuol Sleng confession, CMR 126.20.

94. Chandler (1999a:24). Pon's summary does not always parallel Reap's confession. My account tends to follow the timeline of Pon's summary and the details from Reap's confession.

95. See Becker (1998) on Bou Phat.

96. Reap's confession constructs this incident to associate the Northern Zone network with the Vietnamese by claiming that Sey ordered the executions: "Sey instructed me to clean up these cadres because he was afraid they would reveal something since this group knew about our CIA network. . . . So I cleaned up all of them, working each night until the entire group was gone and could no longer reply." It seems more likely that Pauk simply ordered Reap to execute them.

97. Kha, one of Reap's subordinates, who Khel told me was in charge of the batallion that executed people at Phnom Bros, indirectly referenced the executions at Phnom Bros in his Tuol Sleng confession (confession #P-103, DC-Cam). In addition to detailing how Kha betrayed the revolution by destroying the rice crop, conspiring with local bandits, and plotting against the Party Center, the interrogator's summary of Kha's confession asserts that in July 1977, "when Ângkar ordered them to sweep clean *(boas somat)* the group of April 17 people, including former [Lon Nol] soldiers, subdistrict chiefs, and police officers, Kha and the rest of his clique *(bâk puok)* . . . took the opportunity to destroy the Party line. They smashed thirty families of 'old/base people' from Region 41 who had previously been workers." Here mass murder is only deemed worthy of mention to demonstrate the supposed betrayal of a suspect cadre.

98. See also Chandler (1999a:195n99).

99. DC-Cam document K08273 TSL.

100. Becker (1998:236).

101. "Report of the Activities," in Chandler, Kiernan, and Boua (1988:208).

102. "Hu Nim Confession," in Chandler, Kiernan, and Boua (1988:290, 292, 293).

103. On the purge of the Northwestern Zone, see Becker (1998:233f.); Carney (1989b:105–7); Chandler (1999a:68–70); De Nike, Quigley, and Robinson (2000:401–2); Kiernan (1996:236f., 416f.).

104. See, for example, Chandler (1999a:70).

105. Kiernan (1996:416–23). On the Western Zone purge, see also Chandler (1999a:73); De Nike, Quigley, and Robinson (2000:399); Kiernan (1996:345–48, 390–92).

106. Carney (1989b:86); Kiernan (1996:374).

107. Pol Pot (1977:57).

108. Kiernan (1996). See also Chandler (1999a:72f.); De Nike, Quigley, and Robinson (2000:403); Heder (1997).

109. Kiernan (1996:404).

110. Stuart-Fox (1985:142, 145).

111. On Von Vet's arrest and the final DK purges, see Chandler (1999a:74f.). See also Becker (1998:325); Chandler (1991:298); and Kiernan (1996:437).

PART 2 PREAMBLE

1. Vann Nath (1998:ix). The following account of Vann Nath's experiences is based on interviews I conducted with him in 1995 and 2000, an article about Vann Nath that appeared in the Nov. 2–8, 1992 issue of the *Cambodia Times,* and a rough draft and the published version of Vann Nath's autobiography (Vann Nath 1998).

2. Vann Nath (1998:46).

3. Vann Nath (1998:53, 59, 65).

4. Vann Nath (1998:107).

5. What follows is based on a document Ung Pech wrote during the time he served as the director of the Tuol Sleng Museum of Genocidal Crimes. (After DK, the PRK government turned Tuol into a museum.) While it is possible that some of the details have been exaggerated for anti–Khmer Rouge propaganda purposes, I have tried only to use sections that agree with other survivor testimony and academic scholarship. Ung Pech passed away in late 1996. On the history and politics of memory and representation at the Tuol Sleng museum, see Chandler (1999a); and Ledgerwood (1997).

6. Chandler (1995:22); see also Chandler (1999a); and Hawk (1986:27).

7. Chandler (1999a:130).

8. Smith (1992:7). Like Vann Nath, Im Chan, a former sculptor, was spared because his artistic skills were of use to Duch.

CHAPTER 4

1. CMR 105.4, translated in Chandler (1999a:111). The term "spaces of death" used below is from Taussig (1987).

2. See Ebihara (1968, 1986); Ehrman (1972); Headley et al. (1977); Huffman (1970); Marston (1997).

3. Ehrman (1972:41); Headley et al. (1977:978); *Khmer Dictionary* (1967:1196); Marston (1997:130–31); Pou (1979). On the etymology of *vea,* see Marston (1997:130); Pou (1979).

4. Ehrman (1972:97).

5. Marston (1997:117f.).

6. Marston (1997:117f.). On ordinary and formal registers, see Ehrman (1972).

7. On Khmer kinship, see Ebihara (1968, 1986).

8. *Khmer Dictionary* (1967:169). See also Headley et al. (1977:132).

9. The following etymology and definition of *hierarchy* are based on the *Oxford English Dictionary* (1971:272). See also Dumont (1970); Parish (1996); Williams (1985).

10. *Khmer Dictionary* (1967:417); Headley et al. (1977:356). On Khmer terms related to hierarchy and ranked difference, see *Khmer Dictionary* (1967); Headley et al. (1977).

11. By emphasizing the importance of hierarchy in the Khmer social order, I do not want to construct an orientalizing image of a Cambodian as a *homo hierarchicus* that is the binary opposite of a *homo aequalis* from "the West"

(Dumont 1980; for critiques of Dumont's unidimensional construction of *homo hierarchicus,* see Marriot 1990; Parish 1996). In Cambodia, like the United States and places throughout the world, multiple, sometimes contradictory cultural models for social behavior exist and are variably in play as people move through disparate fields of action. Therefore, in some contexts of Cambodian social life, it is not surprising that we find more egalitarian models foregrounded (Ebihara 1968:187–215).

12. Marston (1997).
13. Hanks (1962); Kirsch (1981).
14. Johnson (1987:xiv).
15. See Shore (1996).
16. For a detailed description of *thvay bângkum,* see Marston (1997:83f.).
17. See Marston (1997:83f.).
18. See Chandler (1999a).
19. Connerton (1989:74).
20. "Sharpen the Consciousness," in Jackson (1989c:289).
21. Carney (1977); Marston (1985, 1997); Marston and Duong (1988); Ponchaud (1978).
22. Marston (1997).
23. Someth May (1986:111).
24. See Marston (1997).
25. Picq (1984:352; 1989:35). See also Marston (1997).
26. Picq (1989:36).
27. Ebihara (1990); Marston (1985, 1997); Picq (1989); Ponchaud (1989).
28. Haing Ngor (1987:190).
29. CMR 187.9; Chandler (1999a:17–18).
30. Vann Nath (1998:49).
31. Haing Ngor (1987:190).
32. See Ebihara (1968); Ledgerwood (1990a, 1996); Smith-Hefner (1999).
33. See Haing Ngor (1987:140, 83); Shapiro (1994:152f., 2002); Ledgerwood (1990a:191f.).
34. See Meisner (1982); Lifton (1989). For an analysis of how the DK regime selectively combined aspects of Marxist-Leninism, Stalinism, and Maoism in the 1976 special issue of *Revolutionary Flags,* see Kiernan (1985b).
35. "Sharpen the Consciousness," in Jackson (1989c:287). This metaphor of sharpening was sometimes used to describe the process of building a proper revolutionary consciousness on the local level. Pin Yathay recalled, "The Khmer Rouge compared us to knives that had to be sharpened regularly. Our political consciousness had to be honed repeatedly by the grindstone of political education. Political conscience and ideological determination, that was all we needed" (1987:171).
36. "Sharpen the Consciousness," in Jackson (1989c:287).
37. *Revolutionary Young Men and Women,* October 1976, p. 1.
38. See Headley et al. (1977:1420); *Khmer Dictionary* (1967:1778); Phra Prayudh Payutto (1995:59); Rhys Davids and Stede (1992:107). I would like to thank Steve Collins, Anne Hansen, and Sophea Mouth for their insights about the meaning of this term.

39. Headley et al. (1977:1059); *Khmer Dictionary* (1967:1283); Phra Prayudh Payutto (1995:254f.); Rhys Davids and Stede (1992:672).

40. Phra Prayudh Payutto (1995:261).

41. See Jackson (1989c:269f.).

42. This and the two following quotations are taken from Jackson (1989c:273–74).

43. See Ponchaud (1978:114, 1989); Criddle and Mam (1987:94).

44. "Pay Attention to Pushing the Work of Building Party and People's Collective Strength Even Stronger," *Revolutionary Flags,* March 1978, in Jackson (1989c:295).

45. Haing Ngor (1987:139).

46. This text was translated by the Cambodia Genocide Program (1998) and is available at: http://www.yale.edu/cgp/translate/index.htm.

47. See, for example, Ly Y (2000:25–27).

48. See Chandler (1999a:89f.); Kiernan (1997:xii). A version of the questionnaire, which I draw on below, is translated on the website of Yale University's Cambodian Genocide Program (http://www.yale.edu/cgp/readings/readings.htm).

49. "Sharpen the Consciousness," in Jackson (1989c: 284). See also Summers (1987:14–15).

50. This and the other quotes in this paragraph are from "Sharpen the Consciousness," in Jackson (1989c: 283–84).

51. Marston (1994:113).

52. "Sharpen the Consciousness," in Jackson (1989c:280). The following three quotations from the article are in Jackson (1989c:286–86, 278, 280).

53. "Sharpen the Consciousness," in Jackson (1989c:276). The following quotations from the article are in Jackson (1989c:282).

54. "Sharpen the Consciousness," in Jackson (1989c:288).

55. On the decimation of Cambodia's Cham population, see Kiernan (1988, 1996); Heder and Tittemore (2001:34); Ysa Osman (2002).

56. For a debate over the extent to which the DK regime manifested Marxist-Leninist or racist tendencies, see Kiernan (1996); Heder (1997); Heder and Tittemore (2001).

57. Cited in Kiernan (1996:280).

58. Kiernan (1996).

59. De Nike, Quigley, and Robinson (2000:318). See also Kiernan (1996:275).

CHAPTER 5

1. FBIS 1978:H3. A roughly similar version of the text had been published in the July 1977 edition of *Revolutionary Flags.*

2. Appadurai (1998).

3. See Appadurai (1998); Feldman (1991); Malkki (1995); Taylor (1999); Taussig (1987).

4. Hinton (1998c:14); Koenigsberg (1975).

5. Summers (1987:14–15). According to Summers, the DK regime further divided the peasant class into mid-level middle peasants (landowners hiring laborers to do 20–60 percent of their farming work), lower-level middle peasants

(subsistence smallholders with enough to eat), and poor peasants (those lacking the means of production, having to work the land of others, and periodically without enough to eat). The working class, in turn, was divided into independent laborers (construction workers, pedicab drivers, plumbers), industrial workers (those working in rubber plantations, shipyards, factories), and party workers (those working in mobile brigades, the revolutionary army, or the revolutionary government).

6. Jackson (1989c:272, 284).

7. *American Heritage Dictionary* (1976:654); Gilroy (1997); Woodward (1997).

8. Chandler (1996, 2000); Edwards (1996). See also Heder and Ledgerwood (1996b); Ledgerwood (1998a).

9. Edwards (1996).

10. Edwards (1996:54).

11. See Chanda (1986:47f.); Chandler (2000:94, 123f.).

12. Democratic Kampuchea (1978:9).

13. See also Ebihara (1968:580–81).

14. Becker (1998); Kamm (1998).

15. See Taylor (1999) for a somewhat parallel explanation of why the bodies of Tutsis were thrown into Rwanda's rivers.

16. Kiernan (1996:296).

17. Edwards (1996); Heder and Ledgerwood (1996b); Jordens (1996).

18. Jordens (1996:139).

19. See Chandler (2000); Kiernan (1996); Morris (1999).

20. Democratic Kampuchea (1978:73). On the 1975 deportations of the ethnic Vietnamese, see Chanda (1986:16); Kiernan (1996:107f., 296f.).

21. Kiernan (1996:296f.). See also Becker (1998:242f.).

22. "About the Standpoint of Politics, Consciousness, and Organization in the Great Revolutionary Movement," *Revolutionary Flags,* June 1977, pp. 11–12.

23. Picq (1989:107–8).

24. Pin Yathay (1987:170–71).

25. Criddle and Mam (1987:90–91).

26. Locard (1996:158). Sophea Mouth (personal communication) told me that the Khmer Rouge would sometimes warn people that their "consciousness wasn't good" *(sâtiarâmma min l'a)*: "In Buddhism, *sâtiarâmma* means to be mindful of an object, such as an object of meditation, whether it's the self, feeling, or other external objects. The Khmer Rouge used the term to mean concentrating one's attention on the revolutionary path. If one was distracted, they would say, 'Your consciousness is not good,' meaning that you did not have good mental concentration on this path. The term suggested having impure thought as well."

27. For a discussion of this and other parallels between the function and production of confessions and psychodynamic processes, see Chandler (1999a:107–8).

28. See Vann Nath (1998:38–40).

29. On the structure, routines, and prison population of Tuol Sleng, see Chandler (1999a:35f.); Vann Nath (1998); Youk Chhang and Phat Kosal (n.d.).

30. Turner (1967); Gennep (1960).

31. Chandler (1999a:36).

32. Chandler, Kiernan, and Boua (1988:183–84).

33. CMR 105.4, Oum Chhan; see Chandler (1999a:131f.).

34. For a detailed description of this torture, see Chandler (1999a:132–34).

35. Both passages are from CMR 99.7, translated in Chandler (1999a:133).

36. Pol Pot (1977:58).

37. CMR 99.7, translated in Chandler (1999a:133).

38. Arendt (1977).

39. DC-Cam document K08359. I would like to thank Youk Chhang and Sue Cook for helping me find documentation on Vaen Kheuan.

40. Chandler (1999a:34); Meng-Try Ea and Sorya Sim (2001).

41. Chandler (1999a:30); Meng-Try Ea and Sorya Sim (2001:35).

42. Chandler (1999a); Meng-Try Ea and Sorya Sim (2001).

43. Hawk (n.d.). See also Chandler (1999a:28–29); Meng-Try Ea and Sorya Sim (2001:28).

44. Meng-Try Ea and Sorya Sim (2001).

45. Chandler (1999a:26).

46. DC-Cam document D06936, translated in Chandler (1999a:82); Meng-Try Ea and Sorya Sim (2001:31).

47. DC-Cam document D06936, translated in Hawk (n.d.). The quotation below is from page 22 of David Chandler's notes on S-21, hereafter referred to as "Chandler notes." I appreciate his generosity in making them available to me.

48. Vann Nath (1998:47, 48).

49. Youk Chhang and Phat Kosal (n.d.). See also Hawk (n.d.).

50. See the extensive DC-Cam holdings on Sreng and CMR 12.25.

51. The following quotes from Siet Chhe are from CMR 138.11, translated by Richard Arant and David Chandler, quoted in Chandler (1999a:84–85).

52. See also Haing Ngor (1987:215f., 239f., 300f.); Vann Nath (1998:27f.).

53. Chandler (1999a:82).

54. DC-Cam document D06936, translated in Hawk (n.d.) and Chandler notes (23).

55. CMR 69.30, translated in Chandler (1999a:129) and Hawk (n.d.).

56. DC-Cam document K08359; Chandler (1999a); Chandler notes (4, 15); Hawk (n.d.).

57. CMR 3.24. See also Hawk (n.d.); Chandler notes (9).

58. Browning (1992); Dyer (1985); Haritos-Fatouros (1988). See also Baumeister (1997); Lifton (1986); Staub (1989); Suedfeld (1990); Waller (2002).

59. See Hinton (1996).

60. Bandura (1986); Kelman and Hamilton (1989). See also Baumeister (1997); Festinger (1957); Milgram (1974); Staub (1989); Waller (2002); Zimbardo et al. (1974).

61. Staub (1989). See also Darley (1992).

62. DC-Cam document D24034, translated in Chandler (1999a:152).

63. On "disciplines" of torture, see Foucault (1979); Rejali (1993).

64. DC-Cam document D06936, translated in Hawk (n.d.).

65. See Chandler (1999a:87f.); Meng-Try Ea and Sorya Sim (2001:21f.).

66. Meng-Try Ea and Sorya Sim (2001:25).

67. CMR 69.30, translated in Chandler (1999a:27).

68. Arendt (1968).

69. Kierkegaard (1941); May (1977). See also Becker (1973); Tillich (1952). On the definition and psychology of anxiety, see Freud (1964); Lazarus (1991); Öhman (2000).

70. Headley et al. (1977:5, 105, 681); *Khmer Buddhist Dictionary* (1967: 28, 138, 592, 828).

71. See Averill (1988); Lazarus (1991); Öhman (2000). There is clearly cultural variation in the form, experience, and meaning of such emotions; for a discussion of the interaction between biological and environmental factors in generating the emotions, see A. Hinton (1999).

72. Hinton, Khin Um, and Phalnarith Ba (2001a, 2001b). See also Marcucci (1986).

73. Neisser (1988).

74. Fromm (1941).

75. For clinical evidence that supports this notion of constriction, see Beck (1999:153).

76. See Locard (1996), Ponchaud (1978), and numerous DK radio broadcasts.

77. Quoted in Meng-Try Ea and Sorya Sim (2001:24).

78. On narcissism and narcissistic rage, see Fromm (1973); Kohut (1972). See also W. L. Hinton (2001a, 2001b); Kernberg (1975); Morrison (1986).

79. Turner (1967:27f.)

80. Turner (1967:28).

81. Turner (1967:28).

82. Klein (1975); Grotstein (1985). See also Born (1998); Hinschelwood (1989); Robben and Suárez-Orozco (2000). Following Grotstein (1985), I will use *projection* and *projective identification* interchangeably.

83. On mastery and torture, see Améry (1980); Scarry (1985). On sadism, violence, and the self, see Fromm (1941, 1973).

84. See also Varela, Thompson, and Rosch (1991).

85. On the five aggregates, see Boisvert (1995); Phra Prayudh Payutto (1995); Varella, Thompson, and Rosch (1991).

86. See Phra Prayudh Payutto (1995:93f.).

CHAPTER 6

1. Headley et al. (1977:748); *Khmer Dictionary* (1967:917–20).

2. Goffman (1967:5) defines a "line" as "a pattern of verbal and nonverbal acts by which [a person] expresses his view of the situation and through this his evaluation of the participants, especially himself." He goes on to define "face" as "the positive social value a person effectively claims for himself by the line others assume he has taken during a particular contact. Face is an image of self delineated in terms of approved social attributes."

3. See Schoenhals (1993) for a Chinese analog.

4. See Ebihara (1968).

5. Kipnis (1995).
6. See Shweder et al. (1997); Miller (1997).
7. Darwin (1965); Ekman (1973).
8. See Cole (1998).
9. Headley et al (1977:101, 1435); *Khmer Dictionary* (1967:136, 1858).
10. On the evolutionary basis of shame, see Fessler (1999). On the development of shame, see Lewis (1992a, 1992b); W. L. Hinton (1999).
11. Hinton, Khin Um, and Phalnarith Ba (2001a, 2001b). See also Eisenbruch (1992); Marcucci (1994).
12. Lebra (1976).
13. Moeun Chhean Nariddh (1995:17).
14. Goffman (1967:11).
15. Headley et al. (1977:36).
16. *Khmer Dictionary* (1967:63).
17. *Oxford English Dictionary* (1989:367).
18. On socialization practices that contribute to the ontological resonance of face and honor, see Ebihara (1968); Hinton (1998b); Smith-Hefner (1999).
19. "Sharpen the Consciousness," in Jackson (1989c:285).
20. Picq (1989). See also Becker (1998:172); Martin (1994:205).
21. See, for example, Picq (1989:14); Pin Yathay (1987:63).
22. "Strengthening the Stand of True Loyalty for the Party, the Revolution, ·and the People All the Time," in *Revolutionary Young Men and Women,* May · 1977, pp. 18–30. I would like to thank Youk Chhang and DC-CAM for providing me with a copy of this document.
23. Headley et al. (1977:949); *Khmer Dictionary* (1968:1163).
24. The word *chett* refers to the psychological "heart," not the physical organ (in Khmer, *beh daung*). Headley et al. define *chett* as "feeling, heart (as the seat of emotion); will(power); intention; thought, opinion, mind" (1977:178). *Chett* is derived from the Pali word *citta,* which means "the heart (psychologically) . . . the centre & focus of man's emotional nature as well as that intellectual element which inheres in & accompanies its manifestations; i. e. thought . . . The meaning of citta is best understood when explaining it by expressions familiar to us, as: with all my heart; heart and soul; I have no heart to do it . . . all of which emphasize the emotional & conative *[sic]* side or "thought" more than its mental and rational side. . . . It may therefore be rendered by intention, impulse, design; mood, disposition, state of mind, reaction to impressions" (Rhys Davids and Stede 1992:266). Finally, the *Khmer Dictionary* states that *chett* "is that which is used for accumulating sensory impressions, for thinking, or for animating consciousness" (1967:220). All of these definitions of *chett* convey the sense of the psychological "heart," an animating and reactive state of mind that results in a feeling, an impulse, or a disposition to act. See also Phra Prayudh Payutto (1995).
25. Chandler (1982); Ponchaud (1989). Teap noted that cadres were given aliases, further detaching them from their victims.
26. See also Chandler (1999a:33).
27. See Chandler (1991); Jackson (1989a).
28. See Becker (1998:207).

29. DeVos (1973).
30. Haing Ngor (1987:229).
31. See, for example, Picq (1989:101f.); Pin Yathay (1987:114); Someth May (1986:205).
32. CMR 3.24. See also Chandler (1999a:95, 131); Hawk (n.d.).
33. Tuol Sleng Confession M226.
34. DC-Cam document D24034.

CONCLUSION

1. De Nike, Quigley, and Robinson (2000: 450). See also Burchett (1981:88); People's Revolutionary Tribunal (1988:58–9).
2. Bou Saroeun (2001:2). See also Pauk's autobiography (Phnom Penh Post Staff 2002:8–9). For a discussion of evidence contradicting Pauk's denials, see Heder and Tittemore (2001).
3. *Oxford English Dictionary* (1989:1962). See also *American Heritage Dictionary* (1976:904).
4. *Oxford English Dictionary* (1989:1962).
5. Headley et al. (1977). *Khmer Dictionary* (1967). I would also like to thank Sophea Mouth (personal communication) for his comments on obedience in Cambodia.
6. Milgram (1974).
7. Milgram (1974:6).
8. Kuper (1981).
9. Hinton (2002a, 2002b).
10. *American Heritage Dictionary* (1976:1040).
11. Although I use metaphors of priming and heat, I do not want to convey the image of genocide as a primordial conflict waiting to explode. In fact, I want to do exactly the opposite — to emphasize that genocide is a *process* that emerges from a variety of factors, or "primes," and always involves impetus and organization from above, or "genocidal activation." For another use of metaphors of heat and cold to describe ethnonationalist violence in a manner that argues against primordialist explanations, see Appadurai (1996:164ff.).
12. The nodes metaphor was suggested by Pradeep Jaganathan at an advanced seminar on "The Cultural Poetics of Violence" at the School of American Research in April 2002.
13. Furthermore, certain constellations of nodes might be broken down into the typologies — such as the distinction between developmental, retributive, and ideological genocides some genocide scholars have proposed — that share a family resemblance.
14. See Bowen (1996) for a discussion of how leaders "push" their followers to engage in violence, often through the generation of panic and fear and the offer of material gain.
15. Kuper (1981). See also Charny (1999); Fein (1984, 1990); Harff and Gurr (1998); Kuper (1985); Lemarchand (2002); Melson (1992); Smith (1987); Stanton (forthcoming); Staub (1989).
16. Kuper (1981). See also Nagengast (2002).

17. Harff and Gurr (1988, 1998); Bateson (1958, 1972).

18. On Genocide Early Warning Systems, see Charny (1999:253f.). Genocide Watch (www.genocidewatch.org; see also www.preventgenocide.org), for example, is an organization devoted to monitoring and issuing warnings about "hot" situations.

19. The order in which I discuss various primes is not meant to be rigid and synchronic: various primes co-occur and mutually influence each other. Moreover, the framework that I am developing is an "ideal typical" one, to use Weber's (1949) term, that provides one way of sifting through and sorting real world complexities. There are certainly other primes that could be discussed and other ways of grouping the material (see, for example, Stanton, forthcoming). Moreover, I should note that the process of priming I describe may be more applicable to what have been called "ideological genocides."

20. See Hinton (forthcoming).

21. See Lindholm (1990).

22. Kuper (1981).

23. Bauman (1989). See also Kaye and Strath (2000).

24. Haing Ngor (1987:230).

25. Douglas (1966:36).

26. See Koenigsberg (1975).

27. See Foucault (1979) on bodily disciplines.

28. In a series of statistical analyses, R. J. Rummel (1997; 1999; see also Charny 1999:157–58) has argued that genocides are much more likely to take place under totalitarian regimes than under democracies (see also Arendt 1968), where power is limited by checks and balances. As the annihilation of indigenous people in the United States and Australia illustrates, however, this finding is a general correlation that should not divert us from examining how genocidal priming unfolds under both systems of political organization.

29. Geertz (1973).

30. Staub (1989).

31. See Martin (1994); Ponchaud (1978, 1989); Sutton (1995).

32. See Chou Ta-Kuan (1987).

33. See, for example, Becker (1986:21); Martin (1994:15); Vickery (1984:4).

34. Thayer (1994:2, 1995b:16); United Nations Center for Human Rights (1997:2). We must be careful not to construct Cambodians as "liver-eating" others, heeding the words of Saruon, a man who cautioned that liver-eating "isn't really a Cambodian characteristic. In a gathering of ten thousand Cambodians, you would find only one person who is savage, one who steals, and one who has eaten human liver. . . . Therefore you can't say that Cambodians eat human liver. It's not true. There is only one person here or there who does this . . . and we Cambodians regard such people as despicable and without value." Just as people in the United States should not be called cannibalistic devil worshippers because of the isolated activities of satanic cults, so too must we recognize that Cambodians should not be stereotyped as "liver-eaters." The practice of human liver-eating is not a regular occurrence in Cambodian society; it usually takes place in extreme contexts, such as DK. At the same time, given the large number of first-hand and documented reports — both from perpetrators and witnesses — of

human liver-eating, we cannot simply dismiss such accounts as a "man-eating myth" (Arens 1979).

35. *Khmer Dictionary* (1967:420).

36. See Smith (1989:28).

37. Chandler (1982).

38. Swearer (1995).

39. Turner (1967).

40. Turner (1980).

41. I want to thank John Ingham (personal communication) for this last connection.

42. For additional discussion of human liver-eating and a related practice, the consumption of human gallbladder *(brâmat)*, see Hinton (1998d).

43. Maha Ghosananda (1992:81).

Bibliography

Ablin, David A., and Marlowe Hood, eds. 1990. *The Cambodian Agony.* Armonk, N.Y.: M. E. Sharpe.

Améry, Jean. 1980. *At the Mind's Limits: Contemplations by a Survivor on Auschwitz and Its Realities.* Bloomington: Indiana University Press.

Anderson, Benedict R. O'G. 1990. *Language and Power: Exploring Political Cultures in Indonesia.* Ithaca, N.Y.: Cornell University Press.

Ang Choulean. 1986. *Les êtres surnaturels dans la religion populaire khmère.* Collection Bibliothèque Khmère, Série Travaux et Recherches. Paris: Cedoreck.

Appadurai, Arjun. 1996. *Modernity at Large: Cultural Dimensions of Globalization.* Minneapolis: University of Minnesota Press.

———. 1998. "Dead Certainty: Ethnic Violence in the Era of Globalization." *Public Culture* 10, no. 2:225–47.

Arendt, Hannah. 1968. *Totalitarianism.* New York: Harcourt, Brace & World.

———. 1977. *Eichmann in Jerusalem: A Report on the Banality of Evil.* New York: Penguin.

Arens, W. 1979. *The Man-Eating Myth: Anthropology and Anthropophagy.* New York: Oxford University Press.

Aretxaga, Begoña. 1995. "Dirty Protest: Symbolic Overdeterminism and Gender in Northern Ireland Ethnic Violence." *Ethos* 23, no. 2:123–48.

Ashley, David W. 1998. "The Failure of Conflict Resolution in Cambodia: Causes and Lessons." In *Cambodia and the International Community: The Quest for Peace, Development, and Democracy,* edited by Frederick Z. Brown and David G. Timberman, 49–78. New York: Asia Society.

Averill, James R. 1988. "Disorders of Emotion." *Journal of Social and Clinical Psychology* 6:247–68.

Ayres, David M. 2000. *Anatomy of a Crisis: Education, Development, and the State in Cambodia, 1953–1998.* Honolulu: University of Hawaii Press.

Bandura, Albert. 1986. Social Foundations of Thought and Action: A Social Cognitive Theory. Englewood Cliffs, N.J.: Prentice Hall.

Barber, Jason. 1997. "Leaner Bun Chhay Vows to Fight On." *Phnom Penh Post,* August. 15, p. 7.

Barber, Jason, and Christine Chaumeau. 1997. "Power Struggle Shatters KR Leadership." *Phnom Penh Post,* June 27–July 10, p. 3.

Barnett, Anthony, Ben Kiernan, and Chanthou Boua. 1980. "Bureaucracy of Death." *New Statesman,* May 2, pp. 668–76.

Barth, Fredrik. 1990. *Cosmologies in the Making: A Generative Approach to Cultural Variation in Inner New Guinea.* New York: Cambridge University Press.

———. 1993. *Balinese Worlds.* Chicago: University of Chicago Press.

———. 1995. "Redefining the Domains of Anthropological Discourse." Paper presented at the University of Chicago, October 9.

———, ed. 1998 [1969]. *Ethnic Groups and Boundaries: The Social Organization of Culture Difference.* Prospect Heights, Ill.: Waveland Press.

Bateson, Gregory. 1958. *Naven.* Stanford, Calif.: Stanford University Press.

———. 1972. *Steps to an Ecology of Mind.* New York: Ballantine.

Bauman, Zygmunt. 1989. *Modernity and the Holocaust.* Ithaca, N.Y.: Cornell University Press.

Baumeister, Roy F. 1997. *Evil: Inside Human Violence and Cruelty.* New York: W. H. Freeman.

Beck, Aaron T. 1999. *Prisoners of Hate: The Cognitive Basis of Anger, Hostility, and Violence.* New York: Harper Collins.

Becker, Elizabeth. 1998. *When the War Was Over: Cambodia and the Khmer Rouge Revolution.* New York: Public Affairs.

Becker, Ernst. 1973. *The Denial of Death.* New York: Free Press.

Besteman, Catherine. 2002. *Violence: A Reader.* New York: Palgrave.

Blass, Thomas. 1993. "Psychological Perspectives on the Perpetrators of the Holocaust: The Role of Situational Pressures, Personal Dispositions, and Their Interactions." *Holocaust and Genocide Studies* 7, no. 1:30–50.

Bloch, Maurice. 1998. *How We Think They Think: Anthropological Approaches to Cognition, Memory, and Literacy.* Boulder, Colo.: Westview.

Boisvert, Mathieu. 1995. *The Five Aggregates: Understanding Theravada Psychology and Soteriology.* Waterloo, Ontario: Wilfrid Laurier University Press.

Born, Georgina. 1998. "Anthropology, Kleinian Psychoanalysis, and the Subject in Culture." *American Anthropologist* 100, no. 2:373–86.

Borofsky, Robert, ed. 1994. *Assessing Cultural Anthropology.* New York: McGraw-Hill.

Bou Saroeun. 2001. "Ke Pauk: 'The Document Is Fiction and Has No Clear Base.'" *Phnom Penh Post* July 20–August 2, p. 9.

Boua, Chanthou. 1991. "Genocide of a Religious Group: Pol Pot and Cambodia's Buddhist Monks." In *State Organized Terror: The Case of Violent Internal Repression,* edited by P. Timothy Bushnell, Vladimir Shlapentokh, Christopher K. Vanderpool, and Jeyaratnam Sundram. Boulder, Colo.: Westview.

Bowen, John R. 1996. "The Myth of Global Ethnic Conflict." *Journal of Democracy* 7, no. 4:3–14.

Breckon, Lydia Ann. 1999. "The Other Side: Ethnic and Transnational Identity among Khmer-Americans in Southern New England." Ph.D. diss., Department of Anthropology, Yale University.

Brereton, Bonnie Pacala. 1994. *The Phra Malai Legend in Thai Buddhist Literature*. Tempe: Arizona State University Press.

Brown, Frederick Z., and David G. Timberman, eds. 1998. *Cambodia and the International Community: The Quest for Peace, Development, and Democracy*. New York: Asia Society.

Brown, MacAlister, and Joseph J. Zasloff. 1998. *Cambodia Confounds the Peacemakers, 1979–1998*. Ithaca, N.Y.: Cornell University Press.

Browning, Christopher R. 1992. *Ordinary Men: Reserve Police Battalion 101 and the Final Solution in Poland*. New York: Harper Collins.

Bun Chân Mol. 1973. *Châret Khmaer [Cambodian Character]*. Phnom Penh: Kehâdtan 79, distributor.

Burchett, Wilfred. 1981. *The China Cambodia Vietnam Triangle*. Chicago: Vanguard.

Burgler, Roel A. 1990. *The Eyes of the Pineapple: Revolutionary Intellectuals and Terror in Democratic Kampuchea*. Fort Lauderdale, Fl.: Verlag Breitenbach.

Caldwell, Malcolm, and Lek Tan. 1973. *Cambodia in the Southeast Asian War*. New York: Monthly Review Press.

Cambodia Genocide Program. 1998. *Ieng Sary's Regime: A Diary of the Khmer Rouge Foreign Ministry, 1976–1979*. Translated by Sorya Sim, Toni Shapiro, and Thavro Phim. New Haven, Conn.: Yale Center for International and Area Studies.

Carney, Timothy. 1977. *Communist Party Power in Kampuchea (Cambodia): Documents and Discussion*. Ithaca, N.Y.: Cornell University Southeast Asia Program.

———. 1989a. "The Unexpected Revolution." In *Cambodia, 1975–1978: Rendezvous with Death*, edited by Karl D. Jackson, 13–35. Princeton, N.J.: Princeton University Press.

———. 1989b. "The Organization of Power." In *Cambodia, 1975–1978: Rendezvous with Death*, edited by Karl D. Jackson, 79–107. Princeton, N.J.: Princeton University Press.

Chanda, Nayan. 1986. *Brother Enemy: The War after the War*. New York: Collier Books.

Chandler, David P. 1982. "Songs at the Edge of the Forest: Perception of Order in Three Cambodian Texts." In *Moral Order and the Question of Change: Essays on Southeast Asian Thought*, edited by David K. Wyatt and Alexander Woodside, 53–77. Monograph Series 24. New Haven, Conn.: Yale University Southeast Asia Studies.

———. 1991. *The Tragedy of Cambodian History: Politics, War and Revolution since 1945*. New Haven, Conn.: Yale University Press.

———. 1995. "Facing Death: Photographs from S-21, 1975–1979." *Photographers International* 19 (April):12–78.

————. 1996. *Facing the Cambodian Past, Selected Essays, 1971–1994.* Chiang Mai, Thailand: Silkworm Books.

————. 1999a. *Voices from S-21: Terror and History in Pol Pot's Secret Prison.* Berkeley: University of California Press.

————. 1999b. *Brother Number One: A Political Biography of Pol Pot.* Rev. ed. Boulder, Colo.: Westview.

————. 2000a. *History of Cambodia.* 3d ed. Boulder, Colo.: Westview.

Chandler, David P., Ben Kiernan, and Chanthou Boua. 1988. *Pol Pot Plans the Future: Confidential Leadership Documents from Democratic Kampuchea, 1976–1977.* Monograph Series 33. New Haven, Conn.: Yale University Southeast Asia Studies.

Chandler, David P., Ben Kiernan, and Muy Hong Lim. 1976. *The Early Phases of Liberation in Northwestern Cambodia: Conversations with Peang Sophi.* Melbourne: Monash University Centre of Southeast Asian Studies Working Papers.

Charny, Israel W., ed. 1999. *Encyclopedia of Genocide.* Santa Barbara, Calif.: ABC-CLIO.

Chigas, George. 2000a. "Draft Translation of *The Story of Tum Teav* by Preah Botumthera Som." M.A. thesis, Asian Studies, Cornell University.

Chou Ta-Kuan. 1987. *The Customs of Cambodia.* Bangkok: Siam Society.

Coedès, G. 1969. *Angkor: An Introduction.* Translated by Emily Floyd Gardiner. Hong Kong: Oxford University Press.

Cole, Jonathan. 1998. *About Face.* Cambridge, Mass.: MIT Press.

Collins, Steven. 1993. "The Discourse on What is Primary (Agganna-Sutta)." *Journal of Indian Philosophy* 21:301–93.

————. 1998. *Nirvana and Other Buddhist Felicities.* Cambridge: Cambridge University Press.

Connerton, Paul. 1989. *How Societies Remember.* New York: Cambridge University Press.

Conze, Edward. 1975. *Buddhism: Its Essence and Development.* New York: Harper Torchbooks.

Coomaraswamy, Ananda K. 1964. *Buddha and the Gospel of Buddhism.* New York: Harper & Row.

Corfield, Justin. 1994. *Khmers Stand Up! A History of the Cambodian Government, 1970–1975.* Clayton, Australia: Monash University Centre of Southeast Asian Studies.

Criddle, Joan D., and Teeda Butt Mam. 1987. *To Destroy You Is No Loss: The Odyssey of a Cambodian Family.* New York: Doubleday.

D'Andrade, Roy. 1995. *The Development of Cognitive Anthropology.* New York: Cambridge University Press.

D'Andrade, Roy, and Claudia Strauss, eds. 1992. *Human Motives and Cultural Models.* New York: Cambridge University Press.

Darley, John M. 1992. "Social Organization for the Production of Evil." *Psychological Inquiry* 3, no. 2:199–218.

Darwin, Charles. 1965. *The Expression of the Emotions in Man and Animals.* Chicago: University of Chicago Press.

Delvert, Jean. 1961. *Le paysan cambodgien.* Paris: Mouton.

Democratic Kampuchea. 1978. *Black Paper: Facts and Evidences of the Acts of Aggression and Annexation of Vietnam against Kampuchea*. Phnom Penh: Ministry of Foreign Affairs.

De Nike, Howard J., John Quigley, and Kenneth J. Robinson, eds. 2000. *Genocide in Cambodia: Documents from the Trial of Pol Pot and Ieng Sary*. Philadelphia: University of Pennsylvania Press.

DeVos, George A. 1973. *Socialization for Achievement: Essays on the Cultural Psychology of the Japanese*. Berkeley: University of California Press.

Dith Pran. 1997. *Children of Cambodia's Killing Fields: Memoirs by Survivors*. New Haven, Conn.: Yale University Press.

Douglas, Mary. 1966. *Purity and Danger: An Analysis of the Concepts of Pollution and Taboo*. New York: Routledge.

Dumont, Louis. 1970. *Homo Hierarchicus: The Caste System and Its Implications*. Translated by Mark Sainsbury, Louis Dumont, and Basia Gulati. Chicago: University of Chicago Press.

Dyer, Gwynne. 1985. *War*. New York: Crown.

Eames, Elizabeth A. 1997. "Navigating Nigerian Bureaucracies." In *Conformity and Conflict: Reading in Cultural Anthropology*, edited by James Spradley and David W. McCurdy, 290–98. New York: Longman.

Ebihara, May Mayko. 1968. "Svay, a Khmer Village in Cambodia." Ph.D. diss., Dept. of Anthropology, Columbia University.

———. 1986. "Kin Terminology and the Idiom of Kinship in Cambodia/Kampuchea." Paper presented at the SSRC/Indochina Studies Program Workshop on Kinship and Gender in Indochina," University of Northern Illinois, July 26–27.

———. 1990. "Revolution and Reformulation in Kampuchean Village Culture." In *The Cambodian Agony*, edited by David Ablin and Marlowe Hood, 16–61. Armonk, N.Y.: M. E. Sharpe.

———. 1993a. " 'Beyond Suffering': The Recent History of a Cambodian Village." In *The Challenge of Reform in Indochina*, edited by Börje Ljunggren, 149–66. Cambridge, Mass.: Harvard Institute for International Development.

———. 1993b. "A Cambodian Village under the Khmer Rouge, 1975–1979." In *Genocide and Democracy in Cambodia: The Khmer Rouge, the United Nations and the International Community*, edited by Ben Kiernan, 51–63. New Haven, Conn.: Yale University Southeast Asia Studies.

———. 2002. "Memories of the Pol Pot Era in a Cambodian Village." In *Cambodia Emerges from the Past: Eight Essays*, edited by Judy Ledgerwood, 91–108. DeKalb: Northern Illinois University Press.

Ebihara, May M., and Judy Ledgerwood. 2002. "Aftermaths of Genocide: Cambodian Villagers." In *Annihilating Difference: The Anthropology of Genocide*, edited by Alexander Laban Hinton, 272–91. Berkeley: University of California Press.

Ebihara, May M., Carol A. Mortland, and Judy Ledgerwood, eds. 1994. *Cambodian Culture since 1975: Homeland and Exile*. Ithaca, N.Y.: Cornell University Press.

Edwards, Penny. 1996. "Imagining the Other in Cambodian Nationalist Discourse before and during the UNTAC Period." In *Propaganda, Politics, and*

Violence in Cambodia: Democratic Transition under United Nations Peace-Keeping, edited by Steve Heder and Judy Ledgerwood, 50–72. Armonk, N.Y.: M. E. Sharpe.

Ehrman, Madeline. 1972. *Contemporary Cambodian Grammatical Sketch*. Washington, D.C.: Foreign Service Institute.

Eisenbruch, Maurice. 1992. "The Ritual Space of Patients and Traditional Healers in Cambodia." *Bulletin de l'Ecole Française d'Extreme-Orient 79*, no. 2:1–35.

Eisenstadt, S. N., and L. Roniger. 1984. *Patrons, Clients and Friends: Interpersonal Relations and the Structure of Trust in Society*. New York: Cambridge University Press.

Ekman, Paul, ed. 1973. *Darwin and Facial Expression: A Century of Research in Review*. New York: Academic Press.

Eller, Jack David. 1999. *From Culture to Ethnicity to Conflict: An Anthropological Perspective on International Ethnic Conflict*. Ann Arbor: University of Michigan Press.

Errington, Shelly. 1989. *Meaning and Power in a Southeast Asian Realm*. Princeton, N.J.: Princeton University Press.

Etcheson, Craig. 1984. *The Rise and Demise of Democratic Kampuchea*. Boulder, Colo.: Westview.

Fein, Helen. 1984. "Scenarios of Genocide: Models of Genocide and Critical Responses." In *Toward the Understanding and Prevention of Genocide: Proceedings of the International Conference on the Holocaust and Genocide*, edited by Israel W. Charny, 3–31. Boulder, Colo.: Westview.

———. 1990. "Genocide: A Sociological Perspective." *Current Sociology 38*, no. 1:1–126.

Feldman, Allen. 1991. *Formations of Violence: The Narrative of the Body and Political Terror in Northern Ireland*. Chicago: University of Chicago Press.

Ferguson, R. Brian. 1989. "Anthropology and War: Theory, Politics, Ethics." In *The Anthropology of War and Peace*, edited by D. Pitt and P. Turner, 141–59. South Hadley, Mass.: Bergin and Garvey.

———. 2003. "Introduction: Violent Conflict and Control of the State." In *The State, Identity and Violence: Political Disintegration in the Post–Cold War World*, edited by R. Brian Ferguson, 1–58. New York: Routledge.

Ferguson, R. Brian, and Leslie Faragher, eds. 1988. *The Anthropology of War: A Bibliography*. New York: Harry Frank Guggenheim Foundation.

Fernando, Basil, and Terrance Wickremasinghe. 1997. "Justice in Name Only— No Genuine Courts." *Phnom Penh Post*, Nov. 21–Dec. 4, p. 11.

Fessler, Daniel M. T. 1999. "Toward an Understanding of the Universality of Second Order Emotions." In *Biocultural Approaches to the Emotions*, edited by Alexander Laban Hinton, 75–116. New York: Cambridge University Press.

Festinger, Leon. 1957a. *Theory of Cognitive Dissonance*. Evanston, Ill: Row, Peterson.

Finkelstein, Norman G., and Ruth Bettina Birn. 1998. *Nation on Trial: The Goldhagen Thesis and Historical Truth*. New York: Owl Books.

Fisher-Nguyen, Karen. 1994. "Khmer Proverbs: Images and Rules." In *Cambodian Culture since 1975: Homeland and Exile*, edited by May M. Ebihara,

Carol A. Mortland, and Judy Ledgerwood, 91–104. Ithaca, N.Y.: Cornell University Press.

Foucault, Michel. 1979. *Discipline and Punish: The Birth of the Prison*. Translated by Alan Sheridan. New York: Vintage Books.

French, Lindsay Cole. 1994. "Enduring Holocaust, Surviving History: Displaced Cambodians on the Thai-Cambodian Border, 1989–1991." Ph.D. diss., Dept. of Anthropology, Harvard University.

Freud, Sigmund. 1964. *The Problem of Anxiety*. New York: W. W. Norton.

Frieson, Kate G. 1991. "The Impact of Revolution on Cambodian Peasants: 1970–1975." Ph.D. diss., Monash University, Australia.

——. 1993. "Revolution and Rural Response in Cambodia: 1970–1975." In *Genocide and Democracy in Cambodia: The Khmer Rouge, the United Nations and the International Community*, edited by Ben Kiernan, 33–50. New Haven, Conn.: Yale University Southeast Asia Studies.

Fromm, Erich. 1941. *Escape from Freedom*. New York: Rinehart.

——. 1973. *The Anatomy of Human Destructiveness*. Greenwich, Conn.: Fawcett.

Geertz, Clifford. 1973. *The Interpretation of Cultures*. New York: Basic Books.

——. 1980. *Negara: The Theatre State in Nineteenth-Century Bali*. Princeton, N.J.: Princeton University Press.

——. 2000. *Local Knowledge: Further Essays in Interpretive Anthropology*. New York: Basic Books.

Gennep, Arnold van. 1960. *The Rites of Passage*. Chicago: University of Chicago Press.

George, Kenneth M. 1996. *Showing Signs of Violence: The Cultural Politics of a Twentieth-Century Headhunting Ritual*. Berkeley: University of California Press.

Giddens, Anthony. 1984. *The Constitution of Society*. Berkeley: University of California Press.

Gilroy, Paul. 1997. "Diaspora and the Detours of Identity." In *Identity and Difference*, edited by Kathryn Woodward, 301–43. London: Sage.

Goffman, Erving. 1967. *Interaction Ritual: Essays on Face-to-Face Behavior*. New York: Pantheon Books.

Goldhagen, Daniel Jonah. 1996. *Hitler's Willing Executioners: Ordinary Germans and the Holocaust*. New York: Alfred A. Knopf.

Gottesman, Evan 2002. *Cambodia after the Khmer Rouge: Inside the Politics of Nation Building*. New Haven, Conn.: Yale University Press.

Grainger, Matthew. 1995. "Chan Dara's Killer Walks, Says Hockry." *Phnom Penh Post*, June 2–15, p. 3.

Grotstein, James S. 1985. *Splitting and Projective Identification*. New York: Jason Aronson.

Haing Ngor. 1987. *A Cambodian Odyssey*. New York: Warner Books.

Hanks, Jane Richardson. 1964. *Maternity and Its Rituals in Bang Chan*. Ithaca, N.Y.: Cornell University Southeast Asia Program.

Hanks, Lucien M. 1962. "Merit and Power in the Thai Social Order." *American Anthropologist* 64, no. 6:1247–61.

———. 1972. *Rice and Man: Agricultural Ecology in Southeast Asia*. Atherton, Ca.: Aldine.

———. 1975. "The Thai Social Order As Entourage and Circle." In *Change and Persistence in Thai Society: Essays in Honor of Lauriston Sharp*, edited by G. William Skinner and A. Thomas Kirsch. Ithaca, N.Y.: Cornell University Press.

Hannerz, Ulf. 1992. *Cultural Complexity: Studies in the Social Organization of Meaning*. New York: Columbia University Press.

———. 1996. *Transnational Connections: Culture, People, Places*. London: Routledge.

Hansen, Anne R. 1999. "Ways of the World: Moral Discernment and Narrative Ethics in a Cambodian Buddhist Text." Ph.D. diss., Department of Religion, Harvard University.

Harff, Barbara, and Ted Gurr. 1988. Toward Empirical Theory of Genocides and Politicides: Identification and Measurement of Cases since 1945. *International Studies Quarterly* 22:359–71.

———. 1998. "Systematic Early Warning of Humanitarian Emergencies." *Journal of Peace Research* 35, no. 5:551–79.

Haritos-Fatouros, Mika. 1988. "The Official Torturer: A Learning Model for Obedience to the Authority of Violence." *Journal of Applied Social Psychology* 18, no. 13:1107–20.

Hawk, David. n.d. *Khmer Rouge Prison Documents from the S-21 (Tuol Sleng) Extermination Center in Phnom Penh*. New York: Cambodian Documentation Commission.

———. 1986. "Tuol Sleng Extermination Centre." *Index on Censorship* 15, no. 1 (Jan):25–31.

Headley, Robert K. Jr., Kylin Chhor, Lam Kheng Lim, Lim Kah Kheang, and Chen Chun. 1977. *Cambodian-English Dictionary*. Washington, D.C.: Catholic University of America Press.

Heder, Steven R. 1980. *Kampuchean Occupation and Resistance*. Bangkok: Chulalongkorn University Institute of Asian Studies.

———. 1991. *Reflections on Cambodian Political History: Backgrounder to Recent Developments*. Working Paper 239. Canberra: Australian National University Strategic and Defence Studies Centre.

———. 1997. "Racism, Marxism, Labeling, and Genocide in Ben Kiernan's *The Pol Pot Regime*." *South East Asia Research* 5, no. 2:101–53.

Heder, Steve, and Judy Ledgerwood, eds. 1996a. *Propaganda, Politics, and Violence in Cambodia: Democratic Transition under United Nations Peace-Keeping*. Armonk, N.Y.: M. E. Sharpe.

Heder, Steve, and Judy Ledgerwood. 1996b. "Politics of Violence: An Introduction." In *Propaganda, Politics, and Violence in Cambodia: Democratic Transition under United Nations Peace-Keeping*, edited by Steve Heder and Judy Ledgerwood, 3–49. Armonk, N.Y.: M. E. Sharpe.

Heder, Steve, and Brian D. Tittemore. 2001. *Seven Candidates for Prosecution: Accountability for the Crimes of the Khmer Rouge*. Washington, D.C.: War Crimes Research Office, American University.

Heine-Geldern, Robert. 1942. "Conceptions of State and Kingship in Southeast Asia." *Far Eastern Quarterly* 2, no. 1:15–30.

Him, Chanrithy. 1997. "When the Owl Cries." In *Children of Cambodia's Killing Fields*, edited by Kim DePaul, compiled by Dith Pran, 147–53. New Haven, Conn.: Yale University Press.

———. 2000. *When Broken Glass Floats: Growing Up under the Khmer Rouge.* New York: W. W. Norton.

Hinschelwood, R. D. 1989a. *Dictionary of Kleinian Thought.* London: Free Association Books.

Hinton, Alexander Laban. 1996. "Agents of Death: Explaining the Cambodian Genocide in Terms of Psychosocial Dissonance." *American Anthropologist* 98, no. 4:818–31.

———. 1997. "Cambodia's Shadow: An Examination of the Cultural Origins of Genocide." Ph.D. diss., Department of Anthropology, Emory University.

———. 1998a. "A Head for an Eye: Revenge in the Cambodian Genocide." *American Ethnologist* 25, no. 3:352–77.

———. 1998b. "Why Did you Kill? The Dark Side of Face and Honor in the Cambodian Genocide." *Journal of Asian Studies* 57, no. 1:93–122.

———. 1998c. "Why Did the Nazis Kill? Anthropology, Genocide, and the Goldhagen Controversy." *Anthropology Today* 14, no. 5:9–15.

———. 1998d. "Genocidal Bricolage: A Reading of Human Liver-Eating in Cambodia." Yale University Genocide Studies Program Working Paper (GS 06): 16–38. New Haven, Conn.: Yale University Genocide Studies Program.

———. 2000. "Under the Shade of Pol Pot's Umbrella: Mandala, Myth, and Politics in the Cambodian Genocide." In *The Vision Thing: Myth, Politics, and Psyche in the World*, edited by Thomas Singer, 170–204. New York: Routledge.

———. 2002a. "Purity and Contamination in the Cambodian Genocide." In *Cambodia Emerges from the Past: Eight Essays*, edited by Judy Ledgerwood, 60–90. DeKalb: Northern Illinois University Press.

———. 2002b. "The Dark Side of Modernity: Toward an Anthropology of Genocide." In *Annihilating Difference: The Anthropology of Genocide*, edited by Alexander Laban Hinton, 1–40. Berkeley: University of California Press.

———. 2004. "Genocide and Modernity." In *A Companion to Psychological Anthropology: Modernity and Psychocultural Change*, edited by Conerly Casey and Robert Edgerton. Malden, Mass.: Blackwell.

———. Forthcoming. *Cambodia's Shadow: Genocide, Modernity, and Revitalization.*

———, ed. 1999. *Biocultural Approaches to the Emotions.* New York: Cambridge University Press.

———. 2002c. *Genocide: An Anthropological Reader.* Malden, Mass.: Blackwell.

———. 2002d. *Annihilating Difference: The Anthropology of Genocide.* Berkeley: University of California Press.

Hinton, Devon, Khin Um, and Phalnarith Ba. 2001a. "*Kyol Goeu* ('Wind Overload'), Part I: A Cultural Syndrome of Orthostatic Panic among Khmer Refugees." *Transcultural Psychiatry* 38, no. 4:403–32.

———. 2001b. "*Kyol Goeu* ('Wind Overload'), Part II: Prevalence, Characteristics, and Mechanisms of *Kyol Goeu* and Near-*Kyol Goeu* Episodes of Khmer Patients Attending a Psychiatric Clinic." *Transcultural Psychiatry* 38, no. 4:433–60.

Hinton, Walter Ladson III. 1999. "Shame As a Teacher: 'Lowly Wisdom' at the Millennium." In *Destruction and Creation: Personal and Cultural Transformations,* edited by Mary Ann Mattoon, 172–85. Einsiedeln, Switzerland: Daimon Verlag.

———. 2001a. "Dreams and the Horizon of the Unknown." *Journal of Jungian Theory and Practice* 3:25–38.

———. 2001b. "Narcissism and Its Vicissitudes." Paper presented to the Jungian Psychotherapists Association, Seattle, Wash., Sept. 22.

Hinton, Walter Ladson IV, Kenneth Fox, and Sue Levkoff. 1999. "Introduction: Exploring the Relationships among Aging, Ethnicity, and Family Dementia Care-Giving," *Culture, Medicine, and Psychiatry* 23, no. 4:403–13.

Hollan, Douglas. 1988. "Staying 'Cool' in Toraja: Informal Strategies for the Management of Anger and Hostility in a Nonviolent Society." *Ethos* 16, no. 1:52–72.

Holland, Dorothy, and Naomi Quinn, eds. 1987. *Cultural Models in Language and Thought.* New York: Cambridge University Press.

Horkheimer, Max, and Theodor W. Adorno. 1944. *Dialectic of Enlightenment.* Translated by John Cumming. New York: Continuum.

Huffman, Franklin E. 1970. *Modern Spoken Cambodian.* New Haven, Conn.: Yale University Press.

Hughes, Caroline 2003. *The Political Economy of Cambodia's Transition, 1991–2001.* New York: Routledge.

Ith Sarin. 1973. *Srânah Proleung Khmaer [Regrets for the Khmer Soul].* Phnom Penh.

Jackson, Karl D. 1989a. "The Ideology of Revolution." In *Cambodia 1975–1978: Rendezvous with Death,* edited by Karl D. Jackson, 37–78. Princeton, N.J.: Princeton University Press.

———. 1989b. "Intellectual Origins of the Khmer Rouge." In *Cambodia 1975–1978: Rendezvous with Death,* edited by Karl D. Jackson, 241–50. Princeton, N.J.: Princeton University Press.

———, ed. 1989c. *Cambodia, 1975–1978: Rendezvous with Death.* Princeton, N.J.: Princeton University Press.

Jatava, D. R. 1968. *The Buddha and Karl Marx.* Jagdishpura, India: Kesari.

Jessup, Helen Ibbitson, and Thierry Zephir, eds. 1997. *Sculpture of Angkor and Ancient Cambodia: Millennium of Glory.* Washington, D.C.: National Gallery. of Art.

Johnson, Mark. 1987. *The Body in the Mind: The Bodily Basis of Meaning, Imagination, and Reason.* Chicago: University of Chicago Press.

———. 1993. *Moral Imagination: Implications of Cognitive Science for Ethics.* Chicago: University of Chicago Press.

Jordens, Jay. 1996. "Persecution of Cambodia's Ethnic Vietnamese Communities during and since the UNTAC Period." In *Propaganda, Politics, and Violence in Cambodia: Democratic Transition under United Nations Peace-Keeping*, edited by Steve Heder and Judy Ledgerwood, 134–58. Armonk, N.Y.: M. E. Sharpe.

Kalab, Milada. 1968. "Study of a Cambodian Village." *Geographical Journal* 134, no. 4:521–37.

Kamm, Henry. 1998. *Cambodia: Report from a Stricken Land*. New York: Arcade.

Kapferer, Bruce. 1988. *Legends of People, Myths of State: Violence, Intolerance, and Political Culture in Sri Lanka and Australia*. Washington: Smithsonian Institution Press.

Kaye, James, and Bo Strath, eds. 2000. *Enlightenment and Genocide, Contradictions of Modernity*. Brussels: P.I.E.—Peter Lang.

Kelman, Herbert C., and V. Lee Hamilton. 1989. *Crimes of Obedience: Toward a Social Psychology of Authority and Responsibility*. New Haven, Conn.: Yale University Press.

Kernberg, Otto. 1975. *Borderline Conditions and Pathological Narcissism*. New York: Aronson.

Keyes, Charles F. 1977. "Millenialism, Theravada Buddhism, and Thai Society." *Journal of Asian Studies* 36, no. 2:283–302.

———. 1983. "Merit-Transference in the Kammic Theory of Popular Theravada Buddhism." In *Karma: An Anthropological Inquiry*, edited by Charles F. Keyes and E. Valentine Daniel, 261–86. Berkeley: University of California Press.

———. 1984. "Mother or Mistress but Never a Monk: Buddhist Notions of Female Gender in Rural Thailand." *American Ethnologist* 11, no. 2:223–41.

———. 1994. "Communist Revolution and the Buddhist Past in Cambodia." In *Asian Visions of Authority: Religion and the Modern States of East and Southeast Asia*, edited by Charles F. Keyes, Laurel Kendall, and Helen Hardacre, 43–341. Honolulu: University of Hawaii Press.

———. 1995. *The Golden Peninsula: Culture and Adaptation in Mainland Southeast Asia*. Honolulu: University of Hawaii Press.

Keyes, Charles F., and E. Valentine Daniel, eds. 1983. *Karma: An Anthropological Inquiry*. Berkeley: University of California Press.

Khieu Samphan. 1979. *Cambodia's Economy and Industrial Development*. Translated by Laura Summers. Ithaca, N.Y.: Cornell University Southeast Asia Program.

Khmer Dictionary [Vochânanukrâm Khmaer]. 1967. Phnom Penh: Buddhist Institute.

Kierkegaard, Søren. 1941. *Sickness unto Death*. Translated by Walter B. Lowrie. Princeton, N.J.: Princeton University Press.

Kiernan, Ben. 1985a. *How Pol Pot Came to Power: A History of Communism in Kampuchea, 1930–1975*. London: Verso.

———. 1985b. "Kampuchea and Stalinism." In *Marxism in Asia*, edited by Colin Mackerras and Nick Knight, 232–49. London: Croom Helm.

———. 1988. "Orphans of Genocide: The Cham Muslims of Kampuchea under Pol Pot." *Bulletin of Concerned Asian Scholars* 20, no. 4:2–33.

———. 1989. "The American Bombardment of Kampuchea, 1969–1973." *Vietnam Generation* 1, no. 1:4–41.

———. 1996. *The Pol Pot Regime: Race, Power, and Genocide in Cambodia under the Khmer Rouge, 1975–79*. New Haven, Conn.: Yale University Press.

———. 1997. "Introduction." In *Children of Cambodia's Killing Fields: Memoirs by Survivors*, compiled by Dith Pran, edited by Kim DePaul, xi–xvii. New Haven, Conn.: Yale University Press.

———, ed. 1993. *Genocide and Democracy in Cambodia: The Khmer Rouge, the United Nations and the International Community*. New Haven, Conn.: Yale University Press.

Kiernan, Ben, and Chanthou Boua, eds. 1982. *Peasants and Politics in Kampuchea, 1942–1981*. Armonk, N.Y.: M. E. Sharpe.

Kipnis, Andrew. 1995. "'Face': An Adaptable Discourse of Social Surfaces." *Positions* 3, no. 1:119–48.

Kirsch, A. Thomas. 1973. *Feasting and Social Oscillation: Religion and Society in Upland Southeast Asia*. Ithaca: Cornell University Southeast Asia Program.

———. 1981. "The Thai Buddhist Quest for Merit." In *Clues to Thai Culture and to Cross Cultural Adjustment, Communication and Innovation*, 120–36. Bangkok: Central Thai Language Committee.

———. 1985. "Text and Context: Buddhist Sex Roles/Culture of Gender Revisited." *American Ethnologist* 12, no. 2:302–20.

Klausner, William J. 1993. *Reflections on Thai Culture*. Bangkok: Siam Society.

Klein, Melanie. 1975. *Envy, Gratitude and Other Works, 1946–1963*. London: Hogarth Press.

Kleinman, Arthur, Veena Das, and Margaret Lock, eds. 1997. *Social Suffering*. Berkeley: University of California Press.

Koenigsberg, Richard A. 1975. *Hitler's Ideology: A Study in Psychoanalytic Sociology*. New York: Library of Social Science.

Kohut, Heinz. 1972. "Thoughts on Narcissism and Narcissistic Rage." *Psychoanalytic Study of the Child* 27:360–400.

Kuper, Leo. 1981. *Genocide: Its Political Use in the Twentieth Century*. New Haven, Conn.: Yale University Press.

———. 1985. *The Prevention of Genocide*. New Haven, Conn.: Yale University Press.

Lakoff, George. 1987. *Women, Fire, and Dangerous Things: What Categories Reveal about the Mind*. Chicago: University of Chicago Press.

Lakoff, Geroge, and Mark Johnson. 1980. *Metaphors We Live By*. Chicago: University of Chicago Press.

———. 1999. *Philosophy in the Flesh: The Embodied Mind and Its Challenge to Western Thought*. New York: Basic Books.

Lazarus, Richard S. 1991. *Emotion and Adaptation*. New York: Oxford University Press.

Lebra, Takie Sugiyama. 1976. *Japanese Patterns of Behavior*. Honolulu: University of Hawaii Press.

Ledgerwood, Judy L. 1990a. "Changing Khmer Conceptions of Gender: Woman, Stories, and the Social Order." Ph.D. diss., Dept. of Anthropology, Cornell University.

———. 1990b. "Portrait of a Conflict: Exploring Changing Khmer-American Social and Political Relationships." *Journal of Refugee Studies* 3, no. 2:135–54.

———. 1992. *Analysis of the Situation of Women in Cambodia: Research on Women in Khmer Society.* Phnom Penh: UNICEF.

———. 1995. "Khmer Kinship: The Matriliny/Matriarchy Myth." *Journal of Anthropological Research* 51, no. 3:247–61.

———. 1996. "Politics and Gender: Negotiating Conceptions of the Ideal Woman in Present Day Cambodia." *Asia Pacific Viewpoint* 37, no. 2:139–52.

———. 1997. "The Cambodian Tuol Sleng Museum of Genocidal Crimes: National Narrative." *Museum Anthropology* 21, no. 1:82–98.

———. 1998a. "Does Cambodia Exist? Nationalism and Diasporic Constructions of a Homeland." In *Diasporic Identity: Selected Papers on Refugees and Immigrants,* vol. 6, edited by Carol A. Mortland, 92–112. Washington: American Anthropological Association.

———. 1998b. "Rural Development in Cambodia: The View from the Village." In *Cambodia and the International Community: The Quest for Peace, Development, and Democracy,* edited by Frederick Z. Brown and David G. Timberman, 127–48. New York: Asia Society.

———, ed. 2002. *Cambodia Emerges from the Past: Eight Essays.* DeKalb: Northern Illinois University Center for Southeast Asian Studies.

Ledgerwood, Judy, May M. Ebihara, and Carol A. Mortland. 1994. "Introduction." In *Cambodian Culture since 1975: Homeland and Exile,* edited by May M. Ebihara, Carol A. Mortland, and Judy Ledgerwood, 1–26. Ithaca, N.Y.: Cornell University Press.

Ledgerwood, Judy, and John Vijghen. 2002. "Decision-Making in Rural Khmer Villages." In *Cambodia Emerges from the Past: Eight Essays,* edited by Judy Ledgerwood, 109–50. DeKalb: Northern Illinois University Center for Southeast Asian Studies.

Lee, Mathew. 1996. "Out of the Loop: Ieng Sary Denies Any Role in Khmer Rouge Atrocities." *Far Eastern Economic Review,* Sept. 19, p. 20.

Lemarchand, René. 2002. "Disconnecting the Threads: Rwanda and the Holocaust Reconsidered." *Journal of Genocide Research* 4, no. 4:499–518.

Lemkin, Raphael. 1944. *Axis Rule in Occupied Europe.* Washington, DC: Carnegie Endowment for International Peace.

Levi-Strauss, Claude. 1966. *The Savage Mind.* Chicago: University of Chicago Press.

Levy, Marc. 1998. Tales of Cambodia's Latest "Killing Field." Camnews v001.n634.3 (June 8) [camnews@lists.best.com].

Lewis, Michael. 1992a. "The Emergence of Human Emotions." In *Handbook of Emotions,* edited by Michael Lewis and Jeannette M. Haviland, 223–35. New York: Guilford Press.

———. 1992b. *Shame: The Exposed Self.* New York: Free Press.

Lifton, Robert Jay. 1986. *The Nazi Doctors: Medical Killing and the Psychology of Genocide.* New York: Basic Books.

———. 1989. *Thought Reform and the Psychology of Totalism: A Study of*

Brainwashing in China. Chapel Hill, N.C.: University of North Carolina Press.

Lindholm, Charles. 1990. *Charisma.* Malden, Mass.: Blackwell.

Locard, Henri. 1996. *Le "Petit livre rouge" de Pol Pot ou les paroles de l'Angkar.* Paris: Harmattan.

———. 1998. "Khmer Rouge Revolutionary Songs and the Cambodian Culture Tradition, or, The Revolution Triumphant." In *Khmer Studies: Knowledge of the Past and Its Contributions to the Rehabilitation and Reconstruction of Cambodia,* vol. 1, edited by Sorn Samnang, 308–48. Phnom Penh: Ministry of Education, Youth and Sports.

Lon Nara. 2001. "Unworkable Verdict for Acid Victim." *Phnom Penh Post,* Nov. 9–22.

Lon Nara and Phelim Kyne. 2000. "Tat Samarina's Family in Terror." *Phnom Penh Post,* Sept. 15–28.

Luong Ung. 2000. *First They Killed My Father: A Daughter of Cambodia Remembers.* New York: Harper Collins.

Ly Y. 2000. Heaven Becomes Hell: A Survivor's Story of Life under the Khmer Rouge. Edited by John S. Driscoll. New Haven, Conn.: Yale University Southeast Asia Studies.

Mabbett, I. W. 1977. "Varnas in Angkor and the Indian Caste System." *Journal of Asian Studies* 36, no. 3:429–42.

Mabbett, Ian, and David Chandler. 1995. *The Khmers.* Cambridge: Blackwell.

Maguire, Peter H. 1998. Unpublished interview with Lor by Peter H. Maquire. Phnom Penh: DC-Cam (uncatalogued).

Maha Gosananda. 1992. *Step by Step: Meditations on Wisdom and Compassion.* Berkeley: Parallax Press.

Mahasi Sayadaw. 1996. *Sallekha Sutta ("A Discourse on the Refinement of Character").* Translated by U Aye Muang. Bangkok: Buddhadhamma Foundation.

Malkki, Liisa H. 1995. *Purity and Exile: Violence, Memory, and National Cosmology among Hutu Refugees in Tanzania.* Chicago: University of Chicago Press.

Mam, Kalyanee E. 1999. *An Oral History of Family Life under the Khmer Rouge.* Working Paper GS 10. New Haven, Conn.: Yale Center for International and Area Studies.

Mannikka, Eleanor. 1996. *Angkor Wat: Time, Space, and Kingship.* Honolulu: University of Hawaii Press.

Marcucci, John Lambert. 1986. "Khmer Refugees in Dallas: Medical Decisions in the Context of Pluralism." Ph.D. diss., Department of Anthropology, Southern Methodist University.

———. 1994. "Sharing the Pain: Critical Values and Behaviors in Khmer Culture." In *Cambodian Culture since 1975: Homeland and Exile,* edited by May M. Ebihara, Carol A. Mortland, and Judy Ledgerwood, 129–40. Ithaca, N.Y.: Cornell University Press.

Marriot, McKim. 1990. *India through Hindu Categories.* New Dehli: Sage.

Marston, John. 1985. "Language Reform in Democratic Kampuchea." M.A. thesis, University of Minnesota.

————. 1994. "Metaphors of the Khmer Rouge." In *Cambodian Culture since 1975 : Homeland and Exile,* edited by May M. Ebihara, Carol A. Mortland,. and Judy Ledgerwood, 105–18. Ithaca, N.Y.: Cornell University Press.

————. 1996. "Cambodian Satirical Cartoons and the Representation of Hierarchy." Paper presented at the Association for Asian Studies Annual Meetings, Honolulu, Hawaii, April 12.

————. 1997. "Cambodia, 1991–1994: Hierarchy, Neutrality and Etiquettes of Discourse." Ph.D. diss., Dept. of Anthropology, University of Washington.

————. 1999. "Cambodia." *Analysis del Anoasia Pacifico* 6:51–82.

————. 2002. "Democratic Kampuchea and the Idea of Modernity." In *Cambodia Emerges from the Past: Eight Essays,* edited by Judy Ledgerwood, 38–59. DeKalb: Northern Illinois University Press.

————. 2003. "Khmer Rouge Songs." *Crossroads: An Interdisciplinary Journal of Southeast Asian Studies* 16, no. 1:100–27.

Marston, John, and Sotheary Duong. 1988. "Language Use and Language Policy in Democratic Kampuchea." Paper delivered at the Indochina Studies Program on Language Use and Language Policy in Laos, Cambodia, and Vietnam: Modern Developments," University of Hawaii, Honolulu, June 27–28.

Martel, Gabrielle. 1975. *Lovea, village des environs d'Angkor.* Paris: Publications de l'Ecole Française d'Extrême-Orient.

Martin, Marie Alexanderine. 1994. *Cambodia: A Shattered Society.* Translated by Mark W. McLeod. Berkeley: University of California Press.

May, Rollo. 1977. *The Meaning of Anxiety.* New York: Norton.

McIntyre, Kevin. 1996. "Geography As Destiny: Cities, Villages and Khmer Rouge Orientalism." *Comparative Studies of Society and History* 38, no. 4:730–58.

Meisner, Maurice. 1982. *Marxism, Maoism, and Utopianism: Eight Essays.* Madison: University of Wisconsin Press.

Melson, Robert. 1992. *Revolution and Genocide: On the Origins of the Armenian Genocide and the Holocaust.* Chicago: University of Chicago Press.

Meng-Try Ea and Sorya Sim. 2001. *Children under the Khmer Rouge Regime.* Phnom Penh: Documentation Center of Cambodia.

Milgram, Stanley. 1974. *Obedience to Authority: An Experimental View.* New York: Harper & Row.

Miller, Joan G. 1997. "Cultural Conceptions of Duty: Implications for Motivation and Morality." In *Motivation and Culture,* edited by Donald Munro, John F. Schumaker, and Stuart C. Carr, 178–92. New York: Routledge.

Moeun Chhean Nariddh. 1995. "Police Blotter." *Phnom Penh Post,* Feb. 10–23, p. 17.

Morris, Stephen J. 1999. *Why Vietnam Invaded Cambodia.* Stanford, Calif.: Stanford University Press.

Morrison, Andrew P. 1986. *Essential Papers on Narcissim.* New York: New York University Press.

Mouth, Sophea. n.d. a. Central Conceptions of Khmer Rouge Ideology. Unpublished manuscript.

————. n.d. b. Jatakas and the Idea of Power. Unpublished manuscript.

Moyer, Nancy. 1991. *Escape from the Killing Fields: One Girl Who Survived the Cambodian Holocaust.* Grand Rapids, Mich.: Zondervan.

Mulder, Niels. 1994. *Inside Thai Society: An Interpretation of Everyday Life.* Bangkok: Editions Duang Kamol.

Nagengast, Carole. 1994. "Violence, Terror, and the Crisis of the State." *Annual Review of Anthropology* 23:109–36.

———. 2002. "Inoculations of Evil in the U.S.-Mexican Border Region: Reflections on the Genocidal Potential of Symbolic Violence." In *Annihilating Difference: The Anthropology of Genocide,* edited by Alexander Laban Hinton, 325–47. Berkeley: University of California Press.

Naranhkiri Tith. 1998. "The Challenge of Sustainable Economic Growth and Development in Cambodia." In *Cambodia and the International Community: The Quest for Peace, Development, and Democracy,* edited by Frederick Z. Brown and David G. Timberman, 101–25. New York: Asia Society.

Neisser, Ulric. 1988. "Five Kinds of Self-Knowledge." *Philosophical Psychology* 1, no. 1:35–59.

Nordstrom, Carolyn, and Antonius C. G. M. Robben, eds. 1995. *Fieldwork under Fire: Contemporary Studies of Violence and Survival.* Berkeley: University of California Press.

Nuckolls, Charles W. 1996. *The Cultural Dialectics of Knowledge and Desire.* Madison: University of Wisconsin Press.

Obeyesekere, Gananath. 1981. *Medusa's Hair: An Essay on Personal Symbols and Religious Experience.* Chicago: University of Chicago Press.

Öhman, Arne 2000. "Fear and Anxiety: Evolutionary, Cognitive, and Clinical Perspectives." In *Handbook of Emotions,* edited by Michael Lewis and Jeannette M. Haviland-Jones., 573–93. New York: Guilford Press.

Ong Thong Hoeung, and Laura J. Summers, eds. 1984. "The Statues of the Communist Party of Kampuchea." In *The Party Statutes of the Communist World,* edited by William B. Simons and Stephen White, 237–59. The Hague: Martinus Nijhoff Publishers.

Ortner, Sherry B. 1989. *High Religion: A Cultural and Political History of Sherpa Buddhism.* Princeton, N.J.: Princeton University Press.

———, ed. 1999. *The Fate of "Culture": Geertz and Beyond.* Berkeley: University of California Press.

Pape, Eric. 1997. " 'Justice is not a wild horse—it must be controlled' [interview with Minister of Justice Chem Snguon]." *Phnom Penh Post,* Nov. 7–20, pp. 13–14.

Parish, Steven M. 1996. *Hierarchy and Its Discontents: Culture and the Politics of Consciousness in Caste Society.* Philadelphia: University of Pennsylvania Press.

Paul, Robert A. 1990. "What Does Anybody Want? Desire, Purpose, and the Acting Subject in the Study of Culture." *Cultural Anthropology* 5, no. 4:431–51.

Peang-Meth, Abdulgaffar. 1991. "Understanding the Khmer: Sociological-Cultural Observations." *Asian Survey* 31, no. 5:442–55.

People's Revolutionary Tribunal. 1988. *People's Revolutionary Tribunal Held in*

Phnom Penh for the Trial of the Genocide Crime of the Pol Pot–Ieng Sary Clique (August 1979). Phnom Penh: Foreign Languages Publishing House.

Phnom Penh Post Staff. 1999a. "Duch and Ta Mok Face Charges Under 'Anti-KR' Law." *Phnom Penh Post,* May. 14–27, p. 1.

———. 1999b. "No Action on Acid Attack." *Phnom Penh Post,* Dec. 10–23, pp. 1, 3.

———. 2002. Autobiography of a Mass Murderer. *Phnom Penh Post,* Mar. 1–14, pp. 8–9.

Phra Prayudh Payutto. 1995. *Buddhadhamma: Natural Laws and Values for Life.* Translated by Grant A. Olson. Albany: State University of New York Press.

Phya Anuman Rajadhon. 1946. "The Khwan and Its Ceremonies." *Journal of the Siam Society* 50, no. 2:119–64.

Piaget, Jean. 1932. *The Development of Moral Reasoning in Children.* Edited by M. Gabain. New York: Free Press.

Picq, Laurence. 1984. "De la reforme linguistique et de l'usage des mots chez les Khmers Rouges." *Asia du Sud-est et Monde Insulindien* 15, nos. 1–4:351–57.

———. 1989. *Beyond the Horizon: Five Years with the Khmer Rouge.* New York: St. Martin's Press.

Pin Yathay. 1987. *Stay Alive, My Son.* New York: Touchstone.

Pol Pot. 1977. "Long Live the 17th Anniversary of the Communist Party of Kampuchea." Phnom Penh: Ministry of Foreign Affairs.

Ponchaud, François. 1978. *Cambodia, Year Zero.* New York: Holt, Rinehart and Winston.

———. 1989. "Social Change in the Vortex of Revolution." In *Cambodia, 1975–1978: Rendezvous with Death,* edited by Karl D. Jackson, 151–77. Princeton, N.J.: Princeton University Press.

Pou, Saveros. 1979. "Les pronoms personnels du Khmer: Origine et evolution." *Southeast Asian Linguistics Studies* 4:155–78.

Power, Samantha. 2002. *"A Problem from Hell": America and the Age of Genocide.* New York: Basic Books.

Quinn, Kenneth M. 1976. "Political Change in Wartime: The Khmer Krahom Revolution in Southern Cambodia, 1970–1974." *U.S. Naval War College Review* (spring):3–31.

———. 1989a. "Pattern and Scope of Violence." In *Cambodia, 1975–1978: Rendezvous with Death,* edited by Karl D. Jackson, 179–208. Princeton, N.J.: Princeton University Press.

———. 1989b. "Explaining the Terror." In *Cambodia, 1975–1978: Rendezvous with Death,* edited by Karl D. Jackson, 215–40. Princeton, N.J.: Princeton University Press.

Quinn, Naomi, and Dorothy Holland. 1987. "Culture and Cognition." In *Cultural Models in Language and Thought,* edited by Dorothy Holland and Naomi Quinn, 3–40. New York: Cambridge University Press.

Rejali, Darius M. 1993. *Torture and Modernity: Self, Society and State in Modern Iran.* Boulder, Colo.: Westview.

Reynolds, Frank E. 1972. "The Two Wheels of Dhamma: A Study of Early Buddhism." In *The Two Wheels of Dhamma: Essays on the Theravada Tradition in India and Ceylon,* edited by Gananath Obeyesekere, Frank Reynolds, and Bardwell L. Smith, 6–30. Chambersburg, Penn.: American Academy of Religion.

———. 1985. "Multiple Cosmogonies and Ethics: The Case of Theravada Buddhism." In *Cosmogony and the Ethical Order: New Studies in Comparative Ethics,* edited by Robin W. Lovin and Frank E. Reynolds, 203–24. Chicago: University of Chicago Press.

Reynolds, Frank E., and Regina T. Clifford. 1980. "Sangha, Society and the Struggle for National Integration: Burma and Thailand." In *Transitions and Transformation in the History of Religions: Essays in Honor of Joseph M. Kitagawa,* edited by Frank E. Reynolds and Theodore M. Ludwig, 56–88. Leiden: E. J. Brill.

Reynolds, Frank E., and Mani B. Reynolds, trans. 1982. *Three Worlds According to King Ruang: A Thai Buddhist Cosmology.* Berkeley: University of California Press.

Rhys Davids, T. W., and William Stede. 1992. *The Pali Text Society's Pali-English Dictionary.* Oxford: Pali Text Society.

Rice, Pranee Liamputtang. 1994. "Childbirth and Health: Cultural Beliefs and Practices among Cambodian Women." In *Asian Mothers, Australian Birth: Pregnancy, Childbirth and Childrearing,* pp. 47–60. Melbourne: Ausmed Publications.

Rizzi, Claudia, and Chea Sotheacheath. 1999. "K. Cham Police at Odds over Vigilante Slaying." *The Cambodian Daily,* August 1:1,6.

Robben, Antonius C. G. M., and Marcelo M. Suárez-Orozco, eds. 2000. *Cultures under Siege: Collective Violence and Trauma.* New York: Cambridge University Press.

Rodseth, Lars. 1998. "Distributive Models of Culture: A Sapirian Alternative to Essentialism." *American Anthropologist* 100, no. 1:55–69.

Roniger, Luis. 1990. *Hierarchy and Trust in Modern Mexico and Brazil.* New York: Praeger.

Rosaldo, Michelle Z. 1980. *Knowledge and Passion: Ilongot Notions of Self and Social Life.* New York: Cambridge University Press.

Rummel, R. J. 1997. *Power Kills: Democracy As a Method of Nonviolence.* New Brunswick, N.J.: Transaction.

———. 1999. *Statistics of Death: Genocide and Mass Murder since 1900.* New Brunswick, N.J.: Transaction.

Sahlins, Marshall. 1981. *Historical Metaphors and Mythical Realities: Structure in the Early History of the Sandwich Islands Kingdom.* Ann Arbor: University of Michigan Press.

Sainsbury, Peter, and Chea Sotheacheath. 2000. "Good Intentions Paved Road to Mass Murder." *Phnom Penh Post,* April 14–27, pp. 8–11.

Samreth Sopha and Beth Moorthy. 1998. "Kem Sokha Still Afraid." *Phnom Penh Post,* Dec. 25, pp. 3, 5.

Saom [Preah Botumthera]. 1986. *Tum Teav.* Paris: Cedoreck.

Sargent, Carolyn, John Marcucci, and Ellen Elliston. 1983. "Tiger Bones, Fire and Wine: Maternity Care in a Kampuchean Refugee Community." *Medical Anthropology* 7, no. 4:67–79.

Scarry, Elaine. 1985. *The Body in Pain: The Making and Unmaking of the World*. New York: Oxford University Press.

Scheper-Hughes, Nancy. 2002. "Coming to Our Senses: Anthropology and Genocide." In *Annihilating Difference: The Anthropology of Genocide*, edited by Alexander Laban Hinton, 348–81. Berkeley: University of California Press.

Schram, Stuart R., ed. 1976. *The Political Thought of Mao Tse-tung*. New York: Praeger.

Schwartz, Theodore. 1978. "Where Is the Culture? Personality As the Distributive Locus of Culture." In *The Making of Psychological Anthropology*, edited by George D. Spindler, 419–41. Berkeley: University of California Press.

Schoenhals, Martin. 1993. *The Paradox of Power in a People's Republic of China Middle School*. Armonk, N.Y.: M. E. Sharpe.

Scott, James C. 1977. "Patron-Client Politics and Political Change in Southeast Asia." In *Friends, Followers, and Factions: A Reader in Political Clientelism*, edited by Steffen W. Schmidt, Laura Guasti, Carl H. Landé, and James C. Scott, 123–46. Berkeley: University of California Press.

———. 1998. *Seeing Like a State: How Certain Schemes to Improve the Human Condition Have Failed*. New Haven: Yale University Press.

Scroggins, Hurley. 1998. "Master of the Mekong Goes Down." *Phnom Penh Post*, Oct. 16–Nov. 12, p. 3.

———. 2000. "New Details on U.S. Devastation, 1970–75." *Phnom Penh Post*, Apr. 14–27, p. 13.

Sedara, Kim. 2001. "Reciprocity: Informal Patterns of Social Interactions in a Cambodian Village near Angkor Park." M.A. thesis, Dept. of Anthropology, Northern Illinois University.

Shandley, Robert R., ed. 1998. *Unwilling Germans? The Goldhagen Debate*. Minneapolis: University of Minnesota Press.

Shapiro, Sophiline Cheam. 1996. "Songs My Enemies Taught Me." In *Children of Cambodia's Killing Fields: Memoirs by Survivors*, compiled by Dith Pran, edited by Kim DePaul, 1–5. New Haven, Conn.: Yale University Press.

Shapiro[-Phim], Toni. 1994. "Dance and the Spirit of Cambodia." Ph.D. diss., Dept. of Anthropology, Cornell University.

———. 2002. "Dance, Music, and the Nature of Terror and Democratic Kampuchea." In *Annihilating Difference: Toward an Anthropology of Genocide*, edited by Alexander Laban Hinton, 179–93. Berkeley: University of California Press.

Shawcross, William. 1985. *The Quality of Mercy: Cambodia, Holocaust and Modern Conscience*. New York: Touchstone.

———. 1987. *Sideshow: Kissinger, Nixon and the Destruction of Cambodia*. New York: Touchstone.

———. 1994. *Cambodia's New Deal*. Washington: Carnegie Endowment for International Peace.

Shore, Bradd. 1996. *Culture in Mind: Cognition, Culture, and the Problem of Meaning*. New York: Oxford University Press.

―――. 1998. *What Culture Means, How Culture Means*. Heinz Werner Lecture Series, vol. 22. Worcester, Mass.: Clark University Press.

Shweder, Richard A. 1991. *Thinking through Cultures: Expeditions in Cultural Psychology*. Cambridge: Harvard University Press.

Shweder, Richard A., Nancy C. Much, Manamohan Mahapatra, and Lawrence Park. 1997. "The 'Big Three' of Morality (Autonomy, Community, Divinity) and the 'Big Three' Explanations of Suffering." In *Morality and Health*, edited by Allan M. Brandt and Paul Rozin, 130–40. New York: Routledge.

Sihanouk, Prince Norodom. 1980. *War and Hope: The Case for Cambodia*. Translated by Mary Feeney. New York: Pantheon.

Simons, Anna. 1999. "War: Back to the Future?" *Annual Review of Anthropology* 8:73–108.

Skidmore, Monique. 1997. "In the Shade of the Bodhi Tree: Dhammayietra and the Re-awakening of Community in Cambodia." *Crossroads: An Interdisciplinary Journal of Southeast Asian Studies* 10, no. 1:1–32.

Smith, Barbara. 1992. "Im Chan—The Sculptor." *Cambodia Times*, Nov. 2–8, p. 7.

Smith, Frank. 1989. *Interpretive Accounts of the Khmer Rouge Years: Personal Experience in Cambodian Peasant World View*. Madison: Center for Southeast Asian Studies, University of Wisconsin.

Smith, Roger W. 1987. "Human Destructiveness and Politics: The Twentieth Century As an Age of Genocide." In *Genocide and the Modern Age: Etiology and Case Studies of Mass Death*, edited by Isidor Wallim, Ann and Michael N. Dobkowski, 21–39. New York: Greenwood.

Smith-Hefner, Nancy J. 1999. *Khmer American: Identity and Moral Education in a Diasporic Community*. Berkeley: University of California Press.

Someth May. 1986. *Cambodian Witness: The Autobiography of Someth May*. New York: Random House.

Soth Polin. 1980. "Pol Pot's Diabolical Sweetness." *Index on Censorship* 5:43–45.

Sperber, Dan. 1985. *Anthropological Knowledge: Three Essays*. New York: Cambridge University Press.

―――. 1996. *Explaining Culture: A Naturalistic Approach*. Malden, Mass.: Blackwell.

Spiro, Mel. 1982. *Buddhism and Society: A Great Tradition and Its Burmese Vicissitudes*. Berkeley: University of California Press.

―――. 1987. "Collective Representations and Mental Representations in Religious Symbol Systems." In *Culture and Human Nature: Theoretical Papers of Melford E. Spiro*, edited by Benjamin Kilbourne and L. L. Langness, 161–84. Chicago: University of Chicago Press.

Stanton, Gregory H. Forthcoming. *The Eight Stages of Genocide: How Governments Can Tell When Genocide Is Coming and What They Can Do to Stop It*. Washington, D.C.: Woodrow Wilson Center Press.

Staub, Ervin. 1989. *The Roots of Evil: The Origins of Genocide and Other Group Violence*. New York: Cambridge University Press.

Strauss, Claudia. 1992. "Models and Motives." In *Human Motives and Cultural*

Models, edited by Roy D'Andrade and Claudia Strauss, 1–20. New York: Cambridge University Press.

Strauss, Claudia, and Naomi Quinn. 1997. *A Cognitive Theory of Cultural Meaning.* New York: Cambridge University Press.

Stuart-Fox, Martin. 1985. *The Murderous Revolution: Life and Death in Pol Pot's Kampuchea Based on the Personal Experiences of Bunheang Ung.* Chippendale, Australia: Alternative Publishing Cooperative.

Suedfeld, Peter, ed. 1990. *Psychology and Torture.* New York: Hemisphere.

Summers, Laura. 1987. "The CPK, Secret Vanguard of Pol Pot's Revolution: A Comment on Nuon Chea's Statement." *Journal of Communist Studies* 3 (March):5–18.

Sutton, Donald S. 1995. "Consuming Counterrevolution: The Ritual and Culture of Cannibalism in Wuxuan, Guangxi, China, May to July 1968." *Comparative Studies of Society and History* 37, no. 1:136–72.

Swearer, Donald K. 1995. *The Buddhist World of Southeast Asia.* Albany: State University of New York Press.

Szymusiak, Molyda. 1986. *The Stones Cry Out: A Cambodian Childhood, 1975–1980.* Translated by Linda Coverdale. New York: Hill and Wang.

Tambiah, Stanley J. 1970. *Buddhism and the Spirit Cults in North-East Thailand.* New York: Cambridge University Press.

———. 1976. *World Conqueror and World Renouncer: A Study of Buddhism and Polity in Thailand against a Historical Background.* New York: Cambridge University Press.

———. 1985. *Culture, Thought, and Social Action: An Anthropological Perspective.* Cambridge: Harvard University Press.

Tannenbaum, Nicola. 1995. *Who Can Compete against the World? Power-Protection and Buddhism in Shan Worldview.* Ann Arbor: Association for Asian Studies.

Tauch Chhuong. 1994. *Battambang during the Time of the Lord Governor.* Edited by Hin Sithan, Carol Mortland, and Judy Ledgerwood. Phnom Penh: Cedorek.

Taussig, Michael. 1987. *Shamanism, Colonialism, and the Wild Man: A Study in Terror and Healing.* Chicago: University of Chicago Press.

Taylor, Christopher C. 1999. *Sacrifice As Terror: The Rwandan Genocide of 1994.* New York: Berg.

Teeda Butt Mam. 1996. "Worms from Our Skin." In *Children of Cambodia's Killing Fields: Memoirs by Survivors,* compiled by Dith Pran, edited by Kim DePaul, 11–17. New Haven, Conn.: Yale University Press.

Thayer, Nate. 1994. "Army's Dossier of Shame." *Phnom Penh Post,* Aug. 12–25, pp. 1–3.

———. 1995a. "Security Jitters while PM's Away." *Phnom Penh Post,* Mar. 24–Apr. 6, pp. 1, 2.

———. 1995b. "Expat Returnees Pose Legal Questions for West." *Phnom Penh Post,* Mar. 10–23, p. 16.

———. 1997a. "Brother Enemy No. 1." *Phnom Penh Post,* Aug. 15–28, pp. 1, 8.

———. 1997b. "Day of Reckoning." *Far Eastern Economic Review,* Oct. 30, pp. 14–20.

———. 1997c. "My Education." *Far Eastern Economic Review*, Oct. 30, p. 21.
———. 1998a. "The Resurrected." *Far Eastern Economic Review*, Apr. 16, pp. 23–4.
———. 1998b. "Dying Breath." *Far Eastern Economic Review*, Apr. 30, pp. 18–21.
———. 1999b. "Party of One." *Far Eastern Economic Review*, Jan. 21, p. 26.
Thion, Serge. 1993. *Watching Cambodia: Ten Paths to Enter the Cambodian Tangle*. Bangkok: White Lotus.
Thompson, Ashley. 1996. *The Calling of the Souls: A Study of the Khmer Ritual [Hav Broleung]*. Clayton, Australia: Monash University Centre of Southeast Asian Studies.
Tillich, Paul. 1952. *The Courage to Be*. New Haven, Conn.: Yale University Press.
Tooze, Ruth. 1962. *Cambodia: The Land of Contrasts*. New York: Viking.
Totten, Samuel, William S. Parsons, and Israel W. Charney, eds. 1997. *Century of Genocide: Eyewitness Accounts and Critical Views*. New York: Garland Publishing.
Turner, Terence. 1980. "The Social Skin." In *Not Work Alone: A Cross-Cultural Study of Activities Superfluous to Surivival*, edited by J. Cherfas and R. Lewin, 112–40. London: Temple Smith.
Turner, Victor. 1967. *The Forest of Symbols: Aspects of Ndembu Ritual*. Ithaca, N.Y.: Cornell University Press.
Twining, Charles H. 1989. "The Economy." In *Cambodia, 1975–1979: Rendezvous with Death*, edited by Karl D. Jackson, 109–50. Princeton, N.J.: Princeton University Press.
Um, Khatharya. 1990. "Brotherhood of the Pure: Nationalism and Communism in Cambodia." Ph.D diss., Dept. of Political Science, University of California, Berkeley.
United Nations Center for Human Rights. 1997. *Evidence of Summary Executioners, Torture and Missing Persons since 2–7 July*. Memorandum to the Royal Government of Cambodia. August 21.
Van Esterik, Penny. 1996. "Nurturance and Reciprocity in Thai Studies." In *State Power and Culture in Thailand*, edited by E. Paul Durrenberger. New Haven, Conn.: Yale University Southeast Asia Studies.
Vann Nath. 1998. *Cambodian Prison Portrait: One Year in the Khmer Rouge's S-21*. Bangkok: White Lotus.
Varela, Francisco J., Evan Thompson, and Eleanor Rosch. 1991. *The Embodied Mind: Cognitive Science and Human Experience*. Cambridge, Mass.: MIT Press.
Vickery, Michael. 1984. *Cambodia, 1975–1982*. Boston: South End Press.
———. 1986. *Kampuchea: Politics, Economics, and Society*. Boulder, Colo.: Lynne Rienner.
Vygotsky, Lev Semenovich. 1978. *Mind in Society: The Development of Higher Psychological Processes*. Cambridge, Mass.: Harvard University Press.
Wallace, Anthony F. C. 1956. "Revitalization Movements." *American Anthropologist* 58:264–81.
———. 1969. *Culture and Personality*. New York: Random House.

Waller, James. 2002. *Becoming Evil: How Ordinary People Commit Genocide and Mass Killing.* New York: Oxford University Press.

Weber, Max. 1949. *The Methodology of the Social Sciences.* New York: Free Press.

———. 1964. *The Theory of Social and Economic Organization,* edited by A. M. Henderson and Talcott Parsons. New York: Free Press.

White, Patrice Michele. 1996. "Crossing the River: A Study of Khmer Women's Beliefs and Practices during Pregnancy, Birth and Postpartum." Ph.D. diss., School of Public Health, University of California, Los Angeles.

Whitehead, Neil L. 2002. *Dark Shamans: Kanaimà and the Poetics of Violent Death.* Durham, N.C.: Duke University Press.

Williams, Raymond. 1985. *Keywords: A Vocabulary of Culture and Society.* New York: Oxford University Press.

Willmott, W. E. 1967. *The Chinese in Cambodia.* Vancouver: University of British Columbia Publications Centre.

———. 1981. "Analytical Errors of the Kampuchea Communist Party." *Pacific Affairs* 54, no. 2:209–27.

Wolters, O. W. 1999. *History, Culture, and Region in Southeast Asian Perspectives.* Ithaca, N.Y.: Cornell University Southeast Asia Program Publications.

Woodward, Kathryn. 1997. "Concepts of Identity and Difference." In *Identity and Difference,* edited by Kathryn Woodward, 8–50. London: Sage.

Worthman, Carol M. 1992. "Cupid and Psyche: Investigative Syncretism in Biological and Psychosocial Anthropology." In *New Directions in Psychological Anthropology,* edited by Theodore Schwartz, Geoffrey M. White, and Catherine A. Lutz, 150–78. New York: Cambridge University Press.

Yimsut, Ronnie. 1997. "The Tonle Sap Lake Massacre." In *Children of Cambodia's Killing Fields: Memoirs by Survivors,* edited by Kim DePaul, compiled by Dith Pran, 185–94. New Haven, Conn.: Yale University Press.

Youk Chhang. 2000. "Shadow." *The Truth* 5 (May):1.

Youk Chhang and Phat Kosal. n.d. *Tuol Sleng As a Prison.* Phnom Penh: Tuol Sleng Genocide Museum and Documentation Center of Cambodia.

Ysa Osman. 2002. *Oukoubah: Justice for the Cham Muslims under the Democratic Kampuchea Regime.* Phnom Penh: Documentation Center of Cambodia.

Zimbardo, Philip G., Craig Haney, W. Curtis Banks, and David Jaffe. 1974. "The Psychology of Imprisonment: Privation, Power, and Pathology." In *Doing unto Others,* edited by Zick Rubin, 61–73. Englewood Cliffs, N.J.: Prentice-Hall.

Index

Compositor: Bookmatters, Berkeley
Text: 10/13 Sabon
Display: Sabon
Printer and binder: Maple-Vail Manufacturing Group